Education, Justice and Cultural Diversity

Education, Justice and Cultural Diversity: An Examination of the Honeyford Affair, 1984–85

Mark Halstead

 The Falmer Press

(A Member of the Taylor & Francis Group)
London • New York • Philadelphia

UK   The Falmer Press, Falmer House, Barcombe, Lewes, East Sussex,
             BN8 5DL

USA   The Falmer Press, Taylor & Francis Inc., 242 Cherry Street,
             Philadelphia, PA 19106-1906

© 1988 J. M. Halstead

*All rights reserved. No part of this publication may be reproduced,
stored in a retrieval system, or transmitted in any form or by any
means, electronic, mechanical, photocopying, recording or otherwise, without permission in writing from the Publisher.*

First published 1988

**Library of Congress Cataloging in Publication Data is available
on request**
ISBN 1 85000 393 9
ISBN 1 85000 394 7 (pbk.)

Jacket design by Caroline Archer

Typeset in Bembo by David John Services Limited, Slough, Berks

*Printed in Great Britain by Taylor & Francis (Printers) Ltd,
Basingstoke*

Contents

Preface   vii

Part One: The Background to the Honeyford Affair   1
1 Ethnic Minorities in Bradford   3
2 LEA Policies: the Growth of Multi-culturalism   21
  in Bradford
3 Honeyford's Articles   55
4 The Campaign against Honeyford, 1984-85   73
5 Some Perspectives on the Affair   117

Part Two: The Underlying Issues   135
6 Racism and Schools   137
7 Free Speech and Accountability   167
8 The Debate about Multi-cultural Education   203

Appendix: A Chronology of Events Relating to   231
(a) Educational Provision for Ethnic Minorities in
Bradford and (b) the Honeyford Affair
Bibliography   285
Index   299

Preface

Following the publication of Ray Honeyford's article, 'Education and Race – an Alternative View' in *The Salisbury Review* early in 1984, a protracted campaign was launched against him, calling for his dismissal from his post as headteacher in Bradford, which culminated almost two years later in his acceptance of an early retirement settlement. The case became an educational *cause célèbre* in the UK; it received extensive media coverage, and had political, legal, social and administrative repercussions both locally and nationally. It is the argument of the present volume that the case also highlights, in a particularly interesting way, a number of issues which are, and are likely to remain in the near future, of crucial importance to contemporary educational policy and practice.

The present volume falls into two parts. The first attempts to provide an objective account of what actually happened in the Honeyford affair and the background against which it took place. The second seeks to encourage some serious thinking about the most important of the issues raised, especially racism, free speech, teachers' accountability and multi-cultural education. The book thus combines elements of a case study with elements of applied social philosophy. It is written in the belief that a close examination of a particular educational incident leads quickly and inevitably to questions of concept and fundamental educational principles, and that it is only through an examination of these underlying issues and principles that the practical lessons of the incident can be understood.

This book has its foundations in the author's twelve years' teaching experience in Bradford and three years' research in philosophy of education at the University of Cambridge, where he has been looking particularly at educational provision for Muslim children in the UK. He acknowledges the help, encouragement and advice of a large number of people in both

Bradford and Cambridge, including LEA officers and advisers, ethnic minority representatives, teachers and others directly involved in the affair, local journalists, librarians, professors, lecturers, fellow research students, family and personal friends. Several parts of the book have been presented over the last two years as lectures and seminars at Homerton College, at Corpus Christi College, Cambridge, at the University of Cambridge Department of Education and at the Peterborough Educational Development Centre, which have provided helpful feedback. A particular debt of gratitude is due to Mr. T.H. McLaughlin for his support and detailed and perceptive criticisms throughout the period of research and writing.

Part One:
The Background to the Honeyford Affair

1 Ethnic Minorities in Bradford

Bradford's population is among the most ethnically diverse to be found outside London. It provides a rich source of information about patterns of immigration and interactions between cultures. The city contains sizable groups with ethnic origins in Ireland, Germany, Poland, the Ukraine, Latvia, Estonia, Bielorussia, Yugoslavia, Lithuania, Italy, Greece, Cyprus, Hungary, the West Indies, Hong Kong, India, Pakistan, Bangladesh and Vietnam, as well as smaller groups from many other areas of the world. This microcosm of contemporary Britain is ripe for investigation, not least because we can gain a better understanding of the current situation of ethnic minorities by looking at how that situation arose, and because future planning, in the field of education as elsewhere, is dependent on accurate knowledge about the present.

The present chapter offers a brief outline of this largely unresearched area. It starts with a historical sketch of immigration into Bradford, divided into two sections: immigration from Europe during the nineteenth and first half of the twentieth centuries, and immigration from the New Commonwealth, Pakistan and Vietnam in the second half of the twentieth century. The next section provides some statistics on ethnic minorities in present-day Bradford, particularly relating to population growth, age range, religion, language, location, employment and housing. The chapter concludes with a consideration of race relations in the city and the Council's response to the situation.

The aim of this chapter is to provide a backcloth to the discussion of Bradford's educational policies for ethnic minority pupils in chapter two, and to the discussion of Honeyford's criticisms of these policies in chapter three.

THE ARRIVAL OF EUROPEAN IMMIGRANTS 1820–1956

Bradford had been a wool-trading centre since at least the fourteenth century, though it was not until after the introduction of steam power and machinery at the turn of the nineteenth century that the city became a byword for wool and worsted manufacture. With the growth of steam-powered mills came a dramatic increase in population, from 13,264 in 1801 to 279,761 in 1901. A significant part of this increase arose as a result of the migration of families into Bradford from surrounding farms and villages and from other parts of Britain, either to work in the mills or to supply the needs of the growing population. However, there was also a large number of arrivals from outside the British mainland; of these, the Irish were the most numerous, and the German Jews the most prosperous.

By 1825 there was already a sufficiently large Irish Catholic community for a small church to be built in the centre of Bradford, but the scale of Irish immigration increased rapidly after the evictions of the poor in the 1830s and 1840s and the Potato Famine of 1845. By 1851, there were 9581 Irish immigrants in Bradford, forming over 8 per cent of the total population. Their numbers were further swelled by Irish navvies leaving the canals and railways they had constructed and coming to work in the mills. The most common occupations for the men were wool-combing, spinning, labouring and hawking, while the women were often servants, washerwomen or charwomen. Immigration from Ireland to Bradford has continued to the present-day, though it is very difficult to estimate how many of Bradford's citizens today are of Irish ancestry. Perhaps the best guide is the number of Catholics in the city, variously estimated at 40–60,000 (Naylor, 1968; Richardson, 1968, 1971; Garnett, 1983; Carroll, 1986).

The experiences of the Irish immigrants in the mid-nineteenth century make an interesting comparison with those of Bradford's Asian communities in the present-day. Coming largely from a rural peasant environment, they had difficulties adapting to an industrial, urban way of life. They were mainly concentrated in ghettos marked out by overcrowding and poor sanitary conditions. In many cases, they did not speak English, and interpreters had to be used in official transactions. They were subjected to strong religious prejudice, for they were predominantly Catholics in a city which was staunchly Protestant. In general, they were despised as illiterate, poverty-stricken, uncivilized and immoral. They tended to be tolerated by the indigenous population so long as they were doing work which no-one else wanted, but resented when there was any danger that they might become a financial burden on the ratepayers. Indeed, Richardson (1971) quotes evidence from the *Bradford Observer* in 1851 and again in 1860 which suggests that there was an active movement in Bradford for the repatriation of the Irish.

It was quite a different story for the immigrants who began to arrive in Bradford from Germany in the 1830s. These were mainly, but not exclusively, merchants of Jewish origin, who were anxious to escape from the oppression and anti-semitism in central Europe, and who were attracted by the blossoming textile industry in Bradford. One of the first to arrive, in 1838, was Jacob Behrens, whose family was in the textile business in Hamburg. By the time of his death in 1889, he was the head of a multi-million pound wool empire with branches in London, Glasgow, Calcutta and Shanghai. The Franco-Prussian War of 1870–71, which disrupted the woollen trade between Germany and France, led more merchants to transfer their headquarters to Bradford. By 1902, twenty-three of the thirty-six yarn manufacturers in the city were of German/Jewish origin; to this day one of the main warehousing districts in the city centre is called 'Little Germany'. From the mid-nineteenth century, the Jews and Germans began to play an active and often leading role in the economic, civic, cultural and academic life of Bradford. Behrens was one of the main figures behind the founding of the Bradford Chamber of Commerce in 1851. Charles Semon, a native of Danzig, became the town's first Jewish mayor in 1864. As their prosperity increased, the Jews and Germans became the main sponsors of the famed Bradford Subscription Concerts and Bradford Festival Choral Society. The father of the Bradford-born painter Sir William Rothenstein had settled in the town in 1859 and set up a warehouse. Similarly, the father of Bradford-born composer Frederick Delius had immigrated from Westphalia and established a firm of wool and yarn merchants. Both sons went to Bradford Grammar School, as did Humbert Wolfe, the poet and author, Ernest Leopold Sichel, the artist and sculptor, and Richard Eurich, the painter, whose fathers were all German-born. Eurich's father, Professor Frederick Eurich, who lived in Bradford most of his life, achieved fame as the conqueror of anthrax. For the Germans and Jews, established religion did not seem a high priority. It was not until 1873 that Bradford's first rabbi, the Rev Dr Joseph Strauss, arrived, though when he did he quickly set up classes in Hebrew and Judaism and established a Jewish burial ground. By this time there were perhaps 300 Jews in the town. A reform synagogue was founded in 1881, the German Evangelical Church having been set up some four years earlier (Pratt, 1971).

J.B. Priestley described the Bradford of his boyhood, in the first decade of the twentieth century, as 'at once one of the most provincial and yet one of the most cosmopolitan of English provincial cities' and called the German-Jewish community a 'curious leaven of intelligent aliens'. In those days, 'a Londoner was a stranger sight than a German' in Bradford (1977, p. 153–5). When he returned to Bradford in the 1930s, Priestley found that a new intolerance which had arisen after the First World War, together with a great slump in the wool trade, had swept away many of the big merchanting houses, particularly the German/Jewish ones. Priestley regretted their departure:

> History shows us that the countries that have opened their doors
> have gained, just as the countries that have driven out large numbers

of its (*sic*) citizens, for racial, religious or political reasons, have always paid dearly for their intolerance (*ibid.* p. 155).

After the initial influx of merchants, there were two later waves of Jewish immigration into Bradford. The first was of Russian and Polish Jews fleeing from the pogroms which had started in 1881. This time, Bradford did not prove as popular a centre as London, Leeds and Manchester. Those who did come were mainly factory workers or tailors. The second wave, beginning in 1930, was of Jews fleeing the growing Nazi influence in Germany, Czechoslovakia, Hungary, Rumania, Austria and Turkey. This group of immigrants was mainly from the professional classes. Neither wave brought large numbers to Bradford, and the current Jewish population is estimated at little over 500. The Jews continue to be very active in local politics, however, and have in recent years produced a disproportionate number of MPs, lord mayors and councillors (Heilbron, 1975; Aronsfeld, 1981; Grizzard, 1983).

The Germans, who had been both welcomed and respected in Bradford in the nineteenth century, suffered some persecution at the start of the First World War. The pork butchers' shops were particular targets. The German Evangelical Church was closed during both World Wars, and in contrast to other European groups the Germans have not maintained their own social club in the city. Since the Second World War, there have been more arrivals from Germany, including some former prisoners of war, some refugees from eastern parts of Germany and some wives of English soldiers who served in post-war Germany (Pratt, 1971).

The next main group of immigrants to arrive in Bradford were the East Europeans who came immediately after the Second World War. Many of these had fought under British command during the war, and, choosing not to return to their home countries because of the political situation there, were happy to accept the offer of employment in Bradford's textile industries. The most numerous among this group of 'European Volunteer Workers' were the Poles, then the Ukrainians, the Latvians, the Yugoslavs, the Estonians, the Bielorussians and the Lithuanians. According to the Census of 1951, the total number of East Europeans in Bradford was 5409, about 2 per cent of the city's population. They formed an easily recognizable group, distinguishable both by their appearance and by their language. Initially, there was some ill-feeling against them, but they were generally accepted in the city because they proved good workers and tended to be undemanding and to keep themselves to themselves, and also perhaps, as Le Lohé (1979, p. 186) points out, because of a general belief that 'many of them had also fought with "Monty" and you couldn't really send 'em back to Communist firing squads'.

The various East European groups sought to preserve their cultural and religious identity by setting up a wide range of clubs, churches and educational activities. There are currently two Ukrainian Catholic churches, one Polish Catholic church and a Russian Orthodox church in the city. The large number of social·clubs ensures the continued celebration of festivals and national days and has encouraged folk-dancing, choirs and many other social activities. As early as 1948, Saturday schools were started, so that children could study their parents' native languages, history, geography, literature, religion and culture. From time to time, the various communities have engaged in anti-Soviet activity, particularly through the Captive Nations Committee. Inevitably, however, the separateness of the communities has declined over the years, especially through intermarriage. A significant number of the immigrants had in fact brought Italian wives with them, and by 1973 it was reported that over one-third of second-generation Poles were marrying outside the community (*Telegraph and Argus*, 19 June 1973). Some have anglicized their surnames, following the earlier Jewish practice. Some have emigrated to Australia and Canada. Nevertheless, there are still sizable East European communities in Bradford. The Bradford Heritage Recording Unit has recently estimated the numbers as 4000 of Polish origin, 3700 of Ukrainian origin, 1200 of Yugoslavian, 500 each of Estonian, Latvian and Bielorussian and 200 of Lithuanian origin (BHRU, 1987 p. 12). More information about the East Europeans is now emerging through the research of the BHRU (*cf* Perks, 1984), and the Ukrainian Video Archives Society (established 1986).

By 1950, the influx of East Europeans had stopped, but workers from Italy, Eire and Austria were still being recruited for the textile industry, often through personal recruiting drives by mill directors (*cf* Cohen and Jenner, 1981, pp. 117–8). The Italian community now numbers about 2000 and has its own community centre and other organizations (CBMC Social Services Directorate, 1983). Apart from a continuing trickle of Italians and Yugoslavs into the city, the last significant group of European immigrants to come to Bradford was from Hungary in 1956. About 250 arrived, fleeing from the political situation in their own country, and were once again largely absorbed by the flourishing textile industry.

THE ARRIVAL OF BLACK IMMIGRANTS 1951 TO THE PRESENT

The term 'black' is now commonly used in Council documents (for example, City of Bradford Metropolitan Council (CMBC) 1984a, 1984c) to describe those immigrants (and their descendants) who began to arrive, often on special work schemes, from the West Indies, India, Pakistan (both West and East) and East Africa during the third quarter of the twentieth century. The term also sometimes includes ethnic Chinese, mainly from Hong Kong and Vietnam.

The West Indians were the first of these groups to arrive, from about 1951 onwards, to fill vacancies in the textile and engineering industries and to work in the short-staffed hospitals and transport services. From the beginning, many brought their families, clearly intent on permanent settlement, and the level of female employment has always been high. The West Indian community in Bradford never became so numerous as that in neighbouring Leeds, and currently stands at about 4500. Almost two-thirds originate from the island of Dominica, though Jamaicans and Barbadans are also well represented. Initially, there was comparative integration with the local population, as the families were dispersed through various housing estates and worshipped in Baptist, Catholic and Pentecostal churches alongside native Bradfordians. In recent years, however, there has developed an increasing sense of the distinct cultural identity of the community, seen in the growth of Rastafarianism and separate black churches such as the Church of God of Prophecy and the New Testament Church of God, and in the establishment of various West Indian societies and organizations. From time to time, the West Indians have complained that the special needs of their community are ignored by the Council in favour of the more numerous Asians, and that the educational system is failing many of their children (there are about 1000 children of 'Afro-Caribbean' origin in Bradford schools). In 1980 the West Indian Parents' Association began to run Saturday classes at Drummond Middle School, with the aim of plugging the gaps left by state schools and providing a curriculum that more closely reflected West Indian experience. Not much (except Hey, 1987) has so far been published about West Indians in Bradford, but in 1986 an oral history project called Black Heritage was set up at Checkpoint, the West Indian community centre, to collect personal histories and reminiscences within the community.

The settlement of Asians in Bradford followed a somewhat different pattern. As the East Europeans and other employees gradually left the textile mills for higher wages elsewhere, so the industry became more dependent on female labour. But when new machinery with greater productive capacity was introduced in the mid-1950s, it needed to be worked twenty-four hours a day to be economic. Women were not allowed by law to work the night-shift, but the single men who began to arrive in increasing numbers from India and Pakistan were seen by the employers as the solution to the problem. Some manufacturers began to advertize for labour in Pakistani newspapers. There is some debate about what set Asian immigration in motion. Certainly the partition of India played its part. Also many Mirpuris used the compensation they were given when their villages were submerged as a result of the construction of the Mangla Dam in the 1960s to pay for the fare to the UK. However, Singh (1986) has argued that it was neither grinding poverty nor the need to re-establish themselves after the partition of the Punjab in 1947 that brought the immigrants to Britain, but the desire for self-advancement and to enhance the social position of their family. Once the process had begun, however, it was self-perpetuating (at least until it was curtailed by the Immigration Acts of 1962 and 1971), for many more came to join relatives already here. Most Asians initially intended to work for a while, earn some money and then return. However, as more relatives arrived, and then wives and children, and as cheap inner-city properties were bought to save the cost of renting accommodation, so the desire and intention to return receded (*cf* Anwar, 1979).

For whatever reasons they came, however, the Asians were welcomed by the textile manufacturers as they provided a cheap and compliant work-force which probably kept the industry competitive for several years longer than it would otherwise have been (Cohen and Jenner, 1981). Though there were occasional strikes (Bentley, S., 1981, p. 232–3), few of the Asians belonged to trade unions (Allen, 1970, p. 106), and they were paid at a rate close to that of female employees. In 1961, when the average manual wage was £15, the Asians were averaging £8.25; ten years later, the corresponding figures were £36.12 and £16.10 (Counter Information Services, 1976, p. 27). But by the 1970s the textile industry was struggling to stay competitive, and more than 10,000 jobs were lost between 1970 and 1976. When the recession began to bite from 1977 onwards, job losses became even more severe, both in the textile mills and in the engineering plants which were either closed entirely or cut back savagely by their multinational owners. By 1984 the Council estimated that there were 37,000 (18 per cent of the working population) unemployed in the district. The immigrants were often the first to be laid off. As one commentator put it, 'the very isolation and low status of black workers that made them so valuable as recruits, now contributes to the ease with which they can be dropped' (*ibid.*, p. 29). Some of the unemployed Asians opened shops, restaurants and small businesses, with the result that the number of Asian businesses in the city increased quite dramatically, from 650 in 1978 to over 1200 in 1984 (Anwar, 1987). As Shepherd (1987) points out,

> The complete range of commercial facilities available is one reinforcer of the separateness of the South Asians. There is little need for contact with the host population except in the areas of education and employment, and it is thus easier to maintain identification with cultural roots (p. 264).

Others, however, were left to compete with the white population for a declining number of jobs. Their success in some areas, such as public transport and supermarket employment, has led to resentment from the white unemployed. In such a situation, there is an increased likelihood that racial prejudice and discrimination could thrive, especially in view of two further factors: the rapid growth in the Asian population (see below) at a time when there are not enough jobs, houses or schools available; and the continued high profile of the cultural differences between the Asians and the white population.

Some of these cultural differences were shared by the earlier waves of immigrants who came to Bradford: the strong emphasis on family and community loyalty; the emotional and other links with their place of origin; the use of unfamiliar language and corresponding inadequate grasp of English; and the desire to maintain their distinctive culture and religion. Other characteristics, however, underline the differences of the Asians from both the native Bradfordians and the earlier European immigrants. These include adherence to totally unfamiliar religions, which has become more noticeable in the city through the rapid growth of temples and mosques. The lack of a common European culture is immediately obvious in the Asians' dress, diet, music, habits of bargaining and in many other areas of behaviour. The practice of arranged marriages has ensured that there has been virtually no intermarriage with other communities. Finally, as with the West Indians, the colour of their skin makes them easily recognizable as a racially distinct group and thus a potential target for racism.

So far I have been concerned with the experiences *shared* by the Asian immigrants in general and their families, but this should not be taken to imply that the Asians form a single cohesive community or that there are not very substantial differences between individuals and groups. The bulk of the 105 organizations affiliated to Bradford's Community Relations Council (set up in the 1960s to offer advice on employment, immigration and discrimination and to monitor local authority policies) are Asian, but represent a wide variety of interests. The main distinctions between groups are in terms of language, country of origin, religion and cultural values, but for the purposes of this chapter I shall concentrate on the differences between the predominantly Hindu and Sikh Indians on the one hand and the Muslims from Pakistan and Bangladesh (East Pakistan until 1971) on the other. The Council estimates that in 1987 there were about 16,000 people of Indian origin and about 46,000 Muslims resident in Bradford (CBMC, 1984b). Allen *et al.* (1981, p. 209) and Ram (1983, 1984) have shown that though the Asians all lived very closely during the initial years of immigration, they have tended more recently to move into separate communities by religion.

The Sikhs, who originated almost entirely from the Eastern Punjab, are probably the most prosperous and the most integrated of the three main religious groups. Their prosperity, seen in their near 100 per cent home ownership, in their recent tendency to seek better accommodation in the suburbs of Bradford and in their comparatively high standard of living (*cf* Singh, 1978, pp. 5–17), is probably largely explained by two facts: they tended to move out of the textile industry and into engineering while there were still jobs available, and they are the only Asian group who have ever had a majority of wives in employment (*ibid.*, p. 12). Their comparative integration, in contrast to the Muslims, may be judged by their frequenting of public houses, by their lack of any principled objection to co-education or Western clothes, and by the willingness of some at least to dispense with turbans and beards to improve their employment chances. On the other hand, many continue to look to the Gurdwaras (Sikh temples) as the focal point for the religious, social, political and educational life of their community. There are now five Gurdwaras in Bradford, and a number of other Sikh organizations including an active Sikh Parents' Association. The Sikhs have also played an important role in several organizations that are not exclusively Sikh in membership, such as the Indian Workers' Association Bradford branch, founded in 1964, and the Asian Youth Movement, founded by Marsha Singh and others in 1977. Both these organizations are significantly involved in campaigning against racism and immigration controls, and were active in the protests against the 'bussing' of ethnic minority children (see chapter two) as well as in the later opposition to Honeyford. Though traditionally Labour voters, the Sikhs have never fielded a candidate in local elections. There are currently nine Sikh and Hindu JPs in Bradford. In spite of the conflicts at Amritsar and elsewhere in 1984–86, the Sikhs in Bradford have tended to be closer to the Hindus than to the Muslims, probably mainly because, as Taylor (1976) found in Newcastle, 'Hindus and Sikhs were less committed than the Muslims to their respective religions' (p. 228).

Somewhat more numerous than the Sikhs, the Hindu community in Bradford is made up of two distinct groups, the larger from Gujerat and the smaller from Punjab. Nearly half the Gujeratis came from East Africa, because of expulsion or the likelihood of it from Kenya and Uganda. Probably because of their different languages (*cf* Bowen, 1981), the social organizations of the Punjabi and Gujerati Hindus have developed independently. Punjabis dominate the Hindu Cultural Society which was formed in 1968, and opened a temple seven years later, to provide a focal point for community activities such as worship, marriages, the celebration of festivals, sporting and musical activities, language classes for children and English classes for women. The largest Gujerati association in Bradford, carrying out similar functions, is the Shree Prajapati Samaj, which was founded in 1975 and set up a temple in 1980. Others included Bharatiya Mandal and Sri Sathya Sai Baba Mandir. Like the Sikhs, the Hindus are comparatively affluent, to judge from their ownership of cars, telephones, videos and washing machines (Ram, 1985). Although there are fewer Hindu working women than Sikhs, they are still four times more likely than Muslim women to be in paid employment (Singh, 1978, p. 13).

Apart from a very small minority of Gujerati Muslims from India, the Muslims come from Bangladesh and from various regions of Pakistan – Azad Kashmiris from Mirpur, Punjabis from Lyallpur and Pathans from Camp-bellpur and Peshawar. Although the Bangladeshi community in the Bradford district numbers only about 2600 people, it has a very rapid growth rate. According to a recent report prepared by Bradford's race relations policy coordinator, Graham Mahoney, they are 'significantly worse off than any other group in the district' on almost any measure of deprivation (quoted in *Yorkshire Post*, 12 October 1987). Nevertheless, they have been able to make their presence felt on the local political scene. Manawar Hussain, the first Asian to be elected to both West Yorkshire County Council and Bradford Metropolitan District Council in 1973, was from Bangladesh, as was another Labour candidate, Choudhury M. Khan, who failed to get elected but later became very influential as president of both the Bangladeshi People's Association and the Council for Mosques and as a leading campaigner against Honeyford. Though the Bangladeshis are separated from the other Muslims by language (Bengali) and by location of settlement (mainly in Manningham and Keighley) and sometimes complain that they are last in the queue for Council aid (for example *Telegraph and Argus*, 3 March 1986), their cultural and religious values are closely in line with the other Muslims. Not unexpectedly (because of their larger numbers), however, the Pakistani Muslims have generally been more successful in local politics, although some commentators have found their political strategies difficult to follow (for example, Le Lohé, 1979, p. 194*ff*). There are at present three who have been elected to Bradford Council. One of these, Muhammad Ajeeb, was the city's first Asian-born Lord Mayor in 1985–86. Although they are involved in local politics, and are increasingly contributing to many aspects of life in Britain (*cf* Anwar, 1987), the Muslims are generally reported as being less in favour of social integration than the Indians (*cf* Evans, 1971), though this may be less true of second generation Muslims. Their separate community existence is focussed on such institutions as the Pakistan Community Centre and particularly the mosques. The number of mosques in Bradford now exceeds thirty, and two purpose-built mosques are now under construction, one of which, when completed, will be the largest in Europe (*cf* Dawe, 1987). More detailed statistics of Bradford's Pakistani community are provided by Anwar (1987), and both Saifullah Khan (1975) and Murphy (1987) offer illuminating insights into the daily life of Pakistanis in Bradford.

Undoubtedly it is the dominance of religion which binds the Muslim community together. This is seen, for example, in the Muslims' belief that the woman's place is in the home; in their expectation that all Muslim children will attend mosque schools in the evenings and at weekends to study the Qur'an and learn Arabic and Urdu: in their request for *halal* meat to be provided for Muslims in schools and hospitals; in their strong opposition to the local activities of the Ahmadiyya movement (a minority sect originating in Pakistan which orthodox Muslims refuse to recognize as Muslim); and in the various educational demands which are described in chapter two. Like all Asians, the Muslims put a very high value on education, but they are anxious that educational provision for their children should be in harmony with their distinctive beliefs and values as Muslims. This has led, *inter alia*, to the insistence on single-sex education at secondary level, to the establishment of an independent school for Muslim girls by the Muslim Association of Bradford and to the call for separate Muslim voluntary-aided schools by the Muslim Parents' Association.

In her research on the Mirpuri villagers in Bradford, Saifullah Khan (1975) has argued that it is the self-appointed leaders of the community, the imams, who have damaged the chances of integration by their emphasis on the fundamental religious principles and traditions of Islam. A recent programme on Pennine Radio in which Asian teenagers from Bradford aired their views on life in Britain seemed to confirm her findings: one claimed that politicians were making integration more difficult and that the provision of *halal* meat in schools was a 'political stunt', another that many Muslims were not particularly interested in 'multi-million pound mosques which the community could not afford' (*cf Telegraph and Argus*, 26 September 1987).

However, this view may be too simplistic: the imams could have no power if the Muslim community did not already have a prior commitment to accept their religious authority. Kitwood and Borrill (1980) have shown that although young Muslim adolescents in Bradford experience conflict between rival value systems, their primary loyalty is still to their own families and Islamic culture. On the other hand, some Muslim youngsters claim to be engaged in the process of educating their parents in Western values, and that they themselves are learning to combine the best qualities of both cultures – respect and an ability to question.

Compared to the Hindus and Sikhs, the Muslims have higher birth-rates, more overcrowded housing, a lower standard of living and higher rate of unemployment (*Telegraph and Argus*, 8 January 1987). But because of the numerical preponderance of Muslims in Bradford, it is *their* experience which determines the overall picture of the city's black population, as will become clear in the next section of the present chapter.

Before we turn to look at the present situation of the black groups in Bradford in more detail, however, mention must be made of one final group of recent immigrants – the Vietnamese. There had been a steady trickle of ethnic Chinese into Bradford since the end of the Second World War, mainly from Hong Kong, but in 1979–81 several hundred Vietnamese refugees arrived in Bradford, first in reception centres run by Save the Children Fund and the Ockenden Venture, and then in permanent accommodation provided mainly by the housing associations. Although their reception in the city has been generally friendly, the chances of more than a handful ever finding employment appear bleak.

BRADFORD'S BLACK POPULATION: SOME CURRENT STATISTICS

(a) Total Numbers

In 1981 the total population of the Bradford Metropolitan District was estimated at about 464,000. The 1981 Census did not ask a question about ethnic origin, but did ask people to record their country of birth. This showed that one in ten of Bradford's residents was born outside the UK. From this information, the Census was able to record the number of people living in households *headed* by someone born outside the UK. Roughly one in seven of Bradford's residents fell into this category. Of these, nearly 75 per cent were black (i.e. from the New Commonwealth or Pakistan). This is still considered to be an underestimate of Bradford's ethnic minority population, however, particularly since some of the descendants of immigrant families now live in completely separate households. Estimates provided by the Council's Policy Unit are probably more accurate.

These show that Bradford's black population grew from 6800 in 1961 to 27,800 in 1971, 52,700 in 1981 and 70,500 in 1987. The ethnic origins of this group are as follows:

Family origin in Pakistan	43,700
Family origin in Bangladesh (mainly Sylhet)	2,600
Family origin in India	16,000
Family origin in the West Indies	4,700
Family origin elsewhere in New Commonwealth (including East Africa)	3,500

About 50 per cent of the black population is under 20 years of age, and in 1981 fewer than 1½ per cent were of pensionable age. Among Pakistanis, males currently outnumber females by almost three to two. (*Sources*: CBMC, 1984a, 1984b, 1984c; Anwar, 1987)

(b) School-Children

In July 1983, there were 87,250 children in Bradford schools. Their ethnic origins were as follows:

77 per cent of UK/Eire origin
20 per cent of Asian origin
        17 per cent Muslim
         2 per cent Sikh
         1 per cent Hindu
1.2 per cent of Afro-Caribbean origin
1.8 per cent of other origins (including EEC, Eastern Europe and Far East)

By 1991 the proportion of black school-children is expected to have risen to about 30 per cent.

In addition to those carried out by the Linguistic Minorities Project in 1981, Bradford Council has carried out several of its own language surveys. The latest, in 1987, reports that a total of sixty-nine languages are known and in use by children in Bradford and that almost 25 per cent of the city's schoolchildren use a language other than English at home. The five most commonly used languages are:

Punjabi Urdu	73.0 per cent
Punjabi Gurmukhi	7.1 per cent
Gujerati	6.2 per cent
Bengali	5.4 per cent
Pushtu	3.3 per cent

The next six, each accounting for less than 1 per cent of the non-English speakers, are Italian, Polish, Hindi, Cantonese, Ukrainian and Creole. (*Sources*: Linguistic Minorities Project, 1983; CBMC, 1983, 1984a, 1984c; *Telegraph and Argus*, 29 June 1987)

(c) Future Growth

Bradford is the fastest growing metropolitan district in Britain, and this growth results mainly from the increase in the city's black population, which is rising by about 3000 people a year. About one-third of these are accounted for by immigration (mainly of women and children and mainly from Pakistan and Bangladesh) and two-thirds by births. It is estimated that by 1996 Bradford's black population will have risen to over 91,000. The birth rate in Bradford's black families is very significantly higher compared to the rest of the city's population, though the difference is gradually decreasing. Currently about 30 per cent of births in the city are to women of Pakistani or New Commonwealth origins.

The bulk of this growth is likely to take place in the inner-city areas where the black population is mainly concentrated. In one inner-city ward (University), 68 per cent of the population is black, and in three others (Bradford North, Toller and Little Horton) the proportion is between 25 per cent and 50 per cent. The highest proportion in Keighley is Keighley North ward with 15 per cent.

Among the implications of this population growth and its distribution, we may note that by 1996:

(i) there will be 10,000 to 12,000 more black children of school age in the city, which will put excessive strain on existing inner-city educational facilities, especially since a significantly higher proportion of ethnic minority pupils stay on at school past the age of sixteen;

(ii) there will be well over 10,000 more black people looking for work, adding to the already desperate employment situation for the black school-leaver and black adult. (In 1981–3 only 7 per cent of black school-leavers looking for work in Bradford found any, compared to over 30 per cent of white school-leavers.) Some look for explanations in terms of levels of proficiency in English and general qualifications (for example, Selbourne, 1987, p. 100*ff*), but research by Campbell and Jones (1983) suggests that the only reason for the different levels of success is skin colour. More recent figures show only minimal improvement);

(iii) there will be more than 5000 additional black families formed, many of whom will seek inner-city accommodation, though there is already serious overcrowding in many such areas, and a shortage of Council housing for larger families. (*Sources*: CBMC, 1984a, 1984b, 1984c; *Bradford Star*, 1 May 1986; *Telegraph and Argus*, 5 March 1986, 29 March 1986)

RACE RELATIONS AND COUNCIL POLICIES

I have already suggested that the increased competition for jobs and housing in Bradford, the rapid growth of the black population and the continuing visible differences of skin colour, culture and religion, could easily combine to create a climate in which racism could thrive. These three factors, together with the greater dissatisfaction felt by many young blacks because of the higher expectations that their education has given them, and the search by some sections of the white population for a scapegoat to take the blame for what they see as the declining quality of life in Bradford (CBMC, 1984a), have made some form of racial conflict almost inevitable.

Racism in Bradford has taken several forms. There has been the racism of the extremist political parties which have sought to stir up resentment of immigrants and sometimes to demand their repatriation. There has been the overt racist behaviour of bullying and intimidation, gang fights, arson attacks, physical assaults (especially on bus and taxi drivers), verbal baiting, graffiti and general rudeness. And there has been what is now usually called institutional racism, resulting from the fact that the city's institutions were designed (or had developed) primarily to meet the needs of white people. The indirect discrimination and disadvantage suffered by black people as a result of this form of racism is now being tackled by the Council in a series of race relations initiatives.

The three main anti-immigrant political parties that have been active in Bradford are the Yorkshire Campaign to Stop Immigration, which was founded in Bradford by J. Merrick in 1970 and which fought several seats in the local elections up to 1975, without much success (*cf* Le Lohé, 1979, p. 198*ff*); the British National Party, which received some publicity when it was joined in 1983 by a former Bradford headmaster, Stanley Garnett; and the National Front, which took over the main anti-immigrant mantle in Bradford in 1976. Although its official activities consist largely in organizing rallies, contesting elections and distributing anti-immigration literature, the main achievement of the National Front in Bradford has been to act as a symbolic focus for much of the intimidation and harassment of blacks by white youths. The activities of the BNP and NF in Bradford schools are discussed further in chapter two, together with the response to their activities by a variety of anti-racist groups.

It is very difficult to estimate the amount of overt racist behaviour experienced by the minority communities of Bradford. It is fairly clear that what is reported in the newspapers is only the tip of the iceberg. Such groups as the Azad Kashmiri Muslim Association and the Asian Youth Movement have claimed that racism is rife in Bradford, and that some children have been too frightened to go to school because of racist attacks. It is true that the violence has not always been one-way, and that Asian gangs have sometimes sought to retaliate. But the trial of the 'Bradford Twelve' brought to light the cloud of fear under which many blacks in the city were living. The Bradford Twelve were a group of Asian youths drawn mainly from the Asian Youth Movement and the United Black Youth League (significantly a mixture of Muslims, Hindus and a Sikh) who were arrested in July 1981 after the discovery of a crate of petrol bombs they had made. The time was a period of racial unrest in various parts of Britain, not only involving attacks on and provocation of Asians in Southall and Walthamstow (*cf* Jacobs, 1986, ch. 6), but also involving clashes between West Indians and police in Brixton, Liverpool and elsewhere (*cf* Cashmore and Troyna, 1983, p. 172*ff*). The defendants claimed that they had made the bombs to protect their community in case a threatened invasion by skinheads materialized. After a six-weeks trial, during which the picture emerged of a community which was under constant fear of attack yet was offered little protection by the police, all the defendants were acquitted in June 1982 (Wilson, A. 1981, 1982; Pierce, 1982; Leeds Other Paper (LOP), 1982).

Partly in response to the heightened racial tensions, the Council embarked on its new race relations initiative in 1981. The expressed aim was to work for social justice for all groups by promoting policies and practices which would create:

i)   equality of esteem between different cultures
ii)   equality of opportunity in employment
iii)   equality of access to council services
iv)   the development of services that were relevant to *all* sections of the community
v)   the elimination of discrimination on racial grounds

(CMBC, 1984c, p. 6)

An all-party Race Relations Advisory Group was set up in the same year, and this produced a twelve-point policy statement for distribution to all Council employees, encouraged the greater use of minority languages in Council documents, called for ethnic records to be kept on recruitment and services within the Council, and carried out a major scheme of consultation with many of the ethnic minority organizations named earlier in the present chapter. The consultations were sometimes fiery affairs (*Yorkshire Post*, 30 April 1982), and the Advisory Group also found itself under attack from some councillors who resented its interference (*Keighley News*, 30 April 1982). Nevertheless, it succeeded in encouraging several changes in Council policy, particularly in the community programme, Council employment, housing, education and the social services. Let us look briefly at the changes in each of these five areas.

First, the share of the community programme (i.e. the distribution of discretionary grants to community organizations and projects) that was allotted to the ethnic minorities had risen by 1985 from less than 10 per cent to about 50 per cent. However, the Council has perhaps not taken enough trouble so far to explain to the general electorate that this is not to be considered as an example of unfairly favouring the minority communities, but of recognizing the parity of needs of all sections of the community and putting money wherever research identifies the greatest need. Secondly, the Council was aware that as the largest employer in the district it should set an example with a genuine equality of opportunity policy. To this end it insisted that all Council employees involved in recruitment should attend Racism Awareness training courses. The aim of recruiting more black staff to Council departments has so far had only limited success; in 1986 only 4 per cent of the Council workforce was black (*Yorkshire Post*, 23 June 1986), and less than 2 per cent of the teaching force, very much lower than the percentage of blacks in the total population. Thirdly, the main problems in housing have been the poor condition of the inner-city housing occupied by black families, and the growing number of such families seeking accommodation. Some 40 per cent of Council expenditure on renovation grants, and 40 per cent of house purchase advances, now goes to ethnic minority families. However, there is still a problem in the shortage of Council housing for large families. Fourthly, the main changes in educational provision to take into account the growing number of ethnic minority schoolchildren are described in chapter two. These have been financed largely under Section 11 provisions, i.e. grants from central government under the terms of the 1966 Local Government Act to meet (currently) 75 per cent of the costs of providing for the 'special needs of immigrants'. Finally, the Council has embarked on a number of initiatives to provide more information to ethnic minorities on what is available through the social services department and to gear that department's provision more closely to the communities' needs.

In spite of the wide range of these policy initiatives, the prospects for black youngsters in Bradford are not rosy. Often brought up in large families living on a low income in sub-standard and overcrowded housing, they experience the kind of disadvantages associated with an inner-city upbringing (*cf* Wedge and Prosser, 1973; Murphy, 1987, ch. 2; West, 1987), in a city which has already suffered disproportionately from the growing North-South divide (CBMC, 1984a; CSO, 1986). Poor qualifications and the experience of discrimination ensure that they are at the bottom of the pile in the search for employment. In addition, they are likely to be under other pressures as they struggle to find their own identity between conflicting cultures, and have to cope with direct experiences of racism at the same time. Education is often held up as the answer, not only to the city's general economic and social problems, but also as the key to good race relations through the development of a parity of esteem for all individuals and an equal respect for all the cultures represented in the city. We must now therefore turn to examine how far the Council's educational policies are succeeding in making a reality of their vision of Bradford as a truly multi-cultural and multi-racial city.

2 LEA Policies: The Growth of Multi-culturalism in Bradford

For more than two decades until the sudden eruption of the Honeyford affair in March 1984, Bradford enjoyed a reputation for its provision for ethnic minority groups that was second to none; and nowhere was this reputation higher than in the field of education. As early as 1970, Allen wrote of Bradford's pride in 'setting an example to other areas in its management of the race situation...particularly in education' (pp. 102–23). In the early 1980s the city earned high praise from successive chairmen of the Commission for Racial Equality, as well as from a number of visiting MPs, and its reputation was further bolstered by a string of articles in *The Times Educational Supplement*, including one entitled 'How Bradford Held on to its Lead in Race' (Spencer, 1983). Even *Race Today* called Bradford 'a trail-blazer and leader in the field of race relations policy' (Morris *et al.*, 1984).

But how accurate is this popular image of Bradford as a multi-racial pace-setter? The image has been criticized from two opposed points of view. On the one hand it is claimed that prior to 1980 Bradford had done nothing to merit its high reputation, which depended on little more than the avoidance of any large-scale disturbances. Grigg (1967, pp. 120, 124) implied as much twenty years ago. On this view, Bradford's policy towards its minority groups before 1980 could best be described as one of benign indifference. The city's Chief Executive, Gordon Moore, commented, 'We used to think we had good race relations when in fact we had no race relations at all' (quoted in Jack, 1985). Action was taken only when it became apparent, in the face of the real possibility of race riots in the city in 1981, that there were no bridges between the communities, indeed nothing to facilitate any sort of communication or negotiation.

On the other hand it is claimed that race relations in the city were no problem before 1980, when the Council started to take matters into its own hands. On this view, the new multi-racial and multi-cultural policies were a major cause of subsequent problems, both because of the way they were introduced and because little attempt was made to ensure popular support for them. In the words of Mike Whittaker, the city's former Policies Development Officer (quoted in Selbourne, 1984a), they were 'imposed from the top' – a notion that Honeyford stressed in his criticism of 'Council diktats' – and some would say imposed too quickly to expect widespread support. Pedley (1986) quotes the Chief Education Officer of another West Yorkshire town as observing, 'Bradford was leading by the chin and would some day pay the penalty'. In such circumstances it was only to be expected that doubts about the wisdom of the policies would be expressed publicly sooner or later; all that was needed was a spokesman. The emergence of Honeyford as the thorn in the side of the local Council, the *bête noir* of the anti-racist movement and, ultimately, the champion of the 'New Right', thus has an air of inevitability. In the words of one commentator, 'If a man like Ray Honeyford did not exist, he would have to be invented' (*Daily Telegraph*, 6 January 1986).

This particular polarization of views over Bradford's multi-racial policies lies at the very heart of the Honeyford affair. Neither the persistence of Honeyford in criticizing current trends in multi-cultural education nor the persistence of his opponents in calling for his dismissal can be understood without reference to it. *He* believed that the policies were misguided and in the final analysis not in the best interests of either the indigenous population or the minority groups; *they* believed that justice could not be achieved for the minorities in Bradford without these policies, and that *he* was the main stumbling block in the way of their smooth implementation. Chapter three examines in more detail the articles in which Honeyford presents his specific criticisms of Bradford's policies and his more general criticisms of what he calls the 'multi-racial lobby'. Chapter four looks at the response of his opponents, and tells the story of the campaign for his dismissal. But first it is necessary to look more closely at the development of the educational policies for minority groups in Bradford. Exactly what were Bradford's race relations policies and innovatory guidelines for schools? What gave rise to them, and what problems were they trying to solve? What values underpinned them, and how controversial were they? How were they introduced, what new demands did they make of Bradford's teachers, and how were the reforms perceived by those they affected most?

The present chapter aims to provide answers to these questions, and is divided into three sections. The first seeks to unravel the complexity of the issues and influences underlying the Council's educational policies, and some of the constraints affecting their implementation. The second outlines the specific demands made by minority groups in Bradford relating to the education of their children, and the detailed policies agreed on by the Council as a response to those demands. The third traces the stages in the development of Bradford's multi-cultural and multi-racial policies, and provides the context in which Honeyford's criticisms of these policies appeared.

UNTANGLING THE ISSUES

The guidelines issued by Bradford Council in 1982 regarding the education of pupils from ethnic minority groups were based on two fundamental beliefs. The first was that all sections of the community in the city had an equal right to the maintenance of their distinctive identities and loyalties of culture, language, religion and custom, and that so far as was compatible with individual needs, the authority's provision of services should respect the strength and variety of each group's cultural values. The second was that all children in Bradford were entitled to equality of treatment, equality of opportunity and equality of services and should be offered a shared educational experience. Both of these fundamental beliefs had been set out in the local authority's policy statement on race relations the previous year. Together, they gave rise to the following statement of the aims of education in Bradford:

1. To seek ways of preparing all children and young people for life in a multi-cultural society.
2. To counter racism and racist attitudes, and the inequalities and discrimination which results (*sic*) from them.
3. To build on and develop the strengths of cultural and linguistic diversity.
4. To respond sensitively to the special needs of minority groups.

The Authority recognizes the organizational difficulties of achieving these aims, while at the same time responding to the individual needs of children, and safeguarding the rights of parents under the terms of the 1944 Education Act. Nevertheless, it is convinced that, with sensitivity and a sympathetic understanding of cultural and religious issues, the educational needs of ethnic minority children can be met within the one educational system and within the framework of a common school curriculum (City of Bradford Local Administrative Memorandum (LAM) No 2/82).

It is not difficult to find evidence in this statement of the influence of the catalysts which speeded up its appearance: the civil disturbances in Toxteth, Bristol, Brixton and Southall in the summer of 1981 and, much nearer home, the arrest of the Bradford Twelve which was described in chapter one; the increasingly vociferous and well-publicized complaints against un-Islamic practices in schools such as mixed swimming; the continued calls for the establishment of single-sex schools for Muslim girls; and, not least, a growing awareness of the legitimate grievances and fears of the ethnic minority groups in Bradford and elsewhere that emerged during the protracted trial of the Bradford Twelve.

What is more difficult to assess is how much political opportunism there was in the new policies. It is true that the voting power of the minority groups was now sufficiently large to have an impact on local elections, particularly since Bradford was a hung Council. Morris *et al.* (1984) argue that the inclusion of racism on the education policy agenda by some Conservative councillors was a clear attempt to attract the black vote, and quote one unnamed Conservative councillor:

> Any political party that tells you that it's doing things for purely altruistic reasons is either a fool or a liar. Clearly both political parties or three political parties are looking to take a chunk of the black and Asian vote. Speaking as a Conservative, I am realistic in realizing that at the moment my party is not receiving a great number of Asian votes.

Selbourne (1985) similarly describes the 'many layers of hypocrisy' which lay behind the 'public facade of local Labour's righteous crusade for mutual respect among the West Riding's races'. On the other hand, there is also evidence to suggest that the local political parties were not merely involved in a scramble for the ethnic minority vote. The race relations policy statement had all-party support, and such disagreements as there were over specific provisions (such as whether *halal* meat should be provided in schools) were not along party lines. Neither is there any evidence to suggest that the policies were motivated by the political radicalism which was apparent, for example, in some London boroughs. It may well be that the development of the new policies had as much to do with a genuine desire to act in justice and fairness to minority groups as with political manoeuvrings.

Whatever considerations lay behind them, however, the policies were generally presented to the public as a practical response to a practical situation. Peter Gilmour, the Conservative chairman of Bradford's Educational Services Committee at the time the policies were approved, drew attention to their pragmatism:

> They're just realistic. One in six of our children come from Asian families. By the turn of the century it will be one in three. The parents are ratepayers. It is the simple duty of the Council to try to satisfy their needs. (quoted in Cross, 1984)

The emerging picture of well-intentioned and widely supported reforms, however, conceals a whole mass of complicating factors. I shall seek to draw attention to some of these by focussing on just one of the controversial concepts contained in the Authority's official statement of aims, the concept of needs.

It has been frequently pointed out (for example, by Dearden, 1966, 1968, pp. 14–18; Gribble, 1969, pp. 80–86; Hirst and Peters, 1970, pp. 32–36) that behind any statement of needs lie certain assumptions about what is valuable or desirable. For to need something implies not only that one has not got that thing, but that to obtain it would be to achieve something that is regarded as desirable. It is thus appropriate, as Dearden (1968, p. 16) points out, 'to look behind statements of needs to the values that are guiding them, for it is here that the issue substantially lies'. This will become clearer as we look at exactly whose special needs are under consideration in the Bradford documents, on what basis these needs are assessed and who is to make the crucial decisions about these needs.

Whose needs are being referred to in the Bradford documents? The Local Administrative Memorandum quoted above (LAM 2/82) mentions the 'educational needs of ethnic minority children' and the 'special needs of minority groups', whereas Gilmour appears to be talking of the needs of Asian families and parents. However, it cannot be assumed that the needs of these various groups are identical. For one thing, it is much easier for adults than for children to define their own needs. When minority groups or parents talk of their needs, they have in mind the achievement of goals which they themselves value or desire, such as the maintenance, preservation and transmission of their distinctive identities or cultural and religious loyalties; and these perceived needs may form the basis of minority group demands such as those discussed later in the present chapter. When we talk of the educational needs of ethnic minority children, however, we are talking of things which others (i.e. adults) consider will be beneficial to them.

Of course it is possible to imagine a situation in which there is general agreement that the educational needs of ethnic minority children do in fact coincide with the needs of their parents and of the community in which they are growing up. For example, a Muslim child no doubt needs a degree of continuity between what she learns at home and what she learns at school if she is to avoid the moral schizophrenia which might arise from being presented with conflicting values before she is able to evaluate these for herself; but such continuity would also facilitate the maintenance of traditional patterns of authority within the family and the strengthening of bonds which tie the child to the minority group to which her family belongs. On the other hand, it is equally possible to envisage a situation in which the needs of ethnic minority children clash directly with the 'needs' of their parents and ethnic community. It is frequently maintained, especially by liberal educationalists, that children need to be helped to see beyond the limited horizons of the present and the particular if they are to develop into autonomous adults (*cf* Bailey, 1984), and that education provides the only way to prevent children from becoming trapped in a restricting culture. In such situations, where there is no agreement over what is desirable for ethnic minority children, the invocation of needs is unhelpful unless it proves possible either for an objective specification to be made of what these children need, or for all parties to agree to accept the judgement of an expert, or for a consensus to be arrived at by negotiation between all the parties concerned. Let us look at each of these possibilities more closely.

Is it possible to specify objectively the special education needs which result from membership of an ethnic minority? One way of attempting this would be to explore the characteristics which distinguish the immigrants and their families from the rest of the population of Bradford, and then to consider the possible educational consequences of these differences. As we saw in chapter one, certain characteristics, such as strong emotional ties with their country of origin, are shared by virtually all the waves of immigrants to arrive in Bradford in the last hundred years. Other characteristics are shared only by those immigrants who have arrived from New Commonwealth countries, Pakistan and Vietnam in the last thirty years: a racial origin and skin colour which immediately makes them distinguishable from the indigenous white population; and the lack of a common European culture, which also makes their 'foreignness' more noticeable. Finally, there is in many cases the attachment to a religion which is unfamiliar to most of the indigenous population, and which appears to be in conflict with some of their basic values. The religion dictates specific patterns of behaviour for believers, forms the primary focus of their loyalty and thus marks them out as a distinctive community. This final characteristic is shared by upwards of 80 per cent of the immigrant families in Bradford, the vast majority of them Muslim.

However, it is not possible to move from factual statements like these about the characteristics of ethnic minorities to a statement about their children's needs, because statements of the latter kind always contain hidden or explicit value assumptions. For example, those who place a high value on social, economic and political integration will no doubt see the special educational needs of ethnic minority pupils in terms of the removal of any barriers (such as inadequate English or cross-cultural understanding, or the experience of racism or other forms of prejudice) which might prevent them from competing on equal terms with their indigenous peers in the employment market and elsewhere. Those who place a high value on the maintenance of a distinct cultural identity, on the other hand, are likely to see the needs of these pupils more in terms of the development of their personal esteem, self respect and sense of belonging, their coming to appreciate the contribution of their group to life in the broader multi-cultural society, or their being protected from the undesirable influences of the broader society (*cf* Husain and Ashraf, 1979, p. 40). It is not difficult to see that these two ways (and they are not the only possibilities) of understanding the special needs of ethnic minority pupils are pulling in different directions: the first towards social integration and cohesion, and the second towards the preservation of religious and cultural differences. I have discussed this apparent incompatibility in more detail elsewhere (Halstead, 1986, pp. 5*ff*), but two examples from the situation in Bradford will serve to illustrate the problem here. The first is the practice of some Asian parents of taking or sending their children on extended trips to the Indian sub-continent. No doubt such trips help their children to develop a greater awareness of their cultural roots, but equally the trips hold back their development of the English language and other skills they require if they are to participate fully in the political, social and economic life of the UK. The second example is the question of co-education, which is widely perceived in this country to have educational advantages. However, the Muslim belief that boys and girls should not mix freely after the age of puberty has made single-sex schools, particularly for Muslim girls, one of the most persistent demands of the Muslim community. In both examples, current Council policy has indicated a value judgment which gives priority to the preservation of cultural identity over the promotion of social integration and cohesion. But there do not appear to be any objective grounds on which this value judgment is based.

If it is not possible to specify objectively the special educational needs of ethnic minority children, is it not best to leave decisions to the judgment of experts? This is broadly the approach adopted by Bradford, both as a general policy, drawing, for example, on such authoritative statements on how children learn as the *Bullock Report* (DES, 1975), and particularly in the early days of its special provision for ethnic minority pupils. Initiatives such as 'bussing' and the establishment of immigrant language centres were set up on the recommendation of the Department of Education and Science (DES), while the individual teacher was left with considerable professional discretion over how to interpret and assess the needs of individual pupils arising, for example, from racism, conflicting cultural demands or poor English. There are several problems with this dependence on expertise, however. The first is that no form of educational expertise licenses a person to make fundamental value judgments on behalf of others; P. White (1983, p. 10) and others have argued strongly that 'there are no moral experts on the good life'. Secondly, even in the area of practical decision-making, the educational experts often do not agree among themselves. This disagreement lies at the heart of several of the changes or reversals of policy in Bradford, such as the abandonment of the policy of 'bussing'; this policy had come increasingly under fire in the mid-1970s from academics such as Professor Terence Lee of the University of Surrey as having a potentially deleterious effect on the education of ethnic minority pupils. Thirdly, there was the danger that the dependence on experts, at least if those experts were drawn exclusively from the majority culture, could perhaps unintentionally legitimize what the minority groups saw as continued cultural domination. The decisions of experts often turned out to be '*our* judgements as to the worth of elements of *their* culture' (Harris, 1982a, p. 227).

It was at least in part a recognition of the unfairness of this conscious or unconscious cultural bias that led Bradford Council to adopt a more cautious approach to the special needs of ethnic minority pupils. This is seen not only in the tendency to introduce new policies (such as the mother-tongue teaching projects or the new regulations for worship in schools) on an experimental basis initially, but also in the willingness to consult more widely and to search for a consensus among all interested parties prior to actual decision-making. This has led both to increased co-operation between the major partners in the educational enterprise, and to a shift to some extent in the relative power of the various partners. In Bradford's case, the initiative seems to be currently in the hands of the local authority, though I want now to take a closer look at the involvement of the government and DES, the teachers, the local community and the parents as well.

The government's major contribution to the debate about the needs of ethnic minority pupils is the commissioning of the *Swann Report* (DES, 1985), but this report has in fact had little impact on Bradford's policies. Indeed, the influence has mainly been the other way round, for Bradford's pioneering policies were well established before the appearance of the report and Bradford was well represented among the members of the Swann Committee. On the other hand, Bradford's policy statements are claimed to be at least in part a clarification and amplification of the existing law. Thus the right of parents to be given information about schools (enshrined in the 1980 Education Act) is extended in Bradford's LAM No 2/82 to their right to receive this information in their own language. Similarly, the right of parents to withdraw their children from religious education and from the school's collective act of worship (enshrined in the 1944 Education Act) is clarified and explained in the LAM. On the other hand, the draft guidelines on school assemblies issued by Bradford's Directorate of Educational Services (CBMC, 1986a, 1986b), which allocate worship to a separate slot on the school timetable from morning assembly and allow for the setting up of non-worship groups in addition to Christian, Muslim, Hindu and Sikh groups, can best be described as following the spirit rather than the letter of the 1944

Education Act. In other cases, the local authority appears to have avoided a strict enforcement of existing laws: breaches of planning regulations by Muslim supplementary schools have sometimes been ignored; it is claimed that a blind eye is turned to the widespread Muslim practice of keeping their daughters at home to protect them from contact with un-Islamic practices at school (though council officers deny that this is in fact a widespread practice); and keeping children away from school for extended periods so that they can visit the Indian sub-continent is now officially viewed as a potentially enriching educational experience rather than a breach of the law.

A large number of the special provisions for the needs of ethnic minority pupils set out in the LAM, however, consist of rules laid down by the local authority. Some of these, such as the provision of *halal* meat in schools, were debated and approved by the full Council after extensive consultation and lobbying. Others were based on established good practice in some schools, which was now extended on a prescriptive basis, on the recommendation of the Directorate of Education, to all schools within the authority. These rules of good practice include permission for children to stay away from school on religious festivals; to receive instruction in their own religion in school time, either in school or elsewhere; to engage in communal prayer led by an imam during the lunch period; to wear traditional dress instead of school uniform, and religious jewellery if their parents wish; and to cover their bodies if they choose, for dancing, PE, swimming and showers. Other special provisions are not prescriptive, however, but merely advise teachers to exercise special tact and sensitivity in areas such as sex education and fund-raising activities involving lotteries and gambling, which Muslims have found offensive.

This increase in the rules which headteachers and staff are required to follow has led to a corresponding decrease in teachers' professional autonomy, by narrowing the scope within which teachers are free to make their own judgments about the educational needs of ethnic minority pupils. The multi-cultural concessions outlined above, as set out in LAM No. 2/82, do not seem to have caused much resentment among Bradford teachers; perhaps they were, as they claimed, merely codifying existing good practice. But the reception of LAM No. 6/83 was a different story. This memorandum gave headteachers new guidelines on how to challenge and correct racist behaviour, and required them to identify, categorize and report any racist incidents in their schools. This time heads baulked at what appeared to them to be increasing central authoritarianism, an affront to their professional expertise and an erosion of their traditional rights and authority. The local association of headteachers voted against implementing the memorandum. This led to a bitter confrontation between heads and councillors, in which heads were called 'power-mad', 'whining' and 'destructive' by both sides of the Council chamber. A local MP, Sir Marcus Fox, on the other hand, supported the heads and dismissed the LAM as a huge 'busybodying exercise'. Many heads also resented having to attend the compulsory race awareness training courses, especially when supply cover was not always provided. Some considered these courses an affront to their professional integrity, and others were offended by what they saw as an aggressiveness and bluntness in the approach adopted by the trainers. A large number of heads felt that educational priorities were getting out of hand, that a disproportionate amount of time, energy and money was being put into the special educational needs of ethnic minority children. Rumours circulated throughout 1984 and 1985, in spite of official denials, that an unusually high number of Bradford heads were seeking early retirement because (in the words of one head) of 'Council bullying'.

As the part played by heads and the teaching profession generally in making the crucial decisions about educational provision for ethnic minority children declined, so the local authority showed an increased willingness to consult and take account of the views and wishes of ethnic minority parents and the local community. Parents were granted more rights in the LAM No. 2/82 than they ever had before (such as the right to withdraw their children on cultural grounds from mixed PE or swimming lessons), and though of course an acceptance of these rights by parents involved an implicit acceptance of the local authority's own right to make such decisions, the local authority did engage in extensive consultations with local community leaders, as seen in chapter one. Often in practice this meant listening to the demands of the leaders of minority pressure groups and community associations. Over fifty such groups are listed in the *Bradford and District Citizens' Guide (Telegraph and Argus*, 1986). On some issues the various pressure groups clearly had different priorities. Saifullah Khan (1975) draws attention to divisions among the Pakistani community in Bradford, and more recent examples of disagreement between pressure groups include the proposal by the Muslim Parents' Association to set up five Muslim voluntary-aided schools in Bradford, which was strongly opposed by the Asian Youth League, while opinion was divided on the issue in the influential Council for Mosques. Similarly, some minority groups supported the decision by Workers Against Racism (an offshoot of the Revolutionary Communist Party) to set up vigilante groups in Bradford in 1986 to protect Asian families and schoolchildren from racist attacks, while others were deeply suspicious of the move. When the various pressure groups were united in support of a cause, however, they appeared always to obtain the concessions they were seeking. This was the case in the call for the provision of *halal* meat in schools; Sikhs and Hindus supported the Muslims in their demands, and were promised support for their own future causes in return. It was also the case, as we shall see, in the calls for Honeyford's dismissal. But whether the primary focus of these various demands was the educational needs of the children or the cultural 'needs' of the parents remains an open question.

With this question of *whose* needs are under discussion, this brief investigation of the theory and origins of Bradford's educational policies for the city's ethnic minority children has come a full circle. What it is hoped the investigation *has* achieved, however, is a greater awareness of the complexities of the situation. In exploring the background to Bradford's special provisions, we are faced with a situation in which a range of different educational needs may be experienced by ethnic minority pupils, resulting, for example, from experiences of racism, conflicting cultural demands or a poor grasp of English. Which particular needs are closest to their experience may vary from pupil to pupil. Sometimes one need is highlighted in the media or in educational research, sometimes another. The situation is further complicated by the necessity for policy to take account of fundamental clashes of principle, as between the right of children not to be trapped in a restricting culture and the right of parents at least to ensure some degree of continuity between what their children learn at home and what they learn at school. These difficulties are clearly open to a variety of possible solutions, and the situation is still further complicated by the not uncommon changes in policy on the part of the Council and the significant opposition to some of these policies from sections of the teaching profession. On top of this comes the activity of a large number of pressure groups among the ethnic minorities, often pulling in different directions, and the efforts of white activists either seeking to win the ethnic minorities to their particular cause (as in the case of Workers Against Racism) or totally opposing a provision decided on by the Council (as in the case of the opposition of animal rights activists to the provision of *halal* meat in schools). The net result is a situation of such complexity that it is easy to get bogged down in detail or to succumb to bias or preconceptions in the representation of events and policies. What is needed is some way of accurately mapping out the issues to give direction to our thinking and to prevent us from wandering aimlessly and indefinitely in this largely uncharted jungle.

I have attempted to provide this initial analysis in three stages. The first involves the provision of a chronology of all the major events in Bradford in the last twenty-five years relating to the city's educational provision for ethnic minorities. The second is an analysis of the specific educational demands made by minority groups and the detailed and varying policies agreed by the local authority in response to those demands. The third outlines the main stages in the development of Bradford's policies towards its ethnic minority children, and provides the context for the appearance of Honeyford's controversial articles.

The first stage of this analysis is contained in the appendix. This comprises a chronological survey of the main events involving ethnic minorities in Bradford in the last twenty-five years, the actions of the Council and the Directorate of Education, the main pieces of educational research conducted on Bradford, and brief references to political decisions or events in other parts of the country where these are deemed relevant to the situation in Bradford. The chronology has been based on as many of the available printed sources as possible, namely, Council publications and unpublished documents, local and national newspaper articles, educational research and other reports on the situation in Bradford published in books and journals, reports by headteachers, educational advisers and the city's Director of Education, and policy statements and press releases from ethnic minority and other pressure groups. This strong emphasis on documentary evidence has been balanced by the personal experience of teaching in Bradford for twelve years during the period under discussion, and by informal conversations with many of the personalities involved. The sources used for information about Bradford included in the appendix are fully referenced, and all of the unacknowledged references to Bradford in the main text are based on material included in the appendix.

The second and third stages of the analysis of Bradford's policies make up the two remaining sections of the present chapter.

MINORITY DEMANDS AND LOCAL AUTHORITY RESPONSES

(1) The Teaching of Islam in State Schools

Not surprisingly, the first demand to be made by the predominantly Muslim ethnic minorities in Bradford was for the teaching of Islam in schools, though this demand was not made until the late 1960s, when the Muslim community was already both sizable and well-established. Up to that time, the transmission of the Islamic faith and culture had been considered the responsibility of the family and the Mosque school. Saifullah Khan (1975) has emphasized particularly the role of Muslim women in the transmission of religious traditions, and, in earlier research, Goodall (1968) reported that most children from Pakistani families in Bradford attended Mosque schools from fifteen to twenty hours a week, to learn Arabic and Urdu and to read the Qur'an.

As Muslim groups became aware of the general right of parents under the 1944 Education Act to arrange denominational religious instruction for their children, either by bringing an outside instructor into the school or by taking their children out of school at the beginning or end of the school day for such lessons, so pressure began to mount for such instruction to be provided for Muslim children in Bradford's secondary schools. The Muslim Association of Bradford and the Muslim Education Trust were the main pressure groups involved at this stage. In 1969, Bradford's Director of Education, F.J. Adams, was worried by these requests, though he recognized the need in principle to respect the rights of minorities. He saw them as running counter to Bradford's policy of integration, and spoke of the danger of 'a divisive element creeping into the schools'. Initially, permission was given for instruction in Islam only at Bradford's immigrant education centres, but in 1972 this was extended to any secondary schools in the district. Commenting on this decision by Bradford's Educational Services Committee, Councillor Albert Swindlehurst said, 'Until there was integration and they perhaps had their own denominational schools, the committee should at least attempt to help them.'

Thus Bradford's LAM No. 2/82 was a clarification and codification of policy which had been instituted ten years earlier. Parents were free to withdraw children from school to receive religious instruction elsewhere, or to arrange for such instruction to be held on school premises. The last hour of school on Fridays was set aside for this purpose. In addition, imams were given permission to enter schools at lunch-time, on the request of parents, to lead Muslim children in prayer.

The demand for the teaching of Islam in state schools had two further repercussions on local authority policy. First, it acted as a catalyst to the development of the city's new agreed syllabus for Religious Education, which sought to give a fair treatment of, and show equal respect for, all the major world faiths. Secondly, the proliferating Mosque schools and other supplementary schools, which remained the main centres for instruction in Islam, were financially supported by the Council. In 1983, a grant of £100,000 was temporarily withheld in an attempt to persuade the supplementary schools to improve standards of health and safety.

Two main doubts hang over local authority policy. On the one hand, there is the question how far, if at all, local authority schools can be used to maintain and transmit *any* religious faith. On the other, it is questionable whether the Council should give financial support to supplementary schools whose methods of teaching and discipline and dogmatic approach are fundamentally in conflict with contemporary educational belief and practice in this country. It has also been claimed that lengthy tuition outside school hours curtails Muslim children's chances of benefitting educationally from normal extra-curricular activities, and perhaps impairs their ability to obtain maximum benefit from their schooling.

(2) The Retention of Single-Sex Schooling

Single-sex schooling, particularly for girls of secondary school age, has been one of the most sustained demands of the Muslims in Bradford (Iqbal, 1975). Islamic law and traditions do not allow the free mixing of the sexes outside the family after the age of puberty, and some Muslim parents have been prepared to keep their daughters away from school altogether, or to send them to Pakistan to complete their education, rather than allow them to attend a co-educational school (cf Selbourne, 1987, p. 103). Apart from an unrealistic request in 1973 by the Muslim Association of Bradford for the law to be changed to allow the girls to leave school at the age of twelve, single-sex schooling appears to offer the only solution to this situation. Initially, the main pressure from groups such as the Muslim Parents' Association, the Jamiyat Tablighul-Islam and the World Islamic Mission was for a separate school for Muslim girls to be established with financial assistance from the Council. Eventually in 1983 a fee-paying school was opened in Bradford by the Muslim Association, with places for 100 senior Muslim girls; however, this school has been criticized by Her Majesty's Inspectorate (HMI) for its inadequate accommodation and resources, its lack of suitably qualified staff, its lack of a balanced curriculum and its low expectations of pupil performance (HMI, 1987). This school could not in any case accept more than a small percentage of the Muslim girls in the city; by 1983, there were approaching 2000 of upper school age, and Muslim pressure groups such as the Council for Mosques began to put their efforts into demanding that Bradford Council should reverse its co-educational policy, and at least retain the status of Belle Vue, the only remaining girls' upper school under its control. Ironically, there is a large Catholic girls' upper school in the city, St. Joseph's College, with significant numbers of pupils of Polish, Ukrainian, Italian and West Indian origin, but as it has voluntary-aided status the governors are entitled to fix the school's admissions policy. 85 per cent of the places are reserved for Catholics, and priority for the remaining places is given to parents specifically seeking a Christian education for their daughters. Many Muslim girls each year are refused admission on these grounds. The third all-girls upper school in the city is the now independent Bradford Girls' Grammar School, which has a small percentage of Muslim pupils.

In the early 1970s, the Council merged most of its single-sex schools to form co-educational comprehensives, and it was Council policy to refuse permission for Muslim girls to transfer on cultural grounds to girls-only schools. This policy was explained by Bradford's acting Director of Education, B.J.R. Parker, in 1974, when he pointed out that if all Muslim girls in Bradford were free to transfer to Belle Vue Girls' School when it became the city's sole girls-only school, it would very soon become an all-

Muslim school. When the policy was changed in 1980, and it was decided to allocate pupils to schools on the basis of parental choice (though pupils within the catchment area were given priority in the case of an over-subscribed school), Parker's prophecy rapidly became true: by 1984 the intake to Belle Vue Girls' School had become more than two-thirds Muslim (McElroy, 1985) and this proportion is still rising. The policy turn-around was completed in 1983 when a Labour motion to merge Belle Vue Girls' and Boys' Upper Schools was narrowly defeated in a Council debate. Since 1983, spokesmen of both main parties have promised to retain the single-sex option (*cf* Dawe, 1987).

As was pointed out earlier in the chapter, the Council's present policy on single-sex schools implies a value judgment that consistency with their parents' beliefs is more important in the education of Muslim children than the benefits of co-education, that the consequent segregation of Muslim girls into what some call 'ghetto schools' is a worthwhile price to pay for such consistency, and that the rights of parents to make educational decisions affecting their own children should take priority over all other consider-ations, even, if necessary, over the rights of the children themselves. Perhaps, however, this is merely another example of a pragmatic policy: at least it tackled the problem of the Muslim girls in the city who were being kept away from school altogether. But even the success of this intention is not guaranteed; in 1984 the headteacher of Belle Vue Girls' School reported that Muslim girls were four times more likely than their indigenous peers to be absent from her school.

(3) The Abandonment of Mono-cultural Education

It would be wrong to claim that before the 1980s there was a demand by any of the minority groups in Bradford for anything called multi-cultural education. However, some of the groups – particularly the Muslims again – did fear that their children were being subjected to moral, cultural and religious indoctrination in schools, although they did not always use those terms. They expressed concern about the effect of 'the permissive British society' on Pakistani girls and about the 'demoralization' of Muslim children. These misgivings about the moral atmosphere of schools tended to focus particularly on sex education, which many Muslims wanted to be discon-tinued, and on authority and discipline, which they wanted tightening up. No doubt this latter point underlies the desire among some Muslims to retain corporal punishment in Mosque schools, which was highlighted in the national press in 1986. There were even greater misgivings about the un-Islamic practices which some Muslim children were being encouraged to engage in – the wearing of skirts, the exposure of girls' bodies in PE, swimming, dancing and showers, and fund-raising activities involving forms of gambling. Some Muslims also objected to their children having to attend Christian assemblies, prayers and religious education classes. The Muslim Parents' Association had been campaigning on these issues since 1974, and in early 1982 launched a vitriolic attack on Bradford Council in the form of a thirty-six page report entited 'Transformation of Muslim Children' (Patel and Shahid, 1982). This report undoubtedly had a major influence on Bradford's LAM No 2/82, which was issued later the same year. Other concessions sought by Muslims to help their children to retain their religious identity included the provision of *halal* meat in schools, which is discussed below, and making the holy days of Eid ul-Fitr and Eid ul-Adha official holidays for Muslim schoolchildren. More recently, some Muslim groups have objected to government plans to include music, art and drama in the proposed national curriculum, for these activities are in danger of violating the teachings of Islam, and some Muslim parents would wish to withdraw their children from such classes. Concern has also been expressed about the possible marginalization of religious education as a result of the proposed legislation (*Telegraph and Argus*, 1.10.87).

The development of multi-cultural education was the response of Bradford Council to these demands. The multi-cultural policies fall into two categories: those which grant multi-cultural concessions to the minority groups, so that schools are never in a position to require pupils to act in a way that is contrary to their (or their parents') religious and cultural beliefs; and those involving the treatment of all religions and cultures with equal respect, so that a positive image of each is presented to all pupils in the city's schools. The first of these objectives was detailed in Bradford's LAM No. 2/82, which has already been discussed: this document was partly prescriptive (children were to be allowed to cover their bodies as they chose for swimming, PE and showers and to wear traditional dress instead of school uniform) and partly advisory (teachers were to exercise tact and discretion in sensitive areas such as health education and lotteries and raffles). The second objective was reflected in the decision to include the variety of faiths in the city in the new RE syllabus published in 1974 under the title 'A Guide to Religious Education in a Multi-faith Community'; this was revised again in 1983. For once, a pragmatic response to the presence of adherents of a variety of world religions in the city went hand in hand with new theoretical approaches to the teaching of Religious Education that had been developing since the late 1960s. An Inter-faith Education Centre for RE teachers and others, catering for the five main faiths in the city, was opened in 1986. Other attempts to treat the major world religions with parity of esteem include the granting of permission for Muslim, Hindu and Sikh children to be absent from school on religious festivals such as Eid ul-Fitr and Diwali, and the experimental proposals for worship in schools which have already been discussed (CBMC, 1986a, 1986b).

The multi-cultural policies were actively disseminated by the LEA advisers and the local T.F. Davies Teachers' Centre, and headteachers were encouraged to organize in-school staff development to ensure that the policies were actually implemented as far as possible. The case of Wyke Manor Upper School provides a well-documented example of the response of one particular school to Bradford's multi-cultural policies and guidelines; after an intensive period of discussion in working parties, faculty meetings and whole staff meetings with outside speakers and LEA advisers, school statements were drawn up on multi-culturalism as well as on anti-racism and prejudice, and the support of parents and governors was actively sought (Duncan, 1985a, 1985b; Lynch, 1986, pp. 82, 152).

The Council's policies sought to tread a middle path between trapping minority children within a restricting culture on the one hand and culturally uprooting and disorienting them on the other; at the same time they sought to inculcate in all children a respect for a variety of cultures and an appreciation of multi-cultural education as an enriching experience. However, they have been criticized for attempting to present too many faiths and cultures to children, in too diluted a fashion, and not helping children to discriminate between them; for emphasizing community differences and thus underlining their separateness; and for not stressing the need to master the dominant culture if one is to thrive economically and politically in society.

(4) The Cessation of the Policy of Dispersal

The policy of dispersing ethnic minority pupils throughout the city's schools (commonly known as 'bussing') was introduced in 1964 in accordance with DES guidelines. The policy had two aims. The first was to assist the language development and general integration of minority children in the city by ensuring that no schools, even in areas of the city where the ethnic minorities were concentrated, had a majority of such children; the original limit of 10 per cent of immigrants in a school was quickly raised to 25 per cent, and raised again in 1969 to 33 per cent. The second was to ensure that all indigenous children had some contact with the ethnic minorities; as Bradford's assistant education officer, P. Bendall, explained in 1972: 'If we can give as many English children as possible the chance of growing up in school with immigrant class-mates, then there is a good chance they will learn to live in harmony with them, and carry on doing so after their schooldays.' Another of the city's education officers, quoted by Troyna and

Williams (1986), put it more bluntly: 'dispersal is...quite simply a system of social engineering' (p. 18).

This policy was never popular with parents. Indigenous parents objected strongly if they found their own children refused a place at a local school to make room for ethnic minority children coming from a distance, and minority group parents were inconvenienced when it came to attending parents' evenings and other activities. Minority pupils were deprived of the benefits of a neighbourhood school, and most of the minority group parents hoped that their own children would not be chosen for 'bussing' (about 15 per cent of ethnic minority children actually were chosen).

Political opposition to the policy developed initially from the far right and the far left. The former objected to any degree of encouragement of racial mixing in schools, the latter to the manifest racial discrimination in the way dispersal was carried out; only children from ethnic minorities were being 'bussed' and this was seen as an example of what Hill and Issacharoff (1971, p. 51) called the 'highly unequal interracial accommodation' which was operating in Bradford. The latter objection only made slow headway, however, for two reasons. First, to challenge intentional racial mixing as discriminatory seemed to be in direct conflict with the American experience of 'bussing' (where it was intentional racial *segregation* which was attacked as discriminatory). Secondly, to call for white children to be 'bussed' into inner-city schools which were already bursting at the seams would appear perverse; 'bussing' was at least in part a response to overcrowding and a way of giving ethnic minority children the benefit of smaller classes. In the event, it was a complaint by a member of the National Front to the Race Relations Board which led to an investigation of Bradford's policy of dispersal, though somewhat ironically the complaint was expressed in terms of which most ethnic minority parents would have approved: 'bussing' was wasting their children's time and denying them the benefits of a neighbourhood school (Kirp, 1979, p. 96). Professor Hawkins of the University of York was appointed by the Race Relations Board to examine whether Bradford's policy of dispersal could be justified in terms of language needs rather than of race. As a result of his report, a few minor modifications were made to the policy.

Council support for the policy remained strong, however, long after it had been phased out in other parts of the country. Indeed the Labour whip was withdrawn from Councillor Rhodes in 1976 for opposing it. In 1978 Councillor Hussain claimed that the 'tremendous social, cultural and educational benefits' of the dispersal policy far outweighed the difficulties it caused for ethnic minority families. He also warned that abandoning the policy would lead to 'segregation and eventually to ghetto schools' and that a massive school-building programme in the inner city would be required. Both of these prophecies have since come true. Opposition to the policy gradually gained momentum, however, in the late 1970s. Councillors Ajeeb and Hameed called the policy racialist and considered it an affront to the freedom and dignity of ethnic minority parents. A petition rejecting 'bussing', with a thousand signatures from teachers, parents and others, was presented to the Council in early 1979. The last straw came when the Commission for Racial Equality decided to reactivate its investigation into the legality of 'bussing', and at the end of 1979 the Council decided to phase the policy out.

Undoubtedly economic factors were a major consideration in the retention of 'bussing' in Bradford for so long. Even when the 33 per cent limit on the number of ethnic minority children in a school had been abandoned as impractical in the mid-1970s, 'bussing' continued, because there was simply not enough space in the inner-city schools for the expanding population, while there was plenty in suburban schools. The political decision to permit all children to attend neighbourhood schools, however, meant that by 1984 there were nineteen schools in the city with over 70 per cent of ethnic minority children, and led to a major new building programme of additional first and middle schools in the inner city. The effect of the decision to abandon 'bussing' on the educational achievement of the children concerned, and on race relations generally, is difficult to assess because of the many other complicating factors, but it seems unlikely that cross-cultural understanding in the city has been improved by the growth of 'ghetto schools'.

(5) The Provision of Mother-tongue Teaching

The special language needs of pupils of Asian origin are not difficult to see. From an early age they are likely to communicate with their parents and elders in Punjabi, Urdu, Gujerati, Bengali or Pushtu; with some of their peers and in all of their contacts with the wider community they speak English; and, in the case of Muslim children, they use Arabic for religious purposes. Since the 1960s Mosque schools and other supplementary schools have catered for these needs by providing tuition in Arabic and a number of mother-tongues; and, as we have seen, such schools have received financial support from the Council. However, demands have not been widespread from the minority communities for mother-tongue teaching in Local Authority schools, though there have been some (for example, from the Hindu Society in 1984); parents have tended to give higher priority to an adequate level of attainment in English. It has been left to the Council to do most of the running in working out children's needs in this area.

Over the last twenty years Bradford Council has tended to place rather less emphasis in its language policies on giving special help with English to ethnic minority pupils, and rather more emphasis on the positive use of minority languages in schools and in official publications. In the 1960s, three Immigrant Language Centres (later simply called Language Centres) were set up in Bradford to ensure that all children had a minimum level of proficiency in English before being transferred to Local Authority schools (Verma, 1986, p. 52). This was considered an efficient use of resources by the Council, particularly in the days of 'bussing'; otherwise every school would have needed an E2L specialist. Doubts developed, however, as to whether such separate provision was really in the best interests of the children concerned. The Language Centres were finally closed in September 1986, with their pupils being catered for henceforth within existing schools.

Mother-tongue teaching has taken two forms in Bradford. First, minority languages, especially Urdu, have been introduced as options alongside French and German in the modern language departments of an increasing number of middle and upper schools. The mother-tongue teaching survey carried out in Bradford and elsewhere as part of the Linguistic Minorities Project reported a total of 183 ethnic minority language classes in the city's schools (Linguistic Minorities Project, 1983). Secondly, there have been experiments in the use of the mother-tongue of Asian pupils as a medium of instruction alongside English for the first two years of their school career. The first was a project sponsored by the EEC, which ran from 1976 to 1980, and the second, the Mother Tongue and English Teaching for Young Asian Children Project (MOTET) was funded by the DES from 1979 to 1981 and carried out jointly by the University of Bradford, Bradford College and the Council's Directorate of Education (Rees and Fitzpatrick, 1981). Its findings provided inconclusive evidence as to the value of such teaching, except perhaps as a means of boosting motivation, confidence and cultural identity, but the practice has been continued in Bradford on a small scale. Undoubtedly the biggest obstacle to the further development of both forms of mother-tongue teaching is the shortage of suitably qualified teachers. Both forms of provision have been criticized, however, for their cost and because it is not clear whether they actually are educationally beneficial for the pupils.

(6) Permission for Extended Trips to the Indian Sub-continent

This was not an issue in the minds of Asian parents until the local authority took steps in 1981 to restrict such trips. The restrictions were proposed because of concern that the education of Asian children was being damaged by trips abroad of anything from two months' duration to a year or more, and because, when there was so much pressure on inner-city school places, it was difficult to keep places open for children who had gone abroad indefinitely. The Council's Multi-cultural Review Body therefore proposed that heads should be allowed to remove pupils from school registers and allocate their places to other children if they were absent for more than six weeks during term-time – an absence considerably longer than the two weeks allowed for in the 1959 Education Act.

At a public meeting held at Drummond Middle School to discuss the proposed rule (a meeting later described by Honeyford in his second *Salisbury Review* article), there were strong objections from Asian parents. They asked the Council to exercise greater flexibility in their approach to the problem, and pointed to the educational and cultural benefits that their children might receive from such trips. The proposals were quietly dropped, but the issue was reopened by Honeyford in the *Head Teachers' Review* two-and-a-half years later, when he claimed that there appeared to be one set of rules for Asian children and another for the rest; his views are discussed in more detail in chapter three.

(7) The Development of Anti-racist Policies in Education

It is a complaint voiced from time to time by people of West Indian origin in Bradford, one of the smallest black minorities in the city, that their own special educational needs are ignored by the Council, which seems to acknowledge only the Asian groups. In one sense it is therefore surprising that they have not until recently been more vociferous in presenting demands to the Council, or more active in anti-racist protests and demonstrations. In fact, the anti-racist movement in Bradford has been mainly spearheaded by white left-wingers and a number of Asian groups. The reasons for this are no doubt complicated, but any explanation would have to include relations between Asian and West Indian groups in the city, and the high degree of shared experience and cultural values among many of the West Indians and sections of the local white working class.

Anti-racism is, of course, a very broad concept, and if taken to include what is now sometimes called 'cultural racism', it encompasses all the demands listed so far in the present chapter; for example, Councillor Hameed's dismissal of the dispersal policy as 'racialist' has already been noted. In the present section I intend to concentrate on two specific demands associated with the development of anti-racist policies in education: the clamping down on overt racist behaviour involving or affecting schoolchildren, and the elimination of factors contributing to unintentional and institutionalized racism in schools. Overt racist behaviour covers everything from the 'unfriendliness, rudeness or indifference' which the Azad Kashmir

Muslim Association said in 1982 was rife in Bradford, to the graffiti, name-calling, racial bullying and gang fights in schools which are reported with increasing frequency in the local press (though the Revolutionary Communist party has claimed that a conspiracy of silence exists between the police, the press and the Council to conceal the real extent of racist attacks). In March 1986, leaders of the Asian Youth Movement called for an official investigation into fighting outside Bell Vue Boys' School which led to the arrest of five pupils; the situation was serious enough for pupils at nearby first and middle schools to be sent home early to avoid getting caught up in the clashes. Sporadic activity in schools by the National Front and other far-right groups has invariably increased tension; trouble flared up at Eccleshill Upper School following distribution of the *British Nationalist*, and some Asian pupils were reported to be 'too scared to return to school'. From time to time allegations are made of racism among Bradford teachers, especially since the announcement that a former Bradford head, Stanley Garnett, had joined the British National Party in 1983. Claims of racism among the staff at Wyke Manor Upper School directed against its black headteacher were made by a supply teacher in the *News of the World*; although the teacher who made the allegations was suspended and the allegations were officially denied, 300 pupils at the school went on strike in 1984 to demand the dismissal of a 'racist' teacher. Marches against racism have become commonplace in Bradford, though education is of course only one of many areas covered by such anti-racist protests. Although activities like marches inevitably attract more media attention, other demands involving less obvious forms of racism, such as the negative patronizing or stereotyped views of some races in school books and the sometimes unintentional racism of 'colour-blindness' (i.e. the denial of significant differences between ethnic groups), continue to be made by some minority groups in Bradford. In 1983 Raminder Singh, the Chairman of Bradford's Community Relations Council, drew attention to the problem of racist school books, and in their publication entitled *Reading, Riting, Rithmetic, Race* in 1984, the Asian Youth Movement attacked complacency on racial issues among teachers and administrators and called for an anti-racist education centre to be set up in Bradford. Shepherd (1987) highlights the low expectations that teachers had of their Asian pupils at one of Bradford's inner-city middle schools.

The Council has sought to respond to both sets of demands. In an initial policy statement distributed to all its employees in 1981, the Council outlined a new twelve-point plan on race relations. This included commitment to a policy 'to encourage equal opportunities, to reduce racial disadvantage and to root out once and for all racial discrimination'. The Race Relations Advisory Group was set up the same year to help other Council departments on racial issues, and the Council was already talking in terms of 'the vetting of books, materials and curricula to ensure that stereotyped images or prejudices are avoided' (CBMC Digest, 1981, p. 23). In 1983, the local authority attempted to standardize procedures in schools on the challenging and correcting of racist behaviour. A Local Administrative Memorandum (LAM No. 6/83) entitled *Racist Behaviour in Schools* was circulated to heads, giving guidelines and rules based on the earlier policy statement, and requiring them to identify and deal firmly and consistently with racist incidents in their schools, and to report them regularly to the local authority. The LAM emphasized the need:

1. to deal with the alleged perpetrators of the racialist behaviour;
2. to aid and support the victim;
3. to lay down firm lines of responsibility for dealing with incidents;
4. to deal with the impact of the incident on the whole community.

Each school was asked to prepare a detailed statement of its own policy against racialist behaviour, based on the general principles set out by the local authority. These general principles included the immediate removal of racialist graffiti or slogans from books or walls; the immediate confiscation of racialist literature, badges or insignia; reporting any activities of extreme political groups inciting racial hatred within the school to the police and the Directorate of Education; informing the parents of pupils responsible for racialist behaviour and involving them in any disciplinary procedures; and informing the victims of such behaviour of the action taken against it. The reasons for the initial opposition of headteachers to this LAM, and the resulting clashes between headteachers and councillors, have already been described earlier in the chapter.

At the same time as attempting to deal with examples of overt racism, however, the Council has also taken some steps to eradicate its underlying causes and less obvious manifestations. The decision to keep ethnic records, made in 1981, represented a clear rejection of the 'colour-blind' approach favoured by some teachers and an attempt to facilitate the monitoring of discrimination resulting from ethnic diversity. The campaign against institutional racism can be seen in the abolition of separate Language Centres in 1986, the drive since 1983 to appoint more ethnic minority governors, the encouragement of schools and libraries to examine critically the image of minority communities presented in the books they use, and, perhaps most controversially, the Racism Awareness Training courses which all heads and others involved in recruitment were required to attend. Though these courses were discontinued in 1986, their activities were incorporated into the regular training and in-service courses run by the local authority.

Perhaps the most important thing to emerge from the Council's actions so far is the great need for tact and sensitivity in bringing racial issues into consciousness and in attempting to correct misunderstandings and to change ingrained attitudes about race. It may be argued that if an anti-racist policy is perceived as a threat, it is almost certain to be counter-productive, and the best solution then is to approach the problem from a different angle. This appears to be the thinking behind the abandonment of the Racism Awareness Training courses, but such tact and sensitivity was not always evident in the Council's handling of the Honeyford affair, as is seen in chapter four.

(8) The Establishment of Muslim Voluntary-aided Schools

In January 1983 the Muslim Parents' Association submitted a request to Bradford Council for permission to take over two first schools, two middle schools and one upper school as Muslim voluntary-aided schools. Among the schools concerned were Honeyford's school, Drummond Middle, and Belle Vue Girls' Upper School. The main reasons for the request were to provide a base for the preservation, maintenance and transmission of the Islamic way of life, to enable Muslim children to have a high level of general education while observing the laws of Islam, to protect children from Westernization, secularization and un-Islamic practices by providing schools with an Islamic ethos, and to ensure that the children were not taught by teachers who had themselves rejected religion. Admission would not be restricted to Muslim children, however. The request was justified in terms of rights granted under the 1944 Education Act, and was seen as a call for parity of treatment with other minority religious groups in the UK, such as Catholics and Jews, who already have voluntary-aided schools. Several respected figures in the British Muslim community visited Bradford to express support for the request, including Yusuf Islam (the former pop star, Cat Stevens). In Bradford, however, opinion within the Muslim community was divided over the value of such schools. The Council for Mosques voted 13-8 against the proposal, and both the Community Relations Council and the Asian Youth Movement strongly opposed it. The latter warned of the dangers of 'voluntary apartheid' and the possibility of a 'racist backlash', and saw the way ahead as depending not on religious schools at all but on a greater openness within a common educational system to ethnic minority needs and a greater commitment to anti-racist education. It was reported that only forty-eight of the pupils at Belle Vue Girls' School supported the MPA's request. Outside the Muslim community, however, the request was universally opposed. The staff at Belle Vue Girls' School were unanimous in threatening resignation, and one parent-governor at Drummond Middle school collected 7000 signatures against Muslim voluntary-aided schools. The local newspaper ran several articles opposing the scheme, but none in favour.

Bradford's Educational Services Committee voted unanimously in September 1983 to reject the MPA's request. The official reasons provided for the refusal are interesting: no mention is made of the dangers of religious segregation, or indeed of any of the points made by the Asian Youth Movement; it was merely claimed that the proposal lacked the support of a sufficiently broad section of the Muslims in Bradford, and that there were neither sufficient financial resources nor the necessary educational and administrative experience within the MPA to carry the project through. This avoidance of a principled stand against Muslim voluntary-aided schools, although many councillors clearly felt that such schools would contravene the whole spirit of the Council's multi-cultural policies (which were directed towards meeting the needs of ethnic minority children within the framework of a common school curriculum), perhaps illustrates the pragmatic and conciliatory nature of the Council's response to Muslim demands. But the Council's response appears to leave the door open for a reapplication at a later date. Indeed, some Muslim groups have tended to wield the threat of such schools as an instrument of persuasion when they meet opposition to their demands (as in the call for Honeyford's dismissal). For many people, it appears that the call for the establishment of Muslim voluntary-aided schools marks the limit of what can be tolerated in a multi-cultural society, and it is the only serious request from a minority group in Bradford so far to meet with an outright refusal. There is little doubt that this fact influenced the local authority's determination to demonstrate its fairhandedness by pressing ahead with the multi-cultural policies such as the provision of *halal* meat in schools.

The call for such schools raises a number of significant questions about the aims of education, which I have discussed in more detail elsewhere (Halstead, 1986). It forms part of the larger debate which was carried on in the correspondence columns of *The Guardian* and *The Times Education Supplement* in the summer of 1986 and again in September 1987 regarding the dual system of education and the justifiability of separate denominational schools. Interviewed on the BBC programme *The Heart of the Matter* on 13 September 1987, Honeyford expressed provisional support for the establishment of Muslim voluntary-aided schools. Early in 1988, it was reported that the Labour Party leadership was dropping its opposition to such schools.

(9) The Provision of Halal Meat in Schools

Halal meat is meat which has been slaughtered in accordance with Islamic law. The animal must be conscious at the time of slaughter, and the name of Allah is invoked as the animal's throat is slit. Meat killed in any other manner is *haram* (forbidden) to Muslims, and this is generally taken to include meat from animals which have been stunned before slaughter in accordance with the 1933 and 1974 Slaughterhouse Acts. These Acts do, however, empower local authorities to allow both Jewish and Muslim methods of slaughter, and Bradford has for many years had a *halal* slaughterhouse to serve the needs of Muslim butchers in the city. But prior to 1983 no *halal* meat was served in public institutions such as schools and hospitals where people of different faiths and cultures intermingle. In practice this meant that many non-vegetarian Muslim schoolchildren in Bradford schools, as elsewhere, were eating only vegetarian dishes in order to avoid contravening Islamic law. During the 1970s and early 1980s, demands intensified from Muslims for an acceptable meat dish to be provided for their children in schools.

In September 1983 the local authority began a pilot scheme involving the provision of *halal* meat in ten schools. Within a year this had been extended to nearly sixty schools, and the eventual intention was to serve *halal* meals in all schools with more than ten Muslim diners. The policy met immediate and vociferous opposition, however, from local animal rights campaigners, and this opposition, highlighted by the refusal of one campaigner to pay her rates, received much attention in the local and national press. Undoubtedly the issue also became a focal point for racial prejudice. The Muslims, worried that the concession they had won might be slipping away from them, began to make their feelings known more forcibly; an estimated 3000 Muslims joined a pro-*halal* demonstration, and a 7000-signature petition was handed in at City Hall. In March 1984 the full Council debated whether to continue the provision of *halal* meat in view of the protests against it. In spite of the opposition of some prominent Labour councillors, including the Lord Mayor, Norman Free, continuation of the policy was supported by fifty-nine votes to fifteen. *Halal* meat now seems to be established as one of the most permanent and secure provisions for Muslim children in the city.

(10) The Removal of Honeyford from the Headship of Drummond Middle School

As the whole of chapter four is devoted to the story surrounding this demand, it will not be discussed further here.

THE DEVELOPING CONCEPT OF MULTI-CULTURALISM IN BRADFORD

The concern of this final section is to bring to light the underlying trends in what has been presented so far as a rather haphazard set of responses on the part of Bradford Council to the demands outlined above. For the purposes of this more interpretative section, I have divided the Council's policies on educational provision for ethnic minority children into three phases, which I shall call integrationism, accommodationism and separatism.

(a) Integrationism

Bradford's policies in the Integrationist Phase appear to have been based on the principle of acting in the public interest. What was perceived to be the primary interest shared by every member of the public equally was the peaceful co-existence of the various groups that made up the broader society in Bradford – in other words, the avoidance of racial and cultural tensions. This was to take priority over considerations such as what might be of benefit to individuals as individuals or members of minority groups. In the Integrationist Phase it was taken for granted that the best way to achieve what was in the public interest (i.e. peaceful co-existence) was through the integration of the minority groups into the social, political and economic life of the broader community. Cultural and religious differences were not ignored, but neither were they encouraged; they were tolerated in general (even to the extent of allowing instruction in Islam to be carried on in schools) so long as they did not conflict with the goal of social integration. Such a goal could only be justified in terms of fairness and equality, however, and so the equal treatment of all people, irrespective of race, colour or religion, became one of the directing principles of Bradford's educational policy. But equality of treatment was understood in the Integrationist Phase to mean treating all pupils the same; the only justification for different treatment was to facilitate identical treatment later in the pupils' school career. This was the rationale behind the establishment of the Immigrant Language Centres in Bradford in 1965, to help minority pupils to gain the proficiency they needed if they were to compete later in the state schools on an equal footing with indigenous children.

The case of Abdullah Patel, which received much publicity in the local press between 1973 and 1975, provides a good example of local authority policy in the Integrationist Phase. He objected on religious grounds to the placement of his daughter Kulsumbanu in a co-educational upper school, and requested her transfer to a girls' school. The local authority refused, and a subsequent appeal to Mrs Thatcher at the DES was turned down on the grounds that the three girls' schools in Bradford were full. When asked whether his strict Qur'anic stance would damage the city's hopes of integration, Patel replied:

> Integration was never possible...Co-existence, yes, but integration
> is the dream of an idealist. Our cultures, religions are too far apart.

When the British were in India, did they integrate? (quoted in
Yorkshire Evening Post, 3 December 1973).

Another Muslim, Riaz Shahid, who later co-ordinated the call for separate
Muslim voluntary-aided schools, left Britain in 1973 after the authority
refused to admit his daughter to a single-sex school. But Patel stood his
ground, and kept his daughter at home until she reached school-leaving age.
He maintained, not without justification (for other girls were being admitted
mid-term to local girls' schools), that the authority appeared to be making an
example of his case. Certainly he was put under strong pressure to conform,
being served with an attendance order and taken to court. What this case
illustrates is that in the Integrationist Phase the local authority was not
prepared to make exceptions in general educational policy on cultural or
religious grounds. To make an exception for parents such as Patel would be
to undermine doubly the Council's policy of treating all pupils the same: he
wanted Muslims treated differently from non-Muslims, and girls treated
differently from boys. If there were sound educational reasons for a policy
such as co-education in the first place, and if the policy were agreed by the
democratic decision of the Council, then it was considered justifiable to
compel parents to conform. Indeed, the Council could defend such
compulsion in terms of protecting the rights of individual children to
equality of treatment, as well as in terms of the promotion of the public
interest.

It would be untrue to claim, however, that local authority policy in this
phase was as fully assimilationist, or as oppressive in intention, as it is
sometimes portrayed. The policy of dispersal, for example, in Bradford's
case at least, was not a measure intended 'to disrupt the education of
indigenous children as little as possible', as the *Swann Report* (DES, 1985, p.
195–6) seems to suggest. Indeed, had such been the intention, it could have
been achieved more effectively by allowing the unchecked growth of 'ghetto
schools'; then indigenous parents would not have found their own children
being refused places at local schools in order to make way for ethnic minority
children who were being bussed in. The primary justification for 'bussing'
was in terms of the public interest: through increased contact, pupils of
different cultures would come to understand each other better and learn
mutual tolerance; and if they could learn to live in harmony in school, this
might carry through to adult life. What was wrong with 'bussing' was not
the intention which lay behind it (to benefit the whole community by
promoting mutual understanding and tolerance, and to benefit minority
children by giving them the best possible introduction to British culture and
language), but the methods used (which involved discrimination: only

minority children were 'bussed') and, more fundamentally, the way the benefits accruing from the policy were conceived. Behind the talk of mutual understanding and tolerance lay a serious imbalance of power. The needs (and the 'problems') of ethnic minority children were being defined by the indigenous majority. The value system on which educational decisions and judgements were based was often alien to the minority groups affected by the decisions. Virtually all the cultural adaptations and transformations were expected from the side of the minority groups. The growing belief that cultural domination, however unintentional, was undesirable and unjust gave rise to the gradual development of the next phase of Bradford's policies.

(b) Accommodationism

What distinguishes the second phase of Bradford's educational provisions for its minority communities is a much greater willingness to take the religious and cultural values and beliefs of these communities seriously. A new concept of integration emerged in Bradford's Race Relations Policy Statement of 1981, which did not 'assume a supremacy of one culture into which others would be easily assimilated', but which aimed instead at the creation of 'a society in which there is a co-operative and peaceful living together based on mutual respect for differences'. The Council was now committed to ensuring that 'so far as is compatible with individual needs, the provision of services will at all times respect the strength and variety of each community's cultural values'. The proviso contained in the phrase 'so far as is compatible with individual needs' was to form one of the foundations of Honeyford's attack on Bradford's multi-cultural policies, as will become clear in chapter three. But what is significant here is that Bradford's policies had ceased to be based on the need to *promote* the public interest as directly as possible, and instead merely acknowledged the necessity to avoid things that were *against* the public interest. This opened the way for policies to develop based on the freedom of individuals and groups to pursue their own good with like-minded people, so long as they respected the rights of others to do likewise. A letter distributed to all Council employees in 1981 pointed out that 'We no longer expect minority communities to integrate and change their ways to suit us', and that 'every section of the community has an equal right to maintain its own identity, culture, language, religion and customs'.

The policy changes ushered in as a result of this new emphasis on respect for the cultures of minority groups fall into two main categories: the first is the increased number of concessions granted to these groups, such as the retention of the option of single-sex education and the provision of *halal* meat in schools; the second is a more positive attempt to increase understanding of and respect for minority cultures by incorporating elements from them into the curriculum of the common school. The detailed policies within these two categories have already been described. It is worth noting, however, that the roots of both categories may be traced back clearly to the Integrationist Phase: the first major concession granted to a minority group was the granting of permission in 1972 for Muslim children to receive instruction in their own faith in secondary schools; and even earlier, in 1970, a committee was set up to revise Bradford's RE syllabus, to ensure that it reflected the variety of faiths in the city.

It must be acknowledged, however, that such talk of cultural concessions to minority groups does itself involve the adoption of a cultural (and some would say a racist) stance. For what is seen by the indigenous population as a cultural concession *to* Muslims (for example, the provision of *halal* meat in schools) may be seen by Muslims as no more than ceasing to demand a cultural concession *from* them (i.e. forcing their children to eat only vegetarian dishes at school dinners). To acknowledge this, however, is to deny the possibility of cultural norms in a multi-cultural situation, and to pave the way for the separatism discussed below.

The Accommodationist Phase involves a recognition of the difficulty of developing an educational policy based solely on the public interest in a pluralistic society where different groups each have their own concept of what sort of education is in the best interests of the child. The aim was to avoid putting minority children into situations where they were required to act in conflict with their parents' beliefs and values, and to present a positive image of their faith and culture to all children in the district. In this way it was hoped to retain the commitment of the minority communities to the principle of common schooling and the continued acceptance of the right of the local authority to make final decisions on educational matters. Such a policy inevitably made demands on the indigenous population, however; they might find traditional modern language options in schools reduced in order to make room for Urdu, or the traditional emphasis on Christianity in RE reduced to make room for the study of Islam, Hinduism and Sikhism. In order to overcome possible tensions resulting from these changes, the local authority began to put less emphasis on the mere *toleration* of cultural differences and more on the need to welcome them as culturally enriching. The problem here, of course, is that the celebration of diversity sits rather uneasily with commitment to a particular set of cultural or religious values and beliefs. There were those among both the indigenous population and the minority groups who doubted that such a policy would work, or was even desirable.

(c) Separatism

The attitude of the local authority towards separatism is currently highly ambivalent. On the one hand, many of its policies appear to be moving in the direction of encouraging separate educational provision for minority groups. But on the other there has been strong opposition to attempts to formalize and institutionalize this tacit trend towards separatism.

Any attempt to satisfy the requirements of all ratepayers in the city was bound to meet up with the problem of minority groups who had 'a strong and distinctive cultural identity intimately bound up with language and religion' and whose main educational goal was the preservation or 'recreation of cultures or societies they have nominally left behind' (the quotations are again from Bradford's 1981 Race Relations Policy Statement). Inevitably, several of the special educational provisions agreed upon by the Council, including some provided for by the 1944 Education Act, involved separating the children of these groups from their class-mates, at least on a temporary basis: permission to withdraw from assemblies or RE; permission to be absent from school on religious festivals; permission to attend Friday prayers led by an imam in or out of school; the provision of separate religious instruction and worship for Muslims in school time; and the development of mother-tongue teaching and bilingual education. Nor is this temporary separation of minority schoolchildren from their class-mates restricted to activities in the school day; by its financial support of Mosque schools, the Council seems to imply approval of the segregation of Muslim and non-Muslim children out of school as well. Potentially even more significant is the concentration of very large numbers of ethnic minority children in some inner-city schools, the direct result of the abandonment of the policy of 'bussing'. The 1984 intake to Drummond Middle School, for example, consisted of 125 children of Asian origin, one West Indian and two indigenous whites, and this is by no means untypical of Bradford's inner-city first and middle schools. It is acknowledged in the report of the Advisers' Inspection of Drummond Middle School (1984, p. 23) that for many British Asian children 'there will be few or no opportunities to meet white children until they go to upper schools'. Yet as already noted, the trend is now continuing into the single-sex upper schools, and it seems to be a distinct possibility that many ethnic minority children will pass through their entire school career with little contact with the indigenous majority, just as the reverse now happens in many suburban schools. The Council has done little to interrupt this trend towards *de facto* separatism since 1980, nor indeed is able to while remaining committed to its policy of seeking to satisfy equally the requirements and demands of all ratepayers.

There is some evidence that when the proportion of ethnic minority pupils in a school reaches a certain level, parents from the majority group will sometimes stop sending their children there (McElroy, 1985), and such schools may then quickly become:

> de facto 'separate' schools for particular ethnic minority groups in all but name and legal status, since they have a considerable majority of ethnic minority pupils (*Swann Report*, DES, 1985, p. 499).

Separatism is thus encouraged by the actions of the white majority; a well-known example is the protest of the parents in the 'Dewsbury affair' in September 1987 (*cf* chapter four below). Perhaps most significantly, the anti-racist policies that have been developed in Bradford in the last five years have tended to provide support for this trend. By highlighting the different needs and experiences of blacks and their distinct identity, anti-racism has provided reasons for treating blacks separately. Bradford's only black upper school head, Carlton Duncan, claimed in a Channel Four programme that the only policy which would meet the needs of the black community was one which was prepared to provide black schools for black children. The well-publicized statement of dissent in the *Swann Report* (DES, 1985, p. 515) was in fact sponsored by two Bradford members of the committee, Carlton Duncan and Akram Khan-Cheema, who argued that in present circumstances separate schools might be the only way of meeting the immediate needs of ethnic minority pupils, and who proposed therefore that positive assistance should be given to ethnic minority communities who wish to establish voluntary-aided schools.

In spite of all this evidence of an underlying trend towards separatism in Council policy, however, it must be admitted that some of the Council's actions give the opposite impression. The closing of the Language Centres is one such example. In particular, the local authority has taken a firm stand against anything that might lead to formal or structural separatism and thus bring about the end of the common educational system. As we have seen, the most direct move towards structural separatism in the city so far was the call for the establishment of five Muslim voluntary-aided schools in 1983, and this was strongly resisted by the Council. 'I don't want separatism in any form,' said Councillor Ajeeb, Bradford's first Asian Lord Mayor. 'It's not on. People can't have it even if they want it. What we want is accommodation of our cultural needs, especially in the educational system' (quoted in Selbourne, 1984a, p. 136).

The evidence seems to suggest that we are still at the start of the Separatist Phase, and how far the trend towards separatism will continue is a matter for speculation at the present time. It seems likely that pressure will be maintained for the appointment of more ethnic minority teachers and governors, particularly in inner-city schools. According to reports prepared for Council departments, only 10 per cent of school governors are Asian, and there are only eighty-six ethnic minority teachers in the district's 300 schools (*Telegraph and Argus*, 29 March 1986). Drummond Middle School again illustrates this imbalance. Over 95 per cent of the children there are from ethnic minorities, but only 36 per cent of the newly constituted governing body and 7 per cent of the teachers (1985 figures). This imbalance seems unfair (and perhaps racist), as it leaves decisions about the education of ethnic minority children in the hands of the indigenous majority, who may not only misunderstand or misinterpret the requirements of these children, but also have the power to disregard their wishes if they choose. But whether the appointment of more governors and teachers from the Muslim community, for example, will lead to increased demands for the Islamification of the curriculum is difficult to predict. A year ago it seemed most likely that demands for Muslim voluntary-aided schools would be renewed and that sooner or later such schools would become a reality in Bradford, particularly since Brent, Bradford's main rival for the lead in multi-cultural and anti-racist initiatives, has already approved one such school in principle. Now, however, it appears that some Muslim parents in Bradford are pinning their hopes on the opting-out section of the Great Education Reform Bill, and Baroness Hooper has acknowledged that racially or culturally segregated schools may be the price the government has to pay for increasing parental choice in education (*The Times Educational Supplement*, 20 November 1987, p. 11).

Further moves of this sort towards separatism, however, are unlikely to be accepted locally without opposition. Apart from opposition within the Council, there is talk of an indigenous backlash if minority groups are perceived to be merely taking advantage of any preferential treatment they may receive in order to further their own plans for 'mono-cultural self-imposed apartheid' (Pedley, 1986). A group's freedom to pursue its own good, even if it involves the tolerance of other groups, cannot operate in a democratic setting without reference to other values, such as justice and respect for persons. Yet the principle of justice raises serious questions about the practice of positive discrimination, and the principle of respect for persons raises questions about the freedom of individuals within the minority groups.

But if the trend towards separatism is not to continue in coming years, it is necessary to consider what alternatives are available. One is a reversion to the accommodationist aproach, and this appears to be what the *Swann Report* is advocating (although it must be acknowledged that for most local authorities such a step would not be a *reversion*). The main difficulty with this alternative, as we have seen, is that it requires that a commitment to fundamental shared values, including the value of pluralism, should take priority over a commitment to specific religious or cultural values; and such a scheme of priorities is not likely to commend itself to Muslims or other minority groups. Another alternative, which Honeyford seems to have been moving towards in his controversial articles, is a reversion to Integrationism. This would involve the re-establishment of a unified approach to educational provision, and an emphasis on common needs and on treating all pupils the same. At this stage it is therefore appropriate to provide a more detailed examination of the arguments about multi-cultural education and related topics contained in Honeyford's articles, which form the subject of the next chapter.

3 Honeyford's Articles

Neither the articles Honeyford wrote before his appointment in April 1980 to the headship of Drummond Middle School, Bradford, nor his book *Starting Teaching* (1982a) provides any hint of the controversy in which he was later to become enmeshed. The former, published in the *British Journal of Disorders of Communication* (1972, 1980) and the *Use of English Quarterly* (1973a, 1973b, 1974), draw on his experience as an English teacher in various schools around Manchester and as a part-time Open University tutor, and on his research for his two masters' degrees (one in Socio-linguistics from the University of Manchester and one in Educational Psychology from Lancaster). The latter is a book of practical advice aimed primarily at the probationary teacher. In view of subsequent events at Drummond Middle School, we might find a certain irony in the book, in his comments on LEA advisers ('practising teachers invariably have a low opinion of them', p. 161) and on governors ('in practice the head tells them what he wants them to know and no more', p. 37). His attitude to teacher autonomy ('an aspect of the job which is immensely prized by teachers', p. 158) also helps to explain his increasing resentment of what he saw as the unjustified interference by the LEA in the running of his school. But his comments on multi-ethnic schools are confined to a single sentence (p. 144) and on the whole the book is as uncontroversial as it is down-to-earth, practical and dull.

Though he was originally a Labour supporter, within two years of his arrival in Bradford his political sympathies and educational ideas had changed dramatically, and so had the tone of his articles. Murphy (1987, pp. 108–9) suggests that his working-class Mancunian origins combined with a reasonable degree of ambition made him vulnerable to the seductions of the New Right. His publications since 1982 fall into two categories: those which illustrate and seek to justify his new right-wing political allegiance, and those which attack both the principles and the practice of multiracial education. His commitment to the educational policies of the New Right is seen in a series of articles and reviews in *The Salisbury Review*, the *Yorkshire Post* and the *Daily Mail* (and indeed in the initial decision to publish in *The Salisbury Review* at all: *cf* chapter five below). In these articles he attacks a wide range of targets: the establishment of comprehensive schools and the introduction of mixed-ability teaching; what he describes as the 'malign influence' of the social-worker mentality, which he feels is creeping into schools; recent curriculum initiatives such as anti-sexist teaching, peace studies, life skills and world studies; and current trends in sex education, which he would like to see countered by greater parental involvement, if they are not to be given the right to withdraw their children completely from lessons. He has also written in support of the voucher system, and has argued, somewhat ironically in view of the campaign against him by parents and others, that parents (whom he describes as the consumers) 'must have a much greater say in their children's education' (1987d). He has acknowledged his indebtedness to the educational thinking of such writers as Honey, Shaw, Marks, Scruton, Cox and Flew. In 1986 he provided confirmation of his political sympathies with a statement on the front page of the Conservative local election manifesto in Bradford (1986d) and by his decision to stand as a Conservative candidate in the 1988 local elections.

Most of Honeyford's articles to date are listed in the bibliography, but for the remainder of the present chapter I shall be concerned only with those publications dealing with race, multi-culturalism and the education of ethnic minority children, particularly those he wrote prior to his departure from Drummond Middle School in December 1985.

ARTICLES ON RACE AND EDUCATION

Honeyford began writing about racial issues with two letters published in July 1982, one to *The Times Educational Supplement* (1982b) and the other to the local *Telegraph and Argus* (1982c). The first expressed dismay that Dr Mortimer's research into the fortunes of successful black children, which had been commissioned for the *Swann Report*, was being dropped as a result of pressure from West Indian organizations. Honeyford felt the research was being suppressed because it was likely to demonstrate a link between the achievement of West Indian children and their family values and backgrounds, whereas the preferred explanation was to link underachievement to racism. This was a theme to which Honeyford reverted in several later articles. The second letter was a response to the suggestion by a regular columnist that Bradford was spending money unnecessarily to placate its ethnic minorities: £70,000 had already been provided for Checkpoint, the West Indian community centre, whose previous premises had been destroyed by fire, because the Council 'feared Toxteth-type riots might occur if they did nothing'; and now £150,000 was to be spent on temporary accommodation for the pupils of a first school that was being repaired, so that the Council would not have to face charges of re-introducing 'bussing' if they followed through their original plan to take the children to a suburban school four miles away while the repairs were carried out. Honeyford's letter expressed concern, on the first count that the Council was yielding to intimidation, and on the second that money was not being spent for 'sound educational and social reasons'. He suggested that some citizen of Bradford should refer the matter to the public auditor. The letter was on school notepaper, and two months later he received a verbal warning from Bradford's director of education.

Honeyford's first article on race and education (1982d) was published in *The Times Educational Supplement* in November 1982. It remains perhaps the clearest explanation of his opposition to multiracial education. His main arguments are:

(1)   that 'the responsibility for the adaptations and adjustments involved in settling in a new country lies entirely with those who have come here to settle', since their initial immigration was an act of free choice;

(2)   that their commitment to a British education (i.e. an education which is deeply embedded in British and European culture) was 'implicit in their decision to become British citizens';

(3)   that the maintenance and transmission of the mother culture of immigrants 'has nothing to do with the English secular school but is a private matter for the immigrant family or community', and that it was a recognition of this fact which enabled earlier Jewish and East European settlers to survive and flourish in this country (*cf* chapter one above);

(4)   that any attempt to 'confer a privileged position' on minority groups, whether through positive discrimination or through attempts to 'enhance the status and self-respect of settler children by teaching the culture of their parents' mother land and a critical view of British imperialism', is misguided, patronizing, and ultimately against their own best interests;

(5)   that the main need of second generation Asian and Caribbean children, who have in any case already absorbed sufficient British culture for them to be considered primarily bi-cultural, is now to master that culture so that they can compete on equal terms in what is in fact 'a pretty ruthless meritocracy' in this country;

(6)   that what is holding black achievement back at the moment is not racism but a 'lack of support for school and its values among West Indian parents', together with the misguided 'cultural revisionism' of

the multi-racial 'bandwagon' (as seen, for example, in the 'literary McCarthyism' of vetting school books for negative references to race and colour);

(7)   that only an emphasis on the 'common needs of all children' and an abandonment of anything promoting an 'artificial and harmful colour consciousness' will help to generate 'a truly equal and harmonious multi-cultural society'.

The article sparked off a considerable debate in the correspondence columns of *The Times Educational Supplement* and elsewhere, and was widely attacked for its insensitivity towards the genuine difficulties faced by the black families in Britain. Again, Honeyford was seen by his director of education, this time in the company of the chairman of Bradford's Educational Services Committee, though this did not constitute a formal disciplinary procedure over the article.

Honeyford's next article in *The Times Educational Supplement* (1983b) did not appear until ten months later, and was quite different in tone and content. The article takes the form of a diary of a week of contacts with Asian parents. He uses actual incidents in his school to convey his opposition to some of the Council's multi-cultural policies which he is obliged to carry out. He criticizes in particular the abandonment of 'bussing', the introduction of *halal* meat for school dinners, and the rule allowing Muslim girls to cover their limbs for PE. He feels that the school's attempts to bridge the gap between the culture of the home and that of the broader community 'are being undermined by a combination of religious fanaticism, official timidity and the misguided race relations lobby'. Some of his incidental descriptions of Asians, although intended to be light-hearted, might be considered offensive (one parent's English 'sounds like that of Peter Sellers' Indian doctor on an off-day'). Not all fall into this category, however; the school's one Asian teacher is described as a 'man of immense patience and courtesy', and the Asian Educational Welfare Officer 'deserves a knighthood for his service to the community'. Indeed, there is a certain implicit admiration for the unsophisticated morality of the Muslim father who firmly chastises his own son for stealing, and for the sense of family responsibility apparent in many of the Asian girls. Nevertheless, the article has two serious flaws. The first is that it concentrates entirely on the *problems* involving Asian parents that Honeyford has to deal with, and has nothing positive or creative to say about the development of cross-cultural friendships, for example, or the benefits the school gains from the variety of cultures represented. Secondly, it gives the impression, perhaps unintentionally, of an 'us-and-them' mentality, since the Muslims are depicted as frequently setting themselves against the values of 'the indigenous population', such as sexual equality or 'the English regard for animal welfare'. Once again, Honeyford was criticized strongly in the correspondence columns of *The Times Educational Supplement* and had an exchange of letters with Bradford's educational directorate. For the first time the Council for Mosques in Bradford was drawn in, as Nazim Naqui, later chairman of the Drummond Parents' Action Committee, drew their attention to the article.

Honeyford was becoming increasingly concerned with the problem of extended visits by Asian children to the Indian sub-continent. This had been mentioned briefly in his previous article, and was now highlighted in a new article in *The Head Teachers' Review* (1983c). The article starts with a favourable picture of the adjustments his school has made, particularly in teacher attitudes, adaptation of the RE curriculum and school – home communications, in response to its increasingly multi-cultural intake. However, the main problem now facing his school, he says, is that an estimated third of his pupils have their education seriously disrupted by term-time visits to the Indian sub-continent. This not only damages the children's language development and general educational progress, but also puts him in an awkward position as headteacher, since he is supposed to uphold the principle of compulsory and regular school attendance yet finds that one particular minority community, the Asians, appear to have 'implicit permission to violate this principle with complete impunity'. He estimates that each year up to 10,000 children may be affected by such trips in the country as a whole, and urges the DES to clarify the legal position and rectify what currently appears to be a 'racially determined attendance policy'.

Honeyford had already had one article published in *The Salisbury Review* (1983a) though this seems to have passed largely unnoticed by those who would have found it offensive. The exciting opportunity to create a harmonious multi-racial society, he argues, by the free and natural interaction of the various racial groups in schools, is now in danger of being lost as a result of the antics of the 'multi-ethnic brigade', whose extremism and insidious intolerance may end up prompting a 'backlash from the overwhelming majority of tolerant teachers and parents'. The questionable ideas of this group include the demands that Indian languages should not only be taught in schools, but used as the medium of instruction; that minority cultures should be fostered in schools, along with a denigration of former British colonialism; that school libraries should be purged of all books that 'fail the multi-ethnic purity test'; that positive discrimination should be provided for young black people; that mono-ethnic minority schools should be allowed to develop in preference to the genuinely balanced multi-ethnic schools that were guaranteed by the Council's former 'humane and sensible' dispersal policy; and that the self-concept of black children should be bolstered by helping them to find their cultural roots rather than helping them to acquire basic skills and qualifications. The multi-culturalists who promote these ideas are a mixture of well-meaning liberals, career-minded teachers, ethnic minority intellectuals and left-wing political extremists, and are further supported by

> an irrelevant, if not positively malign, quango (the 'Commission for Racial Equality'), by a huge ragbag of dubious voluntary organiz-ations, and by a growing army of so-called 'advisers' hired by misguided authorities in order to prove their progressive intentions.

With such a movement committed to the creation of a 'wholly artificial and unhealthy colour consciousness', the prospects of establishing a genuine tolerant and prejudice-free multi-racial society seem increasingly remote.

If the language of this article is somewhat polemical and shrill, that of the next *Salisbury Review* article (1984a) is more so. Several of the items under attack are by this stage very familiar targets for Honeyford's vituperations: the 'purdah mentality' of some Muslim parents; the teaching of minority cultures and languages; the extended trips to the Indian sub-continent; the growing influence of a group of 'aggressive black intellectuals' the distortions of language (especially of terms such as 'racism', 'black', 'uprising', 'cultural enrichment' and 'the celebration of linguistic diversity') engineered by the 'race relations lobby'; and the absence of educational ambition and the values to support it in West Indian homes. Once again, Honeyford draws on his own personal experiences to illustrate the article. In particular, he depicts in some detail a public meeting held at his school in 1981, under the joint auspices of Bradford Council and the Community Relations Council, to discuss the LEA's proposal (which was later withdrawn) to refuse re-admittance to children going abroad for more than six weeks in term time. Honeyford describes the proposal as 'an act of reconciliation' to Asian parents, though the latter unsurprisingly viewed things differently, and expressed their view forcefully. To Honeyford's eyes, the ensuing meeting provides evidence of 'the hysterical political temperament of the Indian sub-continent', and he is particularly critical of a local community relations officer whom he describes as 'a half-educated and volatile Sikh'. He also refers to the reaction to his two earlier articles in *The Times Educational Supplement*. The response from the Haringay Black Pressure Group on Education is described as 'libellous and mindless bombast' and is clearly seen as providing further evidence to support his opinion of black activists and the multi-racial 'bandwagon'.

But the article also raises three points which have not been mentioned before. First, Honeyford claims that freedom of speech is becoming 'difficult to maintain', because the feelings of guilt induced by the 'race lobby' and the fear of giving offence are preventing 'decent people' from writing honestly and openly about their experiences and the reflections they evoke. It is his own reflections on such experiences as the parents' meeting described above, which lead him

> perhaps for the first time to understand why so many fundamentally decent people harbour feelings of resentment.

In consequence, secondly, he now expresses much stronger criticisms of some aspects of ethnic minority cultures than he has before. The 'vast majority' of West Indian homes are described as lacking in educational ambition; a disproportionate number are 'fatherless'; and the West Indian is described as someone who creates 'an ear-splitting cacophony for most of the night to the detriment of his neighbour's sanity'. Pakistan, the country of origin for most of Bradford's ethnic minority families, is described as 'obstinately backward', plagued by 'corruption at every level', and the 'heroin capital of the world'. Finally, he touches for the first time on the educational disadvantage suffered by the white children who now form a minority group in many inner-city schools; they are inevitably not so well initiated into their own language and culture as their parents were, and their plight is likely to become more serious since they lack a spokesman or pressure group to articulate their anxieties.

It was this article, Honeyford's fifth on issues of race and education, which triggered off what has since become known as 'the Honeyford affair'. As soon as the article came to the attention of Bradford Council and the wider public (some two months after its initial publication), it drew a barrage of criticism from many quarters, and set in motion the chain of events, including serious disruption at Drummond Middle School, which eventually led to Honeyford's early retirement. The story of this response, and its wider repercussions, forms the topic of chapter four, and so will not be elaborated on here.

A letter to the *Telegraph and Argus* a month after the affair burst into flames (1984c), and an article in the *Yorkshire Post* (1984d), provide us with Honeyford's initial reaction to what happened. He regards the growing campaign against him as proof of his point that freedom of speech is becoming difficult to maintain, though he has also been encouraged by many messages of support. He argues that teachers in multi-racial schools face problems that are both unprecedented and highly complex, and that they

> have little hope of addressing these problems, let alone solving them, unless we can create a more honest, a more open, and a less fearful intellectual climate than we have at the moment.

He finds his own professional experience in conflict with many of the contemporary multi-racial prescriptions, and therefore feels an urgent need to bring these matters out into open discussion.

At this stage, however, Bradford Council ruled that Honeyford should publish no more articles critical of Council policy – or indeed any articles at all, unless they were first submitted to Council officers for approval. For the next eighteen months, therefore, he published nothing on the topic of race and education, except for one letter to *The Times Educational Supplement* (1985c), which he justified as self-defence against an attack on his personal integrity. Once again he stressed his belief that 'the race relations lobby – the mentality it expresses and the rhetoric it generates – represents a serious threat to intellectual freedom', and that his own role as a head of a multi-racial school 'ought not, in a free society, to prevent me from putting an alternative or unorthodox viewpoint'.

The articles started again within a few days of the announcement of the deal by which Honeyford agreed to take early retirement. The first was the three-part 'exclusive' story written by the head himself for the *Daily Mail*, and published under the title, 'The Hounding of Honeyford' (1985d). This provides the fullest account so far of Honeyford's own version of the events of 1984–85, and will be referred to in detail both below and in chapter four. It also summarizes the substance of his various articles on race and adds a couple of further comments. The first is that multi-cultural education appears often to have a hidden political agenda, to 'change society and inculcate radical attitudes'. The second concerns the best way to tackle racism. Honeyford's view is that 'racism is a failure of the human spirit, and needs to be combatted by general moral education'. To harp constantly on racism, or to deal with it in a different way from any other sort of bad behaviour, is likely to highlight it in pupils' eyes and to increase the chances of its occurrence.

During 1986 Honeyford had further articles on race and education published in *The Salisbury Review*, the *Yorkshire Post*, *The Spectator*, the *Daily Mail*, *Education Today* and in *Anti-Racism: an Assault on Education and Value*, (Palmer, 1986). These gave him an opportunity to amplify his views, respectively, on multi-culturalism and pluralism; on anti-racism and discrimination; on the misguided colour-consciousness of the anti-racists; on the politicizing of anti-racism in Brent; on conflicting cultural values; and on the way language is distorted by the 'race relations lobby'. An article in *The Spectator* (1987a) provides an amusing account of a dispute with a Muslim over his daughter's swimming lessons, and draws attention yet again to the fundamental clash of cultures. In a more recent *Salisbury Review* article (1987e), he criticizes the *Swann report* – on which he is currently reported to be writing a book – and calls for a critical examination of the 'race relations lobby' and for a national debate about the *kind* of multi-cultural society we want Britain to be. He even suggests that a referendum on this issue might be the most appropriate way to consult public opinion. In two *Yorkshire Post* articles in 1987 he has expanded his arguments against mother-tongue teaching (1987g) and against the claim that British society is riddled with racism (1987i). In addition, he has given numerous interviews for television, radio and newspapers and a series of lectures up and down the country. In September 1987, he expressed both sympathy and support through the media for the twenty-six Dewsbury parents who refused to send their children to a school where over 85 per cent of the pupils were Asian. The most significant of the interviews is perhaps the one with Anthony Clare for the Radio Four programme 'In the Psychiatrist's Chair' (reprinted in *The Listener*, 28 August 1986) and of the thirty or so talks he gave in 1986, perhaps the most noteworthy is his speech to the Oxford Union on 20 November in support of the motion 'That the aims of the anti-racist lobby are frustrated by their means'. But in fact there has been no indication, either in the articles or in the interviews and lectures, of any significant shift in his position on education, multi-culturalism and race since his first article on the subject in 1982. He has, however, become increasingly anxious to avoid having his position described as extremist (1987c) and to ensure that his views are given a hearing in any objective accounts of race relations in Britain (1987h).

It may be useful at this stage to summarize Honeyford's views by reference to the terms used in the analysis of Bradford's developing response to ethnic minority demands in chapter two. He is totally opposed to separatism. He believes that it is not the function of the maintained school to preserve or reinforce the values, beliefs and cultural identity of any minority group, and he is totally opposed to anything that might lead to ghettoizing minorities. He fears that separatism of any kind may lead to 'factionalism and inverted prejudice' (1987e). With regard to accommodationism, he is sceptical of concessions granted to parents simply on the basis of membership of a particular group, especially when these might affect the rights of their children. For example, the right to develop a sporting talent might be hindered by the requirement to cover one's legs at all times; more fundamentally, the right to compete on equal terms for scarce jobs might be hindered by squandering vital school time on 'Black Studies', minority languages or other subjects not valued in the broader community. On the other hand, he is happy to encourage the tolerance, understanding and respect that might develop from presenting a range of different beliefs and cultures to all pupils; his school had adopted a multi-faith approach to RE before the new agreed syllabus was introduced to Bradford. His primary sympathies, however, are with integrationism, with its emphasis on treating all pupils the same, on the importance of the English language and on the shared culture and values of the wider British society (1988). We will now turn to examine in more detail the value judgments and assumptions which underlie Honeyford's approach to issues of race and education.

UNDERLYING ASSUMPTIONS IN HONEYFORD'S ARTICLES

Perhaps the biggest problem facing any culturally pluralist society is how to resolve the tensions between the preservation of the distinct cultural identity of minority communities on the one hand and the encouragement of social integration and cohesion on the other. Honeyford's arguments are based on the firm conviction that the former is a private matter for the individuals or communities involved and that the latter is the only legitimate concern of public education in this country. It is this conviction which underlies, and gives unity to, his views on the best approach to education in a multi-racial context and which explains his misgivings about much contemporary practice. The cessation of 'bussing' in Bradford had led to a very dramatic increase in the proportion of ethnic minority pupils in his own school – eventually over 95 per cent. One consequence was the decline in opportunities for the development of cross-cultural friendships, which can contribute significantly to the growth of tolerance:

> It is very difficult for either English or settler children to view each other as odd, much less as inferior, when they have grown up together (1983a).

Cross-cultural friendships also have their part to play in helping children who do not use English at home to consolidate their grasp of fluent, idiomatic English. Honeyford feared that the decline in such friendships, and in the use of English in the playground, would reduce the chances for social integration and make it harder for ethnic minority children to engage on an equal footing with their indigenous peers in an increasingly competitive employment market. The problem was merely made worse by the lengthy absence from school of some Asian children who were taken on extended trips to the Indian sub-continent and by the demands of some parents for concessions to their religious beliefs which would serve to draw further attention to their separateness from the rest of the community. Honeyford maintained that the answer lay not in attempts to enhance the self-concept of ethnic minority children through positive discrimination or the teaching of minority languages or cultures in schools, but in an increased determination to treat all children the same, to encourage social interaction between the various ethnic groups and to put more emphasis on the mastery of the British culture which was equally relevant to the needs of all.

I shall argue in part two of the present book that Honeyford's approach to the education of ethnic minority children is ultimately unsatisfactory because it is dependent on too simplistic an analysis of the situation. His discussion of the 'bi-cultural identity' of young Asians does not take adequate account of the very real clash of loyalties experienced by many Asian children, who may be presented with one set of values and beliefs at home and in their local community and a quite different set at their state school. It fails to consider what legal and moral rights ethnic minority parents have to a say in the education of their children. It fails to explore the extent to which the taken-for-granted values and assumptions on which the British educational system is based are not only alien to many ethnic minority parents, but may force them into a position where they are expected to go against their own fundamental convictions. On the other hand, Honeyford's articles do, as I shall shortly show, raise some pertinent questions about the nature and goals of anti-racist education. In this area, he has been strongly influenced by such American writers as Glazer, Moynihan and especially Sowell.

In fact, many of Honeyford's arguments have a respectable parentage in liberal educational theory, although he himself has never seriously attempted to justify his views in theoretical terms. In a letter to *The Times Educational Supplement* (1985c), he outlines very briefly what seems to him to be the essence of citizenship in a free society – a mixture of human rights and privileges on the one hand, and legal and moral duties and responsibilities on the other, shared by all citizens equally, in a system in which no party is ever immune from criticism. It is this belief which leads him to oppose the practice of positive discrimination, for example, or the apparent exclusion of Asian parents from the duty to send their children to school regularly. Equally, it is this belief which leads him to affirm his right to oppose such practices, and to oppose what he sees as the totalitarian tendencies in anti-racism, which are undermining his professional autonomy as a teacher (1988). Behind the essential pragmatism of Honeyford's own approach to multi-cultural education lies a fundamental commitment to the equality of *all* children, and a fundamental belief that even in a school with a majority of pupils with ethnic origins outside the UK, the aim of education should be to meet the common needs of all children, though he does not spell these out in any detail. It is this commitment that leads him to question the plight of the white minority in schools such as his, to question the value of concessions made to children simply on the grounds of their membership of a particular cultural group, and to oppose privileged treatment of any kind for minority groups. What Honeyford appears to fail to take account of here, however, as I shall point out more fully in part two, is that there can be injustice in treating people the same when in relevant respects they are different, just as much as there can be in treating them differently when in relevant respects they are the same.

Nowhere is this failure clearer than in his understanding of racism. To Honeyford, this word refers to 'the odious doctrines of racial superiority' (1986j, p. 51). To define the word in this way is all well and good, so long as one then proceeds to find another word to describe, for example, the often quite unintentional discrimination experienced by ethnic minorities simply because of the way the institutions in our society are structured. Honeyford nowhere in his articles acknowledges this kind of discrimination as a problem, yet to ignore it in this way actually provides the ideal conditions for it to thrive. Honeyford's statement that 'Britain is not a racist society' (1986b) may be true on his own definition of racism, but is hardly likely to offer much reassurance to those who are daily on the receiving end of gratuitous insults, violence, bullying, threats and other less direct but more insidious forms of discrimination directed at them for no other reason than the colour of their skin. The 'truly equal and harmonious multicultural society' (1982d) which provides Honeyford's vision for the future will never be achieved without an attempt to eradicate current injustices, and his insensitivity to the well-documented difficulties which are the constant experience of the ethnic minorities calls into question his commitment to this goal. Nevertheless, his critique of anti-racist education merits serious examination, particularly because it brings to our attention some crucial questions, both empirical and philosophical, which cannot be side-stepped. For example, to what extent *should* individuals find their identity as members of an ethnic or cultural group (cf. Sowell, 1977, ch. 5)? Is the highlighting of racism in our society likely to increase or decrease its incidence? Should racism be tackled separately in schools, or as part of general moral education? But with these questions we are once again beginning to trespass on the subject matter of part two.

One of the greatest misfortunes about the Honeyford affair was that on the whole his ideas were not challenged in open debate (more recently Murphy, 1987, p. 110–4, has highlighted some of the inconsistencies in his articles) but were merely shouted down. Given the current climate of intense emotional involvement in the anti-racist movement in some quarters, however, perhaps such a response is understandable. Chapter four explores the complicated chain of events that was set in motion as a result of publicity about Honeyford's articles on race and multi-cultural education. Before turning to that topic, I want to look more closely at the specific passages in the articles which gave widespread offence, not only to many of his parents and the local ethnic minority groups, but also to the local education authority in Bradford and to the supporters of multi-cultural and anti-racist education across the country.

WHAT WAS FOUND OFFENSIVE IN HONEYFORD'S ARTICLES

There is no doubt that the articles made Honeyford many enemies. It is much less clear what precisely his opponents objected to. There seem to be significant differences between the objections of councillors and Council officials on the one hand, and parents, leaders of local minority groups and anti-racist activists on the other.

Honeyford's articles alienated the local education authority in a number of ways. First, they objected to his sustained criticisms of Council policies. In fact, his articles criticize almost all the Council's multi-cultural initiatives and responses to ethnic minority demands that were outlined in chapter two. He regrets the ending of the Council's 'bussing' policy and the subsequent growth of 'mono-ethnic, minority... ghetto schools', and discusses the harm done to children's education by extended trips to the Indian sub-continent. He finds it hard to reconcile 'one of the school's values – love of dumb creatures and respect for their welfare' with the LEA decision to provide *halal* meat in his school (1983b). He objects strongly to the call for the use of minority languages as a medium of instruction in state schools. He is opposed to many of the 'diktats' (his term) contained in Bradford's 1983 LAM, *Racialist Behaviour in Schools*, especially the requirements to produce an anti-racist policy statement for his school, to report any racist incident, to keep a file on the children involved, to devote frequent staff meetings to racial matters and to involve parents. He argues that he can see no evidence of racism in his school, and that if he could, he would wish to use his own judgment in dealing with it, on an individual basis (1985d). Secondly, Council officers argued that he had lost the support and trust of many of his parents on account of his insulting and negative statements about ethnic minorities, which were in fact an abuse of his right to free speech. Bradford's director of educational services commented,

> We do not seek to curtail staff's freedoms. If a member of the teaching staff does wish to adopt a public stance on matters related to his work, then our advice to them (*sic*) is that public office holders do have responsibilities as well as rights. If what they say affects parental confidence, it should cause them to reflect on the wisdom of such a stance. (*Yorkshire Post*, 15 May 1984).

Thirdly, Council officers objected to Honeyford's decision to express his opposition to Bradford's multi-cultural policies through the media, rather than through acceptable internal channels such as the advisory service. In an acrimonious exchange of letters with Council officers, Honeyford insisted that he did use the proper channels. Fourthly, his articles were considered professionally irresponsible and lacking in respect and loyalty towards his employers. The assistant director of education in Bradford accused Honeyford of

> discourteous and ungentlemanly conduct towards council officers, and a failure to recognize that there were limits to the criticism he heaped upon them in the press. (*Telegraph and Argus*, 9 June 1985).

In fact, some of Honeyford's strongest personal criticisms of councillors and council officers did not appear until after his early retirement; for example, the title of his article *The Gilmour Syndrome* (1986c) refers to Peter Gilmour, the Conservative chairman of Bradford's Educational Services Committee, who was outspoken in his condemnation of Honeyford's articles.

A different set of objections, relating more directly to Honeyford's voicing of criticisms of West Indian values, Asian temperaments and the political, social and economic conditions in Pakistan, underlay much of the opposition to him which grew up among parents, the minority groups in Bradford and the anti-racist movement generally, although, of course, even among these groups there was a considerable variety of response. Abu Bashir, the chairman of the Asian Workers' Support Group, for example, commented,

> We are more concerned about some of the racist remarks he has made than about his views on the Council's education policy (*Telegraph and Argus*, 18 September 1984)

while Choudhury M. Khan, the president of the local Council for Mosques, said,

> I don't know if he's racist or not, but the smell I get from him is hate. (quoted in Jack, 1985, p. 35).

It is unfortunate that the style of Honeyford's articles made them so open to misrepresentation and quoting out of context. For example, Honeyford's description of the parent of one of his pupils as a 'figure straight out of Kipling' whose 'English sounds like that of Peter Sellers' Indian doctor on an off day' (1983b) has been quoted many times (*cf* Gordon and Klug, 1986, p. 29) as an example of a derogatory statement that is likely to cause offence to Muslim parents. But it is never (to my knowledge) pointed out by his critics that a few lines later Honeyford describes the same man as a 'devout Moslem of the highest moral principle'. An article in *The Times Educational Supplement* (Matthews, 1986) informs us that

> In a TES feature as long ago as November 1982, Mr. Honeyford described black British children as 'strangers in our midst'.

However, a check on the original article (1982d) reveals that the offensive phrase is actually used to refer to immigrants generally, rather than black British children ('communities of immigrants from Poland, Hungary, Yugoslavia, the Ukraine and the innumerable Jewish settlers in this country' are specifically mentioned, as well as people from the New Commonwealth) and the context is not one of alienation, as Matthews implies, but one of welcome. It is clearly possible to argue that there is something insensitive about the use of the phrase at all, however it is contextualized, but this does not justify Matthews' misrepresentation. Sometimes criticisms of the articles appear to lose touch with reality altogether. For example, Seidel (1986, pp. 119, 132) criticizes Honeyford's 1983 *Salisbury Review* article for not mentioning that parents disagreed with his views in 1984. An even more flagrant example of distortion is provided by the leaflet in Urdu that was distributed from Asian community centres in Bradford, purporting to be a translation from Honeyford's *Salisbury Review* article (1984a). A retranslation into English provided by Mrs M. Iqbal, a Honeyford supporter and member of the local Community Relations Council, reads, 'Honeyford means we are illegitimate, we are criminals, we are illiterate... volatile... rascals... useless-...scroungers.' While I do not wish to suggest that all of the distortions in the Honeyford affair were made by his opponents (and in chapter four I shall illustrate some of the distortions of his supporters), the mischievousness of this particular transformation of Honeyford's statement about a high proportion of West Indian families being fatherless into a supreme insult against Muslims makes it necessary for us to accept the possibility that some at least of the opposition to Honeyford resulted not from what he actually wrote, but from what parents were misled into believing that he wrote. Indeed, in other circumstances one could imagine Honeyford proving a more popular headteacher than most with many ethnic minority parents, in view of his emphasis on firm discipline and basic skills and his belief, for example, that parents should have the right to withdraw their children from sex education.

Nevertheless, whatever allowances we make for the misunderstanding, misrepresenting or misquoting of what he wrote in his articles, there remains their largely negative tone and a significant core of insulting statements which would be recognized as offensive not only by the committed anti-racists who view *The Salisbury Review* as a 'contentious and obscene right-wing journal' (Foster-Carter, 1985), but by many of those 'fundamentally decent people' for whom Honeyford claims to speak (1984a, p. 31). Many of these insulting statements succeed in promoting unfavourable stereotypes of West Indians and Asians. The West Indian is portrayed as inconsiderate (creating an 'ear-splitting cacophony for most of the night to the detriment of his neighbour's sanity') and lacking in 'educational ambition and the values to support it' (*ibid.* pp. 30–32). The Asian is portrayed as bent on imposing a 'purdah mentality' in schools, and generally given to 'intense and animated diatribes' which reflect the 'hysterical political temperament of the Indian sub-continent' (*ibid.* pp. 30–1). Both these stereotypes contrast strongly with the very positive image of 'British' people which is conveyed through phrases such as 'the British traditions of... civilized discourse and respect for reason' and 'the British genius for compromise... and for good-natured tolerance' (*ibid*. p. 32). An analysis of the diction of Honeyford's articles reveals a surprisingly high number of negative expressions referring to ethnic minorities, for someone who believes in such traditional British values.

In addition to conducting his argument in terms of stereotypes, Honeyford also makes ethnic minority families the scapegoats for the comparative educational failure of a growing number of white children in inner-city schools. His intuition is that

> it is no more than common sense that if a school contains a disproportionate number of children for whom English is a second language (true of all Asian children, even those born here), or children from homes where educational ambition and the values to support it are conspicuously absent (i.e. the vast majority of West Indian homes – a disproportionate number of which are fatherless), then academic standards are bound to suffer (*ibid*. p. 32).

He even suggests that a growing number of Asians may be exploiting the freedom and privileges they are granted as British citizens in order to 'produce Asian ghettoes', though the real reasons why Asians are concentrated in the inner cities, as was shown in chapter one, have little to do with any such separatist conspiracy.

Finally, when Honeyford decides to contrast the rights and privileges enjoyed by people of Pakistani origin in the UK with the lack of similar rights and privileges in Pakistan, he seems to get carried away with his invective and lose the thread of his argument. He writes,

> Pakistan is a country which cannot cope with democracy; under martial law since 1977, it is ruled by a military tyrant who, in the opinion of at least half his countrymen, had his predecessor judicially murdered. A country, moreover, which, despite disproportionate western aid because of its important strategic position, remains for most of its people obstinately backward. Corruption at every level combines with unspeakable treatment not only of criminals, but of those who dare to question Islamic orthodoxy as interpreted by a despot. Even as I write, wounded dissidents are chained to hospital beds awaiting their fate. Pakistan, too, is the heroin capital of the world. (A fact which is now reflected in the drug problems of English cities with Asian populations.) (*ibid*. p. 31).

However true any or all of these assertions may be, their questionable relevance makes one wonder why they have been included in an article about education at all. The Asian migrants did not introduce the heroin habit into the UK, and the drug problems do not appear to be higher in English cities with Asian populations than elsewhere. Neither can they be held responsible for the present economic plight of Pakistan, or for the actions of a military leader who came to power after the vast majority of them had already left. Nonetheless, it is to be expected that they have retained strong emotional ties to their country of origin, and would be very unhappy to find it traduced in this way.

For a variety of reasons, Honeyford's articles were thus found offensive by a variety of groups. One gains the impression that as he was writing he knew that this was bound to be the case. But it is likely that even he could never have predicted the violence of the response to his articles or the nation-wide repercussions. Chapter four will now describe the story of these events, from the initial flare-up in March 1984, to the eventual retirement of Honeyford in December 1985.

4 The Campaign Against Honeyford, 1984–85

In the previous chapter I suggested that offence was taken at Honeyford's articles not so much because of what he said as because of the way he said it, and that as a result some of the important questions he raised about multi-cultural education and anti-racism were never debated but were lost sight of in the widespread condemnation of his attitude to ethnic minorities. For many people, however, the most crucial issues in the Honeyford affair arise not from his articles at all but from the way that events progressed following the initial demands for his dismissal in March 1984. These issues include questions about the control of education, the accountability of teachers and Council officers, the justifiability of direct action involving the disruption of children's education, and the grounds for dismissing teachers.

CONFLICTING INTERPRETATIONS AND THE NEED FOR OBJECTIVITY

This new set of inter-related issues, further intertwined with the issues mentioned in the last chapter such as racism, cultural identity and minority rights, is made even more difficult to unravel because of the large number of different groups involved and the considerable amount of in-fighting which took place between these groups. For example, all the evidence suggests that the Drummond Parents' Action Committee (DPAC), formed in March 1984 to campaign for the removal of Honeyford from the headship of Drummond Middle School, *did* have the support of the majority of the school's parents, and its candidates were able to win decisive victories in the parent-governor elections. But it is clear that the DPAC did not have the support of *all* Asian parents, as is shown by the well-publicized physical assaults on Asian parents crossing the picket line to take their children to school. Murphy (1987, p. 132) quotes some Asians who strongly disapproved of the picketing.

Increasingly, the DPAC saw itself in conflict not only with Honeyford but also with Bradford Council, though Council officers shared with the DPAC their disapproval of Honeyford's views. The DPAC accused the Council of not implementing its race relations policies, and the Council warned parents of possible legal action if they kept their children away from school. The DPAC also alienated another potential ally, the NUT, which consistently expressed opposition to Honeyford's views, by accusing Drummond Middle School teachers of unprofessionally threatening to punish children who attended the DPAC's alternative school. Honeyford's own union, the NAHT, on the other hand, championed him throughout the affair. The school governors also supported him throughout, though sometimes only by narrow margins and on one crucial occasion only as a result of a tactical error on the part of his opponents: a resolution calling for Honeyford's reinstatement was passed by seven votes to four after four governors had chosen to boycott the meeting. The teachers at the school refused to get publicly involved in the affair. A number of clergymen made statements, some supporting and some opposing Honeyford, but their influence appears to have been very small. Both the DPAC and the Friends of Drummond Middle School (a pro-Honeyford support group) organized petitions, but while the latter attached more importance to the number of signatures they collected (outnumbering the DPAC's petition by more than twenty to one), the former put greater emphasis on protest marches, pupil strikes, pickets and other forms of direct action.

Left-wing Asian groups, such as the Asian Youth Movement (AYM) and the Asian Workers' Support Group, were active in the campaign against Honeyford, and were involved in the formation of the Bradford Drummond Parents' Support Group in October 1985. Among the Muslim groups, on the other hand, some, such as the Azad Kashmir Muslim Association of Bradford (AKMAB), were active, while others, including the Muslim Parents' Association, remained uninvolved. One of the most vociferous opposition groups to Honeyford was the MSC-funded Council for Mosques, which sought to speak for all Muslims in the city (much to the annoyance of the AYM), and which, like the DPAC, found itself increasingly in conflict with Bradford Council. A few individual Muslims made a public stand in support of Honeyford, and two of these were eventually elected as community representatives to the new governing body. The visitor to the picket line, which by October 1985 had become a permanent feature of life at Drummond Middle School, would see two distinct groups of protestors – the white left-wingers and members of anti-racist pressure groups on the one hand, and the Asians on the other. Their physical separateness made an ironic contrast to what appeared to be the complete integration of the children in the school playground on the other side of the wall.

The last two groups involved are the politicians and the media. Nationally, the debate about Honeyford tended to follow party political lines, with Conservatives like Sir Marcus Fox and Nicholas Winterton speaking out in support of him in Parliament, and Labour MPs such as Max Madden speaking against him. In contrast to his successor's handling of the McGoldrick affair, Sir Keith Joseph chose not to intervene, though he called for a full report on the affair and stayed in close contact with local Conservative leaders. However, the invitation to Honeyford to attend an educational seminar with the Prime Minister only two weeks after the rescindment of his suspension was seen by his opponents as either politically inept or intentionally provocative. At the local level, the divisions, at least at first, were less clearly along party lines. In March 1984, the Conservative chairman of the Educational Services Committee was one of Honeyford's most outspoken critics, while his supporters included the Labour Lord Mayor. All three local political parties changed their position on giving Honeyford a financial incentive to take early retirement. As for the media, the local press tended to concentrate on the provision of information, and the two main reporters covering the Honeyford affair, Jim Greenhalf of the *Telegraph and Argus* and Michael Clarke of the *Yorkshire Post*, generally carried out their task with commendable thoroughness and objectivity. The national press, on the other hand, together with a wide range of journals and TV and radio programmes, put more emphasis on commentary on events, and because of the complexity of the issues and the number of groups involved, it is not surprising that a whole range of different and often conflicting interpretations of the Honeyford affair grew up. These interpretations may be divided into eight main categories:

(a)   Honeyford was a sincere headteacher who spoke out from first-hand experience against current trends in multi-cultural and multi-racial education (Flew, 1986, p. 16) and in favour of the traditional values of British education. As a result, he was being unreasonably persecuted by left-wingers, who saw him as a spokesman for the New Right (*cf* Seidel, 1986; Gordon and Klug, 1986), and by anti-racist activists in whose eyes he had 'committed a thought crime' (*The Times* editorial, 26 March 1985). This was the view of the Honeyford affair promoted almost universally in the popular press, as the following headlines illustrate: 'Is it racist to tell the truth?' (*Daily Mail*, 13 June 1984); 'A shameful victory for the bigots' (*Daily Express*, 30 March 1985); 'This decent chap needs a pal' (*News of the World*, 31 March 1985); 'The man who dared to speak his mind' (*Daily Mirror*, 9 April 1985). With the passing of time, the view has become even more distorted. West (1987), for example, somewhat sarcastically comments that Honeyford lost his job apparently for the crime of wanting to teach English children their own language, history and religion (p. 19).

(b)   Honeyford was guilty of insulting ethnic minorities through his articles and whipping up the fears of white people, and had thus proved himself unsuitable for the headship of a multi-ethnic school. The seven racism awareness training officers employed by Bradford Council went so far as to describe him as a 'known racist'. Not unexpectedly, this view was a view generally supported and propagated in publications such as *The Next Step, Searchlight* and the *Caribbean Times*, as well as in press releases from a number of pressure groups such as the AYM and the AKMAB.

(c)   Honeyford was suspended and forced to leave his post as a result of his criticisms of Bradford Council's multi-cultural and race relations policies (Butt, 1985), or because his attitude was deemed to be incompatible with the implementation of these policies. This view was held by many people who, while perhaps disagreeing with Honeyford's opinions, supported his right to express them freely. Meadowcroft, for example, wrote of the dangers to the democratic process in accepting 'that a public employee should be dismissed for his or her views rather than how they carry out their job' (1985) and saw the opposition that developed towards Honeyford (and later for different reasons towards Selbourne at Ruskin College) as 'an attack on political pluralism' (1986). Many Conservatives have viewed the Honeyford affair as primarily an issue of free speech.

(d)   Others (for example, Matthews, 1986) have claimed that opposition to Honeyford developed not because he *criticized* local policies but because he *contravened* them. This was one of the main complaints raised by both the DPAC and the Council for Mosques, and the case presented against Honeyford by the Directorate of Educational Services in Bradford included the charge that he continued to contravene the spirit, if not the letter, of Bradford's policies.

(e)   On another view, Bradford's education officers had made serious errors of strategy in the new multi-racial policies (Pedley, 1986; Murphy, 1987, p. 94), either through incompetence or because they were duped into believing that making concessions to socially and educationally retrogressive Muslim demands would further the cause of racial harmony in the city. They now found themselves in the position, Selbourne (1984a, 1984b, 1987) suggests, where they either had to hand over Honeyford's scalp, which was the latest Muslim demand, or else lose all the goodwill they had so far built up with the Muslim community.

(f)   What was at issue was Honeyford's competence as a headteacher (Husband, E. 1985) and his failure to retain the trust and confidence of a majority of his parents. This is one of the main points of emphasis in the report issued after the advisers' inspection of Drummond Middle School in

June 1984, and in the reports prepared for the special Schools Education Sub-Committee meeting on 22 March 1985.

(g)   Honeyford was a capable, intelligent and questioning headteacher who wanted to be allowed to exercise his professional autonomy in the running of his school. This was the view of Councillor Sunderland, chairman of the school governors (quoted in *Telegraph and Argus*, 26 November 1985), who argued that it was the 'diktats' and constant interference of Council officers in the running of the school that was the main problem.

(h)   Finally, there are those who see Honeyford as primarily a victim of circumstances beyond his control. Bullock (1985) illustrates this view when he claims that Honeyford lost his job 'for attempting to cope with the conflicting demands of the (1944 Education) Act, the Bradford education authority and the minority of non-Asian pupils in his school'.

Rather than take each of these eight main interpretations of the Honeyford affair in turn and evaluate their claims, the present chapter seeks instead to get behind the mythology which has accumulated around the affair and to establish exactly what happened. We cannot draw any justifiable conclusions about the affair until this has been done, and done with as high a degree of objectivity as possible.

Such objectivity, however, is by no means easy to achieve. Many of the written sources (mainly articles in newspapers and journals) are full of distortions, emotive language, factual inaccuracies and various other forms of bias. Several of the main personalities involved have become reluctant to offer for publication any further opinions on the affair, after seeing their opinions distorted and themselves abused in the press; others who do venture opinions often ask not to be named. The chairperson of the DPAC even went so far as to refuse to address a public meeting while any members of the press were present. Both Honeyford himself and his most outspoken critics became targets for hate-mail and death threats. Since Bradford Council found itself threatened with a libel action by the NAHT following the leaking to the press of an internal Council memorandum in which Honeyford was described as a 'known racist', it is not surprising that Council reports on the Honeyford affair were increasingly marked 'confidential'.

It is not too difficult to recognize the emotive language in the descriptions of Honeyford as 'a sacrificial lamb on the altar of race relations' (letter to *Telegraph and Argus*, 27 March 1985), of the chairperson of the DPAC as 'the shrill virago' (*Yorkshire Post*, 8 April 1985, 25 May 1985) or of the race relations movement as 'Thought Police who have bludgeoned Mr Honeyford into submission' (*Daily Express*, 30 March 1985). There is a similar lack of restraint in Selbourne's description of 'the tide of Islam crashing down here and flowing through these terrace houses' (1984a, p. 138) and in demonstrators' portrayal of Honeyford as a devil on banners inscribed 'Honeyford writes in the blood of the blacks'. It is more difficult, without painstaking cross-referencing and checking of original documents, to identify the factual inaccuracies which permeate so many of the articles on the Honeyford affair or to expose the bias in the selection of facts used to justify the various interpretations of the affair mentioned above.

The factual inaccuracies are not necessarily intentional distortions of the truth, but may often result from the uncritical transmission of second-hand information. For example, Brown (1985, p. 9), Jack (1985, p. 34) and Murphy (1987, p. 109) all report that Honeyford's first letter on racial issues (see chapter three) was a response to the claim by a *Telegraph and Argus* columnist that the Council was giving in to blackmail by providing money for a West Indian community centre after it had been threatened by riots if the centre were not built. But what the columnist actually wrote was that the Council provided financial support 'because it *feared* Toxteth-type riots might occur if they did nothing' (*Telegraph and Argus*, 8 July 1982, my emphasis). Such fears might seem wholly justifiable in the wake of events at Toxteth, Brixton, Southall and the trial of the Bradford Twelve, though it was argued in chapters one and two that the primary motivation for the Council's action was more positive, i.e. to provide just and equal treatment for the city's ethnic minorities. But the effect of the distorted version is to incriminate the local West Indian community (by implying that it was public knowledge that it had *threatened* the Council with race riots), thus giving an air of reasonableness to Honeyford's suggestion that some public-spirited citizen should refer the matter to the public auditor. This may be an example of an uncritical acceptance of Honeyford's own version of events, a habit which the *Telegraph and Argus* also occasionally falls into. For example, after the advisers' report on Drummond Middle School, Honeyford was given five months to implement the advisers' recommendations, to forge better links with the parents and local community and to write six reports on various aspects of the school. According to the *Telegraph and Argus* (12 April 1985),

> This plan would appear to have one objective only: the removal of Honeyford from Drummond Middle, to be accomplished by making his professional life as difficult as possible.

This is an exact repetition of Honeyford's own view (*cf Telegraph and Argus*, 15 November 1984), but it is much more likely that the aim of the Council's resolution was actually to force him to think through his commitment to LEA policies and his attitude to the running of his school once again and to try to influence his thinking by making him work closely with advisers. This latter view is confirmed by the report of the Director of Educational Services to the Schools Education Sub-committee on 22 March 1985.

Although views of the Honeyford affair that were biased in the head's favour tended to be dominant in the popular press, it is certainly not true that all the distortions and misleading innuendoes came from Honeyford's supporters. At the end of chapter three, some of the distorted views of Honeyford's articles that were promulgated by his opponents were noted. Indeed, some of his opponents' claims appear totally fanciful, as in this extract from a press release by the Bradford Drummond Parents' Support Group (21 October 1985):

> One wonders whether Mr Honeyford will be the next person to be advocating bird shots fired at the black children at the school.

Picking one's way through such bias and distortion, of which the examples given here are only a tiny proportion, is a lengthy procedure, but one which is indispensible to the attempt to establish exactly what happened in the affair.

Of the hundreds of articles on the Honeyford affair, five deserve special mention. Undoubedly the most colourful is the chapter on the affair in David Selbourne's *Left Behind* (1987, pp. 95–116). This is an expanded, but otherwise neither corrected nor updated, version of an article which first appeared in *New Society* under the title 'The Culture Clash in Bradford' (Selbourne, 1984a). He comments on the irony in the fact that the city's educational planners are conceding the socially and educationally retrogressive demands made by Bradford's Muslim elders 'in the name of "good race relations"; and even, some of them, in the name of "socialist" progress'. But having embarked on a policy of conceding such demands, as a means of developing the confidence and self respect of the minority communities and breaking down the 'ghetto mentality', the planners, in Selbourne's view, have now found themselves in the position where Honeyford's scalp has to be 'thrown to the Muslim lions'. The legitimacy or otherwise of Honeyford's criticisms is no longer the main question; nothing is to be allowed to stand in the way of the implementation of the race relations policies. The trouble is that the 'race-planners' have not succeeded in convincing large sections of the indigenous population (or, indeed, of the leadership of the local Labour party) of the justice of their policies. In Selbourne's words, they 'continue to lean over backwards on "ethnic" issues, only to get further up people's noses'. In spite of its immense readability, however, Selbourne's paper not only significantly misquotes Council officials (*cf* complaints in the *Telegraph and Argus*, 27 April 1984), but also fails to explore questions such as what *should* be done about racism in cities like Bradford, and what rights Muslim parents have or should have in our present society. Nor does he provide any serious examination of the social principles and values underlying Bradford's multicultural policies (*cf* Carling *et al.*, 1984). However, this is not Selbourne's purpose. He is concerned with what he sees as the increasing domination of 'a provincial Yorkshire city in its darkest hours of economic failure' by reactionary, undemocratic and anti-social Muslim imams whose values 'are those of the villages of North Pakistan', and with the failure of the political left to respond adequately to this situation. The paper was written early in the Honeyford affair and is thus, of course, not in a position to comment on its later complexities.

The second is the only complete booklet so far to be devoted to the affair, Andrew Brown's 'Trials of Honeyford' (1985). This has been widely portrayed as a 'usefully detached' account (*The Times Educational Supplement* editorial, 6 December 1985) and as a 'view from the middle' (*Telegraph and Argus*, 3 December 1985). Perhaps this impression was encouraged by the publication of right-wing attacks on the booklet by Cox and Marks for omitting commentary on the political background to the affair and on the involvement of children in the demonstrations against Honeyford (*Daily Telegraph*, 2 December 1985). In fact, Brown's account, like Selbourne's, is strongly biased against Honeyford's opponents, who are pictured as abandoning 'truth and reason alike' (p. 21) in their passionate personal antagonism against Honeyford. Apart from some surprising factual inaccuracies, which may be unintentional, the booklet succeeds in giving a favourable view of Honeyford as much through what it leaves out as through what it says. For example, it invites the reader to study the two articles by Honeyford reprinted in Appendix I, and 'judge for himself the merit of the accusation' that Honeyford's views 'constituted grounds for dismissal' (p. 10). But since the *Salisbury Review* article which set the affair ablaze is not one of those included in the Appendix, the reader is in fact given inadequate grounds on which to make such a judgment, and the criticisms of Honeyford are seen as the more unreasonable. Brown devotes an entire chapter to the advisers' report on their inspection of Drummond Middle School in June 1984, but fails even to mention the most significant of the advisers' recommendations, that the headteacher should

> reconsider his relationships with parents and community groups and the effects of his writings on those relationships and the life of the school.

The third is the supplement, 'The Honeyford Debate', issued with the *Telegraph and Argus* on 26 November 1985 (Greenhalf, 1985b). This contains a chronology of events, a statement of the case for and the case against Honeyford, profiles of the main characters involved in the affair, a summary of the Council's race relations policy, reprints of Honeyford's 1983 *Times Educational Supplement* article and crucial *Salisbury Review* article, an article on the 'cultural racism' of the New Right (based on Seidel, 1986) and an article outlining the complex local political wranglings over the affair. Although this supplement generally maintains a neutral and objective tone, this is marred on occasions, as in the thumbnail sketch of the left-winger and ardent opponent of Honeyford, Councillor Reuben Goldberg. Irrespective of the truth of the allegations, it is hard to find any reasons why his expulsion from his grammar school 'for having long hair, being politically active and repeatedly late' is mentioned except to discredit him by implying that he might be an unsuitable person to appoint as a school governor.

The fourth is Ian Jack's *Sunday Times Magazine* article, 'A Severed Head?' published on 15 December 1985. This is a generally accurate account of events, so far as it goes, brought to life with a considerable amount of local colour. But it makes no attempt to examine the local political response to the Honeyford affair, the disagreements among the Muslims and other Asians, or the attitude towards Honeyford among the broader community in Bradford. Somewhat surprisingly, Jack appears to view the chanting of Honeyford's name at a Bradford City football match as an ironic invocation of a headmaster as a hero, rather than as the use of his name as a racist weapon to insult and drown out the speech being made by the Lord Mayor, Councillor Ajeeb. The article is too sketchy for any significant conclusions to be drawn at the end, though it remains a useful introduction to the affair.

The fifth is contained in Dervla Murphy's 'Tales from Two Cities' (1987). The first half of this volume describes the author's experiences and observations whilst living for several months among the Mirpuris in the Manningham district of Bradford, not far from Drummond Middle School, and concludes with a substantial and generally accurate account of the Honeyford affair (the second half is devoted to Handsworth in Birmingham). Not surprisingly she is mainly concerned to give the local Asian response to the affair, or rather a white liberal outsider's view of the local Asian response to the affair. Those Asians who were happy to chat to her over a pint in the pub are quoted extensively, but there is no evidence that she consulted the imams whose authority is so influential in (and beyond) the Mirpuri community. Somewhat perversely, since most Asian Hindus, Sikhs and especially Muslims do not view themselves as primarily distinguished from other groups in terms of race and colour as much as in terms of religion and culture, she insists on calling them 'the Browns'. Her emphasis on the Asian viewpoint means that the role of whites in the Honeyford affair is generally played down (Peter Gilmour, Richard Knight and Reuben Goldberg are hardly mentioned) and that more attention is paid to the protests and demonstrations which accompanied governors' meetings, for example, than to the meetings themselves. The brief account of the crucial governors' meeting on 22 June 1985, which recommended Honeyford's reinstatement, is both inadequate and misleading (p. 126). Equally misleading is her statement that Honeyford was refused lave to appeal to the House of Lords (p. 141);

leave to appeal was in fact granted on 28 November 1985, and one of the conditions of the early retirement package he eventually accepted was that he should not pursue this appeal.

Although she avoids the trap of coming down too simplistically on one side or the other in the debate, Murphy's evident sympathy with Jenny Woodward (the chairperson of the DPAC), with Honeyford himself (whom she describes as 'an innocent carrier of the New Right virus') and with the Asian protestors against Honeyford (whose demonstrations she frequently joined), inevitably leaves the reader confused. On the other hand, the reader is provided with many perceptive insights into the complexities of life in multi-racial areas, written in an extremely readable style. Sometimes her forthrightness degenerates into merely over-emotive language, as in her invective against the 'lunacy' of Racism Awareness courses and the 'monstrously irresponsible' recommendation by the Swann Committee that the DES should fund an independent evaluation of such courses (p. 122). Her insistence on telling the truth as she sees it, however unpalatable it may be to the parties involved, may in fact cause offence to many: much that she writes is critical of anti-racists, not least the suggestion that many Asians don't take them seriously but prefer to 'seem to ignore racial prejudice' (p. 129); and she may also have offended the Mirpuris by her emphasis on their domestic problems, the Muslims generally by her attack on 'Islamic oppression of women' (p. 27) and the local authority for her dismissal of its 1981 Policy Statement on Race Relations as 'a brave but foolish document' (p. 94). Sometimes indeed she comes perilously close to a re-expression of the very views which from Honeyford's pen caused so much offence in Bradford.

Finally, mention should perhaps be made of Olivia Foster-Carter's account of the Honeyford affair in Barry Troyna's *Racial Inequality in Education* (1987), though this unfortunately contains so many factual inaccuracies and other wild statements that it is of little help to anyone who wants to know what actually happened. For example, Foster-Carter implies (p. 45) that the High Court hearing in September 1985 was concerned with assessing Honeyford's professional competence rather than with the right of the LEA to discipline a teacher against the recommendation of the school governors, and in her version, Michael Beloff (who actually represented Honeyford) is made out to be the judge (p. 54). We are told (p. 44) that unemployment in Bradford 'is now 50 per cent' (in fact it is at most a third of that), and that most of the Asian community 'makes little claim on education' (in fact the percentage of the Asian community in full time education is much higher than that of the white community). The reader will search in vain for an article by Honeyford in the 13 April 1984 edition of *The Times Educational Supplement*, to which she twice makes reference (pp. 46, 58). Though she refers with approval to the claim by Councillor Riaz that

Honeyford has insulted 'the integrity and intellectual capacity of the white working class' (p. 48) and the claim by Alex Fellowes that Honeyford was dangerously dividing the community into black and white (p. 50), neither claim seems to have any foundation in reality. It is surprising that such a careless piece of writing should be included in a serious collection of articles on racial inequality.

Even the best of the accounts which have so far been produced, however, do not appear to contain the degree either of objectivity or of thoroughness which is necessary if we are to come to conclusions with confidence about the affair and the issues which it raises. The first task has therefore been to establish as objectively and fully as possible exactly what happened in the affair. The findings of this investigation are presented as a chronology of the affair in the Appendix. This appendix is based on the examination, comparison and cross-referencing of virtually every local and national newspaper, magazine and journal article so far produced on the Honeyford affair (well over one thousand), and this has been backed up by reference to original documents produced by Bradford's Director of Educational Services, the LEA advisers who inspected Drummond Middle School, Honeyford himself, the DPAC and other pressure groups. This use of printed sources has been supplemented by informal discussions with as many as possible of the parties involved and by a physical presence at events in Bradford such as demonstrations outside Drummond Middle School.

The present chapter is designed to provide a basis of fact for the rest of the book, so that the alternative perspectives presented in chapter five and the underlying issues discussed in part two may be seen to be grounded in an accurate picture of what actually happened. The chapter thus seeks to present the information contained in the Appendix in a more readable and analytical form, and to examine the key documents in more detail, so that the validity of the claims made by the various groups may be assessed and the most crucial issues brought to light. The sources of any unreferenced claims made in the remainder of this chapter may be traced by reference to the Appendix. In the following account, the Honeyford affair is divided into four stages.

STAGE ONE: INITIAL PROTESTS AND COUNCIL INDECISION, MARCH–OCTOBER 1984

In chapter two I attempted to describe the broader context in which the initial reactions to Honeyford's article in 1984 must be understood. Bradford Council had come through a year in which race issues had been constantly highlighted. These included the request by the Muslim Parents Association to take over five local authority schools, the *halal* meat debate and the allegations of racist behaviour by teachers at Wyke Manor Upper School and of racist attacks on pupils at Eccleshill Upper School. All these issues had received substantial attention in the national press and on radio and TV. In December 1983 the local association of headteachers had voted against implementing the Council's LAM 6/83, *Racist Behaviour in Schools*, partly because it was simply another burden on overworked teachers, partly because it was undermining their professional autonomy and partly because some at least felt that drawing attention to racial issues in schools too directly was likely to be counter-productive. In response, members of the Council's all-party Race Relations Advisory Group launched a fierce attack on the city's headteachers. Councillor Barry Thorne, for example, said,

> The crisis we are faced with today is that some of our headmasters are a law unto themselves, and I am getting pig-sick of power-mad headmasters.

The atmosphere was not one in which further dissent from headteachers would be welcomed.

Although Ray Honeyford had been officially encouraged to apply for the headship of Drummond Middle School in 1980, after an unsuccessful application for the headship of a similar Bradford school, by the end of 1983 he was being viewed with deep suspicion by many councillors and education officers, because he, unlike the other headteachers, had used the media rather than the more acceptable internal channels for expressing his criticisms of Bradford's policies, and because he was criticizing increasing LEA authoritarianism as well as the specific provisions of Bradford's new policies. He argued that the policies were ill-conceived and based ultimately on non-educational considerations; and he expressed his views in language which succeeded in offending virtually all the ethnic minority organizations to whom the Council was seeking to build bridges. By the end of 1983, the chairman of the Educational Services Committee, Councillor Peter Gilmour, was convinced that the best thing to do was to 'buy Honeyford off' (Spencer, 1984).

Before March 1984, however, Honeyford was a well-respected headteacher in the eyes of his parents and the local community. His school, like other inner-city schools in Bradford, had been over-subscribed for the previous three years, and appeared to be coping well with the increasing proportion of Asian pupils (from 49 per cent in September 1980 to 87 per cent in September 1983). There had certainly been no complaints about the running of his school.

On 7 March 1984 the bombshell dropped. Mike Whittaker, Bradford's Educational Policies Development officer, informed *Yorkshire Post* reporter

Michael Clarke about Honeyford's second *Salisbury Review* article, and Michael Clarke proceeded to write a news item on it. It is by no means clear why Whittaker took this step. Perhaps he merely thought the item was newsworthy and deserved wider attention. Or perhaps, as Greenhalf (1985a) suggests, he believed that the inevitable publicity would give the Council a good case for getting rid of Honeyford. Whatever his reasons – and by all accounts he took the step without consulting his political masters – the results were dramatic.

The reporters from the local press naturally phoned round to get off-the-cuff reactions to Honeyford's article. Gilmour described it as 'distasteful and highly inaccurate', and Tim Whitfield, Bradford's senior Community Relations Officer, called it 'insulting'. Honeyford acknowledged to the *Telegraph and Argus* that the article might get him into trouble, but said he was 'not happy with the way we as an authority are handling the situation'. Within a few days there were calls from the Community Relations Council, Bradford West Labour Party and various Asian community groups for his dismissal. The local branch of the NUT issued the following press statement:

> We strongly condemn the views expressed by Ray Honeyford in an article in the *Salisbury Review*, winter 1984. We feel that these views contravene the local authority policies on race relations and multi-cultural education. In the light of this we urge the local authority to take immediate action and remove Mr Honeyford from his present post.

On 15 March, the *Telegraph and Argus* published an abridged version of the *Salisbury Review* article and within a few days published two detailed replies to Honeyford by the head of the adjacent Drummond Language Centre and by an advisory teacher for multi-cultural education in Bradford. The national press and the weeklies began to take an interest in Bradford, and several articles were written, from a variety of angles, though at this stage the Honeyford affair was treated as merely one of a whole range of problems Bradford was facing in the area of race relations.

On 15 March, the Drummond Parents' Action Committee (DPAC) was formed, following a meeting between Whitfield, Marsha Singh and others, with a view to informing all 'parents of children in Mr Honeyford's care...of the views and concerns of their headteacher' (*Yorkshire Post*, 9 April 1985). Its chairperson was Jenny Woodward, a former law student whose daughter attended the school. Three days later, the DPAC held its first full meeting for parents with children at the school, and a vote of no confidence in Honeyford was passed. There was a call for a ballot of parents to gauge their reactions to Honeyford's articles. On 2 April, the DPAC had its first meeting with officials from the Directorate of Educational Services, who turned down the idea of a ballot. On 6 April, the school governors rejected a resolution proposed at their termly meeting by their vice-chairman (and DPAC member), Amin Qureshi, calling for Honeyford's dismissal. The parent-governor, through whom the DPAC had been told to direct their complaints, resigned, and in June Jenny Woodward was elected the new parent-governor by a large majority on an anti-Honeyford ticket. On 4 May, an attack on Honeyford's views by Jenny Woodward and six others was published in *The Times Educational Supplement*.

In the meantime, Honeyford claimed that he was deluged with letters and telephone calls of support from all classes of people including university professors and members of ethnic minority communities. One local figure who came to Honeyford's defence was Labour's Lord Mayor, Norman Free, who argued that none of Honeyford's critics was speaking to him personally and that he was merely being tried by the press. Free had further infuriated Honeyford's opponents by telling a Rotary Club meeting that the Council's Race Relations Advisory Group was telling everyone else on the Council what they could and could not do and was exaggerating racial problems. On 10 April, while Free was abroad, his mayoral chambers at City Hall were occupied by a group of anti-racist activists (members of the Asian Youth Movement, the Campaign against Racist Attacks and the Socialist Federation). They were demanding the sacking of Free and Honeyford and the reaffirmation by Council leaders of support for the race relations policies which appeared to be under threat by the public statements of these two men. The occupation lasted only one day, but succeeded in focussing public attention on questions of race again, much to the annoyance of councillors who had been hoping to calm things down before the forthcoming local elections.

Gilmour had made his views on Honeyford's articles plain to *The Times Educational Supplement* in mid-March:

> Clearly Mr Honeyford is at odds with the thrust of council policy. That policy has been through the democratic process at county (*sic*) hall, and received all-party support. We expect our heads to comply with that, and their personal doubts are not matters for the Press.

However, after consulting the city solicitor and the Personnel Office and interviewing Honeyford himself, Council officers decided on 19 April that they had no grounds to discipline him formally. Norman Roper, the assistant director of educational services, wrote to him that though they did not like his comments they did not intend to take any further action. This decision had several important consequences. First, the DPAC now began to direct their protests not only against Honeyford, but also against the Council 'whose failure to take any form of disciplinary action against Mr Honeyford amounted to an insult to black people' (*Caribbean Times*, 11 May 1984). Secondly, Bradford's Community Relations Council alleged in a report on the Honeyford case that political interference may have prevented Council officers from taking proper disciplinary action against Honeyford. Thirdly, Roper's letter set in motion another vehement exchange of letters with Honeyford in which Roper accused him of polarizing opinion and later (on 1 June) of self-righteousness, arrogance and insensitivity. These letters were used the following year by Honeyford's union, the NAHT, to support their claim that Roper was too personally involved in the affair to be able to evaluate the evidence objectively and make the final judgment on Honeyford's future.

In early May 1984, Gilmour lost his seat in the local elections – the only Conservative to do so – at a time when the Conservatives were taking seats from Labour elsewhere in the district. There was a widespread feeling that his public attacks on Honeyford might have had more to do with this result than his defence of the multi-cultural and race relations policies (other councillors who had spoken out in support of these policies had increased their majorities), though his seat was a marginal one anyway. So the unusual partnership between Whittaker, who described himself to Selbourne as 'one of nature's Tories who votes Labour', and Gilmour, surely one of the most socialist Conservatives the Council has seen in recent years, was broken. Between them, according to some local education officers, they had not only adopted a 'Cavalier style of management', but had 'wanted to set up an alternative administration' (Spencer, 1984). Selbourne (1987, p. 97) describes Whittaker as sounding 'like a white bull in an ethnic china shop' in his discussions of the race situation in Bradford, but his extended interview with Selbourne in fact makes him seem more like a red rag to the bull of headteachers and Council officials. With Gilmour gone, however, Whittaker was quickly seconded to the Home Office, and Conservative councillor Eric Pickles moved across from the chair of the Race Relations Advisory Group to that of the Educational Services Committee.

The day after Gilmour's election defeat, the DPAC organized a protest march for parents, children and members of the local community, from Drummond Middle School to the Council offices, to present a 552-signature petition to the Director of Educational Services, calling for Honeyford's dismissal. The protest was filmed for a Panorama programme on Bradford the following week. The rally was addressed by the Labour spokesman on education, Councillor John Lambert, and by Max Madden, MP for Bradford West. A deputation then met Richard Knight, the Director of Educational Services, who responded by announcing his intention to send a team of educational advisers into the school to review the work there and consider specific complaints. In a statement to the press he explained,

> If a member of the teaching staff wishes to adopt a public stance on matters relating to his work...it may result in a check to see that it does not affect the provision in the school.

The DPAC were less than satisfied. They felt that it was wrong that 'the whole school should be placed under stress and the pressures of an inspection which was being conducted only to expose the unsuitability of the headteacher' (*Yorkshire Post*, 9 April 1985). A room was booked by Tim Whitfield in the adjacent Drummond Language Centre for a DPAC meeting to plan their next day of action.

On 7 June, Honeyford gave his version of the campaign against him and the events of the previous three months in a *Yorkshire Post* article entitled 'Taking the Risk of Telling the Truth'. This was openly critical of the official handing of the affair, and claimed in effect that the Director of Educational Services had succumbed to political pressure and ordered the inspection of his school simply to appease his opponents. 'Thus my detractors,' wrote Honeyford, 'had succesfully converted an issue of beliefs into a question of my competence which has never been questioned.' Within five days, he was summoned to appear before the Council's disciplinary body. He was in due course admonished for 'discrediting' both the Council's officers and the authority's policies, and ordered to publish no more articles critical of Council policy. A disciplinary letter was placed on his file. In early October he lost an appeal made by the NAHT on his behalf against this ruling.

The week-long advisers' inspection of Drummond Middle School began on 11 June, with two psychologists and eight LEA advisers taking part. Honeyford had tried, unsuccessfully, to get the inspection postponed until the autumn, because of staffing problems. The Council's Labour group had tried, unsuccessfully, to have Honeyford suspended for the duration of the inspection. The DPAC organized a day of action to coincide with the start of the inspection, and distributed leaflets urging parents to keep their children at home for the day. Pauline Sawyer, a former parent-governor, claimed the leaflet was misleading, however, since it 'had a bold headline saying there was no school on Monday' and implied that the DPAC was officially recognized by the educational directorate. Only about 200 of the 520 pupils attended school that day, though some of the children may have been absent because of Ramadhan, and others were working away on third-year projects. An education officer warned of the possible prosecution of parents who kept their children at home 'on strike', but no action was taken. The activities of the DPAC received national, unsympathetic coverage in Linda Lee Lewis's article, 'Is it racist to tell the truth?' (*Daily Mail*, 13 June 1984). The thirty-two page report on the advisers' inspection was completed by the end of August, although it was not discussed by Drummond's governors and the

Schools Education Sub-Committee until October. The brief given to the advisory team was to consider all areas of the school's provision, but to pay particular attention to the school's relationships with parents and the local community and to its implementation of LEA policies, including the Middle School policy document, the LAMs 2/82 and 6/83 (*Education for a Multi-cultural Society* and *Racist Behaviour in Schools*) and the RE Agreed Syllabus. The report thanked Honeyford and his staff for their co-operation, especially in view of the awkward timing of the inspection, and praised the conscientiousness and 'caring attitude towards all pupils' (p. 27) which existed in spite of unfavourable conditions and facilities in the school. The report was wide-ranging, covering accommodation and resources, staffing and organization, curriculum and standards of work and achievement, communications and the corporate life of the school, and mingled praise with much constructive criticism. For the purposes of this chapter, however, we shall look only at those parts of the report which have a bearing on the claims made by Honeyford in his articles, and the counterclaims made by his opponents.

The report acknowledged the considerable problems facing any school with such a high proportion of children of Asian origin, for whom English was a second language. The special difficulties which some pupils experienced in the use of English was exacerbated by their 'reduced access to models of colloquial, idiomatic English', because for many British Asian children 'there will be few or no opportunities to meet white children until they go to upper schools' (p. 23); and difficulty with English was likely to affect pupils' learning in other areas. Participation in out-of-school activities by Muslim children was severely curtailed both by 'parental concern for Muslim girls' and the fact that 'many pupils attend Islamic religious classes after school' (p. 9). These factors also prevented 'the firm inter-ethnic friendships established between children whilst in school' from continuing beyond the school gate (p. 5). The school was found to be implementing LAM 2/82, especially in relation to clothing for PE and the provision of single-sex swimming lessons, and had already adopted a multi-faith RE syllabus before the adoption of the LEA's Agreed Syllabus. One of the two assemblies the advisers attended was devoted to the significance of Ramadhan the other to the importance of rules. The advisers appeared to accept Honeyford's claim that racial harrassment was not a problem in his school and that the action needed in compliance with LAM 6/83 was minimal.

In other respects, however, Honeyford's views came under criticism. The advisers found no evidence that 'white children as a group were underachieving because they are in a multi-ethnic school' (p. 24), though they conceded that more detailed study was needed on this issue. Nor did they feel that extended visits to the Indian sub-continent should necessarily be viewed as educationally detrimental. Much would depend on the attitude of the head, and his willingness to enter into discussion with parents planning such visits. In general, the tone of Honeyford's communications to parents was criticized as negative and terse (a criticism which Honeyford considers totally unfounded), and the school's aim of encouraging 'understanding and tolerance of diverse religions, cultures and races' was similarly criticized for its rather negative approach to the 'kind of understanding, appreciation and mutual respect that the RE syllabus seeks to promote' (p. 8). One of the main criticisms of the school's provision was that too little use was being made of the linguistic and cultural 'experiences and knowledge which children brought to school' (p. 10), though it was pointed out (p. 21) that this was a common failing among middle schools. Finally, and most crucially, the advisory team met with individual parents and a group from the DPAC and the Community Relations Council. They were told that Asian parents considered that Honeyford had insulted them, their community, religion and culture, and that his articles were having a divisive effect in the school community and beyond. The advisers' conclusion was that

> The situation, as it has emerged, must raise serious questions as to whether it will be possible for the school to continue to function effectively unless the Headteacher is able to regain the trust and confidence of a significant proportion of parents (p. 27).

The report concluded with a series of recommendations, of varying degrees of importance, to the school and to the LEA. However, the advisers made no comments on the effects of the DPAC's activities on the school; perhaps it was beyond their brief to do so, though they had taken the unusual step of listening to complaints about Honeyford from the unofficial DPAC and other groups. There seems to be an element of unfairness in criticizing Honeyford's assembly on the DPAC's day of action for not taking the opportunity to draw the remaining children 'together in the hall to give a greater stress on togetherness and belonging' (p. 9), whilst saying nothing about the group whose day of action had split the pupil body down the middle.

Honeyford criticized the report on several grounds, particularly that it gave too much credence to the DPAC, which he called 'an action group that has got between me and my parents and which has come largely from outside the school' (*Daily Telegraph*, 23 October 1984). There was a general feeling, however, that the report was not unbalanced, and that the impression it gave of Drummond Middle School was not much different from, and certainly no worse than, other schools in similar situations.

While the advisers were writing their report, things were fairly quiet. In July, the local branch of the NAHT published an open letter of support for

Honeyford. Norman Free characterized him as 'an excellent head', and David Selbourne (1984b) wrote of him as 'a lot less wrong than his opponents'. On the other hand, Councillor Ajeeb, who was to become Lord Mayor the following year, called for Honeyford's dismissal. The DPAC, however, waited until the start of the school term before moving their campaign into top gear again. On 18 September, 238 identical letters signed by parents with children at Drummond Middle School were delivered to the Director of Educational Services, requesting their transfer to another school unless Honeyford was removed as headteacher. The signatures had been collected by a door-to-door campaign, and later some parents withdrew their support, claiming that they had been misled about the aim of the letter. On 26 September, the DPAC sent a formal letter of complaint about Honeyford to the Director of Educational Services, and in early October issued *Newsletter No. 1*, outlining their case against the head.

The school governors, who had thrown out another call for Honeyford's dismissal in September, held a special meeting at City Hall on 16 October to discuss the advisers' report. The meeting was picketed loudly by about fifty members of the AYM, the DPAC and the Rank and File teachers' group, and seven governors walked out in protest at Honeyford's presence at the meeting (in his capacity as governor). No public statement was made at the end of the five-hour meeting, since the Schools Education Sub-committee was also due to discuss the report six days later.

Between these two meetings the first discussions took place with Honeyford and Bradford's chief executive Gordon Moore regarding an enhanced settlement if Honeyford were to accept early retirement. An unsubstantiated claim was later made by Honeyford's opponents that he had demanded a £250,000 golden handshake.

At the Schools Education Sub-committee meeting on 22 October, a vote of no-confidence in Honeyford, tabled by the Labour group, was defeated, and then a resolution with a number of provisions moved by the Conservatives was passed unanimously. Honeyford was required to prepare six reports on aspects of the school's provision, for consideration by a sub-group of the governing body. A review of the information prepared for pupils' parents and a plan to involve parents in the school and the school in the local community were to be produced by Christmas, and reviews of the school's aims, of teaching materials, of the use of standardized tests and of methods of making more use of pupils' experiences were to be produced by Easter. A team of advisers and officers was to help Honeyford to implement the advisers' recommendations, to develop better links with the community and to explore ways of putting the LAMs into practice more effectively. A liaison teacher was to be appointed, the principal adviser was to report back to the Sub-committee in March 1985 on the school's progress in implementing the report, and the Director of Educational Services was to monitor any further publications by Honeyford which might affect relations with parents.

This plan raises a number of interesting questions – about the nature of the democratic process, about the wisdom of the resolution and about its ultimate intention. The Labour and Conservative motions here illustrate two distinct approaches to the process of democratic decision-making: the Labour motion (like the earlier governors' votes) was an appeal to a straightforward majority, which was likely to leave a minority group frustrated and embittered, whereas the Conservative motion was an attempt to reach a compromise which all could agree on (though perhaps no-one really wanted it). Indeed, whether the resolution was wise at all is questionable in view of the unwillingness of the DPAC to compromise because of their belief that 'many parents' trust and confidence in the headteacher has been *irrevocably* lost' (*Telegraph and Argus*, 23 October 1984). Councillor Barry Thorne said,

> The Tory resolution was a fudge. It avoided the issue. It is a slow form of Chinese water torture. Mr Honeyford should have been told quite clearly by the sub-committee what he had done wrong. (quoted in Greenhalf, 1985a).

Indeed, the underlying intention behind the resolution was by no means clear. Honeyford believed that the aim was to overload him with work and make his professional life impossible, so that he ended up resigning. A more likely interpretation is the one given by Donald Thompson, Bradford's Principal Officer for Middle Schools, in the report he prepared for the special meeting of the Schools Education Sub-committee on 22 March 1985. He said,

> The headteacher was being provided with a potential opportunity to demonstrate his willingness fully to implement the recommendations contained in the advisory report and thereby both to assuage the 'grave concern' expressed by the sub-committee at its meeting of 22 October 1984 in respect of the advisory team's findings, and to display a basic sympathy with the general thrust of Authority policy in the area of multi-cultural education.

In other words it was hoped that the constant contact with advisers and LEA officials might gradually produce a change in Honeyford's attitude. The very serious practical and moral implications of such an attempt to control a teacher's beliefs (as opposed to his actions and policies) in this way are raised in more detail in chapter seven below. But what no-one appeared to predict was that Honeyford might carry out the requirements of the resolution to the letter without in any way changing his opinion.

In the view of some of his opponents, however, the sub-committee's resolution was merely side-stepping the main problem. As Abu Bashir, chairman of the Asian Workers' Support Group, said,

We are more concerned about some of the racist remarks he has made than about his views on the council's education policy (quoted in *Telegraph and Argus*, 18 September 1984).

The DPAC also felt that the resolution left the problem unchanged. As one member said, 'What about Honeyford? He's still there.'

STAGE TWO: THE SUSPENSION OF HONEYFORD, OCTOBER 1984–MARCH 1985

Bradford's Director of Educational Services, Richard Knight, was more closely involved in the activities of the next few months. On 8 November, in accordance with the sub-committee's resolution, Honeyford submitted an article to Knight which he was considering publishing, and another in January. In both cases, Knight advised against publication and Honeyford complied with the advice, though he saw it as an act of censorship. A third article, entitled 'The Right Education', which was published in the *Salisbury Review* in January, led to calls for his immediate suspension by Labour's education spokesman, John Lambert. Honeyford argued that the article had been submitted before the sub-committee's ruling, and in any case was not about race relations; but Knight felt the article should have been withdrawn. On 15 November, Knight wrote a letter to *The Times* in reply to Roger Scruton's article 'Who are the real racists?'. He argued that the educational achievement of Asian pupils would be harmed 'if there are hidden messages in society or a school telling them that their country, religion or customs, or the parents they respect and admire, are deficient', because 'their emotional ties are a critical factor in their development'. On 30 November, Knight met parents from Drummond Middle School to hear their complaints. Although he emphasized this was not an official meeting with the DPAC, he was later criticized by one school governor for by-passing the normal procedure that complaints should be made directly to the headteacher in the first instance. Following the meeting with parents, there was an exchange of letters between Knight and Honeyford about their complaints.

In the meantime various initiatives were made to link the school more closely to the local community. Honeyford began a scheme of home visits in the company of his Asian Educational Welfare Officer, though since the latter was a Christian convert, he may not have been viewed by some

Muslim parents as sufficiently sympathetic to their Islamic perspective on educational issues. A second Muslim teacher, Mrs Nawaz, was appointed to the school. Mr. Khan was promoted to the position of liaison teacher, and agreed to set up a course in Urdu. The school had already been commended in the advisers' report on the steps it had taken to increase attendance at parents' evenings; these efforts continued, resulting in a 60 per cent attendance at the December meeting.

A governors' meeting on 29 November elected a group of six governors to receive and discuss Honeyford's six reports on aspects of the school's provision. There was some debate about the inclusion of Jenny Woodward in the sub-group since it was felt that her expressed intention of getting Honeyford sacked might affect her capacity to evaluate his reports fairly and objectively (*Yorkshire Post*, 21 March 1985). In fact, no problems material-ized, and in any case the sub-group's chairman, Councillor Kinder, firmly ruled discussion of topics other than Honeyford's reports out of order. The sub-group met three times, together with the authority's principal officer for middle schools and the senior adviser, between 17 December and 4 March 1985, and their comments, both favourable and critical, were recorded and incorporated into the special report prepared for the meeting of the Schools Education Sub-committee on 22 March 1985.

Early in March the DPAC issued a four-page leaflet expressing support for Bradford's race relations policies and calling on the Council 'to publicly recognize the racist nature of Mr Honeyford's published views and his unsuitability as headteacher of Drummond Middle School'. They argued that Honeyford's articles contained 'expressions of prejudice and deliberate misinformation on racial and ethnic distinctions', which was described in Bradford's LAM 6/83 as one of the unacceptable forms of racialist behaviour; that he had shown hostility to black and working class people; and that he had failed 'to respect the strength and variety of each community's cultural values', as required in the Policy Statement on Race Relations issued in 1981. Honeyford's public defence of his views was seen as a declaration of his unwillingness and inability to carry out the Council's policies, and the DPAC therefore called on the Council to take appropriate steps to remove him from his post. 'The danger facing us now,' the leaflet warned, 'is that ethnic minorities and others who may support Bradford's Race Relations Policies are losing confidence in the Council's ability to carry them out'. Both Woodward and Whitfield expressed the belief that if Honeyford was not sacked, there would be a growth in support for separate Muslim schools.

For four months the DPAC had been planning to set up an alternative school 'following anti-racist principles', as a means of continuing their campaign against Honeyford. This school was finally set up at the Pakistan Community Centre on 4 March, and lasted for one week. More than 200 children attended and about twenty qualified teachers offered their services on a voluntary basis. The planning had been careful and thorough, and most of the children's needs were catered for. The lessons included Arabic, Asian languages and Afro-Caribbean culture in addition to more traditional subjects, but there was no provision for sport or PE. Free meals were provided by local Pakistani restaurants. The DPAC refused to give the names of pupils or teachers involved, and turned down requests from Council officials to let an educational welfare officer, a multi-cultural advisory team and a health and safety officer visit the school – though the six Labour members of the Schools Education Sub-committee were allowed a visit. 'As the action was understood to be of five days' duration,' Knight noted in his report to the sub-committee, 'the matter was not pressed.' But Eric Pickles, the Education Committee chairman, was angry. 'The alternative school is a tactic which I deprecate,' he said. 'Actions like this are not the best way to help the reconciliation process.' (*Yorkshire Post*, 5 March 1985). It did serve the ends of the DPAC, however: it achieved maximum publicity for their complaints against Honeyford, and demonstrated to the sub-committee that they meant business. One tactical error was the loss of NUT support. Jenny Woodward alleged to the media that teachers at Drummond Middle School had threatened children with physical abuse if they attended the alternative school, and the NUT retaliated with the threat of legal action if the allegations were not withdrawn.

Support for Honeyford, however, was not lacking. In mid-March, the Friends of Drummond Middle School (FDMS) were formed as a support group for Honeyford. Its founders included Stephen Silverwood, a school governor, and Mrs Mubarik Iqbal, a member of the Community Relations Council. The NAHT reiterated its support for Honeyford and criticized the Council for operating double standards by letting pressure groups flourish while banning Honeyford from making public statements. Pickles, too, spoke out against dismissing Honeyford:

> The fundamental question is whether someone should be hounded out of his job for having exercised the right of free speech on a major issue. Our group would like to see reconciliation. If Mr Honeyford were removed, it would not be the end of a problem but the start. It would leave a scar on this city (*The Times Educational Supplement*, 15 March 1985).

Pickles was in an awkward situation, however, as the date for the special meeting of the Schools Education Sub-committee drew near. He knew that if the vote went against Honeyford, he would incur the wrath of his own back-benchers, and if the vote went in his favour he would incur the wrath of ethnic minority pressure groups, whose respect he had so far retained. One way out was Honeyford's offer to resign – at a price. In the hung Council, the Liberals held the balance of power, and so on 18 March Pickles visited the Liberal leader, Kath Greenwood, in the company of Bradford's chief executive, Gordon Moore, to try to persuade her to agree to a cash settlement for Honeyford. He failed.

On 21 March, the day before the special sub-committee meeting, the school governors met to consider the reports of their own working party, so that their chairman could make a verbal report to the sub-committee. It was clear that a majority of the governors still supported Honeyford. By this stage, the two confidential reports prepared for the meeting, the first giving the advisers' response to Honeyford's six reports and the second, Knight's account of events between October and March, had been leaked to the press. Honeyford claimed that the leaks might prejudice the outcome of the sub-committee's meeting.

The tone of the advisers' comments on Honeyford's reports and on their numerous meetings with him over the preceding five months was much more hostile than that of the previous advisers' report. While conceding that he had generally complied with what was required, they accused him of being negative, defensive and stubborn, and said that as far as his general attitude was concerned,

> We believe that Mr Honeyford's educational thinking is not in keeping with that of the Authority in that it is not in sympathy with our Middle School and other policy documents (p. 48).

They clashed with Honeyford particularly over the concept of multi-cultural education, but also over his alleged lack of commitment to the principle of equal opportunities for girls, the selection of books and materials (the advisers described Honeyford's principle of not interfering in his teachers' choice of books as 'abrogating to his staff the entire responsibility for the selection of material' – p. 47) and the professional autonomy of the head. Some of the criticisms are surprisingly trivial; for example, his *Information to Parents* was criticized because the permission for girls to wear trousers as part of their uniform was put in parenthesis, and because it referred to the *Council's* granting of permission for children to wear items of religious significance. Other criticisms, however, raise issues of crucial importance. In their comments on professional autonomy, we can see an argument of national significance about the control of education being acted out. It is worth quoting their comments in full:

> Mr Honeyford time and again maintained that the LEA could not require him to do things in his own school; it could not dictate what the curriculum should be, nor what the aims of his school should be, nor what materials should be used. If it did it was contravening the

Articles of Government. He would not accept that the Governing Body, and himself as headteacher, act only within the general framework and guidelines as laid down by the Authority. The LEA is responsible for what happens in its schools as the DES indicated by its circular 6/83 which required LEAs to state what guidelines they laid down for their schools and what measures they took to ensure that the curriculum and aims in their schools were within this framework. This is a clear indication at national level that there is not the autonomy that Mr. Honeyford asserts (pp. 6–7).

This on-going debate about the control of education and the complex relationship between heads, LEAs and the DES will be picked up later in the present volume.

Knight's account of events from October to March came to similar conclusions, and again contained a mixture of some trivial and some more significant criticisms of Honeyford. He reported that 'as a result of several enquiries including one from Councillor Goldberg, it emerged that a parent of a white child' was refused permission for her child to wear a tracksuit for PE. The provision in LAM 2/82 had been made for Asian parents on grounds of religious conscience, and Honeyford was applying it to the letter, in spite of an instruction by the Assistant Director of Educational Services to apply the ruling to white children. Knight did not point out in his report that the white parent concerned was Jenny Woodward; indeed, the report avoided any explicit or implicit criticism of the DPAC. What the report *did* refer to was the continuing rift between Honeyford and many of his parents, and Honeyford's apparent preoccupation with his own rights and views. The report concluded:

> In the light of the evaluation by the Advisers of the Headteacher's response to the sub-committee's resolutions and my own contacts with the Headteacher over a period since October 1984, he has not in my view demonstrated any marked change of attitude or commitment to the overall objectives of the sub-committee, particularly in the field of race relations. In this situation I am bound to conclude that I can follow no other course than to consider all the circumstances, including the attitude and commitment of the Headteacher as a senior employee of the Council and whether or not these aspects are, or could be, prejudicial to the future of the school and ultimately, the future of the Headteacher in this school.

The meeting of the Schools Education Sub-committee on 22 March was transferred to the full Council chamber so that the press and members of the public could be accommodated. Feelings ran high, and there was a good deal of barracking and abuse from the public galleries, where Honeyford's opponents formed the dominant group. In all, the meeting lasted over six hours, though perhaps the most important decision was argued out behind closed doors during the 90-minute recess. This concerned the form of the resolution, which was eventually presented in four separate parts: the first accepted the advisers' reports 'with concern'; the second reaffirmed support for the Council's multi-cultural education policies; the third instructed Knight to take steps to solve the 'significant problems' at the school and restore the confidence of the local community; the fourth was a vote of no-confidence in Honeyford. The first three, proposed by the sub-committee's Conservative chairman, were passed unanimously. The fourth, proposed by the Labour group, was opposed by the Conservatives but was eventually passed 8–7 as Labour won the support of the two Alliance members.

The evening's events had several consequences. First, by his tactical construction of the resolution, Pickles succeeded in maintaining his credibility with his own back-benchers *and* with the ethnic minority pressure groups; he had spoken out strongly against the vote of no-confidence while reaffirming his commitment to the Council's race relations and multi-cultural policies. Secondly, the Liberal leader, Kath Greenwood, became the target for a lot of criticism in her own ward for the way she had voted; though Mayor-elect, she lost her seat on the Council a year later. Thirdly, the way was now open for Knight and his assistant director, Norman Roper, to take more decisive action. On 3 April, Honeyford was suspended on full pay, pending a special hearing of the case against him by his school governors, who would in turn make recommendations back to the Directorate of Educational Services. The DPAC were dissatisfied with the speed at which things were progressing, but at least felt they were going in the right direction. Finally, however, the sub-committee's vote of no-confidence marked the start of a massive local and national campaign in support of Honeyford, to which we must now turn.

STAGE THREE: THE REINSTATEMENT OF HONEYFORD, MARCH–SEPTEMBER 1985

After the vote of no confidence in Honeyford, the initiative moved to his supporters. Within two weeks, most of the daily tabloids had run substantial articles in which Honeyford was portrayed as 'gentle and kindly', a 'good man', a 'decent chap', who had been subjected to 'a hate campaign of staggering ferocity', while his opponents were 'the bully boys of the race relations industry', 'Thought Police' and a 'screaming mob'. A very large number of letters was written, particularly to the local press, in support of Honeyford. Three petitions criticizing his treatment and calling for his reinstatement were organized in the next three months, one by Frank Kelly and two by the Friends of Drummond Middle School, and handed in to City Hall. It is claimed that they attracted a total of 23,000 signatures. In March, Nicholas Winterton raised the Honeyford affair in Parliament, and a month later, Shipley MP Marcus Fox secured an adjournment debate, which broke up in a bitter row with Bradford West MP Max Madden, after Fox's speech lashing out at Honeyford's opponents. Although Sir Keith Joseph refused to get publicly involved in the affair, it was reported that he made it clear in a private meeting with Eric Pickles in early May that he did not want to see Honeyford dismissed. The TV EYE documentary on the Honeyford affair (YTV, 2 April 1985) revealed that following a complaint by members of the FDMS that Bradford's education department had acted unfairly, Sir Keith had written to Knight asking for a full report on the handling of the affair.

Meanwhile, Honeyford's opponents made two *faux pas* which unintentionally provided his supporters with more ammunition. The first was the memorandum sent by the seven training officers for the Council's racism awareness courses to the Council's personnel director, Brian McAndrew, and other LEA officers and councillors. As has already been mentioned, this memorandum was leaked to the *Yorkshire Post*, who published it on 27 March. It suggested that Honeyford should be barred from attending one of the compulsory racism awareness courses, because 'to train Honeyford would give him the credibility and power to recruit and show the Council to be colluding with a known racist' and because 'given the racist views Honeyford has experienced, and the disregard he has shown for Council Policy and Training and Race Relations, a five-day course will not change or make him anti-racist'. It claimed that if Honeyford were given credibility by being allowed to attend a course, this would 'give other racists a license to act in a similar way', and would be 'a gross insult to a larger (*sic*) percentage of Bradford's populations', many of whom are losing confidence in the Council's race relations policy anyway. David Hart, general secretary of the NAHT, responded angrily, claiming that the officers were exceeding their brief and engaging in a gross deception by calling Honeyford a racist. Honeyford himself complained that the Council seemed to be assuming that he was guilty until he was proved innocent, and that his chances of receiving a fair hearing were being damaged by such leaks. Councillor Wightman, chairman of the Race Relations Advisory Group, criticized the memorandum and instructed McAndrew to carry out an investigation. Ten Asian groups responded by calling for the inappositely named Wightman's resignation. At the end of April, a disciplinary enquiry into the incident was announced. In June, the NAHT threatened Bradford Council with a libel action unless it paid a substantial sum in damages to Honeyford, fully retracted the document and gave an undertaking that Council employees would not repeat the offence. The final settlement agreed with Honeyford in December included a payment of £5000 in connection with this alleged libel.

The second tactical error by Honeyford's opponents which gave more grist to his supporters' mill was the fact, already described in chapter three, that leaflets in Urdu distributed from five Asian community centres, purporting to be a paraphrase of Honeyford's views, were nothing more than a mischievous distortion of them. It began to seem possible that much of the Asian opposition to Honeyford arose because of misinformation about what he had actually written. However, the woman who revealed this well-publicized distortion, Mrs Mubarik Iqbal, was far from popular with many of the Mirpuri parents at Drummond Middle School; she was herself a right-wing pro-Honeyford Punjabi from another district of Bradford. Her later election to the school's governing body caused much local resentment.

Some of the actions by both supporters and opponents of Honeyford had by this stage become almost ritualistic. In April, the Bradford branch of the NAHT criticized the 'mishandling' of the affair by LEA officers, and voted almost unanimously to call for Honeyford's reinstatement and to express concern at the implications of the case for the free speech of heads. The DPAC continued to promote its views to left-wing groups; Jenny Woodward was booked to address a meeting of Rank and File, and later a fringe meeting at Bradford University's Liberation Festival. Councillor Lambert protested to Knight once again because in his view a letter of self-defence by Honeyford in *The Times Educational Supplement* in mid-May was in breach of the requirement that he should submit all future publications to the director for approval. Tim Whitfield, Bradford's senior community relations officer, continued to make statements criticizing the authority's handling of the affair and laying the blame for the damage to race relations in the city at their door. There were also various attempts to produce a pay-off deal for Honeyford. The first, handled by Gordon Moore in early May, was turned down by Honeyford partly because the details were revealed to the press before he knew them himself. The second, proposed by Councillor Lambert, was not even accepted by his own Labour group, who wanted to see Honeyford sacked. The third was an interesting attempt by the Liberal education spokesman, John Wells, to upstage his two political rivals. He had two secret meetings with Honeyford in early June, to discuss a retirement package including a lump sum payment of £42,000, and an enhanced pension of £6200 a year, with the Council holding the copyright on Honeyford's future articles. However, Labour and Conservative leaders jointly scotched the Wells initiative by ordering the Council representative not to attend any more meetings. Instead, Gordon Moore was to reopen formal talks with Honeyford. Pickles defended this move: 'the longer this goes on, the greater will be the damage to this city and race relations'. The NAHT opened the negotiations on Honeyford's behalf by suggesting that the Council should make an investment to produce £15,000 a year for him. Moore turned this down, and no settlement was agreed.

Amid the continuing polarization of views, there were a few voices of moderation. Carlton Duncan, the black headteacher of Wyke Manor Upper School, was asked at an NUT conference whether he agreed with Honeyford's suspension, but replied that he never commented in public on anything good or bad to do with a colleague. David Smith, the headmaster of Bradford Grammar School, turned down the request from an unnamed Conservative party worker in London to make a public statement in support of Honeyford's views. The local press continued to attempt impartial coverage of the affair; in April, both the *Yorkshire Post* and the *Telegraph and Argus* printed an article by Jenny Woodward recounting and explaining the actions of the DPAC over the previous year. Bradford North Conservative MP, Geoff Lawler, argued that both Honeyford and his opponents were in need of lessons in tolerance. Lord Swann called for an independent enquiry into the Honeyford affair.

The governors of Drummond Middle School met in April to fix a time and place for their special hearing of the case against Honeyford. It was to start on 22 June at Ilkley College, was expected to last for three days, and was to be closed to the public and the press. It was recognized that the governors' final recommendation to Norman Roper would be non-binding, but, in the words of the chairman of governors, Councillor Ernest Kinder, 'we hope he will take heed of our report'. Kinder also said, 'We are going into this with an open mind', though that was not how Jenny Woodward saw it. She commented:

> There is a split in the governors with the majority supporting Honeyford, and this means the outcome of the hearing is a foregone conclusion (*Telegraph and Argus*, 13 May 1985).

Amin Qureshi, secretary of the AKMAB, issued a blunter statement:

> We don't wish to sit in that Tory Madhouse, the so-called Governing Body, which does not represent us.

A major anti-Honeyford demonstration was organized on the eve of the hearing. About 400 joined the march, which culminated in a number of speeches outside City Hall. Honeyford was represented at the hearing by a barrister briefed by the NAHT, and the case against him was presented by the Principal Officer for Middle Schools, Donald Thompson, backed by other education officials. The hearing had a dramatic start when Labour councillor Reuben Goldberg, who had been a governor for only one week, first announced that he, Jenny Woodward and two Asian governors intended to boycott the meeting because they believed it was biased and unrepresentative, and then walked out with a file of confidential documents. A court injunction was quickly obtained ordering the return of the documents, the police were called, and the documents were taken back from Goldberg by the

Council officer acting as clerk to the enquiry. When Goldberg tried later in the day to return to the hearing as an observer, he found that the remaining governors had voted to exclude him from the proceedings. Goldberg later claimed that the incident was blown up out of all proportion in order to divert attention from the boycott. The meeting continued with eleven of the eighteen governors present; apart from those involved in the boycott, one was abroad in Pakistan and two others were absent.

The charges put to the enquiry by Donald Thompson were, in essence, that Honeyford had shown a lack of judgment in his dealings with parents and a lack of loyalty to his employers. He had failed to understand the impact his articles had had on the parents, local community and others with an interest in race relations, and had not considered the possibility that these people might have genuine grievances. Though his articles were negative, unhelpful and written in an abrasive tone, he had refused to acknowledge that some of the responsibility for the present situation must lie with himself, stressing instead his own right of free speech. By his lack of commitment to local authority policies, he had proved himself unworthy of the authority's trust and confidence, and his disregard for counselling and advice and regrettable attitude to Council officers made his suitability for a senior post questionable.

After four days of deliberation and hearing evidence, the governors reached their conclusion, which was announced in the following press statement:

> The governing body has considered all the allegations in detail and concludes that they have not been fully substantiated. We recognize Mr Honeyford's educational contributions to the school. We feel that he should be reinstated to Drummond Middle School with the insistence that with the cooperation of the local authority officers, the harmonious relationship which should exist between the school and the community will be rebuilt. Despite allegations to the contrary, the governors have reached their conclusion after a long, impartial and detailed examination of all the facts.

It transpired that this resolution had been passed by seven votes to four, a fact which must have given the four boycotting governors some misgivings about the wisdom of their action.

Honeyford was jubilant. While acknowledging that Roper still had the final say on his future at the school, he felt that it would be difficult for him to overturn the governors' recommendations. He now looked forward to getting back to his job. There were ominous warnings, however, from the Council for Mosques, the DPAC and the Bradford Labour Party that the governors' decision was not the end of the matter. As far as they were concerned, they still wanted to see Honeyford sacked, and argued that the Council could hardly order the reinstatement of a head in whom they had passed a vote of no confidence.

The expected course for the case to follow was that Honeyford had seven days in which to request a personal meeting with Roper to argue his case for reinstatement. Roper would then have to weigh up the evidence from all sources and make his decision. If the decision went against Honeyford, he could ask for a personal hearing before a sub-committee of councillors. If their ruling went against him, he would then have to take his case to some outside agency such as an industrial tribunal.

The meeting between Honeyford and Roper was fixed for 10 July, but was called off on the last minute on legal advice after the NAHT threatened the Council with High Court action if the hearing went ahead. The NAHT argued first that Roper's position was 'plainly untenable', as he had been involved in formulating the charges against Honeyford and presenting evidence in support of the complaints at the governors' meeting, and was therefore in no position to make an impartial decision about Honeyford's future; and secondly, that Council officers had no right to pursue the case once the governors had called for his reinstatement. The latter point involved the interpretation of the articles of government for the school, particularly the clause which states

> Except when otherwise determined by the Council, a headteacher should not be dismissed except upon the recommendation of the governors (article 9d, Bradford Articles of Government).

The NAHT argued that by calling a governors' hearing, the Council had accepted that Honeyford could not be dismissed except upon the govenors' recommendation; and when the governors recommended reinstatement and not dismissal, as in this case, that was the end of the matter and there was no room for any further review procedures.

At this stage, Pickles pointed out that it seemed to be assumed that Council officers were planning to sack Honeyford, though there was no evidence that this was the case. He himself wanted to see Honeyford back at Drummond Middle School as soon as possible, and thought that this might be the best way of bringing the dispute to an end. Lambert, however, commented that 'to demand his reinstatement is asking for enormous trouble. It is going to divide this city'. Gordon Moore did in fact initiate secret talks with Honeyford and the NAHT about the possibility of reinstatement, but these broke down over the Council's insistence on a 'final warning' disciplinary measure, which could result in Honeyford's dismissal if he transgressed within eighteen months. With the breakdown of these talks, the affair was now left to be settled in the High Court, and thus on 16 July the NAHT served a writ on Bradford Council. In the meantime, Moore carried out an investigation into allegations that a senior Council officer was involved in irregularities in the preparation of evidence against Honeyford, but found the allegations unsubstantiated.

The High Court hearing began on 4 September, with Mr Justice Simon Brown being asked by Michael Beloff QC, representing Honeyford, to grant a declaration that in view of the governors' vote of confidence Honeyford's suspension should be lifted so that he could resume his duties, a declaration that the disciplinary procedures brought against him had been exhausted, and an injunction restraining the defendants from reviewing the decision of the governors. John Melville-Williams, QC, representing Bradford Council, argued on the other hand that the Assistant Director of Educational Services had a duty under Council procedures to review the case. In his ruling the following day, the judge granted the declarations but refused the injunction. He said:

> Once the governors decided against recommending dismissal, that precludes any further disciplinary process on the offences alleged. That situation means the teacher's suspension must fall.

He also called on both sides to resolve their differences and to treat the educational needs of children in Bradford as paramount.

On 11 September, senior Council officials decided to appeal against the court's decision, but to lift Honeyford's suspension in the meantime. Knight said:

> There is an urgent need for reconciliation and it is better that this is faced now rather than later. Lifting the suspension gives all concerned a chance to do this and provides Mr Honeyford the opportunity of restoring the school to as near normality as possible.

He said that if the Council's appeal failed no further action would be taken, but if it was upheld, the Council would continue with its disciplinary procedure.

The acting headteacher, Fred Edmondson, expressed delight at Honeyford's imminent return. Donald Thompson met the staff at Drummond Middle on 13 September to discuss the situation. On 16 September, Honeyford was back at his desk at the school.

STAGE FOUR: THE DEPARTURE OF HONEYFORD, SEPTEMBER–DECEMBER 1985

Honeyford's opponents were horrified at the direction events had taken. The President of Bradford's Council for Mosques, Choudhury M. Khan, threatened to withdraw all Muslim children from Drummond Middle School. Later, in a letter to Gordon Moore, he warned that 'the good relation of the city has been put on stake' (*sic*) and that the Council for Mosques intended to withdraw its representatives from various committees, such as the Multi-cultural Education Support Group and the Race Relations Advisory Group, in protest. On 13 September, the DPAC met at the Pakistan Community Centre to launch a new anti-Honeyford campaign. Its first move was to plan a week's boycott of the school, starting the day Honeyford returned. Up to 200 demonstrators, many having no connection with the school, joined the picket line, and children were encouraged to wear badges with slogans such as 'Ray-cist' and 'I Hate Honeyford'. The daily attendance figures at the school varied from 150 to 200 pupils, out of a possible 530. Much publicity was given to the outbreak of fighting on 18 September when Mr M. Ansari was attacked and beaten by protestors for trying to take his children to school and then speaking to the press about his support for Honeyford. Journalists were also attacked. On 20 September, Knight issued a press release calling on all parents to return their children to school, and the DPAC decided to end the boycott to give the Council a fortnight to remove Honeyford. Children were given a leaflet by the DPAC on their return to school (quoted in full in Murphy (1987, pp. 127–8)). It urged them to make up jokes about Honeyford and to show him no respect in school. This so-called 'Pupils' Charter' was widely condemned, not only by Pickles and Knight, but even by some of Honeyford's strongest opponents. On 24 September, DPAC representatives met teachers at Drummond Middle School to reassure them of their confidence; the *Telegraph and Argus* reported that the teachers responded by saying they wanted nothing to do with the DPAC's campaign. A further half-day boycott was held on 30 September, 'just to remind people we can mount a boycott', according to Councillor Goldberg (quoted in the *Telegraph and Argus*, 30 September 1985). 183 pupils attended the morning session and 350 the afternoon. On 10 October, the boycott of the school was reimposed indefinitely. Attendances fluctuated between 190 and 250 pupils a day.

The announcement that Honeyford was to attend an educational seminar at 10 Downing Street on 2 October with the Prime Minister, cabinet ministers and a number of right-wing educationalists to discuss the long-term direction of the educational system was taken by Honeyford's opponents as an official expression of sympathy for his position. Goldberg said:

Before this row broke out, Mr Honeyford was a nobody in educational terms. It is quite farcical that he has been invited to this high-powered meeting.

On the day of the seminar, a group of London teachers and Asians protested outside 10 Downing Street.

The Lord Mayor, Councillor Ajeeb, told a public meeting called by the Community Relations Council that he could not 'see the unity of our great city being destroyed by one man', and that in his opinion Honeyford should have been suspended until the appeal case was over. Pedley (1986) reports that many people were 'hurt and disappointed' by what they saw as a breach of 'the neutrality of office'. Ajeeb became the target of racist hate mail, and on 28 September he was heckled by football fans shouting 'Honeyford' as he received a cheque at Grimsby for the Bradford City Football Club fire disaster fund. Two weeks later, he made a major speech in Cardiff, attacking race relations in Britain. He called for the scrapping of the Race Relations Act and the Commission for Racial Equality because he thought they had proved ineffective in improving the lot of most black people, who still lived in poverty, bad housing and often in fear. The speech offended local politicians but was praised by Choudhury Khan and Tim Whitfield. A local meeting of the NUT on 24 September passed a motion calling for Honeyford's removal from his school, by 28 votes to 17, and expressed support for the aims of the DPAC. An article by local members of the National Anti-Racist Movement in Education discussed the Honeyford affair particularly in terms of the head's accountability to his employers and parents (*Telegraph and Argus*, 7 October 1985).

In September, new regulations about the constitution of the governing bodies of schools were introduced in Bradford. Each school was to have its own governors, instead of one board covering five schools as in the past. Drummond Middle School was to have fourteen governors, made up of four Council nominees, the headteacher, two members of the teaching staff, one representative of the non-teaching staff, three parent-governors and three community representatives (to be elected by the other governors). On 2 October, three anti-Honeyford parent-governors were elected – N. Naqui, F. Rahman and M. Farooq. The eleven governors already holding office were to have an inaugural meeting on 15 October to elect the three community representatives.

The DPAC chose 15 October for its next major day of action. The usual fifty or so demonstrators outside the school swelled to 250, and the number of children attending dropped to a hundred. A protest march took place from the school to City Hall. The Council for Mosques called on all Muslim children in Bradford (over 16,000) to boycott school for the day in protest against Honeyford; claims varied about the number responding to the call, but the most widely reported figure was one in four. A call for a one-day strike by Council workers failed to materialize; NALGO refused to give its official backing. The day before, an NUT group at Grange School staged an unofficial one-day strike in protest at Honeyford's return to Drummond Middle School; they were later disciplined for this by their union.

The picket reassembled in the evening for the inaugural meeting of the new governing body, who were given a noisy reception when they arrived. Of the twenty nominees for the posts of community governor, three pro-Honeyford candidates were eventually elected. They were Tom Brown, a former Labour councillor, Mrs Mubarik Iqbal, and Azhar Hayat, a lecturer with two sons at the school. These each received six votes, from the Conservative nominees, the two teacher governors, the ancillary staff governor, and Honeyford himself, who exercised his right to be on the governing body. Set against these were the two Labour nominees and the three parent governors. When the result was announced, there were violent scenes both in the school hall and in the playground, with stones and fireworks thrown and school windows broken. Donald Thompson adjourned the meeting. Asian community leaders, notably Nazim Naqui, intervened to help to restore order, and although sporadic fighting continued outside for nearly two hours, the meeting was able to resume. Councillor Eric Sunderland was elected chairman of governors, and Tom Brown deputy chairman. In a brief report at the end of the meeting, Honeyford said he was considering the possibility of setting up a guide and brownie pack in the school.

Widespread reaction to the governors' meeting was reported. In a letter to Gordon Moore, Choudhury Khan expressed concern at the apparent support of the staff at Drummond Middle School for Honeyford. Before this stage, Honeyford's opponents had always emphasized that their quarrel was with him alone, not with his staff. Lambert raised allegations of corruption and vote-rigging with Pickles, and an exchange of letters followed. Pickles in turn urged Lambert to use his influence and party links to persuade the DPAC to call off the boycott and picketing, but Lambert refused. Tom Brown, a Labour member for forty years, was threatened with expulsion by the University Ward Labour Party for backing Honeyford. The Council for Mosques called for an end to picketing at the school for the sake of the children's education, at least until the Appeal Court hearing, and pledged itself to continue the campaign in a peaceful and democratic manner. The AYM issued a press release criticizing this lack of militancy. The Bradford Drummond Parents' Support Group (BDPSG) was set up by an alliance of far-left groups and took over the picketing of the school when it was called off by the DPAC. The BDPSG called for a broader base for the opposition to Honeyford, and called for demonstrations at the school to coincide with the next two governors' meetings.

After threats to his personal safety, police began to keep a watch on Honeyford's house, and alarm systems were fitted there and at the school.

Goldberg and Woodward also claimed to have received death threats, and Council officials began to censor the Lord Mayor's mail to weed out the increasing amount of racist abuse. Fears were expressed at secret talks at City Hall between policiticans, the Chief Constable and the Bishop of Bradford, about the deterioration of race relations in the city and the danger of growing street violence if the Honeyford affair were not resolved. Eight local clergymen issued a statement expressing anxiety about the damage to the community being caused by the affair.

In the meantime, both David Selbourne and Professor Bhikhu Parekh spoke out against the polarization of views which led to Honeyford being seen as the 'racist anti-Christ' by one side and the 'redeemer of the "white minority"' by the other. Selbourne (1985) argued that

> what has been made to appear as a struggle between the 'left' (the Bradford Labour Party, the anti-Honeyford parent activists and the good and the true in general) and the 'right' (Honeyford, Bradford Toryism, *The Salisbury Review* and 'institutionalized racism') is nothing of the sort.

For a start, Selbourne found 'outrageously racist sentiments' being expressed to him 'off the record' by local Labour politicians; also he considered that behind Honeyford's intemperate style there were arguments about race and culture which deserved serious consideration. He concluded that the confrontation in Bradford was not between right and wrong, but between 'rival and alternative conceptions of justice', though the situation was complicated by 'the politicking and calculation of Bradford's mafia of imams', who were using the accusation of racism to further their own obscurantist aims. At the annual meeting of local education authorities in Leeds on 9 November, Professor Bhikhu Parekh, deputy chairman of the Commission for Racial Equality, claimed that Honeyford, like Arthur Scargill, was becoming a symbolic focal point for extreme views, whether of support or opposition. He argued that less attention should be paid to the person, and more to the real issues at stake. In his view, anti-racist education policies were too narrow, and what was needed was a broader, multi-cultural approach, giving a strongly positive emphasis to diversity and respect for other cultures.

On 4 November, the Appeal Court heard the Council's case against the High Court judgment of 5 September. Nine days later, the three judges unanimously overturned the High Court ruling, and said that even after the governors' recommendation for a head's reinstatement, the local education authority still retained the right to consider whether to dismiss him. Lord Justice Dillon emphasized that the court was not concerned with whether Honeyford's views were correct, whether he had expressed them wisely or whether his conduct merited dismissal, but simply with the question of who had the power to dismiss a head, and more specifically with the school's articles of government and the headteacher's contract of service. Lord Justice Lawton ruled that the disciplinary procedures had not been exhausted with the governors' vote of confidence, but that the Council was entitled to continue with disciplinary procedures and to exercise its residual power to dismiss. Lord Justice Dillon further pointed out that the Council still had the power to suspend the head pending a final decision. The Council was awarded costs.

Councillor Goldberg expressed delight at the outcome, and Choudhury Khan said it was a fair judgment. There were renewed demands for Honeyford's sacking by the BDPSG and the Council for Mosques. Council officers, however, ruled out an immediate decision on Honeyford's future, though there appeared to be four options unless he himself volunteered to take early retirement: to sack him after a review of his case, to give him a written warning, to give him an oral warning, or to take no further action. The officers first planned to seek the advice of legal experts. In the meantime, the NAHT announced its intention to petition the House of Lords for leave to appeal against the Appeal Court ruling, and leave was granted on 28 November.

A special meeting of the school's governing body was held on 7 November, to receive the director's report on the current situation and the headteacher's report. Once again the school was picketed, and children used loud-hailers to lead the protest chants against Honeyford. Students at Bradford and Ilkley Community College held a one-day strike to add weight to calls for Honeyford's sacking. At the governors' meeting, the director detailed the school boycotts and described the very great difficulties they were causing in the day-to-day running of the school. He expressed concern about the adverse effects on the children's education, the additional strain on teachers and on relationships within the school, and the question of safety. Honeyford, too, said the staff had been 'saddened and distressed' by being subjected each morning to 'mindless, hateful chanting', and he accused the pickets of destabilizing the school as an institution, undermining the morale of staff, intimidating him as an individual, preventing the proper and civil conduct of affairs and seeking to panic the Council into hasty and ill-considered action. A consideration of Honeyford's report to the governors was held over to the next meeting, on 22 November.

Once again, there was a pupil boycott on the day of this meeting, and a large number of DPAC members attended the meeting itself, in accordance with their rights under paragraph 18 of the *Instrument of Government of Various County Middle Schools, 1985*. Honeyford's report was deliberately uncontroversial, and dealt mainly with staffing, finance and curriculum, but it was still attacked as 'divisive and inflammatory' by Councillor Goldberg, whose call for its rejection was defeated. Parent-governor and DPAC spokesman Nazim Naqui tabled a series of questions for the head to answer, including 'Why have you never apologized for the way you insulted parents in your written articles?', 'Why do you continue to damage the education of our children?' and 'Why don't you help us to resolve this issue by leaving the school?' There was an uproar from the audience when Honeyford refused to comment, saying that the questions were based on a series of false assumptions. Once more the meeting was stopped to restore order.

Four days later Honeyford wrote to Pickles that he was prepared to take early retirement if an appropriate package could be worked out. He indicated that he himself was perfectly fit and willing to continue, but his wife had been suffering from the events of the last twenty months, and also he was worried about the effects of continued disruption by the DPAC and BDPSG on the children's education and on staff morale. A month earlier, the Labour and Liberal groups on the Council had dropped their veto of any financial inducement for Honeyford to take early retirement, and Councillor Tommy Flanagan was sacked as Labour's race relations spokesman for issuing a press statement denouncing this new policy. The Conservatives had shifted ground as well, however, and now insisted that Honeyford should not be made to take early retirement if he did not want to. Liberal councillor John Wells accused the Conservatives of cynically using the Honeyford affair for election purposes, aiming for a 'nasty, right-wing, backlash vote'. 'I urge you to change your position,' he said, 'or you will be accused of fiddling while Bradford burns.'

Once Honeyford had expressed his willingness to depart, however, all three political parties were happy for Gordon Moore to open negotiations with the NAHT about a financial settlement. Agreement was reached on 11 December, ratified by the Council two days later and made public on 14 December. Honeyford was to take early retirement from the end of the month. It was widely reported that his pay-off was worth £161,000, but it was in fact a lump sum of £70,900, plus a pension of £6500, index-linked from the age of 55. The lump sum was made up as follows:

£42,500 – settlement of all outstanding claims against the Council;
£5,000 – settlement of alleged libel by the Council;
£19,600 – DES superannuation;
£3,800 – three months' salary in lieu of notice. (*Telegraph and Argus*, 14 December 1985)

As part of the package, Honeyford agreed not to continue with his appeal to the House of Lords, though no restrictions were placed on his continued writing. The two deputy heads were to run Drummond Middle School until the end of term, and an acting head was appointed (William Haykin, of

Calversyke Middle School, Keighley), so that a permanent appointment need not be made for several months.

Meanwhile, two brief reports in the *Telegraph and Argus* (20 December 1985) captured the essence of one strand of the Honeyford debate. The end of term play at Drummond Middle School was 'Jack and the Beanstalk', avoiding the accusation of Christian indoctrination that might accompany a nativity play, yet still unashamedly British. The end of term play at the adjacent Drummond Language Centre (from where much criticism of Honeyford's views had emanated) was 'Rama and Sita' – progressively multi-cultural, but perhaps almost as alien to the experience of most local Muslims as it would be to the indigenous population.

THE AFTERMATH

There is little doubt that in the short term at least the Honeyford affair had serious repercussions on race relations in Bradford. Both in schools and in the broader community, aggression against the city's Asians appeared to increase. More attacks on Asian taxi-drivers were reported, and the cars, homes and businesses of Asian residents were attacked. The day after the publication of Honeyford's settlement, the Lord Mayor's house was stoned by vandals. Fighting occurred between white and Asian gangs of pupils outside Belle Vue Boys' School, Greenhead Grammar School and elsewhere. Workers against Racism (WAR), an offshoot of the Revolutionary Communist Party, responded by organizing protest marches and setting up vigilante patrols 'to protect blacks from racist attacks'. WAR claimed that there was a conspiracy of silence between the police, the press and the Council to conceal the extent of racial attacks in Bradford. A careers adviser claimed that sixth-formers were staying away from the University of Bradford because the city had a bad name for race relations.

Figures from the so-called New Right found it increasingly difficult to address public meetings, particularly at universities. A planned speech on the Honeyford affair at the University of Bradford by Harvey Proctor was called off on the advice of Gordon Moore, who was worried about serious disruption. An invitation to Roger Scruton to speak at Leeds Civic Hall was withdrawn in March 1986 because it was felt that his safety could not be guaranteed. Honeyford himself had an invitation to speak to Conservative students at Bristol Polytechnic cancelled the month before, and had a very stormy ride at a meeting in Sheffield in September 1986 when he spoke on 'The Myths of Anti-Racism' (Sutherland, 1986; Drew, 1986).

Echoes of the Honeyford affair were heard up and down the country. Jonathan Savery, a teacher at a Bristol multi-cultural education centre, was hailed in the media as the new Honeyford at the end of 1985. He had written an article entitled 'Anti-Racism as Witchcraft' for the *Salisbury Review*, and was also accused by colleagues of making racist remarks. Later, Honeyford and Savery shared the same platform at a meeting at the University of Bristol. Maureen McGoldrick, the headmistress of Sudbury Infants' School in Brent, became the focus of much attention from her local authority, the media and the Secretary of State for Education for a racist remark she was alleged to have made to the effect that she did not want any more black teachers. More locally, after the announcement of Bradford's decision to appoint a Schools' Sex Equality Officer, Keighley teacher Peter Thorpe wrote an article for the *Telegraph and Argus* entitled 'Feminist Line Baffles Me', strongly criticizing the decision. He was investigated by the Directorate of Educational Services, but no action was taken. In September 1987, the parents of twenty-six children in Dewsbury refused to send their children to the school to which they had been allocated, Headfield Middle School, where 85 per cent of the 560 pupils were of Asian origin. Their lengthy protest gained extensive national publicity, partly since it coincided with public discussion of the proposals made in the 1987 Education Bill. Concern was expressed that to increase parental freedom of choice of schools might lead to racially segregated schools – though the Dewsbury parents were at pains to emphasize that their motives were cultural, not racist. Honeyford supported their protest, which he saw as an indication of increasing dissatisfaction with the principle of multi-cultural education, and the Bradford-based Muslim Parents' Association used the occasion to renew their calls for separate Muslim voluntary-aided schools.

In 1987, new Press guidelines relating to publications and radio and television interviews were issued by Bradford Council to all its employees. While there was no prohibition on their right to speak out as private citizens on any matter (as long as it was unlikely to embarrass the Council or breach its confidence), they were not in their capacity as employees to 'criticize politicians, Council policy, other employees or the Council's performance' (*Telegraph and Argus*, 2 October 1987). Though the guidelines were clearly designed in the wake of the Honeyford affair to prevent further public statements by employees that might be embarrassing to the Council, they proved less than easy to apply in practice. At first it was thought that they might have been contravened, for example, by a teacher from Manningham Middle School who had an article published in October 1987 which revealed the negative attitudes of some local teachers to ethnic minority pupils (Shepherd, 1987). The problem was resolved, however, by the ruling that no action could be taken against an employee for publishing academic research.

Bradford meanwhile pressed on with its multi-cultural policies. The draft guidelines for worship in schools, which involved removing worship from morning assemblies and introducing it as an optional activity elsewhere on the timetable, with special provisions for different religions, were introduced on an experimental basis in February 1986 (CBMC, 1986a, 1986b). A new Inter-Faith Education Centre was opened in March. A standing conference on racial harassment was resumed when the Community Relations Council for Council for Mosques ended their boycott of council groups. The Racism Awareness Training Unit was disbanded, and its work amalgamated with the overall training policy of the authority. A new initiative on race relations put forward by Councillor Ajeeb, the chairman since 1986 of the Race Relations Advisory Group, set out guidelines and timetables for the recruitment of black officers to local authority posts. Although this initiative brought to an end the all-party consensus on race relations which the council had maintained for six years, it was criticized by the Community Relations Council and by some black Council officers as a 'toothless tiger'.

The Honeyford affair continued to have repercussions on the local political scene. In March, Honeyford wrote a short statement in support of the Conservatives for their local election newsletter, in which he said that 'the only hope for a genuinely progressive and harmonious education service lies with the Conservatives'. The inclusion of this statement on the front page of the newsletter may have been a miscalculation by senior Conservative councillors, however, for in the local elections they lost sufficient seats for Labour to gain overall control of the Council for the first time in seven years. Councillor Lambert became chairman of the Educational Services Committee and Councillor Goldberg chairman of the Multi-Cultural Education Support Group. The Mayor-elect, Liberal Councillor Kathleen Greenwood, on the other hand, suffered a heavy defeat at the hands of the Conservative candidate, and she herself felt that the Honeyford affair was a significant factor in her defeat; her vote in support of the motion of no-confidence in Honeyford in March 1985 had been resented by a large section of her electorate.

Two of the Racism Awareness training officers who signed the controversial memorandum in which Honeyford was described as a 'known racist' were elected chairman and vice-chairman of Bradford's Community Relations Council (CRC) in May 1987. The CRC, to which over a hundred organizations are affiliated, provides a major link between Bradford Council and ethnic minorities in the city. The two officers, Ishtiaq Ahmed and Mohammed Salam, though currently employed in Calderdale's race relations department, were founder-members of a radical group called the Black Workers Collective (BWC) which was set up in Bradford to organize black workers and defend their interests and democratic rights (*Yorkshire Post*, 13 June 1987). The BWC was viewed with some suspicion in council circles both because of the way it was set up and because of its criticisms of the council's treatment of its ethnic minority workforce. Disquiet was expressed by some Council leaders as well as by some organizations affiliated to the CRC at the apparent transformation of the CRC from an umbrella organization representing minority interests to a black pressure group. The Council for Mosques and the Federation of Sikh organizations both threatened to withdraw their membership, and Councillor Ajeeb questioned whether the CRC was coming to the end of its useful life-span. A new phase in race relations in the city seemed to have arrived, marked by vested interests, political manoeuvring and infighting among the various groups responsible for implementing or monitoring council policy: all of which Honeyford and the New Right at least might take as evidence that the 'race relations industry' is more likely to exacerbate than ease racial problems. On the other hand, Ajeeb expressed the belief that what Bradford was now seeing was healthy disagreement and debate, not civil war or the destruction of council initiatives (*Telegraph and Argus*, 13 July 1987).

Drummond Middle School, under its caretaker head, William Haykin, and then its new head, Leslie Hall, (both of whom had previously been heads of middle schools in the authority), quickly dropped out of the limelight. So did Jenny Woodward, although she was fined in February 1986 for producing a cannabis plant and claimed the police were trying to discredit her. She has been interviewed about her views on the Honeyford affair for the Bradford Heritage Recording Unit, but has put a twelve-year embargo on use of the tapes. Amin Qureshi, one of the most persistent and colourful of the protestors against Honeyford, achieved brief notoriety again in April 1986 when he was invited by Colonel Gadaffi to a four-day all-expenses-paid conference in Libya. Although it transpired that the invitation came to him in his capacity as general secretary of the Azad Kashmir Muslim Association of Bradford, the media took delight in linking an opponent of Honeyford with Gadaffi. Even among the Muslim community, Qureshi's standing was substantially diminished. Honeyford himself, as we saw in chapter three, has written extensively on educational topics for a number of newspapers and journals, and embarked on a series of lectures up and down the country.

How far was Honeyford's departure a triumph for those who had been campaigning against him? Some of his opponents certainly saw it as such. 'We wanted him to go and he's going,' said Goldberg (quoted in *The Sunday Times*, 15 December 1985). 'His removal is a victory for democracy and the wishes of the parents and the children.' (*Telegraph and Argus*, 28 November 1985). For others, it was more a matter of relief. The Lord Mayor, Councillor Ajeeb, said:

> I really am relieved that this long drawn-out saga is now finally over.
> I hope that the city can now move forward in the field of race

relations and that we can still lead the country in spite of the difficulties some of us have faced (*Telegraph and Argus*, 14 December 1985).

In Ajeeb's view, Honeyford was merely an obstacle on the road to good race relations, that had to be bulldozed aside before further progress could be made. The assumption behind the present volume, however, is that the Honeyford affair cannot be pushed aside so easily and forgotten, for it has lessons which we ignore at our peril.

In one sense, therefore, Honeyford's departure *was* a defeat, not only for his supporters but for those occupying the middle ground who believed that behind the stereotypes of Honeyford as martyr or devil lay serious issues which could only be resolved in open, rational debate; it was a defeat because the debate had been foreclosed. Perhaps the insensitivity of his own contributions to the debate was partly to blame for this outcome, although he had himself written of the need to 'create a more honest, a more open and a less fearful intellectual climate' in which issues such as multi-culturalism, anti-racist education, tolerance, cultural continuity and the basis of shared values in our society could be discussed. But the strident tone of his articles was matched by that of the calls for his dismissal, and neither they nor the manner of his eventual departure did anything to bring reasoned discourse to bear on the debate or to facilitate discussion of the issues raised by his articles and by the campaign against him. In an article not directly related to the Honeyford affair, Professor Parekh (1985) had written,

> The school cannot spearhead a political movement and if it ever tried to would lose its educational character and become an arena of struggle between large social and political forces over which it can exercise no control.

The Honeyford affair provides an interesting illustration of this problem.

In part two of the present volume, I intend to examine what seem to me to be the most crucial issues in the Honeyford affair. First, there is a need to explore the ambiguities in the concept of racism, and to consider the justifiability and wisdom of anti-racist education. Secondly, there is the question of the right to free speech, of the extent to which teachers and other educationalists should be responsive to the educational wishes of those they serve, and of the rights of parents to call them to account. Thirdly, there is the problem of what sort of education we should be providing in a pluralist society, how we can evaluate the comparative importance of the goal of social integration as against the goal of cultural preservation, and whether there is a sufficiently broad framework of shared values on which all groups agree for a common curriculum to be worked out which is acceptable to all.

Before we turn to consider these issues, however, it is important to acknowledge that in an affair of this complexity there will be a whole range of possible perspectives, and that depending on the perspective one adopts, so one will focus on different aspects of the affair and produce quite different analyses. Since the perspective that I shall adopt in part two is a broadly philosophical one, I shall first outline very briefly in chapter five some of the possible alternative perspectives on the affair, in particular the psychological, the political, the sociological and the legal and administrative.

5 Some Perspectives on the Affair

There are so many overlapping and intermeshing issues arising from the Honeyford affair that it would be unrealistic to attempt to give detailed coverage to all of them. In part two I have selected for closer analysis three sets of issues which I believe are most central to the affair: racism and anti-racism; free speech and accountability; and integration and cultural continuity. These issues are all related both to Honeyford's articles and to the campaign against him. The aim of the present chapter is to sketch a very brief outline of some of the other major issues raised by the affair.

To some extent, the comparative importance of these secondary issues depends on what one brings to the affair oneself. A feminist may be particularly interested in the active co-operation between feminists and Muslims in the running of the Drummond Parents' Action Committee (DPAC). An administrator may be more interested in the decisions of the High Court and the Appeal Court regarding the education authority's right to dismiss a head after his governors have recommended reinstatement. A sociologist may be more interested in the struggle for power between the various groups involved. Some of these secondary issues may themselves be matters of considerable debate, such as the question whether the class structure was a significant factor in the affair. Others may carry important lessons for future practice, such as the question of how the affair could have been settled more decisively, effectively and quickly. Yet others involve questions which may never be objectively resolved, such as the effect of the dispute on the children at Drummond Middle School who were caught up in it.

These secondary issues are here outlined under four headings: psychological, political, sociological and finally legal and administrative. It is acknowledged that even this categorization is not comprehensive; for example, it gives no space to linguistic issues such as the fascinating variety of styles in evidence in Honeyford's articles. Nor does it discuss media coverage of the affair; this topic was touched on in chapter four, and has been frequently examined by opponents of his views (for example, Drew, 1986; Sutherland, 1986). The aim of this chapter is not to enter into a debate about the comparative importance of these and other issues, but simply to draw attention to some points of interest that have not cropped up elsewhere and where appropriate to indicate the direction further research might take.

1 A PSYCHOLOGICAL APPROACH

In his interview with Honeyford for the Radio Four programme, 'In the Psychiatrist's Chair', Anthony Clare rightly drew attention to the very great feelings that Honeyford's articles aroused in his opponents, and to the fact that their response was more of an emotional than a logical one. In his crucial *Salisbury Review* article, Honeyford had himself shown that he was aware of, and disapproved of, this high level of emotional response to questions of race. He did not see it as a natural and justifiable reaction to extreme aggravation and provocation, as Clare did himself, or to the insensitivity of his own criticisms of ethnic minorities, but explained it in terms of racial or ethnic differences, which somehow also rubbed off on the white members of the 'multi-ethnic brigade' as well. He described how a meeting at his school on extended trips to the Indian sub-continent degenerated into 'a noisy and unseemly demonstration of sectarian bitterness' in which 'the hysterical political temperament of the Indian sub-continent' was seen; he also commented on the 'sound and fury' of criticisms which had been made of his earlier articles.

There appear to be three separate elements, however, in this discussion of the emotional response to Honeyford's articles and to questions of race generally. The first is the anger and frustration which his opponents not unexpectedly felt when they saw their goals being thwarted, which sometimes led to aggressive and hostile acts including death threats, abusive letters and the physical assault by pickets on one parent taking his child to school during the boycott. Honeyford's own description of the reaction of his opponents to the election of three of his supporters to the school's governing body on 15 October 1985 illustrates the way he perceived this fury and aggression:

> Then there was absolute uproar. About three-quarters of the audience rose in fury. There was shouting, swearing, finger-pointing. Chairs were kicked over. A photographer was punched. Bricks were flung through windows. A shrieking harridan (white)

rushed towards the governors' tables. 'Racists! Bastards! Traitors!' she bawled, almost foaming at the mouth (I later learned she was a teacher) (*Daily Mail*, 19 December 1985).

The second is where the tendency to be aggressive or to react strongly to emotional stimuli is seen as part of an individual's temperament or personality. Honeyford implies in his articles that among Asians and Afro-Caribbeans it is often those who share this characteristic that rise to positions of leadership. In the *Salisbury Review* (Winter, 1984) he writes of

> An influential group of black intellectuals of aggressive disposition, who know little of the British traditions of understatement, civilized discourse and respect for reason.

The third element is the psychology of the crowd. What Honeyford describes as 'the baying mob' and the 'jeering, spitting and hissing crowd of enraged militants' (*Daily Mail*, 18 December 1985) has much in common with Gustave Le Bon's description of *La Foule* (1895), which has significantly influenced later studies of crowd behaviour. As members of a crowd, Le Bon maintains, people tend to show more emotionality, irrationality, brutishness and intolerance than they do as individuals. This crowd mentality probably also lies behind the heckling of the Lord Mayor with repeated chants of 'Honeyford' by football supporters, which Honeyford equally condemned.

Another aspect of psychological interest which Clare raised in his interview was Honeyford's 'stubbornness'; Gordon Moore had earlier described him as 'the most stubborn chap I've ever met' (quoted in Jack, 1985). By this, Moore probably meant a refusal to budge in the face of reason, but Honeyford saw it as emotional toughness and a willingness to stand by a principle whatever price he had to pay. Certainly he resisted very considerable pressure from the local authority to conform and change his attitudes, or at least his public expression of them. For him, the crucial question was

> How far can a man push a principle when he knows that other innocent people are suffering? (Clare, 1986)

It was eventually his acknowledgement of the degree to which the children at the school, the teachers, his family and especially his wife were being affected that led him to accept early retirement.

I have already suggested that it may be too late to do more than guess at the effect of the dispute on the children caught up in it. Nevertheless, it does seem likely that the children's socialization, moral development and attitudes to school, to authority and to race relations issues, were influenced to some extent by events at the school. Murphy (1987, p. 130) puts the point more forcefully:

> It disturbed me to think of the possible effects of this prolonged campaign on some children's development. In theory, these pupils were merely being taught how to oppose racism, but I was sickened by the extent to which they had been encouraged to feel and express hatred for one individual.

Children were involved in the protests not only passively, in that they took part in school boycotts and attended the DPAC's alternative school, but also actively by wearing badges with inscriptions such as 'Sack Honeyford Now' and 'Honeyford Out', by ignoring the head in school or making up jokes about him, and by taking part directly in the picket line, holding banners proclaiming such slogans as 'Honeyford, Dead or Alive' and using megaphones to lead the anti-Honeyford chants. While the passive involvement might have been no more than doing what they were told by their parents or others (Honeyford reports that a colleague who asked a child why he was taking part was told, 'A man in glasses said we had to' (*Yorkshire Post*, 7 June 1984).), the active involvement implies that the children had at least to some extent taken on board the attitudes and values of the protestors. Many reports (for example, *New Life*, 29 June 1984) implied that the children were acting off their own initiative, but of course they were not only using materials provided by adults (such as megaphones and badges), but were also modelling themselves on adult behaviour. In view of evidence from psychological research (for example, Bandura *et al.*, 1961) which suggests that children exposed to aggressive models of behaviour are more likely to behave aggressively themselves, there arises the question of the possible long-term effects of the involvement of children in the dispute. Particularly worrying in some people's minds is that their experiences on the picket line might enter their consciousness as part of what it means to be a member of an ethnic minority. Parallels may be drawn with the more long-standing disruption in Northern Ireland, where recent research has explored the possible effects of actual or potential involvement in civil disturbances on the personal and social development of young people (*cf* Taylor and Nelson, 1978; Bell, 1987). The notions of self concept and cultural identity are touched on in more detail in chapter eight.

Finally, again in his interview with Honeyford, Clare raised the question of anxiety and insecurity, as exemplified both in the 'fears of English and indigenous people here' which 'are sometimes underestimated' and in the fears of racial minorities. Honeyford himself placed much more stress on the former than the latter:

some of the offensive reactions that we get from English people towards black and coloured people might be because they themselves feel threatened in their sense of identity and their sense of rootedness and the integrity of their culture. They may, at least initially, feel somewhat threatened by this quite dramatic development in their society (Clare, 1986).

While not denying that ethnic minorities met with prejudice, 'quite spectacular and deplorable prejudice sometimes', he maintained that it would be 'phoney and patronizing' to use this as a reason to avoid passing any critical comments on ethnic minorities or their backgrounds, cultures or histories. What he did not appear to acknowledge was first that there was a need to educate the indigenous population so that they felt less threatened by the minorities, and secondly that the insensitive expression of criticism of minority groups might play directly into the hands of those who were most prejudiced. Chapter six takes this discussion further by tracing the roots of racism in feelings of anxiety, insecurity and threat, combined perhaps with basic human drives such as the need to dominate, to feel superior, to belittle, to snub and to exercise power, which can often lead to acts of direct or misplaced aggression, such as scapegoating and other rationalizations of racial prejudice.

2 A POLITICAL APPROACH

Considerable space has already been devoted to the political dimension of the Honeyford affair in earlier chapters. We saw in chapter two that Bradford's progressive multi-cultural education and race relations policies were not motivated by the kind of political radicalism which is evident in some London boroughs, but were produced as a pragmatic response to the perceived needs of the increasing numbers of ethnic minority children in the city. The degree of political opportunism behind the policies, however, and the vying for the immigrant vote, proved difficult to assess objectively. We noted also that the policies had all-party support, though the chairmen of the committees which piloted the policies through the Council were all Conservatives and according to Selbourne (1985, 1987) at least, there were many covert expressions of racial prejudice from local Labour politicians behind their official support for the policies. We saw in chapter four that at first reaction to Honeyford's articles did not at first divide along party lines, since the Conservative chairman of the Educational Services Committee, Peter Gilmour, was one of his most outspoken critics, while the Labour Lord Mayor supported him. Later, however, opinions became increasingly polarized along party lines, with Conservatives both locally and nationally defending his right to free speech and Labour wanting to see him dismissed. The government maintained a low profile throughout the affair, though there were several hints that they would prefer Honeyford not to lose his job, and this may have been behind the gradual hardening of Conservative opinion in Honeyford's favour locally. The affair had significant repercussions on the local elections, with both Conservative and Liberal councillors who had opposed Honeyford losing their seats.

In this present section I want to outline four further political aspects to the affair which have not so far been given much attention: the implications of the hung Council in Bradford; the relationship between Honeyford and the New Right; the reaction of the extremist political parties to the affair; and the growing politicization of the Asian community in Bradford.

The fact that there had been a hung Council in the city for several years had a number of consequences. There was an increasing tendency to search for policies on which all parties could agree, rather than to depend on straightforward majoritarianism. This was seen, for example, in the lengthy Conservative-sponsored resolution which was passed unanimously by the Schools Education Sub-committee on 22 October 1984 after the Labour motion of no-confidence in Honeyford had been defeated. The resolution included a whole series of requirements designed to bring Honeyford more into line with Council policies and to improve relations between Honeyford and the parents and local community he served. While the search for a solution on which all parties could agree was commendable in many ways, the resolution was perhaps less decisive than it would have been if it had needed the support of just a single party, and may have been responsible for letting the affair drag on and allowing time for opinions to harden on both sides of the debate.

On other matters where no consensus could be reached, the Conservatives, who chaired the committees, were dependent on the handful of Liberal councillors for help to push their policies through. Thus when Eric Pickles, chairman of the Educational Services Committee from May 1984, decided that the best solution to the situation might lie in Honeyford's offer to resign so long as an acceptable financial package could be worked out, he went with the city's Chief Executive on 18 March 1985 to the Liberal leader, Kath Greenwood, to try to persuade her to agree to a financial settlement. She would not agree, however, and in fact three days later voted with Labour and the co-opted SDP member of the Schools Education Sub-committee in support of a new motion of no-confidence in Honeyford, which was thus passed by eight votes to seven. When criticized in her Baildon ward for the way she had voted, she claimed she had been misled and unduly pressurized by Labour councillors who argued that a vote of no-confidence was necessary to reinforce the credibility of the Council's race relations policies. Two months later, however, in a surprise pact between the Labour and Conservative groups, Liberal and SDP representation on Council sub-committees was voted down, and the Alliance was even refused the status of an opposition party. This move was more to do with Liberal voting on the budget than with the Honeyford affair, though it did have repercussions on the affair when Liberal councillor John Wells, perhaps wishing to steal a march on the other parties, initiated secret talks with Honeyford on 7 June 1985 to try to negotiate a settlement. The Wells initiative was blocked by the Conservative and Labour leadership, who together ordered Gordon Moore to open official negotiations with Honeyford instead.

At this stage it appeared that front bench Conservative and Labour councillors agreed that a negotiated deal to bring about Honeyford's early retirement was the best course of action, while the left wing of the Labour party and the right wing of the Conservative party were united in opposing any such financial settlement (the former because they wanted to see Honeyford sacked, the latter because they wanted to see him reinstated). As the Labour leadership gradually won over their backbenchers to the idea of a financial settlement, so Conservative opinion seemed to harden in favour of Honeyford's right to stay at the school – although Councillor Pickles left himself a loophole by saying that he supported Honeyford's case so long as he wished to stay at the school, but if he chose to leave, he would help him to do so with dignity. Throughout the dispute, Pickles had shown considerable political dexterity in balancing the conflicting demands within his own party and the even greater difficulties resulting from the hung Council. The construction of the School Education Sub-committee's motion on 21 March 1985 illustrates this skill: by reaffirming his party's commitment to the Council's race relations policies, he avoided losing the entire credit he had built up with the Asian community, while by opposing the vote of no-confidence and supporting Honeyford's right to free speech, he retained the confidence of his own backbenchers. The inclusion of a statement by Honeyford in the Conservatives' election newsletter in April 1986, however, appears to have been a serious political miscalculation, which may have contributed to the loss of sufficient seats to give Labour their first overall control of the Council for four years. Honeyford's influence can still be traced on the Conservative manifesto for the 1987 local elections, which promised, *inter alia*, to

> respect cultural differences, ensure equal employment within the authority, make English language teaching a high priority, allow debate on alternatives and acknowledge dissenting views (*Telegraph and Argus*, 10 April 1987).

Let us now turn to Honeyford's involvement with the New Right. This term is now commonly used (*cf* Levitas, 1986; Gordon and Klug, 1986; Oldman, 1987) to refer to a political tendency which combines two aspects, a 'neo-liberal laissez-faire economism' and a social authoritarianism. This tendency is being forcefully promoted by a number of pressure groups such as the Centre for Policy Studies and the Salisbury Group. Key figures include Roger Scruton, Anthony Flew, Baroness Cox, John Marks, T.E. Utley, Peregrine Worsthorne, Ronald Butt, Tom Stoppard, John Casey, John Vincent, Maurice Cowling, George Gale, Colin Welch and Kingsley Amis. Through close contacts with the media and having the ear of a large number of Conservative MPs, including Mrs Thatcher, this group is in a position to influence both government decisions and public opinion in a variety of ways. Honeyford's first contacts with this group were accidental, as he answered an advertisement for papers for *The Salisbury Review* after one of his articles was turned down by *The Times Educational Supplement*. Later, he met *The Salisbury Review*'s editor, Roger Scruton, for whom he developed a great personal admiration. Honeyford's views on the inevitability of the central place of British culture in education in this country, and his deep suspicion of the concept of anti-racism and the activities of the 'race relations lobby', were closely in line with the thinking of this group, and Honeyford was gradually drawn into closer involvement (*cf* St. John-Brooks, 1987). He has since written articles on many of the New Right's educational hobby-horses, including the voucher system, sex education and declining standards, though his main interest remains the education of ethnic minorities. In October 1985, he was invited, along with other right-wing educationalists including John Marks, Baroness Cox and John Ashworth, to an educational seminar at 10 Downing Street with Mrs Thatcher, Lord Young, Sir Keith Joseph and other ministers to discuss the future of British education. His views on multi-cultural education were also quoted in the policy paper of the Monday Club. Seidel (1986) claims that the arguments of Honeyford and the New Right regarding the cultural superiority of the traditional British way of life represent a new form of 'cultural racism', a claim which is discussed further in chapter six.

Perhaps surprisingly, the Honeyford affair appeared to encourage little growth in the activities of extreme right-wing groups in Bradford. Indeed, support for such groups was very much on the decline after reaching its zenith in Bradford some ten years earlier. In an inner-city County Council by-election at the height of the affair (April 1985), the British National Party candidate, Stanley Garnett, himself a former Bradford headteacher, who had spoken in support of Honeyford, took less than 4 per cent of the poll with 405 votes. Ten years earlier, the National Front had won 1500 votes in a comparable ward, and in the early 1970s the Yorkshire Campaign to Stop

Immigration had obtained similar results. Honeyford himself said he would be appalled 'if his case had been hijacked by extremist groups' (*The Observer*, 21 April 1985). The involvement of extreme right-wing groups such as the National Front in Bradford schools also seems to have declined since the start of the Honeyford affair; the gang fights which were reported in schools and on the streets in 1986 seem to have been spontaneous activities by small groups rather than the carefully orchestrated actions of political extremists.

Extreme left-wing groups, on the other hand, played a major role in the campaign against Honeyford. The local communist party, which has one of the most consistent records for opposition to any form of racism – in an election address as early as 1968 it was claimed that 'the Communist Party stands for complete racial equality and fights racial discrimination in any form' (Le Lohé, 1979) – was active on the picket line outside Drummond Middle School, as were other left-wing groups. There was usually a group selling *Socialist Worker*. A number of Labour councillors regularly attended the picket line, from moderate left-wingers to those such as Councillor Goldberg whom the press insisted on describing as 'Trotskyists'. The Revolutionary Communist Party, and particularly its off-shoot, Workers against Racism (WAR), was active in the campaign through a variety of marches and pickets including a picket outside Bradford's Conservative Party offices to protest at Honeyford's visit to 10 Downing Street. WAR stepped up its activities in Bradford after the end of the Honeyford affair, organizing what *The Next Step* (4 April 1986) called 'effective defence of the black community against racist thugs' and planning a major march against racism supported by up to a thousand protestors, with Councillor Ajeeb and many other Asians among them.

With few exceptions (such as the pro-Honeyford Mrs Iqbal), the political commitments of the Asians in Bradford are on the left of the political spectrum. There are three Asian councillors at present, and all are Labour Party members; more extreme left-wing groups like WAR have a high percentage of Asian members. The Asian pressure groups are all politicized to a greater or less extent, and fall into two main categories: those with far left leanings, such as the Asian Youth Movement and the Indian Workers Association, and those with a more religious focus, but still with left of centre political leanings, such as the Council for Mosques and the Azad Kashmir Muslim Association. Although there was a certain amount of in-fighting among these groups over the Honeyford affair (for example, over the appropriate degree of militancy for the campaign and over the Council for Mosques' claim to speak for all of Bradford's Muslims), it would be a mistake to place too much emphasis on their differences. They were all united in their opposition to Honeyford because of the way they felt he had insulted their community, their beliefs and their traditions.

3 A SOCIOLOGICAL APPROACH

Although I have suggested that the origins of the protest against Honeyford were very simple, it is undoubtedly true that as the affair proceeded it became the focus for a number of struggles for power and control at a variety of levels. On the political level, as we have just seen, it contributed to such struggles locally (as the three political parties vied with each other to dominate the hung Council), nationally (as the New Right sought more influence and control over government policies) and within the Asian community (as the Council for Mosques and the AYM, for example, tried to extend their respective spheres of influence). On the administrative level, as we saw in chapter four, the staunchly anti-Honeyford partnership between Peter Gilmour, chairman of the Educational Services Committee, and Mike Whittaker, the Policies Development Officer, was resented within some sections of the directorate of educational services because they appeared to want 'to set up an alternative administration' (Spencer, 1984). After the departure of Gilmour and Whittaker, the main administrative struggle for power was between the pro-Honeyford school governors and the directorate of educational services over the question of whether the latter had a right to overrule the former's resolution that the head should be reinstated. On the level of school pressure groups, there was a head-on clash between the anti-Honeyford DPAC and the pro-Honeyford FDMS. The latter swamped the former as far as the number of signatures gathered for their petitions went, whereas the former, who had a head start anyway, placed more emphasis on marches, demonstrations, pickets and school boycotts.

The Honeyford affair also needs to be set in the context of the relationship between Bradford Council and the various Asian community groups. Selbourne (1987) suggests, on the authority of Mike Whittaker, that the 'process of Asian enfranchisement' which began in the early 1980s, by which he means increased financial support for and consultation with Asian community groups and the appointment of some of their key members to positions of influence within the authority, was initiated by the Council as a way of bringing the Asian community more under their control. 'We have trained people to shout,' said Whittaker, 'provided they shout acceptable slogans', by which he meant 'halal meat, mother-tongue teaching. The issues where we can deliver.' This was seen as a way for the Council to stave off demands for separate Muslim schools and 'the destruction of a common education system' (Selbourne, 1987, p. 98). On this analysis, even the demands for Honeyford's dismissal may have been 'stage-managed' by the local authority 'as a sop to avert worse political trouble from the largely unemployed Asian community as the local economy founders' (Selbourne, 1985). For the Honeyford affair was another issue where the Council *could* deliver, though it became increasingly reluctant to do so, because of the likely repercussions not only among other Bradford headteachers but also in the local community. In order to achieve their objective of Honeyford's departure, therefore, the Asian groups had to make full use of the limited power and influence they had over Bradford Council, for example by withdrawing their representatives from the Race Relations Advisory Group, the Multi-cultural Education Support Group and similar bodies, and by issuing vague threats about reopening the campaign for separate schools if Honeyford was not removed.

Selbourne has commented on another dimension of the power struggle between the Asians and the broader community in Bradford – the 'unholy alliance' which developed between the Socialists and the Muslims in the city. He believed that Bradford Socialists 'of left, right and centre, with their own cultural and social complexes', had been 'duped' into thinking that it was

> 'progressive' to defend Islamic reaction; 'Socialist' to promote the anti-social; and 'democratic' to espouse an undemocratic form of cultural private enterprise which, in the Indian sub-continent itself, is regarded with distaste by the Indian left movement, (Selbourne, 1984b)

and that it would advance the prospects of racial harmony to concede the socially and educationally retrogressive demands being made by the Muslims. As an analysis of what was actually happening in Bradford, Selbourne's account here is unsatisfactory because it fails to take note of the significant differences within the Muslim community and shows scant respect for Muslim concern about the lax sexual codes operating in much of British society, which lay behind many of their demands; yet it does draw attention to the complex yet fascinating question of who was using whom, and for what motives, in such alliances between Asians and sections of the broader community.

Another very interesting approach to the Honeyford affair would be to attempt to analyze the dispute in terms of class, though it must be acknowledged that class consciousness is perhaps not so strong in Bradford as other forms of social division. The campaign against Honeyford was frequently depicted as a defence of the rights of both black and working class people. This view can be seen, for example, in DPAC publicity material which claimed that he had attacked 'white working class people as being inarticulate', and has been carried through into later commentaries on the affair, such as that by Gordon and Klug (1986) who argue that 'the superiority of white (middle-class) culture is implicit throughout the writings of Ray Honeyford' (p. 23). Doubts are cast on such a classic Marxist interpretation of the affair, however, by Honeyford's claim to be 'terribly working class' himself (he was born one of twelve children to a Catholic mother in a poor district in Manchester, failed the entrance examination to grammar school, and worked as a clerk in a Manchester confectionery business for ten years after leaving school at fifteen); and by his apparent wish to champion the cause of white lower working class parents whose children formed the new minority in many inner-city schools (*Salisbury Review*, Winter 1984). Even Councillor Ajeeb recognized this; Selbourne (1987, p. 104) quotes him as saying that Honeyford was 'trying to represent the lower working class, the white proletariat'. Evidence from letters to the local press and from Selbourne's interviews with white working class mothers (1987, pp. 107–9) suggests that Honeyford was in fact more in touch with many working class people than were the leaders of the campaign against him, who often turned out to be from liberal/radical middle class backgrounds themselves.

Feminist interest might focus on the place of women in the dispute and on the attitude to female education that emerged. We need to be immediately aware, however, of the danger of oversimplifying the issues in terms of a clear-cut division between conservative or progressive, sexist or non-sexist, Asian or white. One of the main leaders of the predominantly Asian campaign against Honeyford was a white single-parent feminist, Jenny Woodward, while one of his most prominent supporters was an Asian Muslim, Mrs Mubarik Iqbal. Indeed, Honeyford had much support among the women of Bradford, and, significantly, the two letters to the *Telegraph and Argus* which compared him to Christ were both written by women. On female education, Honeyford is fairly middle-of-the-road. He has written of his commitment to equal opportunities for girls (1987a) and has several times criticized the 'purdah mentality' of some Muslim fathers. He was himself criticized on the one hand by local authority advisers for not showing sufficient conviction in encouraging girls to participate in activities traditionally reserved for boys, and on the other hand by some Muslim fathers for allowing boys and girls to face each other over the dinner tables and for insisting on all girls taking swimming lessons. For some people, the biggest question that emerges from all this is how feminists like Jenny Woodward and her friends could ally themselves with what Selbourne (1985) calls 'mosque-led obscurantism – hostile to co-education, sex education, health education, women's emancipation...mixed drama, mixed gymnastics and mixed swimming'. Brown (1985) implies that this gulf was only bridged by some dishonest arguments on Jenny Woodward's part. My own feeling is that the gulf is not so great as is often made out. For a start, the complaints that Honeyford received from some Muslim fathers and reported in his articles were not typical, as Selbourne seems to assume; most were happy to act within the guidelines set out in the Local Authority Memorandum 2/82. Also, both the Muslims and the feminists agreed that girls should not be pushed into conforming to male patterns of behaviour. Jenny Woodward considered it quite natural for many adolescent girls to wish to cover their limbs for sporting activities. Some feminists, moreover, would now no longer wish to urge Muslim women to turn their back on the belief systems in which they have been brought up and adopt Western values (*cf* Halstead, 1987).

A sociological approach to the Honeyford affair would naturally be largely concerned with racism, cultural values, pluralism, integration, socialization, multi-cultural education and minority communities. However, since racism is discussed in more detail in chapter six and the other topics in chapter eight, they will not be developed further at this stage.

4 A LEGAL AND ADMINISTRATIVE APPROACH

Throughout the affair there was considerable emphasis on the legal rights of groups and individuals and the threat of legal action when it was felt that rights had been exceeded or infringed. Thus the requests by 238 parents for their children to be transferred from Drummond Middle School, though handled by the DPAC, were contained in separate letters from each parent to the director of education, to ensure that the requests fell within the parents' legal rights. Careful attention was paid to the rights of the press and the general public under Paragraph 18 of the *Instrument of Government of Various County Middle Schools, 1985* to attend governors' meetings. After complaints from the FDMS, Sir Keith Joseph exercised his legal right as Secretary of State for Education to demand an account of the local authority's handling of the affair. The NUT threatened legal action against the DPAC for alleging that teachers had threatened children attending the DPAC's alternative school with physical punishment. The NAHT took out a writ on Honeyford's behalf against Bradford Council for alleged libel by seven racism awareness training officers who described Honeyford in a memorandum as a 'known racist'.

The only issue actually to reach the High Court was when it was asked to settle the NAHT's claim that the disciplinary procedures against Honeyford had been exhausted following the governors' decision to recommend his reinstatement, and that the Council and its officers had no right to review his case further. In other words, the court was asked to provide a true construction in law of the documents which covered the headteacher's employment, and particularly those sections relating to the power to dismiss. In the event, the outcome was not wholly decisive. The initial High Court finding against the Council was overturned by the Appeal Court, but it was a condition of the settlement agreed with Honeyford in

December 1985 that the final appeal to the House of Lords would be discontinued. Further details have already been given in chapter four. Although the judges were at pains to point out that their decision was concerned only with whether the LEA could in principle revise, review or overturn a governors' recommendation for a head's reinstatement, and not with whether it *should* do so in Honeyford's particular case, this distinction was often lost sight of in popular reaction to the court case, and it was widely believed in some quarters that the judges were considering whether or not Honeyford should be dismissed. One issue which did arise from the case was the anomaly in the position of the assistant director of education, who having assisted in the preparation of the case against Honeyford for the governors' hearing, was then expected to set his own views on one side and to reconsider their recommendation objectively. The judges in the Appeal Court held that there was no reason in principle why he should not be able to do this, and that 'it would be quite wrong to assume, before he has even begun to perform his duties, that he will perform them unfairly' (*Knight's Local Government and Magisterial Reports*, 1986, p. 525).

The case raises broader questions about the control of education, such as the implications of the refusal of the local association of headteachers to implement the Council's LAM 6/83, *Racist Behaviour in Schools*. The 1944 Education Act sets out certain statutory duties for local education authorities, such as the control of secular education in schools, including both what is to be taught and how it is to be taught (section 23), ensuring that the school day begins with a non-denominational act of worship (sections 25-6) and the provision of education which is in general terms in accordance with the wishes of the pupils' parents (section 76). In practice, LEAs carry out these duties with the help of their own officers, the school governors (whose own functions are to be set out, according to section 17 of the Education Act, in local articles of government) and the headteachers. If there is no agreement over how the statutory duties are to be carried out, the LEA has the final decision and may be under a duty to dismiss a head who does not accept its final decision. According to the Bradford articles of government, the school governors are responsible 'through the agency of the headteachers' for implementing council decisions, and therefore the headteacher is 'responsible to the governors for the general conduct, curriculum and discipline of his school' (Article 3). Article 9 (d) stipulates that headteachers are to be employed under a contract of service and concludes,

> Except when otherwise determined by the Council, a headteacher shall not be dismissed except on the recommendation of the governors.

The standard contract of service in use in Bradford provides a disciplinary procedure to be followed if dismissal of a teacher is being considered. First, a written notice of the complaints against him is sent to the teacher concerned. Secondly, the evidence is heard by the governors, who 'may recommend dismissal'. Thirdly, the assistant director of education reviews the decision taken by the governors and makes his own recommendation to the education committee, who alone have the power actually to dismiss the teacher. As we have seen, the court case was to decide whether the disciplinary procedure could continue if the governors do not recommend dismissal. Broader questions about the control of education, the professional autonomy of teachers and the relationship between central government, local government, headteachers and governors will be considered further, along with questions of accountability, in chapter seven.

In spite of suggestions to the contrary by Fairhall (1986), it appears that the 1986 Education Act would have produced a resolution to the Honeyford affair, one that was not in Honeyford's favour. At the meeting to co-opt community governors in October 1985, the pro-Honeyford candidates were elected by a majority of one. However, the new Act's provisions for the structure of the governing body of a school such as Drummond Middle School (a school with 530 pupils) involve dropping the ancillary staff representative and adding a fourth parent governor. This change is likely to have resulted in Honeyford's opponents gaining a majority of one and thus being in a position to co-opt anti-Honeyford community governors. In this case, Honeyford would not have survived any further motions of no-confidence, and the LEA could have proceeded with disciplinary measures with the support of the governing body.

In two other respects, however, the 1986 Education Act did little to resolve questions arising from the Honeyford affair. First, should community representatives co-opted onto the governing body represent the local district served by the school, or the broader district served by the local authority? In the elections of October 1985, the anti-Honeyford candidates of the former category lost to the pro-Honeyford candidates of the latter category. In a polarized situation like this, the Act gives no indication of whose interests the co-opted governors are meant to represent. Nor does the Act tackle the question of whether the governing body should in any way represent the racial or religious balance of the school's pupils. Secondly, one of the main aims of the Act was to clarify the power relationship between governors, LEAs and headteachers and to increase the powers and responsibilities of governors in some areas. While some of the Act's provisions (such as the requirement for governors to produce an annual report for parents and to hold an annual parents' meeting to discuss the running of the school) might have helped to bring the issues in the long-running Tyndale affair out into the open before they did so much damage, the Act offered little practical help towards the resolution of such problems as the refusal of Bradford headteachers to implement the LAM 6/83, a refusal which had much in common with the Poundswick affair, where teachers simply refused to teach pupils whom their governors had suspended and the LEA had reinstated.

There was very widespread criticism of the way Council officials handled the Honeyford affair. But what could have been done to resolve it more quickly and effectively? And what lessons does the affair have for administrative practice within education? I shall conclude this section with five points relating to these questions.

First, the affair underlines the importance of recognizing potential sources of conflict early and taking decisive action at that stage. As we have seen, Council officers had nearly two years' warning before the affair erupted in March 1984 that there was a serious rift between Honeyford's views of multi-cultural education and their own. There were various ways in which the affair could thus have been settled before it had started. Although a head is seldom dismissed except for gross professional misconduct, pressure could have been put on Honeyford at that stage to take early retirement; it is reported (Spencer, 1984) that Peter Gilmour and Mike Whittaker had decided by the end of 1983 that this was likely to be the best course of action. Alternatively, they could have arranged secondment (a course of action later adopted for Whittaker himself) or transferred him to another of the authority's schools where his undoubted abilities could have been put to less controversial use. There is of course no guarantee that such action would have prevented Honeyford from publishing further articles on racial issues, but the postponement of decisive action undoubtedly made the affair more difficult to resolve later.

Secondly, there was a need for much more widespread consultation with headteachers before the two crucial LAMs were introduced as official Council policies. Since headteachers were to be responsible for the implementation of the policies and since they were in the best position to judge the practicability of the policies in their own schools, it seems surprising that the local authority did not involve them more fully in the initial decision-making process. One problem resulting from the lack of effective consultation and involvement in decision-making was that headteachers might find themselves criticized for advocating policies which Council officials had themselves advocated a couple of years earlier but which they now condemned. This happened to Honeyford in connection with the debate about Asian pupils' extended trips to the Indian sub-continent; Roper had shared his views in 1981, but later spoke out against them as Council policy on the issue changed. In fact, the Council's handling of the race relations policies seemed almost designed to put the teachers' backs up. Mike Whittaker told Selbourne (1987, pp. 105–7),

> We're overriding teachers' objections...We're simply not allowing teachers to run schools as they see fit. The smack of firm

government has ruffled their feathers...We told the teachers, 'You will, you must, you have to, or face disciplinary proceedings, like any other Council employee or servant.' At the end of the day, teachers are our line managers. Their job is to see that what we want is done. They may not be used to being talked to in this way, but we're not just paying their salaries and ferrying exercise books and chalk around the city.

Thirdly, if such a high-handed approach was inappropriate for Bradford headteachers generally, it was doubly so for Honeyford. Council officers had had enough meetings with Honeyford prior to 1984 to realize that if he felt he was being pressurized to conform to views he considered misguided, he would simply dig his heels in. If they had firmly decided against putting pressure on him to take early retirement, it would probably have been better to avoid direct confrontation altogether in favour of a more positive and adaptable approach to personnel management. This might have involved first being more prepared to listen to Honeyford's criticisms, however intemperate, and take them seriously; secondly, appealing to him not to do anything which might damage the chances of success for the LEA's policies before anything better could be democratically worked out; and thirdly, searching for agreement over at least the primary objectives of education in a multi-cultural context and attempting to build on that. The unwillingness to adopt such a conciliatory approach might have resulted both from a desire among LEA officers to discourage other heads from following his lead, and from a recognition by certain councillors and others that there was political capital to be made out of the affair.

Fourthly, Council officers adopted a very different approach to the campaigners against Honeyford from the one they adopted towards the head himself. This inevitably left them open to charges of bias. Their approach is of course understandable, as they were afraid that too high-handed an approach might aggravate race relations in the city, and in any case Honeyford was a Council employee whereas most of the protestors were not. However, Council officers appeared to assume that there was no middle course between confrontation with the protestors and non-interference with their activities. One possible course of action would have been to distribute leaflets in appropriate languages to all parents with children at Drummond Middle School describing and justifying the authority's multi-cultural policies and explaining the legal requirement of regular school attendance. It is questionable how far the local authority should have had official consultations with groups such as the AYM and CARA who engaged in acts of civil disobedience (for example, occupying the Lord Mayor's chambers) or with an unofficial body such as the DPAC. In extreme cases, such as when highly inaccurate paraphrases of Honeyford's articles in Urdu were being distributed from Asian community centres, it might have been appropriate for the Council to take some action if they thought that racial tensions were being increased, perhaps by threatening to withdraw financial support from the centres. The Council's failure to take action in such cases undoubtedly contributed to widespread feeling in the city that Honeyford was being 'hounded' while Asians 'could get away with anything'.

Finally, and perhaps most crucially, the Council did not spend sufficient time, energy or money explaining and justifying its new race relations policies to the broader community in Bradford. Pedley (1986) refers to the chief education officer of another West Yorkshire town who claimed that Bradford was introducing

> a programme of positive discrimination which would, if it failed to carry the mass of the people along with it, be ultimately counter-productive.

New directions in policy are most likely to succeed if they are accompanied by a major publicity drive, as we have seen with the sale of British Gas shares. So are campaigns to change people's behaviour and attitudes, as the campaign against AIDS shows. The Honeyford affair may have been, partly at least, the result of the Council's failure to promote and explain its policies with sufficient vigour. Of course, if it had done so, it may have laid itself open to accusations of the illicit or wasteful use of public funds. But such accusations are only likely to arise where the issues being promoted are themselves controversial, and since Bradford's race relations policies had all-party support, there is no reason to suppose that a public relations campaign to promote them would have met with undue opposition.

There is a deeper question, however, that needs investigation – how far the policies themselves are justifiable. This question will underlie much of the discussion in Part Two.

Part Two:
The Underlying Issues

6 Racism and Schools

The question of racism lies at the very heart of the Honeyford affair. The sustained campaign against him did not develop because of his criticism of Council policies or because of widespread discontent at the way he was running his school, but because of his alleged racism. The placards and badges paraded by protestors, the picket-line chants, the press statements by the Drummond Parents' Action Committee and the Parents' Support Group and the articles by his opponents all proclaimed the same message: Honeyford was a racist and as a result of his beliefs had forfeited his right to remain head of his school. Honeyford himself, however, has consistently denied that he is or ever has been a racist. Indeed, he has called racism 'a failure of the human spirit' (1985d, p. 17), has described as 'odious' the doctrine of racial superiority (1986j, p. 51) and has sketched out a vision of society which is 'both multi-racial and free from racial prejudice' (1983a). As we saw in chapter four, a libel action was initiated on his behalf against Bradford Council because a group of Council employees issued a memorandum in which he was described as a 'known racist', though a settlement was agreed as part of his early retirement package without the case ever coming to court.

The assertion and counter-assertion here suggest that different understandings of the term 'racism' are in use, an impression which is reinforced by the discussions of racism in recent writing by the New Right (*cf* Flew, 1986) and the anti-racist left (*cf* Gordon and Klug, 1986). Clearly there is a need for some conceptual clarification before any discussion of the topic can proceed. The main section of the present chapter therefore distinguishes between different types of racism, and considers the criteria according to which an action or a person may justifiably be called 'racist'.

The chapter concludes with an examination of the educational implications of this conceptual enquiry, in terms of educational policy and decision-making on the one hand and practice at school level on the other. Among the questions touched on are how much account should be taken, at all levels of educational planning, of racism as a phenomenon; whether Honeyford is correct when he warns that an anti-racist approach to education may generate 'a wholly artificial and harmful colour consciousness in our schools' and when he advocates in its place an emphasis on the common needs of all children (1982d, p. 21); whether adopting a high profile on racial issues in schools is simply likely to increase the incidence of racism; and whether racism is best combatted by general moral education, as Honeyford (1985d, p. 17) suggests, rather than by teaching children about it directly and encouraging them to adopt an anti-racist stance from an early age.

THE CONCEPT OF RACISM

There are several problems in the way the term 'racism' is currently used. Sometimes racism is portrayed as a deep-rooted problem which pervades the whole of British society and at other times as merely a fringe phenomenon, consisting mainly of deplorable acts of discrimination or violence committed by members of such far-right groups as the National Front. Honeyford (1986b) suggests that Britain is not a racist society at all, but simply suffering from attempts by politically motivated anti-racists to make capital out of feelings of guilt generated by an emphasis on the oppression of blacks in Britain's colonial past. Another debate centres on the claim that only whites can be racist; both Honeyford and *The Swann Report* reject this claim and argue that members of any racial or ethnic group can be guilty of racism.

Honeyford (1986j, p. 52) suggests that the conceptual confusion which lies behind such disagreements can only be avoided by persuading 'those who use the word to stick to its proper meaning'. There are two problems here, however. The first is that even his fellow-contributors to the volume *Anti-Racism: an Assault on Reason and Value* (Palmer, 1986) appear not to agree on what that 'proper meaning' is. In Honeyford's view, 'racism' refers to the 'odious' belief that 'one race is genetically superior to another' (*ibid*. p. 52). For Flew, however, the 'clear and proper understanding' of the term is

> the advantaging or disadvantaging of individuals for no other or better reason than that they happen to be members of this racial group rather than that (*ibid*. pp. 15–16).

In other words, Honeyford defines it primarily in terms of belief, Flew primarily in terms of action. The second problem is that language, like culture, does not remain static. In the last twenty years, on both sides of the Atlantic, the use of the term 'racism' has changed significantly, particularly as a result of research in the social sciences. One example will suffice. Wellman (1977, p. xviii) describes racism as

> culturally sanctioned beliefs which, regardless of the intentions involved, defend the advantages whites have because of the sub-ordinated position of racial minorities.

An attempt to wrench the term back to a supposed authoritative definition can only be justified if a new word is found to describe the institutionalized injustice towards racial minorities which Wellman's definition of racism encompasses. If no new word is found, and the term is restricted to belief in the genetic superiority of certain races, then there is a danger that the 'institutional racism' which has been the subject of considerable research over the last twenty years will simply be ignored or its existence denied completely.

In what follows, I shall distinguish and examine six different types of racism within contemporary writing on the topic. A consideration of what these six types have in common will facilitate a clarification of the concept, of its moral, social and political implications, and of the grounds on which an action or a person may be called 'racist'.

Type One: Pre-reflective Gut Racism

This name is being used instead of the now redundant term 'racialism', implying racial hatred. Its name suggests that it has emotional rather than rational origins and content. It can be observed in both individuals and groups. Its deep psychological roots can be traced to three main factors. First, there is a tendency to feel fear, anxiety, insecurity and suspicion in the presence of any persons and groups who are perceived as strange, foreign or unfamiliar. These emotions can provide a powerful motivation to ethno-centric action of various kinds, as Honeyford himself points out in his interview with Anthony Clare:

> Some of the offensive reactions that we get from English people towards black and coloured people might be because they themselves feel threatened (Clare, 1986, p. 13).

Secondly, there are certain motivational dispositions such as rejection, aggression, dominance and superiority which some psychologists consider fundamental to human personality. For example, Murray *et al.* (1938) include among their list of psychogenic needs the need to snub, ignore or exclude others, the need to belittle, injure or ridicule others, the need to influence, control or dominate others and the need to feel superior to others. These negative dispositions are likely to be directed primarily towards perceptibly different individuals and groups, and if it is true that children or simple-minded adults tend to notice, and put more weight on, physical differences more readily than non-physical ones (*cf* Wilson, 1986, p. 6), it is not surprising that racial minorities become particular targets. The third factor is ignorance of racial minorities, which leaves people open to the too-ready acceptance of myths, stereotypes and other fear-arousing communications. Over the centuries in Britain the black man has become an archetypal image of baseness, savagery, ignorance, ugliness and vice and has been used as a bogeyman for impressionable children rather as the reddleman was, according to Thomas Hardy, in nineteenth century Dorset. Against this background it is easy to see how readily racial myths and stereotypes can gain acceptance. By 'racial myths' is meant statements which have no factual foundation at all or which are necessarily untrue; for example, the claim that 'they all live on social security' is incompatible with the claim that 'they're taking all our jobs'. By 'racial stereotypes' is meant the tendency to see racial groups in terms of a number of supposed distinguishing characteristics, often based on generalizations originating from limited contacts and experience, and to judge individuals in terms of group membership without allowing for individual variation. Thus West Indian children are commonly stereotyped as good at sport and music but badly behaved and unacademic, while Asian children are seen as hardworking but having unrealistic career expectations.

From these three roots racial prejudice can easily develop. Racial prejudice usually involves emotionally charged ethno-centric attitudes, including an antipathy or hostility towards other racial groups. It is extremely difficult to change by argument or the presentation of facts. It may be felt or expressed, acknowledged or hidden, directed towards an entire racial group or towards an individual because of membership of that group (*cf* Allport, 1958, p. 10). Above all, it involves a 'failure of rationality' (Schuman and Harding, 1964, p. 354).

Such prejudice is likely to be expressed in hostile behaviour and in attempts to reject or dominate racial minorities. These may be seen in positive acts of overt racism, the avoidance of social contacts and the process of scapegoating. Positive acts of overt racism include bullying, attacks on property and person, gang fights, murder, verbal abuse and name-calling, rudeness, threats and graffiti. The avoidance of social contacts manifests itself in a general spirit of unfriendliness towards members of other racial groups and often lies behind much of the discrimination in housing and employment in this country, for which there is overwhelming evidence (*cf* Hubbuck and Carter, 1980; Campbell and Jones, 1983; Eggleston *et al.*, 1986). Scape-goating involves relieving one's frustrations or sense of deprivation through displaced aggression directed towards groups of lower status who played no part in causing the initial problem. One example is the tendency to blame minority racial groups for the country's present economic situation. The process of scapegoating completes the vicious circle of gut racism by creating a new set of myths which reinforce racially prejudiced attitudes.

Although it has been assumed in the above discussion that pre-reflective gut racism originates from white people and is directed against blacks, and although white people are clearly in a better position to express certain manifestations of such racism (such as discrimination in housing and employment), there is no reason in principle why this type of racism should be limited to whites only. There may be the same degree of prejudice and hostility in a black who calls a white person 'white racist shit' as in a white who calls a black person a 'black bastard'. As the *Swann Report* (DES, 1985, pp. 27–8) points out, such racism can also exist between minority groups, and this may again take the form of violence, social avoidance or scapegoating.

Pre-reflective gut racism is probably what Honeyford has in mind when he speaks of the 'quite spectacular and deplorable prejudice' which ethnic minorities sometimes encounter (Clare, 1986, p. 13). Elsewhere, however, he has taken care to distinguish between prejudice and discrimination and to argue that the latter need not necessarily follow the former. Prejudice, we are told, is

> the tendency we all have, whatever our colour, to adopt a narrow and rejecting view of others (1982d p. 21).

Discrimination, on the other hand, involves action which penalizes a person for not belonging to one's own group, and is not an inevitable consequence of prejudice. Honeyford writes,

> My hunch, after working for several years in multi-racial areas, is that most people in Britain, whatever their skin colour, are prejudiced non-discriminators (1986j, p. 52).

Honeyford's argument here raises one of the major difficulties about pre-reflective gut racism: is prejudice morally reprehensible in itself, or only insofar as it results in hostility and domination? There is a head-on clash of views on this question between liberals (for example, Allport, 1958) and conservatives (for example, Scruton, 1984, p. 68), the former holding that prejudice is something to be fought and the latter that it is natural and inevitable, so long as it does not lead to reprehensible action.

Perhaps the biggest difficulty in any consideration of pre-reflective gut racism is to ascertain the extent of the racial component in any given hostile behaviour directed towards a member of a racial minority. Certainly factors other than racism may also be involved, and in many cases it is impossible to be categorical in identifying a particular action as racist. But this should not be taken to indicate that reports of such racism are likely to be exaggerated; on the contrary, as has already been shown, there is strong evidence to suggest that the less dramatic manifestations of pre-reflective gut racism form part of the everyday experience of many members of minority groups in Britain and that its more dramatic manifestations are commonly perceived as a very real threat.

A final noteworthy feature of this type of racism is that because of its instinctive emotional origin it sometimes persists in people who have rejected racism in their head. Selbourne (1985), for example, has described the strongly racist opinions expressed to him 'off the record' by Labour Councillors in Bradford who have all officially subscribed to the Council's progressive race relations policy statement. To dismiss this as hypocrisy is perhaps to underestimate the strength and resistance to change of pre-reflective gut feelings, and to oversimplify the way that people react in a situation of cognitive dissonance where their emotional and rational responses make conflicting demands on them.

Type Two: Post-reflective Gut Racism

This type of racism is concerned to provide a *justification* for the continuation of racial privilege, and this may involve the creation of an ideology of racial superiority and domination. Whereas pre-reflective gut racism may be attacked for making arbitrary distinctions between people on the basis of irrelevant differences, post-reflective gut racism counter-attacks by claiming that the differences are not irrelevant.

Post-reflective gut racism therefore involves the *post-hoc* rationalization of practices emanating from racial prejudice, such as social avoidance, scapegoating and overt acts of racism. This rationalization may take two forms: first, the establishment and acceptance of an unfounded system of beliefs which would, if it were true, justify racial discrimination; and secondly, the misapplication of well-founded scientific theories to provide support for racist ideology. Both forms of rationalization may ultimately be the product either of conspiracy or of self-deception (*cf* Jones, 1985, pp. 227–8). Let us look at the two forms in more detail.

The first form, the establishment and acceptance of an unfounded system of beliefs, may make use of either a religious or a scientific framework. British Israelitism, for example, holds that Adam was the progenitor only of the Aryan race, the other races being already in existence when he was created. According to another old belief associated with some fundamentalist Protestant sects, negroes were the descendants of Noah's grandson Canaan and were doomed to perpetual servant status as a punishment for Ham's sin against his father (*cf Genesis* ch. 9 v. 25). In the post-Darwin era, attempts have been made to establish through psychological, genetic and anthropological studies that there are real differences between races in terms of intelligence, personality and moral attributes, which enable the races to be ranked hierarchically and which may thus justify differential treatment and the maintenance of existing inequalities. These attempts usually entail claims that whites of North and West European ancestry are more intelligent, more responsible, more moral, less lazy, less cowardly and have a more significant culture. Thus we find John Tyndall, the former leader of the National Front, claiming

> While every race may have its particular skills and qualities, the capacity to govern and lead and sustain civilization as we understand it lies essentially with the Europeans (quoted in Walker, 1977, p. 81).

A classic example of post-reflective racism is the claim that blacks occupy a subordinate position in our society because they lack the necessary drive and moral stamina to advance themselves, and that this provides an adequate justification for the racial inequalities that currently exist. An example of an extreme form of post-reflective racism is the work in Nazi Germany relating to the distinction between Aryan and other types. This is presumably what Honeyford has in mind when he refers to the 'odious doctrines of racial superiority and the master race' as the 'proper' meaning of the term 'racism' (1986j, p. 51).

Such attempts to establish that individuals' potential as human beings is biologically determined according to their racial membership are, of course, grounded on a false premise: that human beings can be divided up neatly into distinct races on the basis of perceptible biological characteristics such as skin colour which are transmitted genetically from one generation to the next. Research over the last twenty years, however, has provided no scientific foundation for the traditional racial divisions into which the human population is placed (*cf* NUT, 1978; Rose *et al.*, 1984), and suggests that there is as much genetic diversity within groups as between them. This does not make 'race' a vacuous concept (for if that were the case there could be no real racial discrimination or injustice), but suggests that it should be understood as primarily a social rather than a biological construction. In other words, a racial group consists of people who consider themselves or are considered by others to be different from other groups because of perceptible, inherited physical characteristics. If it is accepted that racial categories are shaped by social beliefs and perceptions rather than genetically determined, then the search for genetic differences between races which may justify differential treatment is exposed as irrelevant.

The second form of post-reflective racism, involving the misapplication of well-founded scientific theories to provide support for racist beliefs, may be seen in a new type of racism which has developed in recent years and which is consistent with the belief that racial differences are socially constructed. This 'new racism' (*cf* Barker, 1981; Shallice, 1984; Gordon and Klug, 1986) involves the claim that racism, like nationalism, is simply a more sophisticated form of a natural tribal instinct to group together, to defend one's own territory, to preserve one's distinctive identity, to be loyal to one's kin and to be wary of, and if necessary antagonistic towards, outsiders. On this argument, racial conflict itself is in a sense biologically determined, as it is one aspect of the Darwinian principle of 'the survival of the fittest'. In several speeches Enoch Powell has argued that racial conflict is both natural and inevitable. In 1969, he said,

> We have an identity of our own, as we have a territory of our own, and the instinct to preserve that identity is one of the deepest and strongest implanted in mankind (quoted in Gordon and Klug, 1986, p. 19).

In 1976, he developed the point further:

> Physical and violent conflict must sooner or later supervene where an indigenous population sees no end to the progressive occupation of its heartland by aliens with whom they do not identify and who do not identify themselves with them (*ibid.*).

While such arguments do not depend on the claim that one race is inherently superior to another, they may be considered to typify post-reflective gut racism to the extent that they provide a justification for racial exclusiveness and conflict. In countering such arguments, it is not necessary to reject the underlying anthropological and socio-biological theories. For even if human nature has evolved by a process of competitiveness and aggression, it would be to commit the naturalistic fallacy to argue from this that we should live such a life today. In any case, our active participation in the world depends on much more than can be explained by biological determinism (*cf* Shallice, 1984, p. 8). Honeyford himself recognizes this in a passage already referred to (1986j, p.52), where he argues that although he sees prejudice as a natural human phenomenon, this provides no justification for any form of discrimination.

The case of Arthur Jensen, the Berkeley professor who was caught up in a violent controversy about racial differences in IQ in the late 1960s (Jensen, 1969, 1973), provides an interesting borderline example of the two forms of post-reflective gut racism. If (as some people have suggested) Jensen intentionally used a dubious conception of IQ as a measure of genetically determined intellectual capacity in order to make blacks appear genetically defective as far as intelligence is concerned, then this could be seen as an example of an attempt to justify racial disadvantage through the establishment of an unfounded system of beliefs. It could be best countered by exposing the flaws in Jensen's thesis, as, for example, Dobzhansky (1973) has tried to do. If, however, (as could equally well be argued) Jensen was seeking to draw conclusions in a critically open manner from the best available scientific evidence, then the most he can be charged with is a lack of sensitivity and wisdom in failing to appreciate how his research might play into the hands of racists wishing to justify the continuation of existing white privilege. In this case, the problem is the misapplication by others of his well-founded scientific theories, and it is best countered by exposing the injustice and lack of respect for persons involved. In this latter case, the question arises as to whether it is ever justifiable to suppress scientific research for non-scientific reasons such as fear of the illegitimate or irrational use to which it may be put. As was noted in chapter three, Honeyford argues strongly against any such suppression. He has on several occasions criticized the decision of the Swann Committee to drop the research it had commissioned into the fortunes of successful black children as a result of pressure from West Indian organizations (Honeyford, 1982a; 1986j, pp. 47–8; 1987e).

Like pre-reflective gut racism, post-reflective gut racism appears to be overwhelmingly a white problem, though there is no reason in principle why this should be so. In practice, however, the few examples of black post-reflective gut racism (such as the Black Muslim movement in America: *cf* Essien-Udom, 1966) appear to have originated as a response to white privilege and domination. The main differences between racism of type one and racism of type two are that the latter, unlike the former, is necessarily conscious and intentional and, as its name implies, involves the attempt to provide a rational justification for racial domination.

Type Three: Cultural Racism

This term is being used with increasing frequency (Ben-Tovim, 1978; Saunders, 1982; Greenhalf, 1985b; Seidel, 1986, p. 129; Troyna and Williams, 1986, p. 89; Ashrif and Yaseen, 1987, p. 23; and Gilroy, 1987, p. 61, who applies the term directly to Honeyford) to draw attention to a shift in the focal point of much racism from physical characteristics such as skin colour to cultural characteristics such as social customs, manners and behaviour, religious and moral beliefs and practices, language, aesthetic values and leisure activities. Whereas post-reflective gut racism seeks to explain and justify racist attitudes in religious or scientific terms, cultural racism attempts the same thing in cultural terms. It involves prejudice against individuals because of their culture. The culture of minority groups is seen as flawed in some way, and thus as standing in the way of their progress (*cf* Stone, 1981). Unlike post-reflective gut racism, however, cultural racism does not involve belief in the existence of any biological incapacity to change. On the contrary, change is exactly what is sought. Minorities are encouraged to turn their back on their own culture and to become absorbed by the majority culture. Insofar as they refuse to do so, this is thought to justify inferior treatment and discrimination. Cultural racism, like gut racism, usually involves stereotyping (*cf* Fraser, 1986, p. 59) and is embodied in such statements as 'they've got really dirty habits' and 'why can't they be more like us?'.

Cultural racism demands cultural conformity where it is neither necessary nor perhaps even desirable, and penalizes people unjustly for failure to conform. It may be seen as an attempt to legitimize existing power differences. Opposition to cultural racism does not require the belief that there is no need for any shared values in society; for society would soon disintegrate if there were no respect for law, no acceptance of fundamental principles such as justice and respect for persons and no agreed procedures for resolving conflicts. Nor does it involve the belief that different cultures are all equally good (*cf* Parekh, 1985, p. 23) or that one should never criticize other cultures. What it does involve is the claim that to insist on cultural conformity where such an insistence is not justified is a form of domination and oppression. If teachers take for granted the superiority of white British culture in schools, for example, (as if British culture were not a fluid and constantly changing thing anyway) this is likely to result in an undervaluing of the cultures of children from minority groups and in serious damage being done to their self-awareness. A more open and positive approach to minority cultures, involving an attempt to understand them in their own terms, to explore them with sympathy and sensitivity and to appreciate the enrichment they bring to the broader community is discussed below in chapter eight.

In what sense can the cultural domination under discussion here be viewed as a type of *racism*? Perhaps not at all, in which case we may need to adopt a new term such as 'culturalism' (*cf* Fraser, 1986, p. 41; Seidel, 1986, p. 114), although this has not proved popular so far. On the other hand, racial differences are very frequently accompanied by cultural differences, so much so that it is often impossible to know whether prejudice and discrimination are being focussed on the former rather than the latter. A feeling of biological superiority goes hand in hand with cultural superiority in the quotation already referred to from John Tyndall who speaks of the capacity to sustain civilization lying essentially with the Europeans. In this sense, cultural differences are considered to be the natural consequence of the division of the world's population into a number of distinct racial groups, and thus hostility towards a racial group may find expression in hostility towards that group's 'alien' culture. The hostility may decline to the extent that members of a racial minority are prepared to conform to the cultural expectations of the majority; in this case, they may be accepted as honorary members of the majority group. Most teachers in multi-racial schools are familiar with situations in which white children make overtly racist comments about black people generally, yet at the same time number black children among their closest friends; indeed, the phenomenon is not limited to children. The explanation seems to be that blacks who turn their back on their own distinctive culture and who conform to the cultural values and expectations of the majority may be treated with respect, whereas those who retain their cultural differences are treated with racial hostility.

In her analysis of the early issues of *The Salisbury Review*, Seidel (1986) links cultural racism to the philosophy of the New Right, for whom, she claims (p. 111), 'the problem of race lies in the fact of cultural difference'. The presence of different cultures in a single country, in the view of the New Right, is likely to cause unacceptable social divisions; this problem can only be overcome by the assimilation of minority groups, but if they resist assimilation, the only 'radical policy that would stand a chance of success is repatriation' (Casey, 1982).

Type Four: Institutional Racism

In one sense, this type is closely linked to type three, for the institutions of a society are a product of, and a part of, its culture. But whereas cultural racism focusses attention on the differences or supposed flaws in the culture of minority groups which are said to justify their inferior treatment, institutional racism generally refers to the way that the institutional arrangements and the distribution of resources in our society serve to reinforce the advantages of the white majority.

Since it was first coined twenty years ago (Carmichael and Hamilton, 1967; Knowles and Prewitt, 1969), the term 'institutional racism' has been used with increasing frequency by sociologists, by local authorities and especially by what Banton (1985) and others have called the 'race relations industry'. Inevitably, different writers have understood and expounded the term in different ways. For some, it involves 'manipulating the bureaucratic system to outflank the unwanted' (Humphrey and John, 1971, p. 112); for others, it includes all the material, bureaucratic, legal and ideological forms in which racism expresses itself; yet others talk of racism as 'a basic feature of the entire society, being structured into its political, social and economic institutions' (Spears, 1978). A fuller list of definitions of 'institutional racism' is provided by Troyna and Williams (1986, ch. 3). For the purposes of the present analysis, however, (in order to avoid overlapping with other types of racism, especially type two), a fairly restricted use of the term will be adopted, which accords with the one provided in the *Swann Report*:

> We see institutional racism as describing the way in which a range of long-established systems, practices and procedures, both within education and the wider society, which were originally conceived and devised to meet the needs and aspirations of a relatively homogeneous society, can now be seen not only to fail to take account of the multi-racial nature of Britain today but may also ignore or even actively work against the interests of ethnic minority communities. The kind of practices about which we are concerned include many which, whilst clearly originally well-intentioned and in no way racist in *intent*, can now be seen as racist in *effect*, in depriving members of ethnic minority groups of equality of access to the full range of opportunities which the majority community can take for granted or denying their right to have a say in the future of the society of which they are an integral part (DES, 1985, p. 28).

This passage draws attention to three important features of institutional racism:

(i)   it refers to the adverse effects suffered by racial minorities as a result of institutional 'systems, practices and procedures';
(ii) it is usually unintentional and may be unconscious;
(iii) it is recognized by outcome.

These three features are likely to be generally accepted as essential to the concept of institutional racism (*cf* Williams and Carter, 1985, pp. 4–5), but each is problematic and each is open to a broader or narrower interpretation. First, it is not clear what institutional systems, practices and procedures are under discussion, since the term 'institution' is itself ambiguous. By mentioning 'the staff of an institution' and 'major national academic institutions', the *Swann Report* (DES, 1985, pp. 29–30) appears to adopt the everyday sense of a social organization which brings people together for a common purpose. Much sociological work (for example, Parsons, 1951; Berger and Luckmann, 1967), however, uses the term 'institution' in a specialist sense to refer to normative patterns of behaviour into which people are socialized and which are generally accepted as a fundamental part of a culture; in this sense, one may talk of the 'institution of property' or the 'institution of parenthood'. The difference between these two senses of 'institution' becomes crucial as soon as any attempt is made to eliminate institutional racism. In the former sense, such an attempt will involve revising the rules and regulations that operate in the particular organization, perhaps through government legislation or through the co-operative action of employees. In the latter sense, however, the elimination of institutional racism involves the construction of a new social world in place of the one which individuals have been led, through the process of socialization, to perceive as objective reality. At the very least, it would necessitate a radical re-education.

The second problem is that to describe institutional racism as unintentional or unconscious is to use terms that are appropriate for people, not institutions, and thus to blur the distinction between the institution and the individual. The standard analysis of institutional racism involves four steps:

(a) The historical creation of an institution which is non-racist in intent because it is designed for a homogeneous society. If it contains any elements of racism, these must not be conscious, because if they were the institution would exemplify type two racism.

(b) A change in the context within which the institution exists, so that new minority groups are disadvantaged by the continued existence of the institution. For example, giving preference to the employment of 'the lads of dads' may make it more difficult for new racial minorities to get jobs; and seeing exclusively white faces in school textbook illustrations might give black children a poor self-image.

(c) The power of the white majority over the institution. The institution may be perpetuated intentionally for racist reasons (because the whites perceive it to be to their advantage to do so), intentionally for non-racist reasons (because, for example, tradition and normal procedures are highly valued) or unintentionally (in that customary procedures are adhered to unreflectively).

(d) The moral judgment that once the discriminatory consequences of the institutional practices are raised to consciousness, anyone seeking to perpetuate them is guilty of racism (*cf* Jones, 1985, p. 224). A stronger version of institutional racism involves the claim that merely going about business as usual in such a context makes one an 'accomplice in racism' (Spears, 1978).

The main difficulties with this analysis are its oversimplified view of white individuals as the source of institutional power and its assumption that the raising of individual consciousness is sufficient to bring about institutional change (or at least that if such change does not result, the individuals whose consciousness has been raised are to blame). As Troyna and Williams (1986) point out,

> If one accepts…that routine institutional procedures constitute an independent entity in the production and confirmation of racial inequalitites, then neither the ethnic origin nor the political partialities of individuals operating those procedures are likely to have much impact on this process (p. 57).

The analysis also takes too little account of the control that institutions have over individual conduct, through their very existence as well as through sanctions set up to lend them support (*cf* Berger and Luckmann, 1967, pp. 72–3). The question of the degree of moral blame which may justifiably be attached to white individuals whose advantaged position is maintained through institutional racism is thus an extremely complex one, and most considerations of the question to date (such as those which generally underlie racism awareness courses) have been either too naive or too high-handed.

The third problem arises from the claim that institutional racism is best recognized by its outcome. On this view, the existence of any racial discrimination or other form of racial inequality should alert us to the likely presence of institutional racism. The first difficulty here, as Flew (1987, p. 132) points out, is how to measure the racial inequality. Are we to compare the total black population with the total white population in the country? Or since most black immigrants arrived in this country to take up poorly paid low status jobs and live in deprived inner-city areas, should we compare them with the white lower working class occupying similar roles and status? In other words, are we discussing the various disadvantages experienced for whatever reason by black people, or are we discussing the disadvantages experienced by black people because they are black? If we adopt the former view, and seek to resolve the situation by some form of positive discrimination, then there may be the danger, as Honeyford (1984a) points out, of simply transferring the disadvantage to the white lower working classes in the inner cities, who have few pressure groups or government organizations to represent their interests. The solution proposed in some London boroughs is radical political action which seeks 'to give power to people who do not, in the normal way, have access to it' (Morrell, 1984, p. 206), by ensuring, for example, that black people and other disadvantaged groups are fairly represented in power-wielding organizations such as the civil service, local government, all levels of management, the judiciary, school governing bodies and so on. As well as shifting power to underprivileged groups, this approach involves the systematic reconstruction of institutions into ones which positively promote equality of opportunity, and consciousness-raising at an individual level in order to ensure that hidden racist messages (such as lower expectations) are not programmed into the default system of the institution. However, Williams and Carter (1985) query whether such a project could be successful even within its own terms of reference:

> How far this is a feasible objective within a declining British capitalism is open to question, and the idea that 'sexism, racism and classism' can be 'dismantled' within a society resting on class inequality and exploitation and which materially, ideologically and politically reproduces structures of racial and gender subordination is difficult to sustain (p. 7).

The narrower definition of institutional racism proposed in the *Swann Report* not only is more open to critical investigation but also facilitates an understanding of the kind of institutional changes that might effectively reduce racial injustice. This sense of institutional racism, which I am adopting here as type four, refers to long-established organizational practices which disadvantage members of racial or ethnic minorities for no other reason than that they are members of those minorities. An example is the regulation that children may not be absent from school for more than two weeks a year for family holidays; this rule might be wholly appropriate for families who take their holidays at Clacton, but not for those who take them in Lahore. Another example is that though no examining board would ever dream of setting a public examination on Christmas Day, there have been several examples recently where Muslim children have been expected to sit public examinations in Eid u-Fitr. What this narrower definition of institutional racism excludes, however, is the assumption, for example, that the low number of black people recruited into teaching (*cf* Shallice, 1984) or the over-representation of black children in ESN schools (*cf* Coard, 1971; Ben-Tovim, 1978, p. 208) necessarily point to institutional racism. The kinds of injustice underlying these phenomena may be more complex, or may not be directed towards black people as such. On the other hand, Wellman (1977, pp. 164*ff*, 192*f*) warns that it may just be a way of maintaining white privilege to deny that race plays a part in certain kinds of inequality and discrimination experienced by black people.

Type five: Paternalistic Racism

This type of racism refers to the process whereby the freedom of black people is defined or restricted by generally well-intentioned regulations that are drawn up by whites. As Kirp (1979) points out,

> In all the discussions over the proper place of race in educational policy, non-white voices have seldom been heard. The government

undertook to act in the best interests of a silent constituency. It acted for the racial minorities rather than with them, and in that sense was truly paternalistic (p. 64).

More recently, a minority group leader in Bradford has commented:

The current race relations policy appears to be based on the assumption that white people have a natural right to set the agenda for black people. Such an assumption has more in common with the perpetuation of colonial relationships than the creation of racial harmony (Courtney Hay, quoted in *Yorkshire Post*, 13 June 1987).

It differs in two ways from institutional racism. First, it involves the initiation of new practices and procedures in response to the presence of racial minorities in the country, whereas institutional racism involves the failure to adapt long-standing practices and procedures to new needs. Secondly, it involves a more clear-cut wielding of power by white people, whereas it was argued above that in institutional racism it is a mistake to oversimplify the power that any individuals can wield in established institutions. Paternalistic racism implies that white people have the right to interfere in the lives of blacks for their own good and the power to define that good.

Paternalistic racism can be seen, for example, in the provision of separate language centres for children whose first language is not English, and in the practice of 'bussing' black children (but not white) to ensure a racial mix in local authority schools. It may be seen in some forms of positive discrimination and tokenism, particularly where these are intended as a way of placating agitators and defusing protest without tackling the underlying causes of racial injustice in our society. It may sometimes be benign, as in the case of finance provided by central government under section 11 of the 1966 Local Government Act to cater for the 'special needs of immigrants' (*cf* Willey, 1984, pp. 93–5; Troyna and Williams, 1986, pp. 66f, 108f, 118). Whether or not the paternalism has a harmful outcome, however, and whether or not it is consciously used by white people to reinforce their own privilege, paternalistic racism can be viewed as oppressive of racial minorities in two ways: it denies them the freedom to determine for themselves the pattern of their own future lives; and it implies (sometimes in a rather subtle way) the superiority of the white people who make the decisions.

In sociological terms, paternalistic racism is thus principally concerned with social control. Some writers have suggested that certain forms of multi-cultural education may be examples of paternalistic racism. This is because the terms of reference are generally defined by middle class whites in LEAs and educational institutions and because multi-cultural education is seen as a way of maintaining social stability, increasing the mutual tolerance of different groups and defusing racial conflict without at the same time bringing to light and firmly rejecting the underlying injustices experienced by racial minorities (*cf* Nixon, 1985, p. 31). On this analysis, although multi-cultural education may bring considerable advantages to minority groups, its hidden agenda involves the maintenance of white privilege. Thus Dhondy (1978) sees it as a way of containing black disaffection and Mullard (1980) argues that multi-cultural education

> in its articulated practices is none other than a more sophisticated form of social control which successfully attempts to distort and redefine the reality of racism in schools and society (p. 18).

Elsewhere, Mullard (1984) contrasts (paternalistic) multi-culturalism with anti-racism; the latter is a movement controlled by blacks, directed primarily towards racial justice rather than social integration and harmony, and concerned actively to resist all forms of white dominance and privilege. Of course, there is much to be said in defence of multi-cultural education. Parekh (1985, p. 23) in particular has provided a spirited counter-argument that multi-cultural education provides the only way to challenge and change racist attitudes by tackling their intellectual and moral roots; to encourage respect for and understanding of other cultures; and to help members of minority groups to develop their full potential, acquire pride and self-respect and build up easy social relations with their white peers. These points will be developed further in chapter eight.

Type Six: Colour-Blind Racism

Evidence gathered for the *Swann Report* shows that many people believe that recognizing differences between racial groups is racially divisive and may 'constitute a major obstacle to creating a harmonious multi-racial society' (DES, 1985, p. 26). On these grounds, official policy in the UK (and in America; *cf* Glazer, 1983, p. 126f) has sometimes self-consciously played down the significance of race. In 1973, the DES discontinued the practice of gathering statistics on pupils' ethnic or racial origins (Willey, 1984, p. 95f, examines the arguments for and against this practice). For similar reasons, many teachers have deliberately sought to make no distinction between black and white pupils, but rather to treat them all equally (*cf* Little and Willey, 1983). However, the *Swann Report* concludes that such 'colour-blindness' is

> potentially just as negative as a straightforward rejection of people with a different skin colour since both types of attitude seek to deny the validity of an important aspect of a person's identity (DES, 1985, pp. 26–7).

The problem may go further, since treating racial groups equally without distinction is usually understood as treating them the same, and treating them the same usually implies treating them in accordance with assumptions based on accumulated white experience. In this sense, equal treatment can become a vehicle for white domination.

Colour-blind racism may easily be distinguished from institutional racism as it does not depend on historical institutions but on a policy consciously (but misguidedly) adopted as a response to a contemporary situation. It may be distinguished from paternalistic racism in that it does not depend on an underlying notion of social control and it does not imply a belief in the superiority of white people over black. Colour-blind racism is the type which most closely corresponds to what is commonly called 'unintentional racism'. Even here, however, the notion of intention is problematic, and R.H. Tawney's reference to equal opportunity measures as

> the impertinent courtesy of an invitation offered to unwelcome guests, in the certainty that circumstances will prevent them from accepting it (quoted in Wellman, 1977, p. 220),

alerts us to the possibility that equal treatment may be meted out to black people in the knowledge that they may be unable to take advantage of it.

What is it that makes 'colour-blindness' a type of racism rather than merely a misguided form of action? I want to argue that 'colour-blindness' not only leads to undesirable outcomes (the disadvantaging of black people by ignoring or marginalizing their distinctive needs, experiences and identity), but may also involve racial injustice. It is not a new idea (indeed it can be traced back to Aristotle) that there can be injustice in treating people the same when in relevant respects they are different, just as much as there can be in treating them differently when in relevant respects they are the same. Recently, however, empirical research by feminists has illustrated the effects of this principle: in equal opportunity situations such as co-education, males are generally able to dominate because the terms in which the initial situation is defined are male-oriented and take little account of relevant differences between males and females (*cf* Spender and Sarah, 1980; Deem, 1984; Mahoney, 1985). In the same way, when a 'colour-blind' approach is adopted to any social policy in this country, white people are usually able to dominate because the common experiences are defined in terms which white people can more easily relate to than blacks and which tend to bolster the white self-image at the expense of the black. Thus even if the books which all the children at a school are expected to study are chosen for purely educational reasons, the fact that they all happen to be written by white people is likely to convey the hidden message that white people are cleverer or that what they write is more significant – the more so if similar messages are picked up in other school subjects and activities. As well as the danger of damaging the self-concept of racial minorities through such hidden messages, the 'colour-blind' approach may deny the relevance of the distinctive experiences of minority groups, such as the fact that they are on the receiving end of racial abuse and harassment. 'Colour-blindness' falls down because it is based on an idealistic principle (that all people are equal) which may be valid *sub specie aeternitatis* but which fails to take account of the contingent facts of racial inequality and disadvantage in our present society.

RACISM AS INJUSTICE

If it is justifiable to claim, as I have suggested it is, that racism may manifest itself in any of the above forms, either independently or in combination, then a number of problems immediately arise. The first is that the concept of racism becomes so broad and all-embracing that it loses much of its impact. The second is that racism no longer appears necessarily to imply (as many people think it should) a moral failure in individuals. The third is that most of the measures by which racism is usually recognized and defined turn out to be inadequate. Before we turn to look at the essential characteristics of racism, it is important to examine these problems more closely.

The first problem is that the six types of racism, taken together, cover so much ground that it appears that virtually any action or state of affairs could be described as racist. Activities which may have been assumed for a long time to be non-racist are liable to be suddenly redefined as racist. For example, both collecting racial statistics and refusing to collect racial statistics have at various times been challenged as racist; and as Kirp (1979, p. 40) points out, in Britain intentional racial mixing (as instanced in the policy of dispersing black children throughout the schools of a district) has been condemned and eventually abandoned as racially discriminatory – exactly the reverse of the American pattern. The result of this is that even well-intentioned white people may become confused or discourged in their attempts to avoid racism. Wellman (1977) describes some of the difficulties of a white liberal in adapting to conflicting notions of non-racist behaviour:

> Just as she was coming to evaluate black people as individuals, they demanded to be treated as a group. When she came to recognize that black people needed equal opportunities, they were demanding political power. As she began to locate the causes of discrimination in individual prejudice, black people were referring to the entire society as racist. By the time she recognized that black people needed help, they rejected it (p. 118).

Although some fluidity in the concept of racism is to be expected, what is needed in order to avoid such a high degree of confusion and contradiction is a greater clarity in the criteria of racism and a greater consistency in the application of these criteria to specific situations.

The second problem is that it is no longer easy to know what sort of judgment is implied in the term racism. The level of personal moral culpability, for example, appears to vary from one instance of racism to the next. This becomes clear when racism is analyzed on three planes, the first according to whether it is personal or institutional, the second according to whether it is a matter of practice or beliefs and assumptions, and the third according to whether it is intentional or unintentional. Moral, as opposed to legal, culpability involves intention. The clearest examples where individuals merit moral censure is where they personally and intentionally engage in racist practice. As with the rapist, the moral condemnation is implicit in the description of the action, and the act is considered to merit some form of reprisal. The case of the individual who intentionally holds racist beliefs is less clear-cut. However objectionable the beliefs are, if they remain private and do not impinge in practice on the rights of others, considerations of individual freedom may lead us not to interfere. It is only when the misogynist starts kicking women in the street or inciting others to do so that we restrain him and consider some forcible attitude change.

How far individuals may be blamed for the practices and procedures involved in institutional racism, or for the ideologies, beliefs or assumptions which underlie those practices, is a much more difficult question. Sarup (1986, p. 23) ends up rejecting moral explanations of institutional racism entirely, in favour of economic and political ones, but elsewhere in the anti-racist movement there is a wish to stress individual responsibility (witness the posters which proclaim, 'If you are not part of the solution, you are part of the problem'). Reference has already been made to Spears' claim that merely going about business as usual may make one an 'accomplice in racism'. This is a rather odd phrase, however, just as it would be to call someone an 'accomplice' in institutional elitism, because these things are not crimes (though of course *some* forms of racism are illegal), but social, political and moral issues. What is needed is not the encouragement of individual guilt but careful reflection on the justice of the institutions under consideration, followed by the appropriate social and political action. Indeed, if 'racist' becomes a slogan which is applied indiscriminately to all white people on the grounds that they are all implicated to a greater or less extent in institutional racism, this may have two adverse results. First, the moral force of the term will be diminished (for 'if all whites are racist, it can't be so bad as all that') and secondly, it is likely to drive a wedge between whites and blacks, increase prejudice on both sides and make racial conflict more probable.

There would seem to be much sense in applying the term 'racist' to individuals only if they are personally racist, and applying the term to practices and procedures rather than to people when institutional racism is under consideration.

The third problem is that most of the measures by which racism is traditionally identified turn out to be inadequate. Racism cannot be identified merely in terms of intention (as Honeyford appears to claim), as this would exclude a large part of types four, five and six. Neither can it be identified merely in terms of outcome, for this would suggest that racism could not occur in all-white districts, and it might even form part of an argument for repatriation. The widespread formula that racism equals power plus prejudice and discrimination is equally inadequate, for if power is necessarily involved, this implies that neither lower working class whites nor whites working, for example, in Saudi Arabia can ever be guilty of racism; while if prejudice and discrimination are necessarily involved, this implies that there can be no such thing as colour-blind racism. To identify racism in terms of inequality, whether of treatment, of respect, of access, of opportunity or of outcome may also be unhelpful, for equality of opportunity guarantees future inequalities, equality of respect is impossible to quantify, and equality of treatment (at least when it is taken to mean identity of treatment) is likely to result in the injustices associated with colour-blind racism. In any case, inequality of various sorts is intrinsic to the structure of British society, and anti-racists appear to be divided over whether they are seeking some sort of reshuffling of social goods and power so that these are shared more evenly between blacks and whites, or whether they are seeking a more radical political reform involving the complete abandonment of hierarchical power structures and the principle of competitive individualism wherever these are found. Gaine (1987, pp. 32–8) calls the former approach '"weak" anti-racism, or education for racial equality' and the latter '"strong" anti-racism, making the connections with class'. Behind all these approaches, however, lies the question of justice, and it is to this concept that we must now turn.

The central argument of this chapter is that racism *is* racial injustice. It may involve both isolated instances of injustice on the part of an individual and systematic social injustice which may permeate a whole society. It may be intentional or unintentional, conscious or unconscious. It may emanate from insecurity, from ignorance, from the belief that certain races are genetically superior to others (which, as Honeyford correctly points out, is the original meaning of racism, derived from the Italian *razzismo*), from institutional practices and procedures which were established long before Britain became a multi-racial society, from well-intentioned but misguided responses to the perceived needs and problems of racial minorities, or from the denial that such special needs and problems exist.

To seek to eradicate racism is thus to strive for racial justice. Of course, the appeal to justice is itself not unproblematic, because of the wide variety of views of justice, because of uncertainty over its relationship to other fundamental values such as truth, rationality, liberty and equality, and because of disagreement over how to achieve it in practice (Glazer, 1983, pp. 254*ff*). Some philosophers have sought to classify it in terms of distributive justice, retributive justice and commutative justice. Feinberg (1980), on the other hand, suggests that injustices can more usefully be divided into

> those that discriminate invidiously, those that exploit their victims and those that wrong their victims by means of false derogatory judgments about them (p. 265).

There are further disagreements about justice between utilitarians and rights-based theorists (*cf* Rawls, 1972); between liberals and conservatives (*cf* Scruton, 1984); and between rationalists and religious fundamentalists (*cf* Hourani, 1985).

Without denying the need for an agenda to be set out for further research into the nature of justice and its relevance to our understanding of racism, however, I believe that it is just as important to emphasize the extent of agreement that exists over the concept. For there would seem to be a basic notion of justice which is common to virtually all cultures and views, which could thus provide the basis for identifying and challenging racism in all its forms. It seems probable that very few people would disagree, for example, with Benn and Peters' statement that to act justly is 'to treat all men (*sic*) alike except where there are relevant differences between them' (1959, p. 111).

Ideally, in the context of race relations as in other areas, such justice will need to be tempered with a sense of fraternity, or at least of neighbourliness, because justice alone might be of a grudging, legalistic type which leaves deep-seated negative or hostile feelings untouched. But unless the search for justice takes priority, any attempt to achieve social harmony will have a hollow ring (*cf* Banton, 1985, pp. 12*ff*). This helps to explain the shifting demands of black people that were noted above and the apparently chameleon-like nature of the term racism. For so long as attempts are made to create a spirit of fraternity or neighbourliness without tackling the underlying injustice, these are likely to be rejected as patronizing or insulting, and black people will seek new ways of drawing attention to their sense of unrelieved injustice. Gus John puts the point forcefully:

> To wish to integrate with that which alienates and destroys you, rendering you less than a person, is madness. To accept the challenge to join it and change it from within, when it refuses to accept that you are there in your fullness and refuses to acknowledge the results

of interaction between you and it, is double madness (quoted in
Shallice, 1984, p. 11).

The sort of alienation from social institutions which this quotation typifies
may find expression, for example, in the acceptance of a significantly
different set of cultural values, such as Rastafarianism, or in the eruption of
violence and civil disturbances. In each case, however, the alienation appears
to have the same origin: a perception of injustice and a feeling that no redress
is possible.

To define racism as racial injustice has many advantages. First, it relates
the problem of racism to a fundamental value of our society, indeed, a
fundamental human value. Rawls (1972, p. 3) calls justice 'the first virtue of
social institutions' and as such not a matter for compromise. To define
racism in this way thus underlines the fact that the rejection of racism is not a
matter of interest and relevance only to black people, or to a minority of
extremists, for no morally educated person can be neutral about injustice.

Secondly, by showing racism to be a single manifestation of a broader
moral issue (justice), this definition avoids a narrow focus on racial matters to
the exclusion of all else. On the contrary, an active opposition to racial
injustice not only is fully compatible with working for justice in other areas,
but may also depend on the same 'unifying and overarching theoretical
framework' (Troyna and Williams, 1986, p. 105).

Thirdly, the definition prevents a simple polarization of society into
white and black. Martin Luther King recognized this when, speaking of
Montgomery, Alabama, he said,

> The tension in this city is not between white people and Negro
> people. The tension is, at bottom, between justice and injustice
> (quoted in Grigg, 1967, p. 182).

To campaign against racism could not involve always supporting the
interests of black people under all circumstances, because, as Richards (1980,
p. 5) points out in regard to feminism, a movement in support of a moral
principle such as justice can never take one side automatically, whether to
support women against men or blacks against whites. To campaign against
racism is to campaign against a certain type of injustice, even if that injustice
should be committed by black people against whites. In our present society,
however, it is clear that the elimination of racial injustice would improve the
lot of black people much more than that of whites.

Fourthly, the definition ensures that our understanding of racism is not
tied to a particular political theory or ideology. This is of course not to deny
that justice has far-reaching political implications and is politically mediated
and understood. But if opposition to racial injustice were dependent on a

specifically politicized form of anti-racism (for example, one that was explicitly anti-Tory, as recommended by Hatcher, 1985), two dangers might result. The first is that if the framework of political belief were to become outmoded or discredited, the opposition to racism might be left high and dry. The second is that a rejection of politicized anti-racism might lead to a denial that black people suffer from any sort of racism in our society; Honeyford and other members of the New Right have sometimes been in danger of falling into this trap. To define racism as injustice implies that what is wrong with it is ultimately a matter of moral, not political, concern, though of course the moral shortcoming may be seen in a political and economic context just as much as in a social, cultural or individual one; and if one particular group is always on the receiving end of the injustice, this may have grave social and political consequences.

Finally, to define racism as racial injustice not only increases our awareness of the complexity of the problem, but also provides a framework within which it can be discussed. Philosophical reflection on the nature of justice, at a personal, social and institutional level, would seem to be a vital part of our understanding of racism and how to tackle it. For example, we need to reflect on whether the principles of social justice imply that social benefits should be distributed according to people's rights, according to their deserts or according to their needs, or whether Rawls (1972) is correct that all three criteria can be accommodated in a single theory of justice. Such reflection should both inform and guide our response to racism, not only at the level of theory, but in practice as well. In the final section of this chapter, therefore, we examine briefly the way that in one particular context, that of education, a practical response to racism may be guided by the principles of justice.

TACKLING RACISM IN EDUCATION

The worst form of innovation, it has been said, is to keep things the same when circumstances have changed. And Rawls (1972, p. 3) reminds us that institutions must be reformed or abolished if they are unjust. It is therefore incumbent on us to reflect on the justice of our society's institutions and practices, particularly in view of the significant changes that have occurred in the racial composition of our society in the last four decades. Nowhere is this need stronger than in respect of education. Indeed, it would be unjust not to take account of the effect such social changes may have on the procedures and practices of educational institutions, for the latter encapsulate not only our present conceptions and values but also our future goals and aspirations.

An agenda for such reflection might include three items:

(a)   an appraisal of the racial justice of the whole educational system, including planning, decision-making and the structure of schools;

(b)   the best way to teach children about racial injustice;

(c)   the use of schools to create a better society in terms of racial justice; for, as Bradford's LAM 6/83, *Racialist Behaviour in Schools*, points out, 'racial harmony in the future will very largely be influenced by what happens in schools today'.

The third of these is easily the most problematic, at least conceptually, since it has political overtones which schools are right to be wary of. Schools have to tread a careful path between on the one hand the danger of focussing so strongly on the vision of a harmonious future society that present injustices are overlooked, and on the other the danger of encouraging a politicized type of anti-racism which is likely to get in the way of long-term harmony and fraternity. Certainly schools must avoid getting caught up in the kind of politicized in-fighting on racial issues which has intensified in Bradford since the departure of Honeyford, as described at the end of chapter four. The inclusion of teaching about racial issues on the curriculum must therefore be decided for moral and educational reasons, not political ones. Insofar as schools prepare pupils for social and political life as adult citizens, this is best done (as all LEA policy statements and documents on racial issues agree: *cf* Troyna and Williams, 1986, p. 82) by emphasizing such general principles as justice and democratic rights. Commitment to such fundamental moral principles is ruled into the agenda of schools on educational grounds, whereas more specific political commitments are ruled out. This explains why Jeffcoate (quoted in Nixon, 1985) is wrong to argue that young members of the National Front should be allowed a voice in schools; for the overt post-reflective gut racism which they espouse is manifestly unjust, and schools cannot be neutral about injustice. On the other hand, the ideological anti-Tory stance which Hatcher (1985) and others have claimed is an intrinsic part of anti-racism is politically controversial, and schools would be breaching a basic educational principle (the avoidance of indoctrination) if they were to encourage pupils to adopt such a stance or to accept its tenets as fact.

In an article already referred to, Parekh (1985, p. 23) has argued that schools cannot spearhead a political movement, and that if they tried to do so would be in danger of losing their educational character and becoming 'an arena of struggle between large social and political forces' over which they can exercise no control. It is thus evident that the contribution of schools to (c), the creation of a better society, cannot be directly political but can only be achieved through ensuring (a) that they are based on justice themselves and (b) that their children come to understand and develop a commitment to the principles of racial justice. The present chapter concludes with a brief sketch of the implications of these two points.

(a) Racial Justice in Educational Institutions

Schools can hardly teach justice successfully if they embody injustice in their own structure, organization and curriculum. The forms in which racial injustice is most likely to be found in schools are not to be defined in legal terms (the measure by which Honeyford (1986b) concludes that Britain is not a racist society), but in moral terms. These forms may include, for example, the implicit undervaluing of the history and culture of racial minorities; turning a blind eye to racial insults and other forms of harassment; basing expectations of pupil achievement on racial stereotypes; and consciously or unconsciously reproducing assumptions of white superiority.

Schools are therefore under an obligation to reflect on the way they are organized and on the assumptions which underpin their organization. Such reflection must include all those who are involved in any form of educational decision-making, including the DES, LEAs, examination boards, teacher trainers, textbook writers and school governors, as well as teachers themselves. Such reflection must also take in all aspects of educational decision-making, from the broader political context to the detailed planning of individual schools, including organization and staffing, curriculum, materials and resources, teacher attitudes and expectations, pupil achievement, the school ethos, the hidden curriculum and the school's aims. To take an example from Drummond Middle School, one of the school's aims is

> To encourage understanding and tolerance of diverse religions, cultures and races, whilst maintaining a sense of the school's cultural and historical coherence by stressing the pupils' British identity and the primacy of the English language.

Reflection on this aim would doubtless require both an examination of the concepts of 'British identity' and 'tolerance' and a consideration of whether there is any chance of achieving such an aim without first eradicating all racial injustice within the school. The sort of reflection being described here will to some extent be an individual matter, but should also involve discussion and consultation, particularly with minority groups. In-service courses might provide a suitable forum for such reflection and consultation for teachers and others, but even if they are designed specifically as Racism Awareness courses, they must be seen to promote the interests of racial justice, not of black groups as such. The best race relations training officers will be those who can stimulate such reflection; the contribution that philosophers may be able to make should not be underestimated. As Hare (1963) points out,

> This much can be claimed for philosophy, that it is sometimes easier
> to bring something about if we understand clearly what it is we are
> trying to do (p. 224).

If the aim of the reflection is to ensure that the structure of educational institutions is consistent with the moral principles they teach, the reflection will involve a willingness to adapt and change where necessary. The possible changes will fall into two categories: those which justice demands only when there are pupils from racial minority groups in the school under consideration, and those which are appropriate for all schools irrespective of their racial composition. Into the former category fall cultural provisions such as teaching minority languages and serving *halal* meat for school dinners as well as more clearly racial provisions such as a counselling service for victims of racial abuse. Into the latter category come the rejection of textbooks which carry the hidden message of white racial superiority, and the determination to make use in the learning process of the experiences that *all* children bring to school. These two categories clearly pull in different directions, for the first is concerned with treating members of racial groups differently when there are relevant differences to justify such treatment, the second with treating them the same when there are no such relevant differences. When Honeyford writes of the danger that multi-racial education might 'help to generate a wholly artificial and harmful colour consciousness in our schools' (1982d), he fails to make this distinction. However much we may wish schools to concentrate on initiating children into what is of permanent importance to human beings, they cannot do so in a way which ignores the contingent circumstances of their social environment. In an ideal world, people would perhaps no longer find their identity as members of a particular race or culture. The principle of justice helps us to envisage such a world, but also provides us with rules for organizing our present imperfect world.

(b) Teaching Children about Racial Justice

Certain methods are excluded for educational reasons: indoctrination, political propaganda, and encouraging children to make *political* commitments to anti-racism before they understand the underlying moral principles. Some of the examples of consciousness-raising among primary children quoted with approval by Burgess (1986) certainly fail this test:

Me and Eleanor was looking at the *Dressing Up* book and we found out that there was twelve brown and thirty-nine white and it is not fair (p. 143).

Teaching children about racial justice has five essential elements. These are not stages in the sense that one is superseded by the next, for they may all go on at the same time, though they are probably initiated in the order listed.

1. *Moral Training* This may take the negative form of correcting overtly racist behaviour, even in very young children, and the positive form of encouraging easy social relations between children of different races. It also includes attitudes which children pick up from their teachers and other role models.

2. *The Transmission of Knowledge, Understanding and Attitudes* The provision of accurate information about racial and cultural differences, including a historical perspective, will help to discourage the acceptance of racial myths and stereotypes.

3. *The Development of Moral Commitment* An understanding of the principle of justice and of its place as a fundamental value of our society may involve the examination of a range of different examples (not only ones to do with race). But children must be helped to develop not only an understanding of justice but also a commitment to it, and this will involve the development of other dispositions and qualities of character as well.

4. *The Development of Critical Awareness* As children learn to question attitudes and assumptions, to reflect on their own and other people's beliefs and to become autonomous individuals, so they will be in a position to assess critically both what they read and what they earlier accepted on authority. To the extent that this development of critical awareness is successful, teachers do not need to worry about exposing pupils, for example, to literature which exemplifies attitudes to race which we no longer find acceptable. Indeed, when pupils reach this stage, they are capable of showing teachers where they are wrong.

5. *The Development of Political Understanding* This stage must come last because it depends on the critical application of factual knowledge and moral commitment to current social problems and issues. It implies a willingness to act.

Even if this list proves to be not particularly controversial in principle, there is bound to be very considerable disagreement over the way it is to be put into practice. One example of such disagreement will help to provide a link between this chapter and the next. It concerns who decides in what way overtly racist behaviour is to be corrected. We noted in chapter two the bitter clash between Bradford headteachers and the LEA over the latter's LAM 6/83 which prescribed specific procedures for responding to and recording racialist behaviour in schools. The effect of the mandatory procedures was to diminish the autonomy and discretion of heads, who provided a number of very persuasive arguments against implementing the LAM. But again questions of principle are involved. To what extend are heads and other teachers merely employees who are accountable to their LEAs, and to what extent are they professionals, accountable only to their clients and to their own professional body? How far are they free to criticize the decisions made by their LEAs which affect the day-to-day running of their schools? To these questions we now turn in chapter seven.

7 Free Speech and Accountability

To Honeyford himself, the question of free speech was at the very heart of the affair. In a letter to the *Yorkshire Post* shortly after the affair erupted (19 March 1984), he wrote:

At rock-bottom this is not a debate about multi-racial schooling. It is about that great but fragile British tradition – intellectual freedom.

Elsewhere, he called on 'all who believe in free speech as passionately as I do' to lend their support (1984c). In this way he gained the sympathy of many who, while not necessarily agreeing with what he said, nevertheless believed in his right to say it. He was presented in large sections of the press as a man of courage, who was prepared to stand up and say what he thought about racial issues in the country regardless of the consequences.

To his opponents, on the other hand, this talk of free speech was a red herring. What was at issue was Honeyford's accountability to parents and pupils, to his employers and to the local community. On this view, his criticisms of ethnic minorities had caused him to lose the confidence of many parents, who no longer wished to entrust their children to him. Council officers also queried whether he could carry out his responsibilities as an LEA employee when he was so implacably opposed to crucial LEA policies. Honeyford's own view of accountability, according to which he was obliged to *take account of* the wishes of interested parties while retaining a high degree of professional autonomy in the organization and running of his school, was thus under challenge from a stronger view of accountability in which he could be *called to account* by his employers or parents.

Free speech and accountability have both become very topical issues in education in recent years, but it is clear that different people have used these terms in different ways and that the terms are in danger, like 'racism', of becoming political slogans. The interplay between the two concepts and the

Honeyford affair forms the subject of the present chapter. It is hoped that an examination of the Honeyford affair will help to illustrate and clarify the concepts, and equally, that a clarification of the two concepts will throw light on some of the main issues in the affair.

1. FREE SPEECH

Honeyford's arguments about free speech have their origin in his practical experience as a teacher in multi-racial Bradford. He claims that the 'multi-racial lobby' has become a powerful influence on both national and local policy and has convinced many people that there is a broad agreement on racial issues 'from which dissent must be due either to ignorance or malice' (1984d). The problem is that his own experience does not accord with the current orthodoxies, yet he feels under strong moral pressure to remain silent. The crucial *Salisbury Review* article (1984a) starts with an expansion of this problem:

> As the headteacher of a school in the middle of a predominantly Asian area, I am often...the recipient of vehement criticism whenever I question some of the current educational orthodoxies connected with race. It is very difficult to write honestly and openly of my experiences, and the reflections they evoke, since the race relations lobby is extremely powerful in the state education service. The propaganda generated by multi-racial zealots is now augmented by a growing bureaucracy of race in local authorities. And this makes freedom of speech difficult to maintain. By exploiting the enormous tolerance traditional in this country, the race lobby has so managed to induce and maintain feelings of guilt in the well-disposed majority, that decent people are not only afraid of voicing certain thoughts, they are uncertain even of their right to think those thoughts. They are intimidated not only by their fear of giving offence by voicing their own reasonable concerns about the inner cities, but by the necessity of conducting the debate in a language which is dishonest.

Elsewhere, he focusses not so much on the moral pressure he feels himself under from the 'race lobby' as on their refusal to countenance the expression of 'an alternative or unorthodox viewpoint' (1985c). He sees both the mentality and the rhetoric of the 'race lobby' as a 'threat to intellectual freedom' (*ibid.*) and argues that

> there can be no more powerful criticism of any doctrine than that it cannot bear to have its assertions examined (1986b).

He rejects the notion that there should be a 'taboo' on any subject (except, presumably, those expressly restricted by legislation) in a 'society such as ours which professes to permit free speech' (1984d). He therefore pledges himself to attempt to open up a genuine debate on racial issues by seeking a more honest climate for discussion and by challenging 'the dubious arguments of vested interest – both professional and political – which dominate the debate' (*ibid.*). He acknowledges that to do so is to take a huge risk: he may have his remarks distorted or misconstrued, he may give offence to minorities, he may even lose his job. But he is not prepared to allow these dangers to stand in the way of 'the free and open exchange of opinion on these vital matters' (quoted in *Telegraph and Argus*, 15 March 1984).

It appears that Honeyford has his opponents trapped: anyone who does not welcome his alternative, unorthodox viewpoint can be branded as an enemy to free speech. Indeed, when Billingham (1985) argues that the debate has more to do with Honeyford's running of his school and the right of the local community to some respect than with his right to free speech, Honeyford's reply concludes that 'those like Mr Billingham...do little to advance the principle of free and open debate' (1985c). Several events both during and after the affair served to confirm in Honeyford's mind that the principle of freedom of expression was at stake. One example was the insistence by the Director of Educational Services in Bradford in late 1984 that all future articles by Honeyford should be submitted to his office prior to publication; another was Bristol Polytechnic's decision to refuse permission for him to address a meeting there after he had been invited by the Conservative Club. Nor was it simply the principle of freedom of expression which appeared to be at risk. When Honeyford writes that by winning an inspection of his school, his opponents succeeded in converting 'an issue of beliefs into a question of my competence' (1984d), he introduces the even more fundamental principle of freedom of opinion. There is some evidence that the local authority has sometimes engaged in attempts to change teachers' opinions and attitudes; this emerges in the memorandum produced by the Racism Awareness Training Officers discussed in chapter four, and in the confidential report issued by the Director of Educational Services to the Schools Education Sub-committee in March 1985, which says,

> There are still concerns about the appropriateness of the philosophy that the head has outlined... He has not in my view demonstrated any marked change of attitude or commitment to the overall objectives of the sub-committee, particularly in the field of race relations.

Increasingly, both Honeyford and his supporters have talked in terms of 'Thought Police', whose task is to ensure that all teachers have the '"correct", officially sponsored attitudes towards "multi-culturalism" and race' (1986j).

An initial response to these claims is that behind the very obvious strength of feeling with which they are expressed there is some confusion over what the principle of free speech is, how it is justified, and what kind of constraints may be brought to bear on it. First, it is not clear whether Honeyford is arguing from within a legal, a political or a moral framework. Secondly, it is not clear whether it is ideas or people, policies or cultures which he is demanding the right openly to criticize, and whether he thinks that the same kind of constraints (if any at all) are applicable in each case. Thirdly, it is not clear if he sees free speech as an end in itself, or as a means to an end. Fourthly, it is not clear if he is writing as an individual citizen, or as an expert, and whether any claim to speak as an authority on the grounds of extensive experience as a teacher should be tempered with greater professional reticence and discretion than might be the case if the views expressed were merely an instinctive, unreflective response to a situation by a private individual. He appears not to have paid adequate attention to the difficulty for a headteacher of separating mere private opinion from the constraints of holding public office.

It is tempting to question, particularly in view of the large number of articles that Honeyford has published on racial issues in education and the wide publicity given to his views, whether he has any grounds at all for claiming that his freedom of speech is being restricted by his opponents; and to conclude that the appeal to free speech (like the strongly emotive language in some of his articles) is being used rhetorically, to help him to take the high moral ground in his arguments about race and multi-cultural education. It is equally possible to argue, however, that he is doing more than this, and is in fact seeking to make a genuine contribution to the political debate about free speech. But either way, the Honeyford affair forces us to reflect on political disagreements over the principle of free speech and the legitimacy of an appeal to the principle in any given context.

From a legal perspective, the principle of freedom of expression is to set out in the European Convention on Human Rights and Fundamental Freedoms which is considered binding on signatory countries such as Britain. Article 10 (which contains similar wording to the earlier Universal Declaration of Human Rights) reads:

1. Everyone has the right to freedom of expression. This right shall include freedom to hold opinions and to receive and impart information and ideas without interference by public authority and regardless of frontiers. This article shall not prevent states from requiring the licensing of broadcasting, television or cinema enterprises.

2. The exercise of these freedoms, since it carries with it duties and responsibilities, may be subject to such formalitites and conditions, restrictions or penalties as are prescribed by law and are necessary in a democratic society in the interests of national security, territorial integrity or public safety, for the prevention of disorder or crime, for the protection of health or morals, for the protection of the reputation or rights of others, for preventing the disclosure of information received in confidence or for maintaining the authority and impartiality of the judiciary.

There are three main kinds of justification for this principle of freedom of expression: the first is that the truth is most likely to emerge when there is an open market-place of ideas with no restriction in the expression of any idea; the second is that free speech is necessary in a democracy so that no information is withheld from the electorate which turns out to be relevant to the decision-making process and so that citizens can criticize government officials and hold them to account; the third is that free speech is an intrinsic good, the removal of which involves a loss of dignity and autonomy for the individual. Schauer (1982) has provided a careful critical examination of these three justifications of free speech, and there is no need to rehearse all his arguments in detail here. However, it will be helpful to look more closely at the political dimensions of the principle of free speech, for it is primarily on the political level that most of Honeyford's arguments are expressed.

From a political perspective, there are many different shades of emphasis on the principle of free speech. For the purposes of the present analysis, however, I intend to concentrate on just four, two of which are inside a liberal framework and two outside. For each I shall select a representative proponent.

On the Outside Right is the view which subordinates individual freedom, of whatever kind, to the authority of the institution, and particularly to the authority of established government. This authority is embodied in the law, and more generally in the fundamental values of our society, and any freedom which claims not to be subject to the constraints of such authority is illusory. Scruton, in *The Meaning of Conservatism* (1984) upholds this view and argues that

constraint should be upheld, until it can be shown that society is not damaged by its removal (p. 17).

This implies that however highly free speech is valued, it cannot be identified as a principle separately from the institutions in which it originates and by which it is defined. Scruton thus concludes that

there cannot be freedom of speech in a healthy society, if by freedom is meant the absolute untrammelled right to say what one wishes and utter one's views on anything, at any time, and anywhere (*ibid.*).

On the Inside Right is the view that freedom is the highest value and that freedom is to be understood in terms of the individual will being unimpeded except by the right of others to similar freedom. When individuals are not allowed room to exercise their autonomy, this impedes their capacity for rational action and effectively denies their separate existence. Thus the political order, which exists for the benefit of individuals, must not interfere with the framework of rights which enables individuals to exercise autonomous choice. Nozick provides an extreme example of this view in *Anarchy, State and Utopia* (1974) where he argues that morality is grounded in a set of individual rights which 'express the inviolability of persons' (p. 32). These include the right to life and freedom from assault, the right to ownership, enjoyment and transfer of property, the right to be free from all forms of coercion, and the right to protect oneself against the violation of one's rights. The last of these may be transferred to the state, but the state's function should not go beyond the protection of individuals against violence, fraud, theft or breaches of contract. According to Nozick, the state cannot justifiably interfere in a social system to relieve suffering, satisfy needs, balance out inequalities or provide for the general welfare, but only to protect the above rights. Outside the state's function as guardian of these rights, the individual has a general or residual right to liberty. Freedom of speech on this view is a component of general liberty (*cf* Schauer, 1982, ch. 4); in Berlin's terms (1969), it is 'an absence of obstructions on roads along which a man can decide to walk'. The Inside Right view of freedom of speech is not necessarily tied to such an extreme libertarian view as Nozick's, however. There are two arguments from a broader liberal perspective which support the principle of free speech. First, insofar as liberalism embodies respect for individuals as individuals rather than as members of a social group, its emphasis on individual choice is bound to result in individual differences. Such diversity, as Schauer (1982, p. 61) points out, 'lies at the core of liberalism'. When such diversity is freely expressed, it increases the range of alternatives available to the individual, and at a more objective level, it increases the chances of recognizing weaknesses in established views and thus of advancing knowledge. Secondly, the liberal emphasis on rationality and on individual choice points to the argument that individuals need to be as well informed as possible. Thus Scanlon (1972) asserts that to restrict the flow of information to individuals may prevent them from hearing all sides of an issue and thus from making the best informed choices, whether individually or collectively. The principle of free speech may thus be derived from liberal arguments relating to the autonomy of the individual.

On the Inside Left is the view that the supreme value is equality of concern and respect. Dworkin (1977), for example, holds that there is no general right to liberty; people only have specific rights such as freedom of speech, freedom of worship, freedom of political activity and free choice in personal and sexual relations, and these specific rights are derived from the fundamental duty of governments to treat citizens with equal concern and respect. This fundamental duty gives governments wide-ranging inter-ventionist powers, including the right to prohibit racial or sexual discrimi-nation, to enforce desegregation, even to allow reverse discrimination: for such interventions are directed towards the equal treatment of all individuals. Other forms of intervention, such as preventing an individual from speaking his mind on political issues, may well improve the general welfare, but at the cost of a loss of equal concern and respect for certain individuals; on Dworkin's view, such forms of intervention are not permissible, and the citizen is protected from them by a series of specific rights, as listed above. Concerning free speech, Dworkin (1977) writes,

> the government is not entitled to constrain liberty of speech, for example, whenever it thinks that would improve the general welfare (p. 270).

Schauer (1982) reaches a similar conclusion by a different route when he discusses the extent to which a minority is morally obliged to obey a particular law which has been enacted by the majority, overruling the objections by the minority. He argues that

> One reason for precluding the majority from withdrawing the minority's freedom to dissent is that the minority's right to object, to attempt to influence the majority, to have some say in the formulation of final policy, provides the moral basis for binding everyone to the rule ultimately adopted (p. 42).

On this view, individual dignity and equality requires the moral right to equal participation, and this moral right presupposes freedom of speech.

On the Outside Left is the view that the rights of individuals may sometimes be overruled by considerations of the general interest, and in particular that the principle of free speech should in some cases 'take second place to other imperatives' (Arblaster, 1974, p. 168). Marcuse (1969), for example, sees existing political liberties and liberal values as a cloak hiding the reality of manipulation and repression. These render ordinary citizens impotent and prevent them from being open to rational moral persuasion because they have been subjected to 'the indoctrination processes of affluent capitalism' (Carter, 1973, p. 132). The attempt by the right-wing British press in 1986 to discredit the anti-racist policies of certain London councils by publishing reports that they were banning the use of black bin-liners and the singing of 'Baa Baa Black Sheep' because they were 'racist', illustrates the way that the media can attempt to influence independent judgment by the creation of 'pseudo-events'. Marcuse argues that it is not possible to tackle such grievances through existing political channels, and that direct confrontation is needed in order to bring to light the manipulation and underlying repressiveness of the existing system. In his view, tolerance is a relative, not an absolute, value and is no longer justified when it is used to perpetuate repression and injustice. On these grounds, he argues that free speech should not be allowed to racists, fascists or other proponents of inhuman policies, and that disruptive action in such cases may be the only valid response. Though there is some uncertainty about Marcuse's position (*cf* Bridges, 1982a, pp. 50–1; Skillen, 1982, p. 140–1), it appears that he accepts that free speech and other freedoms would not vanish permanently under the radical socialism which he envisages, but would re-emerge in a different form (*cf* Carter, 1973, p. 132). Freedom of speech under contemporary liberalism is seen as providing little more than a safety valve for letting off steam; in the view of the Outside Left, true political liberty must be subordinated to the constraints of political principles. There are obvious parallels here with the views of the Outside Right.

It should be noted that the nomenclature I have used to identify these four political positions relating to the principle of free speech is primarily designed to distinguish between views that are inside a liberal framework and views that are outside. The terms should not be taken to imply, for example, that the Inside Right view is necessarily less politically extreme than the Outside Right. On the contrary, there is every likelihood that far right political groups such as the National Front would be more attracted to the Inside Right's strong emphasis on individual freedom than to the Outside Right's emphasis on governmental restraint, at least while they remain a minority group with little political influence. Nor should the terms be identified too readily with party political allegiance. While Scruton presents what I have called the Outside Right view as essentially conservative, this does not mean that it is the official view of the Conservative party. Indeed, the Conservative leadership which steered the multi-cultural and race relations policies through Bradford Council in the early 1980s exemplifies the Inside Left view, giving priority to the fair and equal treatment of all groups. More recently, the local Conservative party has shown more sympathy with the Inside Right position; their manifesto for the 1987 elections to Bradford Council specifically mentions that in the field of race relations they will 'allow debate on alternatives and acknowledge dissenting views' (*Telegraph and Argus*, 10 April 1987). However, the Press guidelines issued to employees of Bradford Council in 1987 under its Labour leadership, as described at the end of chapter four, appear to have more in common with the Outside Left position. Nationally, the Conservative party seems to be veering increasingly towards the Inside Right; as Scruton (1984) himself admits, the party

> has begun to see itself as the defender of individual freedom against the encroachments of the state, concerned to return to the people their natural right of choice... The concept of freedom – and in particular, such constitutionally derived freedoms as the freedom of speech, the freedom of assembly, the 'freedom of conscience' and the 'right to strike' – this concept has until recently been the only one that has been presented by contemporary Conservatism as a contribution to the ideological battle which it assumes to be raging (pp. 15, 17).

Nowhere is the Conservative preoccupation with freedom seen more clearly than in section 43 of the 1986 Education (No. 2) Act which obliges universities and polytechnics to take reasonable steps to ensure that no guest speaker is denied free speech 'on any grounds connected with the views or beliefs of that individual'. In effect, this requires universities to provide a platform for any speaker however offensive his or her views may be so long as they are within the law. No doubt Scruton would agree with Zellick's (1987) dismissal of this 'absolutist' view of freedom of speech as 'wholly unprecedented and quite out of keeping with this country's traditions and practices'.

Although Honeyford at one stage (when discussing his opponents' rights) quotes Burke with approval to the effect that 'liberty, too, must be limited in order to be possessed' (1985c), he does not generally follow his mentor Scruton in dismissing the present Conservative emphasis on the freedom of the individual as a 'passing fashion' (1984, p. 16). On the contrary, his staunch defence of personal freedom as a fundamental value is an archetypal example of the Inside Right position. He strongly opposes any policy or practice tinged with suppression (hence his dismay at the Swann Committee's dropping of research it had commissioned into the fortunes of successful black children) and appears genuinely concerned about the lower priority given to freedom of expression by groups with views to the left of his own. In fact, Honeyford's positive arguments about free speech can be seen as a defence of the Inside Right position against both Inside and Outside Left, and as an example of the kind of free speech he is advocating. As such, it is a valid contribution to a political debate, although it should be noted that Honeyford's position logically requires that he must recognize and respect the right of those who do not agree with him to argue equally strongly for their own position.

The other side of Honeyford's argument about free speech, however, involves the claim that the 'multi-racial lobby' is obstructing free speech by seeking to make racial issues a 'taboo' subject. This claim seems to be based on a particular view of what constitute legitimate constraints on free speech, but the argument is confused because it is not clear either whom precisely Honeyford is attacking under the heading of the 'multi-racial lobby' or on what grounds he is attacking them. At some points his attack is directed against anti-racist campaigners; but he does not recognize that their opportunities to suppress free speech are limited and that they themselves are to a large extent dependent on the principle of freedom of expression in the presentation of their case to those in authority. At other points he directly criticizes ethnic minorities and their cultures and argues against the assumption which he believes to be operating in some quarters that the toleration of minority groups requires their immunity from criticism; but he does not acknowledge that the mutual respect between parents and teachers which is necessary for a successful school is likely to be damaged if teachers express public criticism of the parents and their culture. At other points again, he attacks educational decision-makers, and local councils and LEAs in particular; but he fails to acknowledge that his right as an individual to criticize their policies must be balanced against the Council's mandate from the local electorate both to formulate policies and to ensure that their employees carry them out. Let us look at these three targets of Honeyford's attack in closer detail.

(1) Insofar as Honeyford is attacking anti-racist campaigners who may engage in direct action to achieve their ends, he fails to distinguish between the kind of protest which seeks to draw attention to the erosion or ineffectiveness of specific liberal values in society (such as the equal treatment of all the members of that society) and the kind which seeks to use confrontation as a means of expediting a wished-for revolution. The former type of protest is in keeping with the Inside Left position, the latter with the Outside Left. The crucial question therefore seems to be at what stage protest becomes a potential enemy to free speech, rather than an expression of it.

Much that was written on this subject in the aftermath of the student unrest in the late 1960s (for example, Carter, 1973; Arblaster, 1974; Honderich, 1976) is relevant to our understanding of the campaign against Honeyford (I am here assuming that we can take this campaign as an example of the type of protest which Honeyford claims is likely to damage the cause of free speech). Kent (1976, p. 42f), for example, distinguishes four techniques of protest, all of which were used in the campaign against Honeyford: attention-grabbing publicity, seen for example in the DPAC's organization of a demonstration outside Drummond Middle School to coincide with the visit to Bradford of a film crew from the BBC programme *Panorama*; legal resistance, seen in the request from 238 parents for their children to be transferred to another school; illegal resistance, seen in the practice of keeping children away from school, and in the refusal of permission for Council health and safety officers to inspect the premises of the alternative school that the DPAC set up; and violence, seen in the attack on an Asian parent taking his children to school during the boycott.

To what extent does the use of such techniques suggest that the campaign against Honeyford was an unjustifiable affront to his right to freedom of expression? Various arguments might be marshalled in support of such a conclusion: in particular, that the techniques of protest used are undemocratic and irrational, that they display intolerance and that violence is never justified in civil protest. In reply, however, it may be argued that violence is not always aimed at confrontation and revolution, but may simply be an extension of other forms of dissent (*cf* Marcuse, 1969, pp. 130–1). In the campaign against Honeyford, violence did not seem to be an intrinsic part of the protest at all, but an occasional and spontaneous overflow of zeal in the response to what were perceived to be provocative and offensive statements by Honeyford himself. Indeed, although a sense of disgust and outrage were considered by the campaigners to be appropriate moral responses to what Honeyford wrote (and were perceived as no more emotional or intemperate than the head's own language in his *Salisbury Review* articles), the high level of feeling generated rarely became detached from its rational underpinnings (i.e. a considered rejection of the intolerance and denial of equal concern and respect for all which the articles were thought to typify). The charge that the protest was undemocratic is hard to make stick, since the campaigners were at pains to make clear that they were demonstrating in support of, not against, the Council's democratically agreed policies. Jenny Woodward (1985), the chairperson of the DPAC, writes,

> To the suggestion that the action committee is out to curtail freedom of speech, we would reply that no one is being criticized for expressing their feelings. But once certain feelings have been expressed by an employee it begs the following questions: Are those feelings in accordance with the agreed policies of the employers? Are we as consumers of the educational services, paid for by public funds, bound to accept the attitudes of one headteacher who finds himself in conflict with the policies he is under contract to follow?

If the impetus behind the campaign against Honeyford really was a desire for the fair and equal treatment for all rather than the wish to limit the free expression of political ideas, then this view is closer to the position of the Inside Left than the Outside Left. On this view, Council policies were supported by the protestors since they upheld the same principles, and this support was expressed in the desire to call to account an employee avowedly opposed to those policies. No doubt the protest would attract some campaigners bent on confrontation and radical change, but the principles on which this particular campaign was run appear to involve an acceptance of free speech rather than a rejection of it. Thus in spite of its occasional regrettable use of force, the campaign against Honeyford, like his own articles, may be judged to be a valid form of political debate. This is of course not to claim that all activities of anti-racists are necessarily equally unimpeachable; each case must be examined on its own merits.

(2)   Honeyford's insistence on the right to criticize ethnic minorities and their cultures raises other difficulties. He claims,

> No one is immune from criticism nor is any group or community. But...(certain anti-racists) appear to believe that the ethnic minorities are beyond and above criticism. This not only violates the notion of genuine liberty, it is deeply patronizing, since it suggests that the ethnic minorities are not responsible for their attitudes and behaviour. It also suggests the ethnic minorities have access to an unspecified but ever-present right to special protections not afforded to other citizens. The majority population rightly resents the double standards this sort of special pleading implies. My strictures on the ethnic minorities arise not from 'stereotyping'...but on observed behaviour and published information. I believe that the race relations lobby – the mentality it expresses and the rhetoric it generates – represents a serious threat to intellectual freedom (1985c).

In part, this passage involves a restatement of certain fundamental liberal principles. On the one hand, the liberal is committed to the pursuit of truth in all its forms and to free critical debate as the most rational means of advancing this pursuit; this implies a willingness to denounce falsehood and evil, not to treat them as though they did not matter. On the other hand, the liberal is committed to an open, pluralist, democratic society where there is a maximum tolerance of diversity; such tolerance implies a willingness to let others speak, a willingness to give them a fair hearing and an openness to the possibility of being persuaded by them (*cf* Skillen, 1982, pp. 140–1).

It is not these principles which Honeyford's opponents object to, however, for they are fundamental to our liberal democratic heritage. Their objection is to the way he applies them to ethnic minorities in Britain, which involves two dubious empirical claims: (a) that ethnic minorities are intolerant of, and wish to silence, any legitimate criticisms directed towards themselves, and (b) that his own criticisms are legitimate because they are based on 'observed behaviour and published information'. One example from the list given in chapter three of what was found offensive in Honeyford's articles will serve to cast doubt on claim (b). In *The Salisbury*

Review, Honeyford asserts that 'educational ambition and the values to support it are conspicuously absent' from 'the vast majority of West Indian homes' (1984a). Clearly he has not *observed* the vast majority of West Indian homes, but even if there is published socio-economic data which could be related to the complex notion of educational ambition, he has attempted neither to explain this nor even to refer to it. In spite of his denial, it is hard to avoid the conclusion that this is an example of stereotyping as it was defined in chapter six, involving generalizations drawn from limited experience in a way which takes inadequate account of individual variation. The fact that Honeyford's articles contain even a few such unjustified and unjust assertions and innuendoes (among a larger number of valid and perceptive arguments) raises the question of what sort of response is appropriate. Insofar as the assertions are an insult to the dignity of ethnic minorities and fail to treat them with equality of concern and respect, it is not surprising that they were found offensive and helped to drive the ethnic minorities in Bradford into an alliance with the anti-racists in their political campaign against Honeyford.

But the question is whether ethnic minorities would be justified in seeking to curb the expression of unjust and offensive assertions. To put the question more concisely, must one tolerate the intolerable? Mill (1972b) provides us with a starting point when he describes the principle

> that the sole end for which mankind is warranted, individually or collectively, in interfering with the liberty of action of any of their number, is self-protection. That the only purpose for which power can be rightfully exercised over any member of a civilized community, against his will, is to prevent harm to others...He cannot rightfully be compelled to do or forbear because..., in the opinion of others, to do so would be wise, or even right. These are good reasons for remonstrating with him, or reasoning with him, or persuading him, or entreating him, but not for compelling him, or visiting him with any evil in case he do otherwise... The only part of the conduct of anyone, for which he is amenable to society, is that which concerns others. In the part which merely concerns himself, his independence is, of right, absolute (pp. 72–3).

If we accept this principle, the question is whether the expression of unjust and offensive assertions has more in common with the holding of unpopular or dissenting opinions (as in the case of the National Front member, Patrick Harrington, at North London Polytechnic in 1984: *cf Education*, 15 June 1984), or with the performance of unjust or offensive actions (such as polluting the atmosphere or practising cardio-vascular surgery without a medical degree: *cf* Schauer, 1982, p. 64). In the former case, Mill has provided very compelling arguments that individual freedom is paramount; and Sieghart (1985, p. 142) shows that in law the freedom to communicate information and ideas is not confined to those that are inoffensive (*cf* Skillen, 1982, pp. 140–2; Harris, 1982a). In the latter case, however, the need to prevent harm to others may justify suppression.

Almond (1987) proposes as a solution a 'toleration continuum':

> a continuum that stretches from opinion through the expression of opinion, to proselytizing for an opinion, to inciting to action, and finally to action itself, (p. 55).

and argues that the line which marks the limits of tolerance must be drawn before action and incitement to action 'at that point where the principle of protection of the defenceless must take priority'. On this view, since Honeyford's articles in *The Salisbury Review* are clearly an example of 'proselytizing for an opinion', his claim to the right to freedom of expression is justified. Almond also discusses the question of the freedom of association of those whose views are offensive or deeply repugnant to others (*ibid.*, pp. 54–5) and she concludes that if separation proves the only solution, it should be brought about 'by the objector removing himself or herself rather than by the expulsion of the person whose presence is found offensive'. This view would appear to leave Honeyford doubly secure: secure in his job, and secure in his right to criticize ethnic minorities.

But this conclusion fails to take account of Norris's point that to demonstrate the desirability of freedom of expression is not the same as demonstrating that there should be 'no restrictions concerning who is to be permitted to voice an opinion' (1976, p. 16). Let us take an extreme example, of a headmaster who writes an article arguing the case for the repeal of the law against paederasty. Let us suppose also that his running of his school is carried out with unimpeachable integrity, so that the principle of protecting the defenceless from harm is not invoked, and the article is simply an instance of 'proselytizing for an opinion'. Even so, the parents of children at the school might be justified in expressing a lack of confidence in the headmaster and in not wishing their children to be under his care. This would not be tantamount to denying his freedom of expression as an individual, but would be a reaction to his failure, as a person in a position of authority and control, to live up to the responsibilities and duties attached to that position. For it would appear that the right of headteachers to free speech, like that of doctors, social workers and priests, is to some extent circumscribed by their role. Honeyford himself writes that

> citizenship in a free society not only confers certain rights and privileges; it also carries with it duties and responsibilities. This

mixture of human rights and legal and moral duties seems to me to be the essence of liberty in a free society (1985c).

If this applies to citizenship, how much more must it apply to positions of trust and authority in our society.

In the opinion of a large part of the ethnic minority communities served by his school, Honeyford's insensitive and irresponsible promulgation of unjustified opinions provided sufficient grounds for them to lose confidence in him as a headteacher and to wish their children not to be taught by him any more. 238 parents were prepared to request that their children should be transferred to another school, and in these circumstances his employers, the LEA, were bound to consider whether it would be in the interests of all concerned to remove the head rather than to transfer so many children. However, nothing in this process of calling Honeyford to account implies either that he was being denied his right to freedom of expression as an individual or that the ethnic minorities considered themselves to be beyond or above criticism.

(3)   Finally, Honeyford demands the democratic right as a citizen to criticize LEA policies. This demand is based on the liberal belief that the freedoms of speech, expression and the press are fundamental to any free, open and democratic society, as Sieghart (1985) points out:

> They are needed in order to restrain the excesses of rulers by making their subjects aware of abuses, corruption or incompetence, both in government and in other organizations; they serve to promote public debate about policies and issues that concern everyone (p. 142).

However, in Honeyford's case, the situation is complicated by two factors. First, the policies he criticizes were agreed by the democratic processes of local government; indeed, as we saw earlier, they had the agreement of all the political parties on Bradford Council. Secondly, Honeyford was a public employee responsible for putting those policies into effect. He could, of course, justifiably argue that he had a right as a professional to participate in the shaping of the policies, but it is clear that once the Council had agreed on specific policies, it could not be expected to be neutral on the issue of whether they are carried out. What Schauer (1982) says about the state seems to apply equally to local government:

> It seems more reasonable to hold that if a law is indeed just, then the state is politically and morally authorized to enforce compliance (p. 70).

Faced with an employee whose views are diametrically opposed to those underlying official policies, the least an LEA could do would be to check that the employee's views were not adversely affecting his or her capacity or willingness to carry out the policies. The LEA might also question the appropriateness of leaving responsibility for carrying out the policies in the hands of someone who had publicly expressed opposition to them. Neither of these responses involves the denial of free speech to an individual, however; they are more to do with the accountability of a public employee, as Bradford's Director of Educational Services points out:

> We do not seek to curtail staff's freedoms. If a member of the teaching staff does wish to adopt a public stance on matters related to his work, then our advice to them is that public office holders do have responsibilities as well as rights. If what they say affects parental confidence, it should cause them to reflect on the wisdom of such a stance. It may result in a check to see that it does not affect the provision in the schools (quoted in *Yorkshire Post*, 15 May 1984).

To sum up, Honeyford is justified in claiming the right as an individual to express his opinions freely within the law, whether he is engaged in political debate or in criticizing public policies, individuals or cultures. He is also justified in claiming that any attempt to suppress his right to free speech as an individual on the grounds that the opinions he expressed are offensive would be an intrusion on his personal liberty. For toleration is not limited to what is inoffensive, and to tolerate the expression of an opinion does not in any way imply endorsement of that opinion. However, as a public employee in a position of authority and responsibility, he is operating within tighter moral constraints than he would be as merely a private individual, and these constraints are defined in terms of his accountability to his employer and his clients. It is these constraints, not a more sinister attempt to suppress free speech, which create the strong moral pressure on him to remain silent, which was mentioned at the start of this chapter. However, several types of accountability have emerged in the discussion of free speech, and we must now turn to examine the concept of accountability more closely.

2. ACCOUNTABILITY

The accountability of a headteacher to his employers and to his parents was regularly invoked by Honeyford's opponents as an unproblematic indication of his responsibility to live up to the expectations of those he served. Thus the Bradford members of the National Anti-racist Movement in Education (NAME) write,

The second question is that of accountability. Mr Honeyford has shown himself to be opposed to the Council's educational policies, which have been developed over several years and have all-party support. Rather than join constructively in Bradford's ongoing debate about such policies, or resign his post because he cannot support them, he has chosen to disparage them – insulting, in the process, the minority communities which provide most of his pupils. Mr Honeyford is accountable to his employers and his parents. The majority of his parents have signed a petition showing that they have no confidence in him; as for his employers, the Education Sub-committee's 'no confidence' decision has been confirmed by the advisory team which reported that there is 'too much stress on the weaknesses and deficiencies of pupils' at Drummond Middle School (NAME, 1985).

Such an assertion is far from unproblematic, however. Behind Bradford's innovative multi-cultural policies lies a belief in the right of all interested parties to have their wishes and needs *taken into account* in educational planning and decision-making. Implicit in this developing notion of *moral and legal accountability* on the part of the LEA, however, is the idea that headteachers are paid employees of the LEA with the technical expertise necessary to implement the policies but with less individual autonomy than professionals have traditionally taken for granted. This idea was stated explicitly both by the former chairman of Bradford's Educational Services Committee, who is quoted as saying, 'We expect our heads to comply' (*The Times Educational Supplement*, 16 March 1984) and by the former Policies Development Officer who commented, 'We're simply not allowing teachers to run their schools as they see fit' (quoted in Selbourne, 1987, p. 105). The moral and legal accountability of the LEA to the electorate thus involves a strong emphasis on the *contractual accountability* of heads and other teachers to the LEA. Not surprisingly, Honeyford, in common with other Bradford headteachers, resented this erosion of their professional autonomy; *professional accountability* in their view involves the freedom to make judgments on educational matters according to appropriate educational criteria and the responsibility to *offer an account* of these in accordance with professional codes of practice when required to do so by interested parties. When the DPAC attempted to *call Honeyford to account*, however, their main objection was that he was not being sensitive to their cultures or responsive to their special needs. *Responsive accountability* implies an obligation to *take account of* the wishes of interested parties beyond the letter of the law or the teacher's contract; but the term gives no clue as to who the interested parties are or whose claim must take priority in the event that the interests of the parents, the children, the local community or the general public are not compatible. To talk in an unqualified way of Honeyford's accountability to his employers and his parents may therefore be doubly misleading, since it implies that the form of accountability is the same in both cases and that the parents and LEA were in alliance against Honeyford; in fact, as we saw in chapter four, the DPAC and other pressure groups came increasingly to hold the LEA to account, while the LEA at one stage threatened the parents with legal action over the non-attendance of their children.

Two needs emerge from this brief review of accountability in relation to the Honeyford affair. The first is a clarification of the concept itself. Accountability is one of the few areas where some attempt has already been made in recent years to match philosophy of education and educational practice (for example, Becher *et al.*, 1979; Sockett *et al.*, 1980; Elliott *et al.*, 1981a; Kogan, 1986), but these attempts have often been based on conflicting conceptual frameworks. The second is an examination of the arguments for the professional autonomy of teachers, on which Honeyford placed strong emphasis, to see how well they stand up, particularly in a pluralist society, to the concerted challenge of increased centralized control of education on the one hand and of increased demands for accountability to the consumer on the other. These two issues will occupy the remainder of the present chapter.

THE CONCEPT OF ACCOUNTABILITY

Dictionaries (for example, the *Concise Oxford*) usually define 'accountability' either in terms of an agent's obligation to 'give an account' of his actions or as 'responsibility'. Neither definition is adequate without qualification. To define accountability in terms of delivering an account is inadequate since it is clear that a headmaster who harangued his assembled school with political propaganda for half an hour every morning would not have fulfilled the requirements of accountability so long as he was happy to describe or explain his actions to anyone who required him to do so. Educational accountability also involves taking into account the requirements of the law, the values of the broader society, the guidelines of the local authority, the professional code of conduct, the rights of the parents, the interests of the children and so on. In addition, accountability implies that the educators' account of their actions should (implicitly if not explicitly) be judged to be satisfactory by those who have a legitimate stake in the educational process. Accountability thus inevitably raises questions about who should have a stake in the educational process, and is never far removed from questions about the control of education. As Bridges (1981) points out, an explanation of educational accountability couched simply in terms of a school's concern to communicate what it is doing to an outside audience fails to tell us enough about educational accountability as a political concept located among discussions about the *control* of education (p. 224).

The equation of accountability with responsibility involves different problems, not least that it provides too easy a justification for the claim that the teacher should be accountable in the main 'to his or her own informed conception of the role of a general educator' (Bailey, 1983, p. 11). Bailey argues that

> the more I am morally responsible or accountable for my own actions, the less it is reasonable to expect me to be responsible or accountable *to* anyone else in the sense of simply obeying them; though it might indeed be reasonable to expect me to give an account of, explain or justify my actions, if only to show publicly that I am acting in a morally responsible way (*ibid.*, p. 14).

The trouble with this argument is that 'responsibility' is a much broader concept than 'accountability', and one cannot therefore make distinctions that relate to the former and apply them uncritically to the latter. The primary force of the sentence, 'Titty is responsible for her own actions' is that the origin of her actions can be traced back to Titty herself. This implies (a) that she is capable of rational conduct and (b) that she is free to choose between courses of action. It may also, but need not, imply that she is liable to be called on to answer for her actions. Accountability, however, means responsibility only in this latter, narrower sense of answerability. But to be answerable implies an audience (whether explicitly referred to or merely understood) in a way which acting in a morally responsible manner does not, and thus it is not possible to discuss educational accountability without asking to whom the educator is to be accountable. It may be possible under certain conditions to justify a professional model of accountability which lays stress on the teacher's autonomy, as I shall argue later, but a justification that is based on too broad an understanding of the concept will not do.

An adequate account of educational accountability must therefore steer a middle path between control and autonomy. The autonomy of educators will be tempered by the fact that they are accountable to those they serve, and that those they serve have legitimate expectations and requirements which should be satisfied. On the other hand, the control of education can never be so tight that educators are reduced to the status of conveyor belts carrying precious nuggets from the mines of knowledge to the lines of empty minds waiting to be filled. From what has been said so far, it appears that there are six conditions which any case of educational accountability must satisfy:

(1)   The person who is accountable is the holder of a defined role.

(2)   The role-holder's accountability relates to actions carried out in connection with the requirements of the role.

(3)   The role-holder's accountability is to one or more specific audiences – those who have delegated the responsibilities of his role to him, and/or those who are on the receiving end of his actions.

(4)   The audience has certain legitimate expectations which the role-holder should take into account, and has grounds for insisting that those expectations be satisfied.

(5)   The role-holder should be willing to accept that some account of how the expectations are being satisfied should be prepared if the audience requires it, or at least that evidence should be made available to the aidience so that some assessment of how the expectations are being satisfied can be made.

(6)   Sanctions or other forms of appropriate action (including professional advice, remedial help, further feedback) are available if the account or assessment indicate that the legitimate expectations are not being satisfied.

Two main types of question emerge from these six conditions. The first concerns who defines the responsibilities of the specific role – the role-holder himself relying on his own professional expertise, or the audience; and if it is the latter, does this refer to those who foot the bill, or those who receive the service? The second concerns the level of control implicit in the notion of accountability to a specific audience. Should the role-holder merely be *responsive* to the expectations and requirements of those he serves, or is he *answerable* to them? The way in which educational accountability is understood in practice depends on the answers given to these two questions. Let us look at the two questions in more detail.

Accountability is usually invoked when there are three parties to an agreement rather than just two, i.e. when the role-holder is engaged to provide a service but is paid by someone other than the person who receives the service. In other words, a is paid by b to provide a service for c, and a is accountable to both b and c for providing that service. Thus a bus driver is accountable both to the bus company which hires him and to the passengers he serves, though on some occasions he might allow his own claims to expertise to override the requirements of the other two parties ('I've been driving buses fifteen years, and I know what I'm doing'). Accountability procedures are less likely to be invoked in a situation where b pays for a service which she herself receives from a, since the direct control she can exert (for example, by refusing to pay for the service) normally obviates the need for a more time-consuming and less clear-cut calling to account. In education, there is some uncertainty about who b actually is (the local government, the national government, the tax payer or the rate payer), about who c actually is (the child, the parent, the local community or society as a whole) and about the legitimacy of the claims of other groups (employers, unions, universities and so on) to have a say in the process. The situation is further complicated by the fact that parents may well pay for education as taxpayers as well as being on the receiving end as consumers. Nevertheless, the crude distinction between a (the educator), b (those who employ him) and c (those for whom he carries out a service) still has some validity. The question of which of these should have the greatest say in determining the responsibilities of educators lies at the heart of the debate about account-ability.

The second question requires a distinction between on the one hand the answerability of educators, their responsibility to demonstrate that they are satisfying the expectations of the audience and that, for example, pupils are in fact learning what they are supposed to learn (which I shall call 'contractual accountability'), and on the other the process of taking into account the requirements of all interested parties when making educational decisions (which I shall call 'responsive accountability'). The former category is exemplified in the question whether we are getting value for money from our educational service, the latter in the question which figured highly in Callaghan's 'Great Debate' launched in 1976, whether education should be more accountable to industry. Contractual accountability is primarily concerned with educational outcomes and results, whereas responsive accountability, while not ignoring these, puts more emphasis on educational processes and decision-making. Contractual accountability is directed more towards control (though, as we shall see, self-accounting procedures are an attempt to fulfil the requirements of contractual accountability while playing down the element of control); responsive accountability is directed more towards involvement and interaction between the decision-makers and those whom the decisions affect. In contractual accountability, the requirement for educators to give an account of their actions means no more than that they should give a description of them; in responsive accountability, on the other hand, giving an account of one's actions involves explaining and justifying them.

An analysis which combines the distinction between contractual and responsive accountability with the dominance of one of the three main parties to the accountability process – the employer (i.e. the LEA, the governing body or other employer), the autonomous professional and the consumer – produces six possible models of educational accountability. These are:

1. The Central Control Model (contractual, employer dominant).
2. The Self-Accounting Model (contractual, professional dominant).
3. The Consumerist Model (contractual, consumer dominant).
4. The Chain of Responsibility Model (responsive, employer dominant).
5. The Professional Model (responsive, professional dominant).
6. The Partnership Model (responsive, consumer dominant).

These models are, of course, ideal types, but it is hoped that, in spite of the inevitable oversimplification, a brief examination of each will help to shed light on the understanding of accountability in the Honeyford affair.

THE SIX MODELS OF ACCOUNTABILITY

The Central Control Model lays stress on teachers' status as employees with a contract of employment (at least in some sense), who are under the obligation to demonstrate that they are in fact doing what they are paid to do (*cf* Gibson, 1980). Even after payment by results was abandoned, the accountability of educators was for many years judged primarily in terms of their students' success in public examinations. The requirement of the 1980 Education Act that schools should publish a detailed analysis of their examination results for the benefit of prospective parents, and the proposal in the 1987 Education Bill to test pupils at the ages of 7, 11, 14 and 16, both reflect this view of accountability. One of the purposes of the proposed national curriculum is to

> enable schools to be more accountable for the education they offer to
> their pupils, individually and collectively (DES, 1987, p. 4).

A similar approach has been much in vogue in the USA since the 1960s: the educator is accountable to the general public (who pay for the education through taxes) for the achievement of pre-specified objectives by the children he teaches, and this achievement is assessed on the basis of the test scores gained by the children. Test results thus loom large in the accountability process, and the question of whether the tax payer is getting value for money from the educational system can be answered in terms of what results are achieved from what outlay of resources. The main objections to this approach to accountability have been set out by Sockett (1980, pp. 17–19). A much less crude approach to central control, which takes account of the fact that the success of a school can never more than partially be judged by test or examination results, is seen in the external monitoring of schools carried out by representatives of the teachers' employers (HMI at the national level and LEA advisers or inspectors at the local level).

The Self Accounting Model involves schools and teachers monitoring their own activities in an attempt to satisfy the requirements of contractual accountability while holding on to as much professional autonomy as possible and avoiding increased bureaucratic control of education. The Cambridge Accountability Project (Elliott *et al.*, 1981a, 1981b) was mainly concerned with investigating schools that were committed to the Self-Accounting Model. Both Scrimshaw (1980) and Becher *et al.* (1981, pp. 75*ff*) offer a number of arguments in favour of a school offering an account of its activities rather than being called to account by an external body. Sockett (1982, p. 544), on the other hand, questions whether self-accounting is a credible alternative to the bureaucratic centralism of the first model, since 'accountability without redress is empty'.

The Consumerist Model introduces the mechanisms of the free market in place of central or professional control as the primary means of enforcing educational accountability (*cf* Kogan, 1986, pp. 51ff). The model is based on the belief that if schools or LEAs no longer have a guaranteed clientele, this will create an incentive to compete which will in turn push up educational standards. The model is exemplified in proposals for a voucher system such as that advocated by Coons and Sugarman (1978) and more recently by Seldon (1986), whereby parents' influence on the character of the school would be strengthened by their freedom to spend their vouchers at the school of their choice. Honeyford has himself argued that under such a system

> parents would become much more involved in the accountability of schools, since they possess 'the power of exit' and control the purse strings (1986f).

Of course, individual parents who are dissatisfied with the educational provision at one school have always had the right to transfer their children to another. The William Tyndale affair, for example, started with a considerable number of parents transferring their children to other schools before the ILEA began to investigate what was going on at the school (Gretton and Jackson, 1976; Ellis *et al.*, 1976; Scrimshaw and Horton, 1981). But the Consumerist Model goes beyond this in that it involves a radical redistribution of power and authority in educational matters. A modified form of the model is seen in the provisions of the 1987 Education Bill which allow the governing bodies of schools to opt out of local authority control.

The Chain of Responsibility Model is a form of responsive accountability based on an acknowledgement of the complexity of the relationship between employer, practitioner and client in the field of education, and an acknowledgement that different types of educational decisions may reasonably be considered the domain of different groups. The model has three main features. The first is that an initial distinction is made between those who make educational decisions and those whose wishes, interests, requirements or opinions are merely taken into account by the decision-makers. The second is that the various groups of decision-makers, who consist of different categories of elected representatives and their employees, are ranked in a chain which extends from parliament and the DES, to local councils and LEAs, to school governors, to headteachers, to senior staff and finally to assistant teachers. In some respects the relationship between the links in the chain is hierarchical, in that each link can control, to a greater or less extent, the practice of subsequent links, and the autonomy of any given link is subject to the constraints which may be placed upon its freedom of action by the preceding links. However, to describe the relationship as hierarchical or as one of control is to oversimplify it. For the elected representatives are unlikely to act without at least seeking the professional advice of their employees, and those at the teaching end of the chain have a variety of means open to them for diminishing the effectiveness of policies initiated without their approval. These include tacitly ignoring the policy, going through the motions of compliance, campaigning against the policy through their unions, working to rule and so on. The third characteristic feature of the model is that each link in the chain has a special responsibility to particular interest groups, as set out in figure one below. Each link demonstrates its responsiveness to its interest groups in two ways: sounding out opinion and engaging in dialogue on the particular educational decisions for which it has responsibility, and delivering an account of the decisions it has made. One disadvantage of the Chain of Responsibility Model is that it might lead to a growth of bureaucracy and to power struggles between different links in the chain. Another disadvantage is the implicit hierarchy of interests which results from the more or less explicit hierarchy of educational decision-making and control. Thus the interests of the parent qua parent rank lower than the interest of the parent qua rate payer, and both rank lower than the interests of national industry. An interest group may appeal to a higher link in the chain if it believes the response to its wishes and demands has been unsatisfactory, but has no guarantee of a sympathetic hearing. Sir Keith Joseph, for example, was very responsive to a small number of complaints about Peace Studies in schools (Joseph, 1984), but refused to get involved in the Honeyford affair; and Kenneth Baker, who intervened in the McGoldrick affair, has so far held back from involvement in the dispute at Headfield Middle School in Dewsbury.

The Professional Model avoids the problem of a hierarchy of interests by leaving educational decisions (except on matters on which they are contractually accountable) to the judgment of the professional educators – or of the school, though I tend to agree with Sockett (1980, p. 13) that school accountability is reducible to the accountability of the head and other

Figure One: The Chain of Responsibility Model

THE CHAIN	responsive to . . .	THE INTEREST GROUPS
Parliament/DES	. . .	General public, CBI, TUC, universities, national pressure groups.
Local government/LEA	. . .	Rate payers, local electorate, employees, local industry
Governors	. . .	Parents and local community
Head	. . .	Parents, higher education, colleagues
Senior staff	. . .	Parents, pupils, colleagues, unions, other educational institutions
Assistant teachers	. . .	Parents, pupils, colleagues, unions, other educational institutions

teachers. On this model, which is set out in more detail by Bailey (1980, 1983), professional educators seek to retain control over educational decisions which affect themselves, and see themselves as the arbiter when they are faced with conflicting demands from different interested parties. Their professional status requires them to take account of all the expectations, wishes and criticisms emanating from those with a legitimate interest in the education they are providing, but as they are ultimately responsible for educational practice, so they claim the right to make final judgments and to define the boundaries of their own accountability. This right is based on their professional training and expertise, on the standards they have implicitly committed themselves to when entering the profession, and on the professional autonomy that teachers have traditionally been allowed in this country. How far the claim of teachers to be professionally autonomous is rationally justifiable will be considered in the final section of the present chapter.

The Partnership Model combines two main principles. The first is that the responsibility for educational decisions should not lie with one dominant group, but with a partnership of all those directly affected by a particular decision or with a legitimate interest in it. The second is that all the parties to the partnership are not merely consulted before the decisions are taken, but have a share in the actual decision-making, either directly or through their representatives (the distinction between representation and direct partici-pation, which Pateman (1970) makes much of, is not central to the argument here). There are likely to be three stages in decision-making on this model: (a) the pooling of ideas and the critical discussion of options; (b) 'the negotiation through argument and compromise of whatever can satisfy most people as being the most rational, or, failing that, the most reasonable solution' (Bridges, 1978, p. 118); and (c) the acceptance of the obligation to abide by and help carry through the decisions which have been reached in this democratic manner. This model therefore provides a quite different approach to accountability from the Chain of Responsibility and Professional Models. Each member of the partnership is accountable to the other members in the sense of being under an obligation to take their views and interests into account, but is not accountable to any outside interest group (unless of course he has been elected as a representative of a broader group, in which case he will be answerable to them for the way in which he represents their interests).

A major obstacle facing the Partnership Model is the difficulty of gathering all the parties with a legitimate interest into a single manageable committee which can actually make decisions. Usually in practice only some of the main interested parties are brought together on a decision-making body. The Schools Council was one such attempt, but was perhaps too dominated by teachers (Plaskow, 1985). Prior to the 1986 Education (No. 2) Act, governing bodies were often dominated by political nominees. The theory behind the encouragement of greater extra-professional participation in educational planning and decision-making is set out in the *Taylor Report*, to which the roots of the 1986 Act can be traced:

> The Secretaries of State have pointed out that curricula must meet, and be responsive to, the needs of society...If ordinary people do not, as some teachers suggest, understand what schools are trying to do, it is in part because they have traditionally not taken an active

part in determining the educational policy of the schools (DES, 1977).

Elliott (1980, p. 82), however, has argued against the participation of non-professional bodies in final decisions about educational policy, and in any case it has been suggested (Bridges, 1982b, p. 14) that many parents do not see PTA committees and parent governors as a genuine vehicle for the expression of their concerns.

It may be helpful at this stage to look back at the Honeyford affair in light of the distinctions which have so far been made.

The accommodationist and post-accommodationist phases of Bradford's policy towards its minority communities described in chapter two provide an archetypal example of the Chain of Responsibility Model. A number of features of the policy make this clear. First, the council and LEA were attempting to respond to the perceived needs and wishes of the particular interest groups to which they were responsible. As the former chairman of the Educational Services Committee points out,

> One in six of our children come from Asian families...It is the simple duty of the Council to tre to satisfy their needs (quoted in *The Times Educational Supplement*, 25 May 1984).

Secondly, though they took care to engage in dialogue with the minority communities, the Council and LEA emphasized their own right to interpret and evaluate the requirements of those communities. Thirdly, the Council and LEA drew attention to the fact that they were acting within the guidelines defined by the government or the DES; usually, they claimed to be 'clarifying' or 'interpreting' or 'acting within the spirit of' the 1944 Education Act. Fourthly, the Council and LEA expected subsequent links in the chain of responsibility to take account of their guidelines and definitions of good practice and to act in accordance with them.

Honeyford's stance, on the other hand, provides an equally clear example of the Professional Model. Where LEA guidelines were specific, he took these to form part of his contractual obligations and carried them out to the letter. But where LEA guidelines were expressed in general terms as recommendations for good practice, he considered these as advice which he as an autonomous professional could weigh alongside other considerations before making decisions about educational practice within his own school. The high value which Honeyford put on professional autonomy is made clear in his guide for probationary teachers (1982a, p. 158) as well as in the reports he was required to prepare for the special meeting of the Schools (Education) Sub-committee on 22 March 1985.

The view of accountability which emerges from the protests against Honeyford, however, is much less straightforward. In chapter four I divided the protest into four stages. The first stage involved the two logical courses of action open to parents according to the analysis of responsive accountability which has been offered: organizing a protest group (the DPAC) to co-ordinate action against Honeyford and to put pressure on the LEA to respond to their demands (in keeping with the Chain of Responsibility Model); and urging the school's parent governor to press the claims of the DPAC on the governing body as a whole (in keeping with the Partnership Model). In the event, the existing parent governor could not handle the demands and resigned, and the election of the DPAC chairperson as the new parent governor by a large majority put her in a strong position to urge both governors and LEA to call Honeyford to account. The LEA's response to this first stage of the protest appeared to miss the point, however; the DPAC were objecting to Honeyford's failure to be responsive to their wishes and needs, but the LEA sent in a team of inspectors to Honeyford's school to check that its educational provision was in line with LEA policies. In other words, complaints about a lack of *responsive* accountability were being met in terms of the *contractual* accountability of the Central Control Model.

In the second stage of the protest, the DPAC began to call the LEA to account. They claimed to be supporting LEA policies on race relations, and called on the LEA to take what was in their eyes the necessary step of dismissing a head who was contravening these policies. The Council's response this time was to require Honeyford to prepare six reviews of aspects of his school's provision – a requirement which was closely in line with the Self-Accounting Model, except that there was still a strong element of central control in the advisers' evaluation of these reports. The main complaints against Honeyford in the second report by the advisers were that he had not changed his attitude in any way and that he was not sufficiently responsive to the requirements of the particular interest groups that according to the Chain of Responsibility Model were primarily his responsibility – the parents and the local community. As a result of this report he was suspended.

The final stage of the protest, after Honeyford had been reinstated, had much more in common with the Consumerist Model. This stage was marked by direct action aimed at making his school unworkable and thus his departure inevitable. The justification for this action was based on the claim that the parents had the right, as the representatives and trustees of the children at the school, to call a head directly to account themselves. This of course raises the question whether the wishes and judgments of parents should be paramount in the education of their children, a question which has been much debated in recent years (*cf* Coons and Sugarman, 1978; O'Neill and Ruddick, 1979; Bridges, 1984; Hobson, 1984; McLaughlin, 1984, 1985).

The mode of Honeyford's actual departure, however, was such that he could claim it was an autonomous decision on his part, in line with the Professional Model; although he was willing and able to carry on as head, he weighed the effect the dispute was having on his wife's health, the morale of the staff and the education of the pupils and decided that the best course of action was to accept early retirement.

The fact that all six models were thus operating in the Honeyford affair helps us to understand the confusion and talking at cross purposes which typifies the affair. More significantly, it highlights the central questions which underlie any discussion of accountability. How should educational decisions be reached? How much account should be taken of the wishes of interested parties? Is it in fact possible to take account of conflicting wishes, and if not, whose interests are to take priority? Are there basic criteria according to which educational problems should be resolved irrespective of the wishes of interested parties? If there are, are teachers in the best position to understand these criteria and should they therefore have the final responsibility for decisions relating to educational policy and practice? The final section of the present chapter briefly examines the response to these questions implicit in Honeyford's position and the difficulties facing any attempt at professional accountability in a pluralist society.

PROFESSIONAL AUTONOMY IN A PLURALIST SOCIETY

Like other headteachers in Bradford, Honeyford objected to what he saw as the encroachment of the LEA into areas which had traditionally been left up to the independent judgment of the teacher. He has consistently attached high value to professional autonomy (Honeyford, 1982a, p. 158), and this had led him to stress a relationship of trust between the various parties involved in the educational enterprise, rather than one of compulsion, and to stress the professional judgment of the individual teacher rather than the following of externally imposed rules and guidelines. Accountability according to this view thus involves profesional responsibility, plus a willingness of offer an account of one's actions when this is required of one (for example, by the governors). This view is not very different from that widely supported by liberal educationalists and taken for granted by a large section of the teaching profession. It appears, for example, to be broadly in line with the following description of the autonomous teacher provided by Bailey (1980):

An autonomous teacher does not ignore the wishes and interests of others – parents, pupils, governments and employers – but such a teacher does reserve the right to consider such wishes and interests in the light of appropriate criteria. The wants and wishes cannot simply be taken as given starting points. An autonomous teacher does not necessarily refuse to submit to the judgment of others, but again such a teacher would need to satisfy himself concerning the criteria of judgment and the procedures by which he is asked to accept the judgments of others. In particular he might consider it proper to be subject in some matters to the judgment of his professional associates (p. 99).

Bailey offers three main justifications for linking accountability to professional autonomy. First, he argues that accountability necessarily involves autonomy and that accounts of moral and professional action only make sense where the agent is considered to be autonomous (although he points out that autonomy is always a matter of degree; *cf* 1980, p. 104; 1983, pp. 11, 15). If the agent is merely responsible to his superiors in the sense of working strictly to their orders, then it is they, not he, who should provide the explanation and justification of his actions. The second argument is that teachers in fact have to be accountable within considerably diverse contexts, and that the best way to help teachers to fulfil their role satisfactorily in these differing school conditions and arrangements is to encourage them to develop the capacity to reflect critically on the possible ways of applying general educational principles to specific situations and to act on the basis of this rational reflection. Only if teachers are professionally autonomous will there be a system of decision-making flexible enough to take into account the needs of individual children and the requirements of specific contexts: a centrally imposed system could not be sufficiently adaptable. The third argument is a refinement of the assumption held in some quarters that teachers' professional knowledge and expertise justifies them in holding themselves aloof from non-expert interference and criticism, or at least that if their actions are questioned by parents, for example, the appropriate response is for teachers to attempt to 'educate' the parents (*cf* Nias, 1981, p. 202) by patiently explaining what they are seeking to do and why. Bailey (1983, pp. 13–14) argues that teachers' professional expertise consists not in the possession of specialized packages of information and skills but in the capacity to apply broadly generalizable knowledge, skills and attitudes to whatever situations they find themselves in. The capacity to make autonomous decisions is thus a major part of teachers' expertise, and to instil that capacity in their pupils is one of their major goals; but it is because their decisions are autonomous ones that they have a duty to explain them or give an account of them to all interested parties.

The first of these arguments is broadly acceptable, so long as it is acknowledged that accountability involves at least a minimal degree of autonomy *and* a minimal sense of responding to, or being constrained by the legitimate claims of, interested parties. Indeed, it is this very tension between autonomous action and legitimate constraint that is picked out by the term 'accountability'.

If the second argument relates primarily to questions of practical detail requiring immediate resolution, then few would dispute that these are best dealt with by the person on the spot; and much educational decision-making belongs to this category. But Bailey appears to argue that more fundamental decisions, such as educational aims and priorities, should also be the exclusive domain of the professionally autonomous teacher. This does not mean that the wishes and requirements of interested parties would be ignored, but simply that they would be put through the filter of the teacher's own rationality, expertise and professional judgment. In Bailey's view, the teacher, who has an informed and rational conception of what education is and where it should be leading, fights for education as he or she sees it and tries to stop it being domesticated to other ends. The resulting decisions and actions would thus inevitably be dependent on the teacher's perception and understanding of the situation. It is clear that if a system of autonomous decision-making by professional teachers is to be found acceptable, there has to be a high level of trust in the teacher's perception and understanding of the situation and an agreement over the basic criteria according to which the autonomous decisions should be made. Our contemporary multi-cultural context underlines the difficulties in achieving either of these conditions. Teachers' perceptions, preconceptions and tacit cultural assumptions are no longer universally shared (if they ever were), and teachers themselves are in any case notoriously divided on many issues, including the aims of education. It is doubtful if there is a sufficient agreement over 'values which are basic to our shared form of life' (Bonnett, 1979, p. 166) to provide a framework of basic educational criteria. This point will be discussed in more detail in the next chapter.

Teachers can count on public and parental support most readily when they are perceived to be doing their best to achieve educational goals which are shared by all interested parties. Such trust is clearly much more readily achieved in a mono-cultural than in a multi-cultural context. Nias comes to more or less the same conclusion in an intuitive article of considerable insight (1981, pp. 211*ff*), where she argues that trust, at least in an educational context, involves (a) predictability of personal and institutional behaviour and (b) agreement over ends. Where these two conditions prevail, parents and the general public appear happy to leave educational decision-making to the autonomous professional, confident

> both that the school was doing what they would broadly wish it to do and that it could apparently be trusted to get on with the job (Bridges, 1982b, p. 14).

In the absence of such predictability and agreement, however, the claim of teachers to professional autonomy is likely to be seen as a barrier to, rather than as a way of facilitating, accountability. A common educational system in a pluralist context is bound to produce conflict over the aims of the education provided, and thus over educational practice, and there will be increasing dissatisfaction with the policy of leaving the decisions to the teachers.

There are two ways of breaking through this impasse: weakening the common educational system or restricting the professional autonomy of teachers. Scrimshaw draws attention to the first possibility, Nias to the second. Scrimshaw (1980, p. 52*f*) acknowledges that professional autonomy can work only when there is a broadly shared framework of educational assumptions, and argues that this shared framework can only be achieved under two conditions: that 'virtually everyone in the school knows what these assumptions are before joining it and has some fair measure of sympathy with them'; and that 'parents in any given area must have some measure of real choice between schools for their children'. Parental choice has become a slogan of Conservative educational policy in recent years, but events in Dewsbury in 1987 have suggested how the movement to racial and cultural segregation may be accelerated if the provisions of the 1987 Education Bill become law. Arguing from the assumption that the common school is axiomatic, on the other hand, Nias suggests that professional autonomy will have to be tempered with what she calls 'formal procedures' of accountability, by which she appears to mean forms of organization which structuralize relationships, responsibilities and roles within the school. The Chain of Responsibility Model as described above is one such system, which perhaps has more potential for coping with the fundamentally conflicting educational values, goals and assumptions held by different groups in our society than does the Professional Model. Insofar as he acknowledges the need for 'a structural framework for policy-forming discussion', Bailey (1980, p. 107) concedes the existence of constraints on teachers' professional autonomy.

Bailey's third argument, which defines teachers' professional expertise in terms of the ability to make autonomous decisions about what and how to teach children, is also problematic. Clearly teachers cannot exercise their professional autonomy in total isolation and independence from their professional colleagues. But as soon as Bailey concedes that professional autonomy includes 'the right to participate in the formation of policy to be collectively implemented' (1980, p. 107), we are forced to ask why this right to participate is restricted to professional educators. If the parents (or politicians, employers, trade unionists, social workers or other interested parties) share the fundamental knowledge and commitment to autonomy which in Bailey's view form the basis of teachers' professional expertise, on what grounds are they to be excluded from participation in decisions affecting the future generation? Even if parents do not share this knowledge and commitment, to exclude them from the decision-making process has every appearance of oppression and a lack of respect for the rights and opinions of others.

Bridges (1979, p. 161*f*) and White (1980, p. 27*f*) take this point further and argue that decisions about what to teach in school are dependent on conceptions of the good life and the good society, and that teachers cannot claim any special expertise which would justify leaving such decisions in their hands. Decisions can only be reached through rational debate among all interested parties. White (1980) argues that such rational public debate must take place to establish a consensus of values which could form a framework for fundamental educational decisions, and that

> if there is no reason why this overall framework should differ from child to child, there is every reason why it should be worked out centrally (p. 40).

The main problem here is that the argument proceeds from an ideal situation (a consensus of values) to actual practice (central educational decision-making), but does not consider whether the practice is justifiable or appropriate in a less than ideal situation where a consensus of values does not exist. White concedes (*ibid.*, p. 37*f*) that unless an objective framework of values can be established, there may be no case for the state control of fundamental educational decisions. What actually happens, however, since such decisions still have to be made, is that they are based on majority agreement; indeed this is all that is needed to make the Chain of Responsibility Model workable. But in a pluralist context, simple majoritarianism is likely to leave some groups dissatisfied and anxious to opt out of the current system.

This leads Bridges (1979), and more recently White (1987) and Haydon (1987), to emphasize the value of the democratic process *per se*, according to which all interested parties have a share in the actual decision-making. Drawing heavily on Mill (1972a), Bridges argues that co-operation in a common cause is a value in itself (1980, p. 67) and that participatory democracy enhances the quality of life (1979, p. 164) both for the community as a whole and for the individual participants (1978, pp. 118–121). The final decisions reached would ideally represent some kind of balance of individual interests, settled amicably by mutual consent after free and open discussion, or else settled by a vote if disagreements remain too strong to do otherwise.

There are a number of practical difficulties with this Partnership Model, however: how to decide whose interests in educational decision-making are legitimate; how to balance the partnership between numerically uneven parties such as parents, teachers, the general public, LEAs and industry; how to justify the extensive demands participation makes on the time, effort and commitment of those involved; how to avoid conflict and divisiveness as groups realize that their chances of gaining concessions increase with the intensity of feeling with which they express their views; and how to ensure that the decisions reached through democratic participation are actually good ones. There is a danger that democratic participation may become more of a power struggle between rival factions than an impartial way of resolving disagreements in a spirit of co-operation. Dunlop (1979, p. 48) juxtaposes a different type of co-operation in which identity with the community is achieved through the sharing of customs, traditions, values and tacit assumptions, and sees this identity with the community as taking the sting out of any disagreements that might arise and enabling a common mind to emerge. Within a homogeneous, mono-cultural society, such a spirit of co-operation is quite compatible with the professional autonomy which Honeyford claims. In a multi-cultural society, however, it is only likely to be achieved within separate cultural groups, and the professional autonomy of teachers could therefore only be viable under a system whereby parents were genuinely free to choose schools which shared their own fundamental values and beliefs.

Bonnett (1979, p. 166) reminds us that there is a danger in what I have called the Partnership Model of losing sight of the fact that there are objective criteria that provide 'a firm and limiting framework' within which democratic decisions can be made. He points out that 'consistency with the values upon which the idea of democracy rests would seem to demand set limits upon the content' of decisions reached by participatory democracy. A corollary of this (and here I am extending Bonnett's argument) is that a dissenting minority need not consider itself bound by a democratic decision unless that decision satisfies such objective criteria as the demands of justice; otherwise, as Bridges (1980, p. 69) concedes, corporate decision-making would be oppressive of individual freedom and smack of totalitarianism. This highlights the need, before democratic decision-making can even start, to endeavour to establish the criteria according to which those decisions can be made, criteria which are consistent with our fundamental shared beliefs and values. The Swann Committee recognized this need and based its report (DES, 1985) on what it saw as rationally justifiable axioms for a democratic pluralist society – though the values which underlie the committee's educational recommendations have been far from universally accepted (*cf* Ashraf, 1986; Khan-Cheema *et al.*, 1986).

I have argued in the present chapter that attacks on Honeyford in terms of his failure to be accountable to those he served involve an oversimplification that obscures the real point. Accountability *is* an important part of Honeyford's educational philosophy; but the question is whether the model of professional accountability to which he appears committed is appropriate to the context in which he was working. I have argued that it is virtually impossible to have (a) the professional autonomy of teachers, (b) the common school, and (c) a pluralist society at the same time: any two of these conditions precludes the third. (a) and (b) may perhaps be compatible only in a homogeneous, mono-cultural society where there is broad agreement over educational goals and values; they are thus likely to be able to continue in those parts of the UK which have so far been untouched by cultural and ethnic diversity. (a) and (c) can exist only where schools have made explicit their educational values and assumptions and parents have some measure of free choice between schools so that they can choose a school with whose goals they are in sympathy. In both these cases, parents will trust the professional judgment of teachers mainly because it is reasonable to expect that the teachers' decisions about what is in the best interests of the children will coincide with the parents'. But under conditions (b) and (c), where some groups are likely not to share either the tacit assumptions or the stated educational goals of the school, parental rights may be invoked which are ignored when there is a consensus of values, and teachers' actions are likely to come under much closer scrutiny. If the common school is to survive such a situation, it seems inevitable that what Nias calls 'formal procedures' will have to be developed, which will make explicit the educational criteria by which decisions are made, and clarify the roles and responsibilities of teachers. This will involve increased central control, but may also open up greater participation in decision-making among other interested groups. All this acts as a strong constraint on the traditional concept of teachers' professional autonomy, as Honeyford found to his cost. It is no longer possible in a pluralist society which provides a common educational experience for all its children to think of accountability in terms of

> teachers acting with a proper sense of professional responsibility while remaining personally autonomous in their professional actions (Bailey, 1980, p. 99).

A more structured view of accountability now seems inevitable.

What this discussion of accountability has done, however, is to open up another debate, about multi-cultural education. Is the appropriate response to the education of children in a pluralist society one which seeks to provide them with a common educational experience based on fundamental democratic values, as the *Swann Report* proposes? Or is freedom of parental choice, which may lead to diverse educational provision, a more fundamental value? This question will form a major theme of the final chapter.

8 The Debate About Multi-cultural Education

In chapter two a distinction was made between two senses of multi-cultural education. The first refers to the attempt in schools to respond positively to the cultural requirements and sensitivities of children and parents from minority groups, as far as this can be achieved without contravening fundamental educational objectives. The second refers to the sort of education which is considered appropriate for *all* children if they are to be adequately prepared for life in a pluralist society. The first is grounded on the wish to demonstrate respect for the religious and cultural beliefs of the minority groups. It may be seen in the conscious avoidance of putting children in the position where they are expected to act in a way that is contrary to their deeply held beliefs; it therefore includes matters of clothing and diet, the observation of religious festivals, and so on. More positively, it may involve making educational use, for children from minority groups, of the cultural identity and experiences which they bring to their school; hence it will seek to make use of pupils' mother tongues. The second is based on a positive view of cultural and religious diversity as a source of enrichment and breath of perspective. It entails encouraging *all* children to develop a spirit of enquiry in relation to other cultures, an openness to and sympathetic understanding of a variety of ways of looking at the world, a willingness to enter into the spirit of different civilizations and societies, and a sensitive respect for those with different religious beliefs and cultural values from their own.

These two senses of multi-cultural education are of course closely connected and inter-dependent. In particular, schools can hardly encourage children to respect other beliefs and cultures (type two) if they do not demonstrate such respect in their own dealings with ethnic minority pupils (type one). However, the distinction remains a valid one in a number of ways. The first type is possible only for schools which contain children from minority groups, whereas the second is considered by its advocates to be just as important for schools with no such pupils. As was noted in chapter two, multi-cultural education of the first type has been campaigned for, sometimes quite passionately, by various minority groups; multi-cultural education of the second type, however, has not generally been campaigned for by minority groups (*cf Swann Report*, DES, 1985, p. 238), but has been devised as a rational response to the educational requirements of our contemporary pluralist society. Although Honeyford himself does not explicitly distinguish between the two types of multi-cultural education, his arguments, as we shall shortly see, can only be understood by invoking some such distinction.

Multi-cultural education in both senses is closely linked to the search for racial justice. A desire to avoid the domination associated with what was in chapter six called cultural racism has clearly provided a significant impetus to multi-cultural education of the first type. Similarly, the wish to discourage racism, prejudice, bias and ethnocentricity has been a major factor behind the development of the second type. Even critics of multi-cultural education acknowledge this. Those on the left often see it as having similar aims to anti-racist education, though watered down and ineffective in comparison; those on the right, in the other hand, including Honeyford, criticize it for damaging the possibility of social integration by accentuating both cultural and racial differences. The currently popular concept of ethnicity combines racial and cultural identity into a single term, and helps to reinforce the impression that questions of race and culture are ultimately inseparable. Some writers have indeed come to use the terms 'multi-cultural' and 'multi-racial' almost interchangeably. Honeyford himself is quoted as saying in connection with the Dewsbury school boycott that

> there is a ground swell of parental opinion against multi-cultural education. You really have to emphasize that a school is English, instead of having the nonsense of a multi-racial school. Multi-cultural education is a fashionable bandwagon which will do considerable harm (*Telegraph and Argus*, 4 September 1987).

In spite of the obvious connections between race and culture, however, the present chapter is written in the belief that from an educational point of view they raise quite different questions and issues. In chapter six it is argued that the most crucial question linking race and education is how schools could best promote racial justice; the goal of racial justice is not itself in dispute. Multi-cultural education, on the other hand, raises much more intractable questions. Should children from different cultural backgrounds be provided with a culturally uniform or culturally differentiated curriculum? If schools are not to play a part in preserving minority cultures, is it possible to avoid cultural domination by the majority? Are the preservation of cultural identity and the pursuit of social cohesion and integration actually compatible as educational objectives? In what ways and to what extent should schools reflect the diversity which exists in a culturally pluralist society? Is Britain in fact a culturally pluralist society? And how far is cultural transmission a primary function of schools anyway?

It is with questions such as these that the present chapter is concerned. It starts with an exposition of Honeyford's criticisms of multi-cultural education, and explores some of the fundamental problems raised by his criticisms, particularly relating to cultural pluralism, shared values and individual and group rights. It considers the educational arguments in support of multi-cultural education, and finally examines a Muslim challenge to these arguments which does not accept their basic liberal assumptions.

HONEYFORD'S CRITICISMS OF MULTI-CULTURAL EDUCATION

Although Honeyford has frequently been described in the media as the 'race-row head', he is much more concerned in his articles with questions of culture than with questions of race. His criticisms of minority cultures themselves have already been discussed in chapters three and seven, but our present concern is with his views concerning the account that schools should take of the culture of the minority groups.

Some of his fiercest criticism is reserved for what I have called type one multi-cultural education. He objects to making concessions to the cultural sensitivities of children from minority groups both in principle and in practice. He argues that granting such concessions may sometimes undermine some of the most fundamental principles on which education in the UK is based, such as equal opportunities. Thus when a Muslim father tried to withdraw his daughter from swimming lessons on religious grounds, Honeyford saw this as a direct clash over educational principles:

> I had to run a school which was obliged both from conviction and legal necessity to ensure equal opportunities for girls. And denying a little girl the right to swim clearly violated *our* principles... I had no right to restrict her human possibilities in the way her father wanted (1987a).

In such situations, in Honeyford's view, no compromise is desirable or even possible: it is a straight choice between basing educational decisions on a 'purdah mentality' (1984a) or seeking to protect children's rights and liberate them from the restricting cultures of their parents. His commitment to the latter alternative is absolute. In other contexts, where fundamental values are not at stake, he still generally argues against making concessions to minority groups in schools. Of course, each concession requested by such groups raises different issues, and Honeyford did during his headship make a number of adaptations to minority requirements in his school (including adaptations to assemblies and the RE syllabus, changes in what clothing was considered acceptable, single-sex grouping for some activities and the teaching of Urdu), but he feels that some of the concessions which are still being demanded are not in practice in the interests of the children concerned. For example, wearing cumbersome clothing may prevent Muslim girls from developing their sporting talents (1983b); more seriously, the use of mother-tongues as a means of instruction, the practice of making extended trips to the Indian sub-continent, and the teaching of 'Black Studies' or other subjects not valued in the broader community may make it more difficult for minority children to master the culture 'in which they live out their lives outside the home' (1982d). Even if such concessions result from parents' natural desire for cultural continuity in the upbringing of their children, supporters of such an approach

> may well be involved in a process which actually limits the settler child's chances in a pretty ruthless meritocracy — which is what our society now is. And they are thereby delaying the emergence of a 'black' professional and managerial class, which could play such a vital part in establishing a truly equal and harmonious multi-cultural society (*ibid*).

Finally Honeyford objects to many of the cultural concessions demanded by minority groups because he sees them as socially divisive; they emphasize the difference between the groups, and if some groups are perceived as being granted special privileges (such as having their cultures treated as immune from criticism: *cf* 1985c), this is likely to increase suspicion and resentment elsewhere. Schools have a part to play in developing social cohesion and integration, and this requires an emphasis on the common needs of all children and a determination to apply the same rules and policies and teach the same things to all children.

In arguing that the maintenance, presentation and transmission of minority cultures is not the role of the maintained school but ultimately a private matter and that schools should provide basically the same educational experiences for *all* children, Honeyford is broadly in line with the recommendation of the *Swann Report*. Where he differs is in his view of what the common educational experience should consist of. He objects to attempts to bring that experience more into line with the cultural diversity which is in evidence in Britain today. His objections to what I have called type two multi-cultural education fall into five main categories. First, he thinks of multi-cultural education as a 'fashionable bandwagon', which has little to do with the real needs of children, whatever the colour of their skin, but is the product of the sort of progressive thinking which has already caused much damage to the state system of schooling (1985d). Secondly, he complains that multi-cultural education lacks any kind of roots. In his opinion, it has no attachment to history, tradition, natural development or actual, common experience — in other words, no attachment to those things which give the concept of 'culture' real, human meaning (1986c). He believes that education should be deeply rooted in a country's long-standing culture and values. He has on several occasions (1986c; Clare, 1986) expounded what 'Englishness' means to him: it is tied up with language, history, tradition, a Christian heritage, parliamentary democracy, the rule of law, and distinctive achievements in learning, the arts, science, literature, warfare and diplomacy. He argues that a commitment to a British education based on such values was implicit in the decision of immigrants to become British citizens, and that the responsibility for adaptation and adjustment lies with them (as the earlier waves of immigrants to Britain described in chapter one appear to have accepted: *cf* 1982d), not with the schools which now find themselves with significant numbers of ethnic minority pupils (1987e). Thirdly, Honeyford argues that multi-cultural education has no popular mandate, but has been imposed from above by 'official diktat' (1986c). He suspects that multi-cultural policies violate the wishes of the majority of parents, who prefer a 'unitary notion of culture' to prevail and minorities to be left to sustain their own cultures 'through private initiatives' (*ibid.*), and he argues that the public should now be consulted through a national referendum on multi-cultural education in Britain (1987e). Fourthly, he is anxious about the implicit relativism in the belief that 'all cultures now represented in this country should have equal status' (1986c) and the institutional consequences of such relativism. Fifthly, he expresses concern that multi-cultural education often appears to have a hidden political agenda. He sees it as part of a movement which aims to use schools, not for educating children in accordance with their parents' wishes, but to change 'society' and inculcate radical attitudes. The neo-Marxist rhetoric in which multi-cultural concepts are so often couched suggests to him that the purpose is basically political (1985d). In a similar vein, he accuses the Commission for Racial Equality of seeking to impose 'some sort of officially sponsored cultural pluralism' (1986c), while boroughs such as Brent, he says, are not only taking steps to ensure that all educationalists have 'the "correct", officially-sponsored attitudes towards multi-culturalism and race' but are also creating 'powerful racial bureaucracies' bent on inner-city revolution (1986i).

While some of these criticisms may be superficial (for example, the dismissal of multi-cultural education as a 'fashionable bandwagon') and others only loosely thought out (for example, the proposal for a referendum on multi-cultural education), they represent, especially when considered in the broader context of Honeyford's writings on race, immigration and traditional English culture discussed in chapter three, a serious challenge to the concept of multi-cultural education, and they raise a number of fundamental questions about its philosophical underpinnings. These questions fall into three main categories: those involving notions of pluralism, those involving social and cultural values and those involving the rights of children and parents.

The first of these categories is important because we cannot explore the question of what sort of education we should be providing in a pluralist society unless we can establish in what ways, if any, ours is a pluralist society. While Honeyford accepts that there is a plurality of races, cultures, beliefs and values in our society, he does not appear to accept that existing structures should be adapted in any way to take account of this diversity; indeed, he is deeply suspicious of the desire to transform such structures (*cf* Bullivant, 1984, p. 71), fearing that behind it lies sinister political motivation. For him, pluralism is not a matter of different groups vying with each other in a struggle for power, nor does it involve individuals showing primary loyalty to their own group rather than to the broader society. He sees pluralism as involving diversity in the private domain, but integration into the existing public structures of society. When he uses the metaphor of the school as a 'cultural bridge' (1983b), he appears to envisage that the traffic on it is only travelling one way, from the 'purdah mentality' of the home to the freedom, openness and toleration of the broader society. The gradual assimilation of minorities to the majority group which is likely to result from this approach to public education also requires the majority to make plain their commitment to their own traditional culture and values; this presumably lies behind Honeyford's plea for a referendum on multi-cultural education.

Secondly, if we accept that it is axiomatic to educational planning that all children should receive a common educational experience — and towards the end of this chapter I shall discuss a Muslim challenge to this assumption — then we are forced to consider on what values that common educational experience is, implicitly or explicitly, to be based. The strong cultural relativism which Honeyford fears lies behind much thinking about multi-cultural education probably in fact has few supporters today (*cf* Zec, 1980; Walkling, 1980); but the search for a set of shared values to which all groups will make a commitment is itself problematic. What could provide the basis for any such set of shared values in our pluralist society? Honeyford argues that they must be rooted in British culture, history and traditions; but there is the danger that this might be seen by the minority groups that are now well established in the UK as cultural domination. The more liberal *Swann Report* argues that they must be rooted in rationality, and appears to use the term 'shared values' primarily to refer to those that can 'justifiably be presented as universally appropriate' (DES, 1985, p.4). A Muslim response would claim that all cultural values, even those of our contemporary secular society, have roots in religion, and it is only by exploring 'those fundamental absolute values which all religions share' (Ashraf, 1986, p. vi) that we can arrive at an adequate conceptualization of 'shared values'. Unless this debate about shared values can be resolved, the notion of the celebration of diversity, which lies at the heart of multi-cultural education, also becomes mere rhetoric, and one may be tempted to conclude, as Sir Keith Joseph did in his retirement speech on 21 May 1986, that 'multi-cultural education has become an almost meaningless phrase'.

The third category involves questions of rights. The right of minority groups to preserve, maintain and transmit their distinctive beliefs and values to the next generation is closely tied up with the concept of pluralism, but the rights of parents and children as individuals raise different questions. To what extent do parents have the right to bring up their own children in their own culture and religion, and to what extent do children have the right to be liberated from the restricting beliefs of their parents? Do schools have a duty to encourage all children to develop into autonomous individuals, as Honeyford believes, even if this involves creating a serious clash of loyalties in some minority groups, or should schools give priority to the development of emotional stability and security in their children by ensuring that there is some degree of consistency between the values to which they are exposed at home and those to which they are exposed at school? Questions regarding the rights of children thus merge into questions of educational theory and practice. Honeyford was criticized by LEA advisers for not drawing more extensively on the experiences that children brought with them to school: but perhaps such an approach to teaching is part of the 'fashionable progressive bandwagon' which he whole-heartedly rejects. On the other hand Honeyford does not discuss the argument by Parekh (1985) that multi-cultural education is in fact in the liberal tradition, since education can only open children's minds and develop their critical awareness if it presents them with alternatives and forces them to enter sympathetically into the experiences of others.

These three issues — pluralism, shared values and rights — lie at the very heart of the debate about multi-cultural education. Each deserves a much more extensive treatment than it is possible to provide in the remaining pages of this volume. All I can hope to do is to sketch out briefly the direction which a fuller examination of each of them might follow, and thus take a little further the debate on multi-cultural education which Honeyford himself hoped his articles would open up.

PLURALISM

In classical liberal theory, as Crittenden (1982, p. 13) points out, the fundamental units of society are the individual and the state, and intermediate groups are understood wholly in instrumental terms — to protect and advance the interests of individuals. Contemporary liberalism, on the other hand, has come to place more value on groups, since individuals need social contact, tend to find their identity through common institutions and activities and do in fact have shared final ends (*cf* Gaus, 1983, p. 108). Groups tend to be socially cohesive because their members share characteristics which distinguish them from other groups. Only some of these dis-tinguishing characteristics, however, are sufficiently significant for the members of the group to be considered a separate *community*; language, culture, race and religion are among the most important of these. A society will generally be considered pluralist if it is made up of different communities in this sense, distinguished from each other by language, culture, race or religion but living side by side in mutual tolerance. In the West, this kind of pluralism is seen as a way of preserving fundamental freedoms (such as freedom of conscience and religion), particularly for minority groups, against oppression by a powerful central government or by crude majoritarianism. Such pluralism involves the encouragement of diversity as good for the health of democracy, indeed, as the very essence of democracy. On a liberal view, however, diversity can only be celebrated under certain conditions; it is clear, for example, that indiscriminate tolerance may become a license for intolerance if it facilitates the existence of groups that deny such fundamental values as freedom, justice and equality (*cf.* Marcuse, 1969, p. 90). Freedom therefore can be granted to a group, on a liberal view, only if it satisfies certain conditions. These conditions include respect for individual freedom (including freedom of action, freedom of conscience, freedom to leave the group); recognition that other groups have the right to enjoy the same freedoms and privileges that it enjoys for itself within the wider society; and respect for the interests of the wider society (which presupposes a commitment to certain social and moral values, such as justice and an acceptance of the rule of law). Any discussion of pluralism therefore involves the interplay between the freedom of the individual, the freedom of the group and the interests of the broader society; but even on a contemporary liberal view, it is the freedom of the group which most frequently has to give way in the face of constraints from the other two.

Various attempts have been made by social and political theorists to justify the placing of greater stress on the group than liberalism allows, but, as we shall see, none of these attempts is directly related to the dominant form of pluralism in British society — the presence alongside the indigenous majority of ethnic minority groups with diverse and sometimes opposed cultural values and ways of life. Nicholls (1974, 1975) has distinguished three types of social and political pluralism which stress the importance of the group; I shall call these the American Model, the Colonial Model and the English Model.

On the American Model, (seen in the writings of Bentley, Truman, Dahl and others, and more recently Sowell and Glazer), groups are said to compete to influence the policy of government at different levels in the interests of their own members, through expensive electioneering or civil rights campaigns, for example. The state is seen as 'a regulator and adjustor among them; defining the limits of their actions, preventing and settling conflicts' (Dewey, 1920, p. 203). Wolff, however, argues that such a system favours those groups already in existence (1968, pp. 149, 152), among which there is in any case already a considerable degree of cultural uniformity (cf Van den Berghe, 1967). The new ethnic minorities are unlikely to gain the power, skills and resources to urge their cause against entrenched interests, unless they conform more fully to existing political and cultural values. Marcuse (1968, p. 61) therefore concludes that such 'harmonizing pluralism' in the United States is a manifestation of a new totalitarianism.

On the Colonial Model (which emerges in the writings of Furnivall, Boeke, M. G. Smith and Despres), group affiliations do not form a cross-cutting network or web, but reinforce one another so that the state is made up of different segments, separated from each other by social, cultural, religious and racial factors. Consequently, the members of the groups live almost all their lives within the single groups, meeting members of other groups only 'in the market place'. The whole state is kept together by two factors — by a common economic system and by force. Though the sociologists and social anthropologists on whose work this model is based are not concerned with contemporary Western pluralist societies so much as with colonial or post-colonial territories such as Burma or the Dutch East Indies, much of what they write does seem relevant to the situation of disadvantaged ethnic minority groups in industrial societies. Where ethnic identity is paralleled by corresponding patterns of dwelling, occupation, language, religion, dress and recreation, the group is set apart from the rest of the society as having a distinctive cultural identity and way of life. However, if a society becomes segmented in this way, the likelihood of social and political instability is thought to increase. Also the use of force to hold the state together (unless in exceptional circumstances) offends fundamental democratic values.

On the English Model (based on the work of Figgis, Maitland, Cole and the early Harold Laski), groups were seen as voluntary associations which the individual could freely join or withdraw from, but they could not be understood fully in terms of the lives of their individual members. The assumption was that most people would belong to a number of different groups (cultural, religious, economic, civic or other) and they would have a cross-cutting membership: thus people of different races might belong to the same trade unions and people of differing religious persuasions might share the same leisure interests. According to Figgis at least, people's membership of the state is dependent on their membership of societies like the church, the trade union or the family, and the state is best understood as a *communitas communitatum*. Though the state has some authority to regulate and control group activities, it has a corresponding duty to respect the *internal* development and functioning of the group (Figgis, 1913, pp. 121–4), and there may be occasions when groups are justified in resisting the state (Nicholls, 1974, p. 14). However, it is hard to imagine any modern state being prepared to allow minority groups total freedom in their internal functioning. A democratic state would inevitably seek to protect itself from the twin dangers of anarchy if the group refused to accept the state's authority and the possible suppression of individual rights within the group (Selznick, 1969, p. 38; Kerr, 1955, p. 14). While the English Model avoids some of the dangers of segmentation, it is dependent on membership of the different groups being cross-cutting; but this is not the case in practice with minority groups in the UK such as the Muslims, despite Honeyford's claim to the contrary (1982d), since they tend not to belong to a network of groups which also have members of other cultural and ethnic communities. The English Model turns out to be no less unsatisfactory than the other two in resolving the pluralist dilemma of modern democratic states: how to preserve the unity of the state based on democratic principles without threatening the existence of ethnic, cultural, and religious minorities which may have values and ways of life in direct conflict with those taken for granted by the majority. It seems unlikely that this can be achieved without some transformation of state controlled institutions such as schools. How much transformation is likely to be involved, and how it is to be achieved, however, depends on what sort of balance is to be struck between conflicting demands and conflicting underlying values.

Even within a liberal framework of values there is room for very considerable disagreement. Thus we find one liberal taking a comparatively hard line with the ethnic minorities: he somewhat reluctantly accepts toleration of communities whose culture does not support autonomy, for example, so long as they are 'viable communities', and he hopes for their gradual transformation. At the same time, he claims that if the life they offer their young is too impoverished and unrewarding, compulsory assimilation (by force if necessary) may be 'the only humane course' (Raz, 1986, pp. 423–4). On the other hand, we find another liberal arguing that ethnic minorities should be permitted unrestricted freedom to follow their own customs and religious practices, be governed by their personal law and receive education in their language and cultural tradition.

This freedom would be subject to just two limitations: any practice leading to severe physical abuse would be disallowed, and impractical institutional accommodations to minority beliefs and values would not be required (Lustgarten, 1983, p. 101f).

The former of these views adopts an approach of negative freedom (reluctant non-interference), which is very much in line with Honeyford's position, whereas the latter involves positive freedom, particularly in the sphere of education, where the transmission of the cultural values of minority communities would be provided out of public resources.

A more moderate liberal view of pluralism is provided in the *Swann Report* (DES, 1985). This had among its terms of reference to 'review in relation to schools the educational needs and attainments of children from ethnic minority groups' (p. vii). It starts by attempting to reflect upon the relationship between the ethnic majority community and the ethnic minority communities in the context of the kind of society for which in its view the educational system should seek to prepare all youngsters:

> The ethnic community in a truly pluralist society cannot expect to remain untouched and unchanged by the presence of ethnic minority groups — indeed the concept of pluralism implies seeing the very diversity of such a society, in terms for example of the range of religious experience and the variety of languages and language forms, as an enrichment of the experience of all those within it. Similarly, however, the ethnic minority communities cannot in practice preserve all elements of their cultures and lifestyles un-changed and in their entirety — indeed if they were to wish to do so it would in many cases be impossible for them to take on the shared values of the wider pluralist society. In order to retain their identities when faced with the pervasive influences of the lifestyle of the majority community, ethnic minority groups must nevertheless be free within the democratic framework to maintain those elements which they themselves consider to be the most essential to their sense of ethnic identity — whether these take the form of adherence to a particular religious faith or the maintenance of their own language for use within the home and their ethnic community — without fear of prejudice or persecution by other groups. It is important to emphasize here free choice for individuals, so that all may move and develop as they wish within the structure of the pluralist society. We

would thus regard a democratic pluralist society as seeking to achieve a balance between, on the one hand, the maintenance and active support of the essential elements of the cultures and lifestyles of all the ethnic groups within it, and, on the other, the acceptance by all groups of a set of shared values distinctive of society as a whole. This then is our view of a genuinely pluralist society, as both socially cohesive and culturally diverse (pp. 5–6).

This passage appears to suggest that in a pluralist society there should be freedom for the members of minority groups to maintain their distinctive cultures and lifestyles, since assimilation unjustly seeks to deny the fundamental freedom of individuals to differ in areas 'where no single way can justifiably be presented as universally appropriate' (p.4); but this freedom is subject to two major constraints: first, priority must be given to taking on 'the shared values of the wider pluralist society' (for without these there would be the danger that society would fragment along ethnic lines, and this would 'seriously threaten the stability and cohesion of society as a whole' (p. 7)); and secondly, the group's authority and control over the individual is constrained by the requirement of 'free choice for individuals'. These constraints suggest that in spite of the claim in the last two sentences of the passage, the goal of social cohesion is taken more seriously than that of cultural diversity. Indeed, the tentative vision of society at the end of the Report's first chapter confirms this impression:

We are perhaps looking for the 'assimilation' of *all* groups within a redefined concept of what it means to live in British society today (p. 8).

These two constraints on the freedom of the group are very much in evidence in the Report's educational recommendations. Stress is placed on the role of education in laying the foundations of, and helping to shape, a 'genuinely pluralist society' (p. 316). Three goals are mentioned for education: first, educating all children to an understanding of the shared values of our society; secondly, helping children to appreciate the diversity of lifestyles and backgrounds which make up our society; and thirdly, meeting the individual educational needs of all pupils (pp. 316–7). The first of these aims is based on the first constraint mentioned earlier, the avoidance of social fragmentation. The second aim again seeks to avoid fragmentation by encouraging the celebration of diversity, while at the same time opening the door to genuine individual choice between alternative ways of life. The third aim raises the question of how the 'individual educational needs' of the pupils are to be assessed, and by whom. The Report appears to suggest that the danger which Harris (1982a, p. 227) draws attention to, that any selection is bound to reflect the cultural values of the selector (he writes of '*our* judgements as to the worth of elements of *their* culture'), is to be avoided by assessing such needs according to rational, educational criteria. The third aim therefore inevitably involves the right of all children to decide for themselves their future way of life. There seems to be an unresolved tension in the *Swann Report* between its claim that education should at least partly be concerned to enable and assist ethnic minorities 'to maintain what they regard as the essential elements of their cultural identities' (p, 465–6) and its approval of a statement by Banks to the effect that if schools were to reinforce the values and beliefs that students bring with them from home, such an approach would be too 'culturally encapsulating' (p. 322). Presumably it is the need for education to promote the shared values of the broader society and to respect the rights of the individual pupil which leads the report to conclude that

> the role of education cannot be and cannot be expected to be to reinforce the values, beliefs and cultural identity which each child brings to the school (p. 321).

Before we can examine what sort of multi-cultural education is compatible with such a perspective, however, we must consider these two constraints — shared values and individual rights — in more detail.

SHARED VALUES

In Honeyford's view the only set of shared values which schools are justified in presenting to their children are those based on traditional British beliefs, culture and ways of life. As we have already seen, he maintains that such values provide an appropriate framework for education in this country, because they have deep roots in our national heritage, because the majority of parents support them and because to abandon them may leave education a prey to fashion or to political extremism. Indeed, the wish to jettison traditional values he considers to be indicative of a dangerously revolutionary tendency.

The *Swann Report* pours scorn on such a view that pluralism and multi-cultural education are undermining what it calls 'an ill-defined and nebulous concept of "true Britishness"' (DES, 1985, p. 7). It argues that the wish to base education on traditional British values and culture is no more justifiable than the wish to use education to preserve minority beliefs and values. Schools, in the Report's view, do not have a responsibility for any kind of cultural preservation (p. 322), and certainly not to reinforce a single cultural view (p. 321), for this would unjustifiably restrict a child's freedom to decide his own future way of life (p. 323). In any case, culture is not a static thing, but is constantly changing as it adapts and absorbs new ideas and influences (pp. 7, 323). Since

> the reality of British society now and in the future, is that a variety of ethnic groups, with their own distinctive lifestyles and value systems, will be living together (p. 324),

good education must reflect this diversity, encourage a sensitive understanding and appreciation of a variety of cultures and lifestyles, and avoid an 'anachronistically Anglo-centric view of the world' in both curriculum and school ethos (p. 318). There is therefore no onus on ethnic minorities to feel under an obligation to 'conform to the traditional British way of life' (p. 6); on the contrary, the Report envisages a society

> which both values the diversity within it, whilst united by the cohesive force of the common aims, attitudes and values which we all share (p. 7),

and sees education as having a major role in creating such a society (p. 316).

The *Swann Report* thus makes it abundantly clear that it does not equate the concept of 'shared values' with traditional British values. How the concept *is* to be understood in the Report, however, is by no means clear. At times, for example when it discusses 'the common...values which we all share' (p. 7), it seems to refer to an HCF of values, that is, to a set of values which is shared as a matter of empirical fact by all the major cultural groups that make up contemporary British society. Such a view, as I have pointed out elsewhere (Halstead, 1986, pp. 7, 17) would be quite acceptable to Muslims and other minority groups in the UK. At other times, however, for example when it discusses the need for the minority groups to '*take on* the shared values of the wider pluralist society' (p. 5, my emphasis), the Report appears no longer to have in mind an HCF of values but to be pointing, as White (1987, p. 17) suggests, in the direction of what our shared values *should* be, even if they are not in practice shared by all the groups in our society. References to what can 'justifiably be presented as universally appropriate' (p. 4) suggest that the *Swann Report* accepts that there are criteria of rationality which 'shared values' must satisfy if their acceptance as universal principles is to be justified. The view of the task of education which emerges from this is a fundamentally liberal one. First, education should encourage a commitment to the framework of shared values and an understanding of the rational principles on which they are based. Secondly, education should provide children with objective information about and insight into a wide range of non-shared cultural values; encourage them to respond sympathetically and indeed to value diversity in this area; and leave them free to determine their own individual identities and develop into autonomous individuals. Minority groups such as Muslims, however, may be much less happy with this second account of 'shared values', since it is based on liberal assumptions which they do not necessarily share, yet their freedom to opt out of the educational system to which it gives rise would be very limited.

Various attempts have been made to tighten up the rather loose concept of 'shared values' in the *Swann Report* (for example, White, 1987; Haydon, 1987). I want to argue that the term consists of two distinct elements: those values which all groups in a pluralist society do in practice have in common, and those values which, though not currently shared by all groups, need to be agreed upon in order to provide a basis for the establishment of common institutions in the broader pluralist society. Clearly there could be no society at all without a minimum set of common values and standards of behaviour. These are likely to include, first a basic social morality without which no form of social life would be possible (in particular, a respect for justice and a recognition that other groups have as much right as one's own to avoid physical pain and death among their members); secondly, a commitment to values presupposed by the pluralist ideal (in particular, the toleration of groups with different ideals to one's own and the rejection of violence as a means of persuasion); and thirdly, the acceptance of a common system of law and government by all groups within the broader society (though the systems need not be the same for all 'broader societies') and a commitment to seek to change these only through democratic means.

So far so good. But, as White (1987, p. 16) points out, this minimum framework of common values is a very *thin* one, certainly not sufficient to support a common system of education as extensive as we have today. The need for such a common system, in order to prevent social disintegration resulting from racial, cultural and religious diversity in our society, might in itself provide adequate justification for the liberal desire to expand this minimum framework of values into a complete scheme of social morality beyond which lies merely an area of legitimate diversity (itself a matter for celebration) and individual choice. But Crittenden (1982) and White (1987) offer a number of further justifications. If a pluralist society is *a* society, there must be interaction between its constituent groups. Political and economic systems cannot exist in isolation from cultural factors (language is an example), and if the former characterize the society as a whole, the latter cannot be left totally to the society's constituent groups. It is impossible for a political order to function 'without making at least some assumptions about the ingredients of a worthwhile human life' (Crittenden, 1982, p. 30). Though the liberal vision of pluralism is not compatible with Honeyford's view that all groups should be initiated into the culture of the dominant group, it anticipates that there will be a 'gradual merging of outlooks' (White, 1987, pp. 15, 21–2) and that traditional ethnic, religious or class-based groups will correspondingly decline (Crittenden, 1982, p. 37). Crittenden at least is aware of a tension between his depiction of diversity as desirable and the homogenizing tendencies of the type of pluralism he supports, but he nevertheless believes that such 'open pluralism' with its high degree of interaction between groups is the most justifiable kind of pluralism.

How might such an expansion of the minimum framework of common values take place? White (1987) and Haydon (1987) both propose some form of democratic negotiation which would directly involve far more of the general population than representative government does, and which would be carried on at various levels and in various contexts, including the school. Democratic participation itself, however, already presupposes certain shared values and an underlying shared goal, and if such a basic consensus among the various groups in our society does not exist, then the proposal may be perceived by minority groups as constituting a threat to their existence or way of life by undermining their traditional identity. Indeed, these anxieties seem well founded in view of White's hypothesis that as an increasing convergence in values appears, so 'a further decline among religiously-based values' may be expected (1987, p. 22)

One of the main values presupposed by the process of democratic participation is a commitment to rationality. There could be no basis for the negotiation of an expanded framework of common values if there were no general acceptance of rationality as a means of assessing beliefs and values. To the liberal, the value of rationality is self-evident; as Crittenden (1982) says,

> it cannot be seriously doubted that the practice of critical, reflective rationality is preferable to any that relies largely on the unquestioning acceptance of received beliefs and the pronouncements of established authority (p. 42).

Critical rationality does not require, as Crittenden is at pains to point out (pp. 44 *ff*), that individuals should be constantly calling everything into question, or that they should refuse to acknowledge the possibility of areas of experience that surpass rational understanding, or that they should deny the importance of feeling in human experience, or that they should assume that there must always be a single best answer to complex moral problems. What critical rationality *does* require of members of the pluralist society is an active willingness to review all beliefs and values in the light of the evidence of rationality and experience and to reject or modify them where the evidence becomes strongly weighted against them. Such a view will undoubtedly appeal more to liberals than to minority groups such as the Muslims in the UK whose way of life is based on 'commitment to a "sacred" order of authority that dominates every aspect of human life'. The price that the latter must pay for general toleration in a pluralist society, on Crittenden's view (p. 50), is 'the acceptance of a public order at odds with its fundamental ideals'.

Like the English pluralists discussed above, some minority groups may naturally be suspicious of tolerance on these terms. The liberal wish to expand the framework of common values in order to promote the common good and the public interest and to reflect the essential unity of the state may well be seen as a disguised wish to impose majority values on unwilling minorities. Such groups are likely to be dubious about the possibility of creating any set of common values beyond the purely political framework necessary for the maintenance of order (Nicholls, 1974, pp. 46, 62). Insofar as they see any 'common good' worth considering, they see it as structural rather than substantive in nature (Nicholls, 1975, pp. 9–10); it involves the provision of a suitable context for separate groups to continue to live their own more or less autonomous lives.

Two further points emerge from this discussion of shared values. The first is that there are clear educational consequences that arise from a commitment to liberal pluralism. In particular, the uncritical presentation of any concept of the good or of any understanding of the world and human life is ruled out. Children of all groups need to be taught to question their assumptions, to grapple with existing world views, to engage in rational debate and thus to value the diversity of outlooks which makes such critical engagement possible. The second is that the biggest challenge to this dominant liberal view comes not from those like Honeyford who wish the expanded framework of common values to be tied in much more closely to the traditional British way of life, but from those groups whose fundamental commitments include the acceptance of a divine order of authority that affects every area of their lives and prevents them from *celebrating* a diversity which includes groups totally antipathetic to their own beliefs and values.

Both of these points will be discussed in more detail below, but first, attention must be given to the claim made by White (1987, p. 24) and others that although liberal pluralism is generally happy to allow the values of minority groups to flourish or wither 'as the reflective judgements of their members determine', there is one area where such freedom cannot flourish unchecked:

> The one area in which the larger community may sometimes have to interfere with local values is in the upbringing of children . . . (There are) limits to how far they can be brought up to believe that the values of their community are the only ones they should follow.

This leads straight to the vexed question of parental and children's rights.

RIGHTS

As we have already seen, Honeyford argues that ethnic minority parents have no right to restrict the education of their children to the narrow framework of their own beliefs and values. He argues, first, that this would be against the interests of the broader society, since it would militate against social harmony and integration; secondly, that it would be against the interests of the children themselves, since they have a right to find their own way in life and the right to expect education to prepare them for this as well as helping them to compete on equal terms with others in political, economic and social life; and thirdly, that if schools were merely to reinforce children's existing values, beliefs and cultural identity, this would be too culturally encapsulating and ultimately anti-educational.

It is not clear whether Honeyford objects only to schools helping ethnic minority parents to bring up their children in their own religion (because he claims this would weaken the overarching traditional British culture and way of life and reinforce the separateness of minority communities) or whether he is expressing a more principled objection to attempts by any group, majority or minority, to foreclose children's options through an education restricted to a single set of cultural or religious beliefs and values. If the former is intended, then he lays himself open to charges of cultural racism as defined in chapter six; but if the latter is intended, he is raising a question that has come increasingly to the fore in educational thinking in recent years (*cf* Coons and Sugarman, 1978; McLaughlin, 1984): how far parents who are religious believers have the right to bring up their children in their own religion and to expect schools to reinforce this upbringing. This latter question lies at the heart of any discussion about what concessions within public education can justfiably be made to religious believers so that their children are never put in a position where they are expected to act contrary to their deeply held beliefs.

P. White (1983) argues that

> there are no, so to speak, self-standing parental rights. That is, there are no rights possessed by parents qua parents which permit them to direct their children's lives along certain tracks (p. 159*f*)

Though she goes on to concede that parents do have two types of rights (the first is to enable them to carry out their parental responsibilities — though it is not clear precisely what would be licensed by such a right — and the second, held in common with all citizens of a democratic society, allows them to try to interest others, including children, in their own interests), her claim offends widely held 'commonsense' assumptions about parental rights. Parents have traditionally been considered to have the right to develop particular talents in their children, to buy superior education, to withdraw their children from RE lessons, to send them to a religious school, and so on. At first blush, White's view seems totalitarian in the sense that it denies parents a freedom that they have traditionally held. Her view is, however, a practical attempt to resolve a problem that liberals (for example, Fishkin, 1983) have been becoming increasingly aware of, that the autonomy of the family sits uneasily with other liberal values such as the equality of life chances and the principle of personal autonomy.

Before we can consider whether parents have the right to bring up their children in their own religion, we must therefore consider whether parents have the right in principle to make *any* fundamental decisions about the education and upbringing of their own children. It is clear that children are physically, psychologically and morally immature, and that at least young children lack the rational capacity to exercise the responsibilities of citizenship. This is taken to justify paternalism (the right to interfere in the life of another person for his or her own good), although the *extent* to which paternalism should be applied towards children is a matter of much debate (*cf* Harris, 1982b). Strike (1982a, p. 128) argues that the present freedom of the child may be justifiably infringed to prevent him from harming himself, to develop his rational capacities, to expand his future opportunities, to maximize his future happiness and to prevent him from making immature, uninformed decisions. The question is whether the parents or the state should be primary paternalistic agent in respect of the child. Though the extension of the state's general control over the child at the expense of the family in the last century has been viewed with concern in some quarters (e.g. Geach and Szwed, 1983, pp. 1–2), such control is generally limited to the public development of the child (i.e. as a future citizen). The state recognizes that the child can only learn what it is to be a person and develop communal feelings and social attitudes from other individuals, and this task is likely to be best carried out by those who have the strongest sense of duty and commitment to the child, who know the child and its needs most intimately and who are attached most closely to it by bonds of affection. This relationship between child, parent and state can perhaps be expressed most clearly in terms of a hypothetical social contract made between parents and the state on the birth of a child. The biological parents are appointed trustees of the child; the terms of the trusteeship require them to make decisions that are in the best interests of the child and not against the public interest; in return they are allowed to determine the course of their family life without undue interference from the state. The state remains the final arbiter when the terms of the trusteeship are abused by the natural parents, and thus has the right to find substitute parents or to take over the trusteeship itself if the natural parents are clearly either not acting in the interests of the child (for example, child abuse) or acting in conflict with the public interest (for example, allowing the child to commit crimes). Otherwise, state involvement in the upbringing of children is limited to situations where the state has an interest in what happens (for example, to increase industrial performance, to develop social competencies, to prepare children for democratic citizenship). Thus parents are not barred in principle from making fundamental decisions about the education or upbringing of their children — unless those decisions conflict with either the public interest or their children's own interests.

What sort of parental decisions *could* clash with the public interest? The general public has both a positive and a negative interest in education. First, there is the concern that children should develop competencies which will help to create a stable and democratic society. Since all citizens share the same laws, the same political rights and the same economic system, it is important that they should be able to 'interact harmoniously and communicate intelligibly' and 'function properly in a just society' (Strike, 1982a, p. 159). Secondly, there is the concern to protect the public interest from harm. If parents sought to bring up their children, for example, in a way which was seen to 'fuel intolerance and undermine social co-operation' (Coons and Sugarman, 1978, p. 91), the state would have the right to overrule the parents to prevent the public interest from being harmed.

But is the public interest in either respect likely to be harmed by the religious upbringing of children or by the attempt to respond positively to the cultural requirements and sensitivities of children from ethnic or religious minorities? So long as the concessions do not stand in the way of the children coming to understand and share the common values of the broader society, there seems to be no reason why the public interest should be damaged. On the contrary, children are more likely to develop loyalty towards a state which respects their own religious beliefs and values, and the greater emotional and social stability which is likely to result if children's public education is not in conflict with the values of the home may again be in the public interest.

Strike (1982a, pp. 160–1) argues convincingly that although schools are publicly financed and administered, they normally provide instruction in excess of what is required by the public interest. From the standpoint of the English pluralists, this additional education would primarily be concerned to initiate children into the shared values and beliefs of the group; but on a liberal view, which is presumably the perspective from which Honeyford is writing, such additional education can only be justified on the grounds that it is in the interests of the child. What remains now to be decided is whether there are objective, educational criteria according to which the best interests of the child can be judged, or whether they are to be judged by parents exercising their own paternalistic discretion. This can only be resolved by a closer examination of the concept of the interests of the child.

There is in fact no clear liberal view of the sense in which children have interests. P. White (1983, pp. 139–41), for example, insists on talking of the autonomy (not the potential autonomy) of the child, while Mill (1972a, p. 73) specifically excludes children from all that he says about the principle of liberty. Child liberationists such as Holt (1975), however, have argued that children should have the right to decide for themselves matters which affect them most directly, and partly as a result of the influence of the liberationists the dividing line between childhood and adulthood is gradually being eroded (*cf* Harris, 1982; Postman, 1983). The recent emphasis on children's rights (Wald, 1979; Houlgate, 1980; Wringe, 1981) has led to family relationships being increasingly discussed in terms of the conflicting rights and interests of parents and children (Ackerman, 1980, pp. 15–4); this is because rights are not usually invoked except to redress injustice, and the injustice suffered by children is usually at the hands of those who make decisions on their behalf (i.e. the parents). Since children have no power to support their own rights, the state intervenes on their behalf when it sees fit. State paternalism is typically seen in the child-saving movement (Freeman, 1983, p. 29–35; Goldstein *et al.*, 1973, 1979, 1986), with its emphasis on the protection of children from inadequate care. However, the debate comes a full circle with Goodman's claim (1971) that talk of children's 'rights' obscures their more fundamental needs for love and security. The unhappy situation of children, he says,

> is not something to cope with polemically or to understand in terms of 'freedom', 'democracy', 'rights' and 'power', like bringing lawyers into a family quarrel. It has to be solved by wise traditions in organic communities with considerable stability, with equity instead of law and compassion more than either.

A middle-of-the-road liberal view considers children to be persons, objects of respect and ends in themselves, but sees them as autonomous, rational, moral agents only in the sense of belonging to the class of beings who share those characteristics: their capacity in this respect is unactualized potential. It is the fact that they are objects of respect and that they are potential autonomous rational moral agents that justifies us in talking of the interests of the child. It is the fact that children are immature and only potentially rational and autonomous that makes them dependent on adults for the early years of their life and justifies paternalism.

The interests of children are, of course, not necessarily paramount in decision-making which affects them. In matters in which the public interest is involved (for example, the financing of education), the interests of an individual child must be weighed against those of other children and other interested parties, such as the state and the broader society. Within the family, the child's interests are weighed against those of other members of the family. There may be some situations in which a parent finds herself wearing three hats simultaneously: representative of her own interests, trustee of the interests of her child, and objective arbiter of these perhaps conflicting interests. This problem may only recede if we acknowledge the existence of values which are supernumerary to the basic liberal framework — the wider moral context of love, care and concern in which people make sacrifices for their children, seek a better future for them than they had themselves, and so on.

If we concede, however, that children have rights as potentially autonomous agents, and that parents (at least when they are wearing their trustee hat) are bound to take into account the interests of the child, there is still a difficulty in establishing where, exactly, the interests of the child lie. Coons and Sugarman (1978, ch. 3) argue that there is no general consensus about the best interests of the child, though most liberals would want to say that at least one thing, the development of personal and moral autonomy, is in the general interest of *all* children (Crittenden, 1978; McLaughlin, 1984).

Of course, it is not sufficient to argue that children are potentially autonomous and that we have a duty to help them to achieve their potential, for they may be potentially racist or murderous; the decision to help them to achieve the particular potential of personal and moral autonomy requires a prior judgment about the value of this potential. This prior judgment may be based on the claim that children have a right to certain 'primary goods', among which would be an education designed to give them a knowledge of competing conceptions of the good life and to develop their capacity to choose freely and rationally between them (*cf* Bridges, 1984, p. 56; Gutmann, 1980). According to Rawls (1972), paternalistic decisions, as far as these are justified,

> are to be guided by the individual's own settled preferences and interests insofar as they are not irrational, or failing a knowledge of these (as in the case of children), by the theory of primary goods. As we know less and less about a person, we act for him as we would act for ourselves from the standpoint of the original position (pp. 209, 248–50).

A primary good is something rational people want whatever else they want — rights and liberties, opportunities and powers, income and wealth and self-respect (*ibid.*, pp. 62, 92). This list of primary goods may thus be taken to provide the general criteria 'according to which we can judge the interest of persons under paternalism' (Strike, 1982b, p. 135). This list also provides for many liberals the general criteria according to which a common curriculum can be built. Rights, liberties and self-respect all point in the direction of personal and moral automony: if one is to help children to be free to do something, they must be helped to develop the power and the means to do it. White (1973) and others have argued that people can make an informed choice between alternative activities and ways of life only if they have been introduced to the range of possibilities. A child can become a responsible citizen in a democratic society only by means of a basic general education of sufficient breadth and openness.

Liberalism can thus produce a framework of both public and personal values which can elucidate the interests of the child and thus provide a basis for educational decision-making. The public values involve preparation for citizenship in a democratic society; the child is to come to understand, and develop a commitment to, those values in the broader society which can justifiably be claimed as universally appropriate. The personal values involve the development of personal and moral autonomy, based on rationality combined with the child's right to freedom and self-respect: the child needs to become aware of the diversity of beliefs and lifestyles that exist in the world and to develop the capacity to make rational, informed choices between alternatives.

THE JUSTIFIABILITY OF MULTI-CULTURAL EDUCATION

We are now in a position to ask whether multi-cultural education, of whatever type, is or could be in conflict with the interests of the broader society, with the interests of the child or with fundamental educational principles, as Honeyford argues. It appears from the above discussion that parents as primary paternalistic agents have the right on a liberal view to make demands relating to their children's education so long as these demands do not conflict with either the public interest or with the children's interests as liberals perceive them. Ethnic minority parents have in fact been demanding that education should respect their religious and cultural beliefs and not put their children in a position where they are required to act contrary to those beliefs. It is clearly in the interests of the state to show respect towards such beliefs and to avoid any appearance of majoritarian domination, for this will encourage minority groups to develop a sense of loyalty to the broader community, and social harmony and cohesion will be increased. It is also in the interests of the state to demonstrate the justice, tolerance and celebration of diversity which it expects its component groups to show towards each other. It is in the interests of children to be encouraged to develop a coherent self-identity, and not to be put in a position where the values they are presented with in school are in serious conflict with those they have encountered at home. A strong argument can therefore be developed that type one multi-cultural education (respecting the cultural requirements and sensitivies of minority groups) is in the interests of both the broader society (by encouraging social stability) and in the interests of the individual child (by providing a more stable base for a consistent self-concept to develop). The aim of the concessions involved in this type of multi-cultural education is not to 'inculcate an uncritical acceptance of any conception of the good life' (Ackerman, 1980, p. 163), which would, of course, be unjustifiable on a liberal view, but to provide children with continuity and stability and to avoid unnecessarily disorienting them.

Type two multi-cultural education, which seeks to prepare children for life in a pluralist society by encouraging them to respect those whose beliefs and values differ from their own, to see diversity as a source of enrichment, and to be open to a variety of ways of looking at the world, is even more in line with a liberal view of education. As Parekh (1985) points out, if children never get beyond the framework of their own culture and beliefs (even if these are shared by the majority in their country), they are unlikely to develop lively, enquiring minds, imagination or a critical faculty. A mono-cultural diet is likely to breed 'arrogance and insensitivity' among children from the majority culture and 'profound self-alienation' and a distorted self-concept among minority children. Multi-cultural education, on the other hand, is

> an education in freedom — freedom from inherited biases and narrow feelings and sentiments, as well as freedom to explore other cultures and perspectives and make choices in full awareness of the available and practicable alternatives. Multi-cultural education is, therefore, not a departure from, nor incompatible with, but a further refinement of, the liberal idea of education. It does not cut off children from their own culture. Rather it enables them to enrich, refine and take a broader view of it without losing their roots in it... If education is concerned to develop such basic human capacities as curiosity, self-criticism, capacity for reflection, ability to form an independent judgment, sensitivity, intellectual humility and respect for others, and to open the pupil's mind to the great achievements of mankind, then it must be multi-cultural in orientation (Parekh, 1985, pp. 22–3).

In the same article, Parekh dismisses the view that multi-cultural education is necessarily based on cultural relativism, as has been implied by Scruton

(1986) and others. Parekh argues that different cultures have a right to be understood in their own terms, and that they need to be explored sympathetically, not judged superficially on the basis of the norms and values of another culture; but this is not to claim that they are above all criticism and judgment. The debate about cultural relativism is, of course, an extended one (*cf* Warnock, 1979; Cooper, 1980, pp. 138*ff*; Walkling, 1980; Zec, 1980; etc.), but in view of Parekh's statement, it would seem that the onus is now on those who believe that multi-cultural education is based on relativist assumptions to justify their view. Finally, Parekh points out that even if a culture is ultimately judged to be defective, this must not be taken to mean that its adherents are less deserving of respect as human beings or have a weaker claim to basic human rights.

If we accept these arguments, none of Honeyford's criticisms of multi-cultural education stands up to close examination. It does not go against the interests of the child or the interests of the broader society, nor does it offend fundamental educational principles. It is not a 'fashionable progressive bandwagon', but an attempt to relate long-established liberal educational principles to a new social situation. It is not part of a sinister left-wing plot to overthrow the traditional order of things, but a rational response to the presence of ethnic minorities in this country, based on the values of freedom, equality and justice. It does not lack attachment to history and tradition, for its roots can be traced through the long history of liberal education. It does not necessitate an acceptance of cultural relativism or claim that different cultures cannot be criticized and evaluated, but simply requires any judgments that are made to avoid superficiality, ignorance and bias. In particular, it attempts to avoid unacceptable forms of cultural domination, such as a crude form of majoritarianism which may totally exclude minority cultures from public institutions like schools and thus leave minorities with a sense of grievance.

A MUSLIM CHALLENGE TO MULTI-CULTURAL EDUCATION

Honeyford's criticisms of multi-cultural education, which appear to be presented from a liberal perspective, can thus be answered convincingly from within that perspective. And to the extent that contemporary educational practice in authorities such as Bradford is based on such a perspective, his worries seem unfounded.

However, a problem remains — to which I have alluded from time to time throughout the present chapter — relating to those groups who are reluctant to accept a liberal framework of values as a basis for educational decision-making (*cf.* Ashraf, 1988a, 1988b). To such groups, the principles of liberal education may appear as just one more challengeable version of what is good for children. Bridges (1984) summarizes the problem:

> We are faced then with a conflict of world views which cannot be resolved except within a framework of premises which constitute one such world view and therefore cannot (except perhaps by a convenient coincidence of opinions) resolve conflicts between such views (p. 57).

The Muslims in the UK are one such group. Many are afraid that the rational principles and democratic participation, which liberalism sees as justifying an expansion of the framework of common values, will intentionally or unintentionally produce a new form of cultural domination. They resent Crittenden's claim that the price they must pay for general toleration in a pluralist society is 'the acceptance of a public order at odds with (their) fundamental ideals' (1982, p. 50). They do not accept that religion should be treated as one of a possible range of cultural options open to the individual child, for to them its basis in revelation gives it a fixedness which is quite alien to culture, and religion provides the foundation for the unity, indeed the very existence, of the community of which, by birth and upbringing, they are a part. They despair when they find their own presence in the UK being used by liberal educationalists to justify policies quite alien to their wishes. This last point has been explored in more detail elsewhere (Halstead and Khan-Cheema, 1987), but for now a couple of examples will suffice. Although there is considerable evidence that many Muslims would like to have the same choice which is available to Catholics, Jews and others, to send their children to a county school or to a voluntary-aided school, the Swann Committee has in response urged a reconsideration of the whole dual system of education (DES, 1985, p. 514), and this appears to imply a belief that the system is no longer justifiable and should be abandoned. The argument seems to be that there are no grounds under present legislation to refuse Muslims permission to establish such schools; but the existence of Muslim voluntary-aided schools may strongly militate against the harmonious pluralist society envisaged by the committee, by encouraging socially divisive attitudes in minority groups and racism in the majority; therefore the best course of action is to reconsider the legislation. Haldane (1986) has drawn attention to the irony of this proposal:

> How could it satisfy the Muslim wish for their own religious schools, to be required to send their children to secular institutions? And what view should they form of a society that would respond to their expression of deep attachment to tradition by casting off its own inheritance? (p.164).

Similarly, the presence of Muslim and other non-Christian children in our schools is commonly used as a major argument (for example, in the *Swann Report*, DES, 1985, pp. 497, 519) against the continuation of a compulsory daily act of collective worship. However, many Muslim organizations have made it clear that they do not wish such worship to be discontinued, merely to be adapted so that it does not conflict with the different faiths represented in schools (*cf* Khan-Cheema *et al.*, 1986, pp. 13, 16).

Muslims have shown no reluctance to accept the minimum set of common values (including a basic social morality and a common system of law and government) without which there could be no society at all, and to accept that these should occupy a prominent place in public education. However, they also believe that insofar as schools provide instruction in excess of what is required by the public interest, this additional education should be determined by the need to initiate children into the shared values and beliefs of the local community or the religious or cultural community to which they belong. They believe that the interests of the individual child do not exist in isolation from the group. For the Islamic community, religion provides

> a comprehensive viewpoint from which perspective on other areas of
> life is gained. Other domains are not adequately grasped until they
> are assimilated into the religious outlook (Strike, 1982b, p. 88).

If this dominance of religion over all aspects of life is accepted, it will have profound educational consequences. It may involve rejecting the autonomy of the academic discipline, which has traditionally been cherished in liberal education; Husain and Ashraf (1979) and Ashraf (1985), for example, have called for the disciplines to be Islamicized. It may also involve a reassessment of the meaning of personal and moral autonomy; if it means simply that one consents oneself (*autos*) to be bound by a rule (*nomos*), this would be quite consistent with a religious perspective on education, but tighter concepts of autonomy would not (*cf* Halstead, 1986, ch. 4). The creation of a school ethos in which religious values might be picked up, might also be considered just as valuable as the direct transmission of these values.

To fight for such principles within a common system of education must seem like an uphill task for even the most optimistic Muslim, and hence the possibility of some form of segregated education comes into question. So far, no Muslim voluntary-aided schools have been established, though there have been applications in Bradford, Brent and Kirklees. But there now seems to be a very real chance that the opting-out clause in the educational legislation currently under discussion at the time of writing, may provide Muslim parents in schools where they are the majority with the opportunity to create institutions much more in keeping with their own beliefs and values. Some Muslim groups are already actively considering this possibility (*The Times*

Educational Supplement, 16 October 1987, p. 1), though others are concerned about the social implications of such strengthening of cultural barriers (Ashraf, 1988a). The long-running debate between the need for social integration and cohesion on the one hand and the right of minority groups to preserve their own culture on the other looks set to take a new turn, in view of the present government's stress on freedom of choice for parents. Distinctively Islamic schools may well result from the new legislation, particularly in view of the trend towards the *de facto* segregation of education for Muslim communities which has already been identified in chapter two.

The case for such Muslim schools is a strong one, as I have pointed out elsewhere (Halstead, 1986). However, they also raise a number of fundamental problems, especially from a liberal perspective, relating to the nature and aims of education. For many people, it is the prospect of such schools which heightens and underlines the dangers to which Honeyford has been drawing attention. If such schools do in fact come into being, then it seems likely that his warnings about the dangers of social divisiveness will gain a more sympathetic hearing than they have up to now.

Appendix

A CHRONOLOGY OF EVENTS RELATING TO (a) EDUCATIONAL PROVISION FOR ETHNIC MINORITIES IN BRADFORD AND (b) THE HONEYFORD AFFAIR

(N.B. Events directly related to the Honeyford affair and Drummond Middle School are printed in italics.)

1964   There are sufficient immigrant children (mainly of Pakistani origin) in some of Bradford's inner city districts for a policy of dispersal ('bussing') to be introduced by the Labour-controlled council. The aim is to aid assimilation by ensuring that no school has more than 10 per cent immigrants, though this figure is soon raised to 25 per cent. By December 1965, twelve Bradford schools have already reached the 25 per cent limit (*Yorkshire Post*, 25 February 1966). In 1969, the figure is raised again, to 33 per cent, and Bradford announces a major review of its dispersal policy. Support remains strong within the council, if not among parents, for several more years, as the policy is seen as a way of avoiding ghetto schools (*Telegraph and Argus*, 27 June 1969, 29 March 1972).

1965   By January, immigrant children form 3.6 per cent of Bradford's school population (*Yorkshire Post*, 25 February 1966). The first immigrant language centre is set up for Asians in Bradford (*Yorkshire Post*, 9 July 1965) and by January 1967 two more have been added (*Yorkshire Post*, 28 January 1967). These continue until 1986 to offer crash courses in English as a Second Language and to prepare pupils to cope with mainstream education in Bradford schools (Verma, 1986, p. 52).

1986   By October, there are 3361 children of Asian origin in Bradford schools (*Telegraph and Argus*, 27 November 1968). The Council publishes an information book about its services in five Asian languages (*Telegraph and Argus*, 25 October 1968). J. Goodall notes that in Bradford most Pakistani children attend one of the two mosques for 15–20 hours a week on average, either before or after school on weekdays or on Saturday or Sunday mornings, to receive instruction by the imam in Arabic and Urdu and to learn to read the Qur'an (Goodall, 1968; Taylor with Hegarty, 1985, p. 385).

October 1969   The Muslim Association of Bradford requests that instruction in Islam should be provided for Muslim children in Bradford secondary schools. While recognizing that this request is in accordance with the 1944 Education Act and that the rights of minorities should be respected, the city's director of education sees the request as running counter to Bradford's policy of integration (*Telegraph and Argus*, 17 October 1969). In 1971, Muslims renew this request, since Islam is only taught so far at Bradford's immigrant education centres, at the end of the main school day (*Telegraph and Argus*, 15 October 1971). In response to continued pressure from the Muslim Educational Trust, the Educational Services Committee eventually gives permission in July 1972 for Muslim leaders to give religious instruction in the city's secondary schools after school hours (*Telegraph and Argus*, 11 July 1972).

April 1970   A committee is set up to revise Bradford's Religious Education syllabus and to ensure that it reflects the variety of faiths in the city (*Telegraph and Argus*, 10 April 1970). In 1974, the new 'Guide to Religious Education in a Multi-Faith Community' is published by Bradford's Educational Services Committee (*Telegraph and Argus*, 1 March 1974).

1971   P. Evans reports that out of a sample of 150 young male immigrants in Bradford, 21 per cent of the Pakistanis plan to return to Pakistan to make their career (Taylor with Hegarty, 1985, p. 41). The majority (59 per cent) think that people should maintain their different customs but live peacefully side by side; the Pakistanis are generally less in favour of integration than the Indians (*ibid*, p. 423f; Evans, 1971).

1973   First demands are made for a separate school for Muslim girls (*Telegraph and Argus*, 21 December 1973). Indigenous opposition is expressed in letters to the press (*Telegraph and Argus*, 16 April 1973) and in editorials (*Telegraph and Argus*, 8 January 1974). A major feature is published in the local press on the Muslim girls controversy (*Telegraph and Argus*, 11 January 1974).

May 1973   Abdullah Patel objects to the placement of his daughter in Hanson Upper School on the grounds that it is co-educational. His appeal is turned down in June, but he writes to the DES and Mrs Thatcher personally looks into the case; once again, his appeal is unsuccessful. In spite of being served with an attendance order, he keeps his daughter at home until she reaches school-leaving age in July 1975. The City's acting director of education expresses the fear that if all Muslim girls are allowed to transfer to Belle Vue school when it becomes the sole girls-only school in Bradford in 1975, then it will quickly become an all-Muslim school (*Telegraph and Argus*, 2 June 1973, 18 August 1974, 11 July 1975; *Yorkshire Post*, 27 December 1973, 23 January 1974, 11 July 1975; *Yorkshire Evening Post*, 3 December 1973). In December 1973, Riaz Shahid, an immigration consultant, leaves the UK after 15 years' residence to avoid sending his 13-year-old daughter to a mixed school (*Telegraph and Argus*, 8 December 1973; *Yorkshire Post*, 10 December 1973).

January 1974   Abdullah Patel helps to found the Muslim Parents' Association (MPA) with a 21-member committee and a 7-man executive to co-ordinate demands for concessions for Muslims in existing Bradford schools and the establishment of a separate school for Muslim girls (*Telegraph and Argus*, 15 December 1973, 7 January 1974). It is planned to open a Muslim girls' school in March, but the plans are shelved owing to lack of interest among Muslim parents. Patel resigns from the MPA in April (*Yorkshire Post*, 4 February 1974, *Telegraph and Argus*, 6 March 1974, 8 April 1974).

Early 1975   A Bradford University lecturer attacks Bradford's 'bussing' policy (*Telegraph and Argus*, 21 January 1975). Over the next four years, opposition to 'bussing' increases from Asian community groups, from many individual parents (both white and black), from the Community Relations Council and gradually from the political parties as well. In 1976, a Council working party recommends that the policy of 'bussing' should be continued with a few minor modifications, after a review of the policy on the instructions of the Race Relations Board was carried out by Professor Hawkins of York University (Kirp, 1979; *Telegraph and Argus*, 13 November 1976). The Labour whip is withdrawn from Councillor Rhodes for opposing it (*Yorkshire Post*, 31 December 1976). In 1977, however, Councillor Ajeeb, Chairman of the Community Relations Council, speaks out against it (*Telegraph and Argus*, 11 March 1977). In 1978, Councillor Hameed calls the policy 'racialist' (*Telegraph and Argus*, 14 October 1978), but Councillor Hussain supports it in a speech to the Labour group (*Yorkshire Post*, 20 December 1978; *Telegraph and Argus*, 1 March 1979). In November 1978, the Trades Council expresses opposition to 'bussing' (*Telegraph and Argus*, 17 November 1978) and a meeting is held between teachers' groups opposed to 'bussing' and representatives of the Asian communities to discuss tactics; the National Front disrupt the meeting (*Telegraph and Argus*, 29 November 1978). Opposition to 'bussing' gains momentum and a 1000-signature petition is presented early in 1979 (*Telegraph and Argus*, 1 March 1979). Councillor Arthur makes a last stand for 'bussing' (*Telegraph and Argus*, 22 March 1979), but when the Commission for Racial Equality questions the legality of the policy (*Keighley News*, 20 April 1979), it is announced that the policy is to be investigated (*Telegraph and Argus*, 28 June 1979; *Times Educational Supplement*, 7 October 1983) and the local Labour party withdraws its support for the policy (*Telegraph and Argus*, 11 September 1979). 'Bussing' is phased out at the end of 1979 (*Telegraph and Argus*, 23 January 1980), though the 1500 pupils already being 'bussed' (approximately 14 per cent of the ethnic minority children in Bradford schools) are to continue at their present schools (*Telegraph and Argus*, 21 April 1980, 10 June 1980). Support for 'bussing' has never entirely died out in the city (*Bradford Star*, 17 September 1987, 8 October 1987).

March 1975   Muhammad Iqbal prepares a report for the Union of Muslim Organizations recommending that the DES should help to set up separate Muslim schools (*Yorkshire Post*, 21 March 1975; *Telegraph and Argus*, 13 June 1975). In 1977, the World Islamic Mission holds a conference at St George's Hall, Bradford, and passes several resolutions demanding concessions for Muslims, including the establishment of single-sex schools for Muslim girls (*Telegraph and Argus*, 8 August 1977). Meanwhile, the Muslim Parents' Association, which has previously held talks with a Pakistan Embassy official (*Telegraph and Argus*, 12 March 1975), hopes for a gift from Pakistan or Saudi Arabia to build a girls-only school. The international conference on Islam held in London in 1976 serves to increase expectations (*Telegraph and Argus*, 3 April 1976, 20 April 1976, 1 December 1976).

1975   V. Saifullah Kahn's PhD at the University of Bradford on Mirpuri villagers in Bradford is completed. Her main points include the high value placed on education by Muslim parents and their expectations on authority and discipline; the role of self-appointed leaders of the community who have damaged chances of integration by stressing the fundamental religious principles and traditions of Islam; the role of women in the transmission of religious traditions to children; and the divisions within the Pakistani community (Saifullah Khan, 1975). A smaller survey of the Sikh community in Bradford is published in 1978 by Ramindar Singh (Singh, 1978).

1976   G. Beaumont reports that heads of language centres and Asian teachers in Bradford are unanimous that English should be the prime medium for teaching and learning at all stages (Beaumont, G. 1976; Taylor with Hegarty, 1985, p. 231).

1977   The Asian Youth League (AYL) is founded in Bradford. Its founders include Johnny Rashid and Marsha Singh, a former pupil of Belle Vue Boys' School, who in 1983 is appointed multi-cultural affairs officer for Bradford (*New Statesman*, 13 January 1984, *Telegraph and Argus*, 24 June 1983).

1977–81   A major feature in the local press exposing some of the racist myths about Bradford's Asians is published (*Telegraph and Argus*, 31 May 1977). Cater and Jones' article 'Asians in Bradford' is published (*New Society*, 13 April 1978). In 1979, a debate develops around Bradford Council's publication, 'District Trends'. There is an angry reaction in Bradford to the article, 'City Lives on Immigration Time Bomb' (*Daily Telegraph*, 6 May 1979). In 1981, Paul Barker's article on Bradford, 'In Ethnic England', is published (*New Society*, 15 October 1981).

October 1978   An experiment is started at Bradford University into mother-tongue teaching for five-year-old Asians in Bradford and Keighley, and lasts for two years (*Telegraph and Argus*, 26 October 1978). This Mother Tongue and English Teaching Project (MOTET), funded by the DES, provides inconclusive results on the value of mother-tongue teaching, except as a means of boosting the children's motivation and confidence (Fitzpatrick and Rees, 1980; Taylor with Hegarty, 1985, pp. 226, 242–4). In September 1980, a mother-tongue teaching conference is held by the CRE at Bradford College, with a report published later in the year. Bradford College has run mother-tongue courses for several years, but by 1982 there are only four mother-tongue teachers in Bradford; this rises to thirteen by 1983 (excluding supplementary school teachers) (Linguistics Minorities Project, 1983; CBMC (1984d); Taylor with Hegarty, 1985, p. 234).

1980   M. Campbell and D. Jones carry out a project at Bradford College looking at Asian school-leavers aged 16 in Bradford. Their results, published in 1982, present a bleak picture of the prospect of unemployment (Campbell and Jones, 1983; Taylor with Hegarty, 1985, pp. 307, 324, 330, 334). T. Kitwood and C. Borrill recount research on young Muslim adolescents in Bradford which suggests that they experience conflict between rival systems of meaning and value, but that their primary loyalty is to their own families and their Islamic culture (Kitwood and Borrill, 1980; Taylor with Hegarty, 1985, p. 439).

April 1980   *Ray Honeyford, aged 46, takes over as head of Drummond Middle School. He previously applied for the headship of Manningham Middle School, Bradford, and was advised to apply again; Manningham and Drummond have the same governing body. Drummond has been a middle school since 1974, having been built in the late 1880s as a board school and having been subsequently an elementary, a secondary modern and a junior high (*Telegraph and Argus, *23 November 1984). As a consequence of the phasing out of Bradford's policy of 'bussing', 49 per cent of the pupils at Drummond Middle School are now from ethnic minorities (mainly Muslims). This percentage rises to 65 per cent in September 1981, 74 per cent in September 1982, 87 per cent in September 1983 and about 95 per cent by the time of Honeyford's departure (Brown, 1985; City of Bradford Metropolitan Council, 1984e).*

March 1981   Bradford's Policy Unit publishes 'Turning Point', proposing a new approach to race relations (City of Bradford Metropolitan Council Digest, 1981). A Race Relations Policy Statement follows in due course, and the Council sends out a letter outlining its twelve-point plan on race relations to each of its employees. The plan includes keeping ethnic records, adopting an equal opportunity employment policy, consulting ethnic communities over issues which affect them and fighting racial discrimination. Racism Awareness Training (RAT) courses are set up, primarily to help those involved in recruitment (*Telegraph and Argus*, 15 March 1982; *Keighley News*, 30 April 1982; *Times Educational Supplement*, 7 October 1983; Twitchin and Demuth, 1981, pp. 161–74). The CRE praises Bradford's race relations policies (*Telegraph and Argus*, 28 April 1982, 28 May 1983; *Yorkshire Post*, 29 April 1982).

April 1981   Bradford's Education Panel discusses the proposal to refuse automatic readmission to children going abroad for more than six weeks in term-time. Many Asians object strongly (*Telegraph and Argus*, 14 April 1981, 28 April 1981).
A public meeting is held at Drummond Middle School, organized

jointly by Bradford Council and the Community Relations Council, to discuss the proposed six-weeks rule (Telegraph and Argus, *15 June 1981, 16 June 1981). Honeyford later raises the topic in his article in the* Head Teachers' Review *(1983c) and describes this meeting in his second* Salisbury Review *article (1984a).*

Norman Roper, Bradford's assistant director of educational services, supports the proposals (*Times Educational Supplement*, 19 June 1981), but in view of Asian protests, the controlling Labour group asks the multi-cultural review body, which made the original recommendation, to reconsider. Eventually, the proposal is scrapped (*Telegraph and Argus*, 30 July 1981).

11 July 1981   Asian youths in Bradford preparing to face attacks similar to those at Southall are arrested. Twelve are charged with conspiracy, but claim they were acting in legitimate self-defence, because they had reason to believe attacks on the Asian community in Bradford were imminent. After a 31-day trial, they were cleared in June 1982 (*New Statesman*, 4 September 1981, 11 June 1982; *Guardian*, 21 June 1982; *Telegraph and Argus*, 22 April 1982, 28 April 1982, 16 June 1982; *Race Today*, April 1983).

August 1981   Bradford Council sets up a new consultative group, the Race Relations Advisory Group, with Councillor Barry Thorne as chairman (*Telegraph and Argus*, 12 August 1981).

December 1981 Riaz Shahid, now parent-governor at Belle Vue Girls' School, expresses his objections to the school's un-Islamic practices, such as discos, tombolas, lotteries, raffles, sex education and mixed bathing (*Telegraph and Argus*, 15 December 1981, 18 February 1982; *Yorkshire Post*, 13 February 1982). In February 1982, The Muslim Parents' Association (MPA), of which Shahid is secretary, publishes a 36-page report, 'The Transformation of Muslim Children', which claims that Bradford Council has not honoured an agreement made in 1974 about the education of Muslim children. It lists eleven points demanded by the MPA, including excusing Muslim children from assemblies, RE and sex education. It also calls for the resignation of Educational Services Committee chairman, Doris Birdsall (Patel and Shahid, 1982; *Yorkshire Post*, 16 February 1982).

Later, Shahid calls for Muslims to be co-opted onto the Educational Services Committee (*Yorkshire Post*, 12 September 1983).

February 1982 Councillor Birdsall announces that revised guidelines on teaching Asian pupils are already being drawn up (*Yorkshire Post*, 18 February 1982). The first of these guidelines is prepared by March 1982 (*Telegraph and Argus*, 10 March 1982, 18 March 1982).

March 1982 'Any Questions' is broadcast live from Eastbrook Hall, Bradford, with Enoch Powell as a member of the panel. Angry protests are staged outside the hall (*Telegraph and Argus*, 16 March 1982, 18 March 1982, 22 March 1982).

April 1982 A survey of minorities in Bradford reveals that West Indians consider themselves ignored by council services, that Asians fear their children are being indoctrinated with Christianity and that Pakistanis represented by the Azad Kashmir Muslim Association believe that racism is rife in Bradford (*Yorkshire Post*, 30 April 1982).

July 1982 *Honeyford writes to* Times Educational Supplement *(1982b), regretting the suppression of research commissioned for the Swann Report on black achievement. He also writes to* Telegraph and Argus *(1982c), on school notepaper, criticizing the Council for giving a cash grant to Checkpoint, a West Indian Association, for a new community centre (as reported in* Telegraph and Argus, *8 July 1982), and suggesting that the district auditors be brought in. In September, he receives a verbal warning from Richard Knight, Bradford's director of educational services, as a result of this letter (*Telegraph and Argus, *26 November 1985).*

October 1982 A new policy document is prepared on educational provision for ethnic minorities in Bradford. The main issues covered include separate PE for girls, permission for Friday prayers for Muslims to be held in schools led by imams, permission for Muslim pupils to be absent on religious festivals and to wear traditional dress and jewellery, permission for parents to withdraw their children from RE and assemblies, and the future provision of *halal* meat in schools (*Telegraph and Argus*, 8 October 1982). The *Times Educational Supplement* (1

October 1982) calls Bradford's multi-cultural policies 'admirable' and runs a major article on them. In November, the policy is set out and distributed to schools in a Local Administrative Memorandum: 'Education for a Multi-cultural Society: Provision for Pupils of Ethnic Minority Communities' (LAM 2/82). Michael Whittaker is appointed by Peter Gilmour, chairman of the Educational Services Committee, to oversee the implementation of the new multi-cultural policies (*New Society*, 26 April 1984).

November 1982
A conference is organized to discuss a new RE syllabus for Bradford (*Yorkshire Post*, 5 November 1982; *Jang* (Urdu daily paper published in Bradford), 6 November 1982). The new seventeen-page agreed syllabus, 'Religious Education for living in today's world', 19 November 1982, emphasizing a multi-faith approach, is eventually published in June 1983 (*Telegraph and Argus*, 21 July 1983; *Yorkshire Post*, 26 March 1984).

19 November 1982
Honeyford's article 'Multi-racial Myths' (1982d) is published in the Times Educational Supplement. *The* Caribbean Times *carries a long reply by the 'Haringay Black Pressure Group on Education'. The article also produces substantial discussion in the TES's correspondence pages throughout December. Honeyford is seen by Knight and Gilmour, though this was not a formal disciplinary procedure over the article.*

January 1983
The Muslim Parents' Association submits a request to take over two first schools, two middle schools and Belle Vue Girls' Upper School as Muslim voluntary-aided schools (Muslim Parents' Association statement; *Times Educational Supplement*, 11 February 1983; *Guardian*, 19 February 1983). *Drummond is one of the two middle schools involved, along with two of its feeder schools, Whetley and Green Lane First Schools. Pauline Sawyer, parent governor of Drummond Middle, is active in collecting signatures from parents and others for a 7,000-signature petition against Muslim voluntary-aided schools. A meeting is held on 14 June at Drummond Middle School for parents to express their views on the proposal (*Jang, 24 May 1983).*

Articles strongly opposing the proposal are written by John Salmon (*Telegraph and Argus*, 5 July 1983) and Aziz Khan

(*Telegraph and Argus*, 14 July 1983). All forty-nine staff at Belle Vue Girls' School threaten resignation if it becomes a Muslim voluntary-aided school (*Times Educational Supplement*, 17 June 1983). A survey suggests that only forty-eight out of 600 girls at the school agreed with the Muslim plan (*Telegraph and Argus*, 25 May 1983). The Asian Youth Movement (1983) and the Community Relations Council oppose the plan, and Bradford's Council for Mosques votes 13 to 8 against supporting separate Muslim voluntary-aided schools. In September, the Educational Services Committee votes unanimously to reject the MPA plan, on the grounds that it does not have the support of many Muslim parents or of the rest of the community and that it lacks the finance and the educational and administrative abilities to carry out its proposals. Councillor Thorne calls the MPA 'crackpots', but claims that it was the refusal of some heads to carry out the Council's multi-racial policies which led to the MPA's proposal (*Telegraph and Argus*, 7 September 1983; *Jang*, 6 September 1983; *Times Educational Supplement*, 9 September 1983). In October, the MPA appeals to Sir Keith Joseph over the Council's decision (*Times Educational Supplement*, 7 October 1983; Taylor with Hegarty, 1985, p. 380). The Socialist Education Association urges Labour-controlled LEAs to oppose Muslim voluntary-aided schools (*Education*, 30 March 1984). An NUT discussion paper, *Religious Education in a Multi-faith Society*, comes out strongly against separate Muslim schools (*Education*, 19 October 1984). Meanwhile, Kirklees Council rejects a call for a similar voluntary-aided school at Batley, while Brent eventually gives conditional approval to the application for Islamia primary school at Brondesbury Park to be given voluntary-aided status (*Times Educational Supplement*, 30 August 1985, 13 September 1985, 21 February 1986, 7 March 1986, 14 March 1986; *Race and Immigration*, publication of the Runnymede Trust, June 86). In March 1988, the Labour Party leadership drops its opposition to Muslim voluntary-aided schools, (*Times Educational Supplement*, 11 March 1988).

March 1983   Bradford's Educational Services Committee requests £100,000 for supplementary schools and mother-tongue teaching, but the request fails to get past the full Council (*Times Educational Supplement*, 4 March 1983). In November, the grant is still withheld, as a lever to persuade the supplementary schools to improve their standards of health and safety (*Telegraph and Argus*, 8 November 1983).

May 1983   Bradford Council publishes a booklet in Urdu, Gujerati and Bengali on the arrangements in schools for Muslim children.

22 May 1983   Bradford's Council for Mosques organizes a meeting at St George's Hall to give Muslim parents the opportunity to meet Bradford councillors, especially Peter Gilmour. Nearly 1,000 parents attend. Single-sex education is the main item of discussion. Fourteen resolutions are passed, including a request for *halal* meat, the ending of sex education and the retention of Belle Vue Girls' School (*Jang*, 24 May 1983; *Times Educational Supplement*, 27 May 1983).

June 1983   *Honeyford's article 'Multi-Ethnic Intolerance' (1983a) is published in the* Salisbury Review.

July 1983   The number of children of Asian and Afro-Caribbean origin in Bradford schools rises to 18,325, out of a total of 87,358 pupils (*Telegraph and Argus*, 8 April 1985). This compares with 13,686 in 1979 and 11,547 in 1977. 77 per cent of Bradford's schoolchildren are of UK/Eire origin, 17 per cent Muslim and 3 per cent other Asian, 1.2 per cent Afro-Caribbean and 1.8 per cent other origins or unspecified. 30 per cent of births in Bradford are of children of Asian or Afro-Caribbean descent, and this is expected to be the proportion of the school population by 1990 (City of Bradford Metropolitan Council, 1983). More detailed statistics are available in *Bradford in Figures*, (City of Bradford Metropolitan Council, 1984b). The Linguistic Minorities Project reports that in March 1981, 14,201 pupils in Bradford spoke a language other than English at home, and that there were sixty-four languages in use the city (Linguistics Minorities Project, 1983). Bradford Council now carries out its own regular language surveys. The 1987 survey shows that 25 per cent of the city's schoolchildren speak a language other than English at home, with Punjabi Urdu being spoken by more than 15,000 children (*Telegraph and Argus*, 29 June 1987).

September
1983

A fee-paying school for Muslim girls opens in Ryan Street, Bradford. It is owned by the Muslim Association of Bradford, whose president is Sher Azam, and has places for 100 girls (*Times Educational Supplement*, 6 May 1983; *Yorkshire Post*, 16 January 1985). An HMI report in 1987 criticizes several aspects of the school's provision (HMI, 1987).

2 September
1983

Honeyford's article 'When East is West' (1983b) is published in the Times Educational Supplement. *The article again provokes correspondence in the* Times Educational Supplement *(16 September 1983) and Nazim Naqui (later chairman of the DPAC) informs Bradford's education department that he will raise this article at the Council for Mosques. Norman Roper, the assistant director of educational services, summons Honeyford to City Hall to discuss the article with Knight and himself, and this leads to an angry exchange of letters between Honeyford and Roper (*Yorkshire Post*, 6 September 1985).*

September
1983

Bradford Council plans to introduce *halal* meat, initially into ten Bradford schools, later to another twenty, and eventually into all schools with more than ten Muslim diners. There is widespread debate about the policy (*Times Educational Supplement*, 7 October 1983, 21 October 1983) and Mrs Reynolds leads a protest against it on the grounds of animal rights, and stops paying her rates (*Times Educational Supplement*, 3 February 1984).

September
1983

Bradford is described as a 'multi-racial pace-setter' (*Times Educational Supplement*, 9 September 1983, 7 October 1983), although not all think that Bradford is spending enough on anti-racist teaching (*Times Educational Supplement*, 21 October 1983). A substantial increase in the number of Asian school governors in Bradford is reported (*Ravi*, local Asian newspaper, 16 September 1983). John Salmon, in the catalogue to the 'Petals from a Lotus' exhibition, calls the notion of an integrated multi-racial city a myth (*Telegraph and Argus*, 25 October 1983).

September
1983

The opposition Labour group's move to merge Belle Vue Boys' and Belle Vue Girls' Upper Schools is narrowly defeated (*Ravi*, 1 October 1983; *Sunday Times*, 2 October

1983; *Times Educational Supplement*, 7 October 1983; Taylor with Hegarty, 1985, p. 380).

September
1983

The Race Relations Advisory Group criticizes a memorandum drawn up by the Education Department about preventing racial harassment in schools. Ramindar Singh, chairman of the Community Relations Council, points out the link between attitudes and behaviour, and raises the question of racist school books (a working group is already considering this problem) (*Ravi*, 30 September 1983). In November, Graham Mahoney is appointed to Bradford's Policy Unit with responsibility for Race Relations (*Telegraph and Argus*, 10 November 1983). A Local Administrative Memorandum is sent to headteachers on racist behaviour in schools, giving new guidelines on how to recognize, challenge and correct racist behaviour (LAM 6/83). Teachers on the Professional Association Committee are asked to compile a list of racist attacks on ethnic minority children in schools; they report back that hardly any such attacks have taken place (*Yorkshire Post*, 26 March 1984).

November
1983

TV Calendar programme links racism and Eccleshill Upper School, Bradford. Kenneth Lickley, head of the school, says that tension has been exacerbated by press coverage and by the LAM 6/83. On 5 December, there is a racist fight at Eccleshill following the distribution of 'British Nationalist' in the school. One Asian boy is expelled, one white boy suspended. The Council launches an enquiry (*Telegraph and Argus*, 29 November 1983; *Times Educational Supplement*, 23 December 1983). David Hamilton's article on Bradford, 'Schools of Racism', is published (*New Statesman*, 13 January 1984; *Telegraph and Argus*, 5 January 1984).

December
1983

Honeyford's article 'The School Attendance of British/Asian Children' (1983c) is published in Head Teachers' Review. *The article is discussed in* Times Educational Supplement, *(9 December 1983, 30 December 1983).*

December
1983

Claims of racism among the staff at Wyke Manor Upper School against its head, Carlton Duncan (Bradford's only black head, appointed earlier in 1983), are made by supply teacher Christopher Perry in the *News of the World*. An official enquiry is set up and Perry, a former Liverpool city councillor and locum education officer for Brent CRC, is suspended. He is arrested after refusing to leave the school (*Yorkshire Post*, 5 December 1983, 11 December 1983; *Yorkshire Evening Post*, 11 December 1983; *Times Educational Supplement*, 23 December 1983; *New Statesman*, 13 January 1984). In February 1984, 300 pupils at Wyke Manor strike, demanding the sacking of a racist teacher (*Race Today*, July–August, 1984). In June 1984, Perry is bound over to keep the peace, and Knight and Gilmour are cleared of charges of assault for removing him from the school. In November 1984, a team of four advisers is sent to Wyke Manor for four days for a consultative exercise (*Observer*, 5 May 1985; *Yorkshire Post*, 2 May 1985; *Education*, 10 May 1985). In November 1985, Perry returns to Bradford to sell copies of his 216-page report detailing his complaints of racism among teachers at Wyke Manor. At the end of 1985, Carlton Duncan, who had been a member of the Swann Committee and a prominent supporter of separate schools for blacks (*Times Educational Supplement*, 24 January 1986), leaves Bradford for a post in Birmingham (*Telegraph and Argus*, 6 February 1986). Under his headship, Wyke Manor had taken a lead in multi-cultural and anti-racist education (Lynch, 1986, pp. 82, 152; Duncan, 1985a and 1985b).

December 1983

After the local Association of Headteachers votes against implementing LAM 6/83, members of the Race Relations Advisory Group accuse heads of being 'power-mad' (Labour Councillor Barry Thorne) and 'whining and... destructive' (Tory Councillor Ronnie Farley). Marcus Fox, MP, however, supports heads' autonomy in this matter (*Telegraph and Argus*, 5 January 1984). The heads demand supply cover for attending the compulsory racism awareness training courses (*New Statesman*, 13 January 1984). Already by April 1983, every recruitment panel in Bradford had to contain one trained member of staff (*Times Educational Supplement*, 7 October 1983); after April 1986 for all other departments and January 1988 for Education, it is planned that no-one will be able to take part in the selection of new staff who has not attended a racism awareness training course. Altogether, 2000 local authority employees are expected to attend (*Telegraph and Argus*, 15 February 1984). The racism awareness workshops, which are described in *Telegraph and Argus* (17 February 1984), have already been running for eighteen months. They are paid for from the £250,000 race relations budget. Shirley Woodman, secretary of the local NAHT branch, expresses her dislike of the whole concept of racism awareness training (*Daily Mail*, 15 March 1984). Later, she claims that nineteen heads in Bradford are retiring because of Council bullying, particularly in the area of race relations, and that forty-five more are considering it (*Yorkshire Post*, 12 March 1984; *Times Educational Supplement*, 16 March 1984). Gilmour and Knight both question her claims (*Yorkshire Post*, 14 March 1984; *Education*, 25 March 1984). She repeats the claim in 1985 (*Yorkshire Post*, 10 April 1985; *Yorkshire Evening Post*, 10 April 1985).

1984　　　　　　*G.K. Verma and K. Mallick's 'Children's Books and Ethnic Minorities' is published as chapter nine in Verma and Bagley (1984). The case study part of the research, carried out about 1980, is based partly on Drummond Middle School and is the work of Olivia Foster-Carter, who is active in the DPAC (Brown, 1985, p. 17ff) and later writes about the Honeyford affair (Foster-Carter, 1985).*

January 1984　　Stanley Garnett, a former Bradford headmaster now living in Leeds, joins the British National Party (*Telegraph and Argus*, 5 January 1984, 24 May 1985; *New Statesman*, 13 October 1984; *Times Educational Supplement*, 13 October 1984). He later expresses support for Honeyford (*Observer*, 21 April 1985; Foster-Carter, 1987, p. 50).

January 1984　　*Honeyford's article 'Education and Race – an Alternative View' (1984a) is published in the* Salisbury Review *(Winter 1984).*

February 1984　The head of Belle Vue Girls' School reports high absenteeism among the Muslim girls at her school. Although only 50 per cent of the pupils are Muslims, 80 per cent of the absentees are (*Jang*, 10 February 1984).

March 1984　　The Asian Youth Movement (AYM) circulates a pamphlet attacking racist and complacent teachers and administrators (Asian Youth Movement, 1984). It also calls for more black teachers in Bradford, and an anti-racist education centre (*Yorkshire Post*, 6 March 1984; *Observer*, 11 March 1984; *Education*, 16 March 1984).

6 March 1984

Bradford Council debates whether to discontinue the provision of *halal* meat in view of opposition to it, especially from animal rights campaigners. Lord Mayor Norman Free opposes continuing the provision, going against the official Labour group policy (he is later expelled from the Labour group for this). An estimated 3000 Muslims join a pro-*halal* demonstration, and a 7000-signature petition is handed to the city's chief executive. The vote is 59 to 15 in favour of retaining the provision (*Guardian*, 5 March 1984; *Yorkshire Post*, 6 March 1984; *Education*, 9 March 1984; *Meat Trades Journal*, 22 March 1984; *The Listener*, 17 May 1984; *Arabia: the Islamic World Review*, May 1984). Animal rights campaigners later oppose the provision of *halal* meat to Muslim hospital patients (*Yorkshire Post*, 4 January 1986; *Telegraph and Argus*, 13 February 1986).

7 March 1984

Yorkshire Post *publishes a story about Honeyford's latest* Salisbury Review *article, having been told about it by Mike Whittaker, Bradford's Educational Policies Development Officer. A storm breaks about the article. Gilmour calls it 'distasteful and highly inaccurate', and Honeyford acknowledges in an interview that the article might get him into trouble, 'but I'm not happy about the way we as an authority are handling the situation' (*Telegraph and Argus, 8 March 1984). Bradford's Council for Mosques condemns the article and his dismissal is called for by the education panel of the Community Relations Council (*Telegraph and Argus, 9 March 1984), by Bradford West Labour Party (*Telegraph and Argus, 12 March 1984), by Bradford NUT (*Telegraph and Argus, 17 March 1984, Yorkshire Post, 19 March 1984; Times, 24 April 1984), by the Federation of Bangladeshi Youth Organisations (*Telegraph and Argus, 4 May 1984), by Max Madden, MP for Bradford West (*Telegraph and Argus, 8 May 1984), by Councillor Ajeeb (Lord Mayor from 22 May 1985) and others. Honeyford is defended by Labour's Lord Mayor, Norman Free, who claims that none of his critics is speaking to him personally, he is merely being tried by the press (*Telegraph and Argus, 10 March 1984, 15 November 1984). Honeyford claims that he has received many letters and telephone* *calls of support (*Yorkshire Post, *19 March 1984). An abridged version of the* Salisbury Review *article is published in the local press, together with an interview in which he defends the article (*Telegraph and Argus, *15 March 1984). 'A Divisive View which can only Hurt Children', a reply to Honeyford by Alex Fellowes, the head of Drummond Language Centre (no connection with Drummond Middle School), is published (*Telegraph and Argus, *22 March 1984), and within a week another reply, entitled 'Fair Words – Foul Intentions' by Bernard Campbell, an advisory teacher for multi-cultural education in Bradford (*Telegraph and Argus, *29 March 1984). Marsha Singh's response about visits to the Indian sub-continent emphasises a positive approach to such trips (*Education, *16 March 1984).*

11 March 1984 The article, 'Bradford Torn by Racial Tensions as Asians Speak out' (*Observer*, 11 March 1984), heralds a whole flood of articles on the situation in Bradford in national newspapers and magazines in the next few months. These include an article on *halal* meat and Bradford's race policies (*Guardian*, 26 March 1984); an article on Bradford's policies, 'Memo for Disharmony', by Demeter Messenger (*Yorkshire Post*, 26 March 1984); an article by F. Hanley on the effects of the Community Relations Council on Bradford's employment policies (*Employment*, March 1984); an article mainly on problems in Wyke Manor School, 'Children Fight Racism in Bradford Schools' (*Searchlight*, magazine of the Campaign against Racism and Fascism, April); two articles by Colin Hughes on Bradford's 'prescriptive' multi-cultural education policies and the problems of ethnic minorities (*Times*, 16–17 April 1984); an article on Honeyford and Bradford's multi-cultural policies by David Selbourne, 'The Culture Clash in Bradford' (*New Society*, 26 April 1984) — Mike Whittaker protests strongly over the tone of this article, which does not show him in a favourable light (*Telegraph and Argus*, 27 April 1984) — and a reply presenting an alternative view by Carling, Husband and Palmer (*New Society*, 10 May 1984); an article by David Lomax, 'We Haven't Forgotten Brixton and Toxteth' (*The Listener*, 17 May 1984); a review of Bradford's policies by Jack Cross, 'When in Bradford...' (*Times Educational Supplement*, 25 May 1984); a lurid picture of the racial climate in Bradford (*Sunday Telegraph*, 13 May 1984); and 'Schooling Crisis in Bradford' (*Race Today*, July–August 1984).

15 March
1984

The Drummond Parents' Action Committee (DPAC) is formed to demand Honeyford's dismissal. Jenny Woodward, a former law student whose daughter Jessica attends Drummond Middle School, is elected chairperson. On 18 March, the DPAC holds its first major public meeting for parents and passes a vote of no confidence in Honeyford. It calls for a ballot of parents' opinions of Honeyford's articles. On 2 April, it meets with Education department officials (Murphy, 1987). On 6 April (and again in September), the termly meeting of Drummond Middle School governors rejects a resolution calling for Honeyford's dismissal.

10 April
1984

*The Lord Mayor's chambers are occupied in his absence by members of the Asian Youth Movement and other anti-racist groups calling for the sacking of both Free and Honeyford (*The Listener, *17 May 1984;* Telegraph and Argus, *15 November 1984).*

10–19 April
1984

Honeyford replies to his critics in a letter to the Telegraph and Argus *(10 April 1984). Eric Pickles meets Sir Keith Joseph; the official Tory line at this time is that Honeyford should go, but quietly. Bert Lodge writes a profile of Honeyford in the* Times Educational Supplement *(13 April 1984). On 17 April, Roper writes to Honeyford claiming that his articles are polarizing opinion in Bradford. After being interviewed at Provincial House two days later, Honeyford is told that his comments are not welcome, but he will not be formally disciplined for them (*Yorkshire Post, *23 April 1984;* Telegraph and Argus, *19 April 1984). In a letter to Roper on 1 May, Honeyford calls the LAMs 'misguided' and writes of his concern about the dangerous consequences of the imbalanced ethnic intake in schools like his. On 1 June, Roper replies, mentioning the 'self-righteous and arrogant tone' of Honeyford's letter, and the exchange of letters continues (*Yorkshire Post, *6 September 1985).*

23 April
1984

The Council for Mosques holds a meeting at Queen's Hall, Bradford, for local Muslims, Hindus and Sikhs to air their views on racial and multi-cultural issues with Bradford councillors (*Ravi*, 27 April 1984). The Council for Mosques appoints a committee to make recommendations on a campaign for single-sex schools; it estimates that up to 1,000 Muslim girls do not attend school because of their mixed composition, though the local authority dismisses this figure as fantasy. Gilmour (and Neil Kinnock on a visit to Bradford) expresses support for single-sex schools (*Arabia:*

the Islamic World Review, May 1984). In July, the Labour Party Young Socialists' Asian Youth Conference is held in the Queen's Hall, with Max Madden, Pat Wall and others as speakers. As early as 1974, the LPYS had organized a 5000-strong demonstration against increasing racial attacks in Bradford (*Militant* 6 July 1984).

April 1984   *Honeyford's article 'Teacher and Social Worker — an Inevitable Conflict' (1984b) is published in* Salisbury Review. *It is reprinted in the* Times *(21 May 1984), using Scruton's usual space, under the title, 'Do-gooders Doing a Disservice'.*

3 May 1984   In the district council elections, Peter Gilmour, the architect of Bradford's progressive multi-cultural policies and chairman of the educational services committee, is the only Conservative to lose his seat (Keighley North) to Labour (*Times Educational Supplement*, 11 May 1984). In later interviews, he describes Bradford's policies as neither radical nor based on ideology; 'they're just realistic' (*Times Educational Supplement*, 25 May 1984; 16 November 1984). He later leaves the district (*Times Educational Supplement*, 24 January 1986). Eric Pickles takes over as chairman of the Educational Services Committee, and Whittaker is soon afterwards seconded away from Bradford (*Times Educational Supplement*, 16 November 1984).

4 May 1984   *'Racism in Bradford', by Jenny Woodward and others, is published in* Times Educational Supplement *(4 May 1984). The same day, the DPAC organizes a protest march from Drummond Middle School to Provincial House, with representatives from the Asian Youth Movement, the Council for Mosques, the local West Indian Parents' Association, Al Falah (the Islamic Youth Movement), the Bangladeshi People's Association and Mothers against Racism (Foster-Carter, 1987). The petition which is presented, calling for Honeyford's dismissal, has 552 signatures, seventy-five of which are parents' (*Telegraph and Argus, 6 June 1984). Knight promises to arrange an advisory inspection of Drummond Middle (*Telegraph and Argus, 5 May 1984; Yorkshire Post, 5 May 1984; Times Educational Supplement, 11 May 1984; Caribbean Times, 11 May 1984). On 20 May, the DPAC meets at Drummond Language Centre (which has been booked on its behalf by Tim Whitfield, secretary of the Community Relations Council) to plan its next day of action.*

14 May 1984   *The 'Panorama' report on 'The Bradford Experiment' is broadcast* (The Listener, *17 May 1984). Knight had previously written to Honeyford offering guidelines for his contribution to the programme* (Yorkshire Post, *6 September 1985).*

June 1984   *Jenny Woodward is elected parent-governor of Drummond Middle School by a large majority on an anti-Honeyford ticket.*

7 June 1984   *Honeyford's article 'Taking the Risk of Telling the Truth' (1984d) is published in the* Yorkshire Post. *Five days later, he is summoned to appear before the Council's disciplinary body in connection with this article (Yorkshire Post, 14 June 1984). On 18 July, he attends the disciplinary hearing and five days later receives a written warning about the article. On 25 July, he appeals against the formal warning, and David Hart of the NAHT seeks to have the warning set aside (*Times Educational Supplement, *31 August 1984). In early October, he loses an appeal against Bradford Council's ruling that he should publish no more articles critical of Council policy (*Times Educational Supplement, *12 October 1984).*

11 June 1984   *The Community Relations Council queries Bradford Council's handling of the Honeyford affair (*Telegraph and Argus, *12 June 1984). A month later, the city's chief executive, Gordon Moore, launches an enquiry into their allegations that political interference stopped Council officers from disciplining Honeyford properly after his articles (*Telegraph and Argus, *12 July 1984, 13 July 1984). The DPAC organizes a day of action to coincide with the start of the advisers' inspection of Drummond Middle School; it takes the form of a one-day strike by pupils, and in fact about 60 per cent are absent. Pauline Sawyer, a former Drummond parent-governor, complains that parents were misled by the DPAC's leaflet about the strike (*Yorkshire Post, *14 June 1984). Two psychologists and eight LEA advisers start their week-long inspection of Drummond Middle School, having been instructed to report back to the Schools (Education) Sub-Committee. Both the advisers and Honeyford consider that the timing of the inspection is awkward (City of Bradford Metropolitan Council, 1984e, p. 3). The 32-page report is completed in August (*Times Educational Supplement, *31 August 1984). The report praises the caring attitude in the school (p. 27) in spite of unfavourable conditions and facilities (p. 4), but the crucial question raised is whether the school will be able to 'function effectively unless the Headteacher is able to regain*

> the trust and confidence of a significant proportion of parents' (p. 26). The report concludes with thirty-seven recommendations to the school and seven to the LEA.

13 June 1984   *Lynda Lee Lewis's article 'Is it Racist to Tell the Truth?' is published in the* Daily Mail.

July–August   *The Bradford branch of the NAHT publishes an open letter of*
1984   *support for Honeyford (*Times Educational Supplement, *12 October 1984). His union renews its support in October (*York-shire Post, *22 October 1984). An article by Morris, Hussain and Aura discusses Bradford's race relations and multicultural education policies (*Race Today, *July–August 1984). A letter by David Selbourne discusses the Honeyford affair in terms of tolerance, freedom of speech and democracy. He suggests that Muslims are duping Bradford Council into satisfying their demands (*Yorkshire Post, *28 August 1984).*

September   *The new intake at Drummond Middle School is 128 pupils (125*
1984   *Asian, two indigenous whites and one West Indian), bringing the total to 532 pupils (Headmaster's report to governors, 7 November 1985).*

18 September   *Abu Bashir, chairman of the Asian Workers' Support Group, is*
1984   *quoted as saying, 'We are more concerned about some of the racist remarks he has made than his views on the council's education policy' (*Telegraph and Argus, *18 September 1984).
                *The parents of 238 children send identical letters (prepared by the DPAC) to Knight requesting their transfer to another school. Woodward explains that the purpose of the request is not to achieve the transfer but to put pressure on the Council to remove Honeyford (*Yorkshire Post, *3 October 1984;* Times Educational Supplement, *12 October 1984;;* Telegraph and Argus, *15 October 1984;* Education, *19 October 1984). On 23 September, the DPAC meets at Drummond Centre to draw up a letter of complaint about Honeyford which it sends to the Educational Directorate three days later. In early October, the DPAC issues Newsletter No 1 which outlines its case against Honeyford.*

30 September   *Honeyford speaks out on Radio Four's 'Poles Apart' programme*
1984   *against racial discrimination (*Telegraph and Argus, *1 October 1984).*

16 October 1984   *A special meeting of the governors of Drummond Middle School is held at City Hall to discuss the Advisers' Report. The meeting is picketed by about fifty placard-waving demonstrators, who later hammer on the doors of the meeting room, chanting and heckling. Seven governors, including Jenny Woodward, walk out* (Telegraph and Argus, 17 October 1984).

18 October 1984   *First discussions take place regarding an early retirement offer for Honeyford* (Telegraph and Argus, 19 October 1984). *Lambert (Labour's education spokesman) and Madden (MP for Bradford West) both later claim that Honeyford demanded a £250,000 golden handshake* (Telegraph and Argus, 17 April 1985, 19 April 1985).

22 October 1984   *District Trends 1984: the Changing Face of Bradford* is published by the Council (1984a). It claims that Bradford, said to be the cheapest place in Britain to live, is in reality a 'poverty zone' where people cannot make ends meet, where one-third of all families are on state benefits, and the inner-city unemployment is as high as 50 per cent. There is a substantial section on race relations and its effect on housing, education, employment and the social services. The report receives substantial media attention, on BBC TV Newsnight (23 October 1984) and in *Daily Star* (25 October 1984), *Daily Mail* (23 October 1984), *Daily Mirror* (22 October 1984), *Daily Telegraph* (23 October 1984), *Financial Times* (25 October 1984), *The Listener* (1 November 1984) and elsewhere.

22 October 1984   *Bradford Schools (Education) Sub-committee holds a special meeting to discuss the Advisers' Report. Honeyford survives a vote of no-confidence. A detailed resolution is passed giving Honeyford six months to restore parental confidence and to write six reports on various aspects of the school* (Report prepared for the special meeting of the Committee on 22 March 1985, p. 50). *He is to have the support of eight council officers in implementing the recommendations* (Telegraph and Argus, 23 October 1984, 15 November 1984; Daily Telegraph, 23 October 1984; Times Educational Supplement, 26 October 1984; Race and Immigration, December 1984). *Knight meets Honeyford on 7 November to discuss these requirements. Honeyford is also instructed to submit future articles to Knight prior to publication; he does in fact*

> *submit two further articles (on 8 November 1984 and 22 January 1985) to Knight, who in both cases advises against publication. This leads to a further exchange of correspondence, as Honeyford sees it as an act of censorship (Director's report to the Schools (Education) Sub-Committee on events 20 October 1984 — 16 March 1985).*

27 October 1984
*Anti-Honeyford parents plan to set up their own school (*Telegraph and Argus, *26 November 1985). Plans continue over the next four months (*Telegraph and Argus, *19 February 1985;* Yorkshire Post, *19 February 1985;* Times Educational Supplement, *22 February 1985) until the school is eventually set up on 4 March 1985 (q.v.).*

30 October 1984
Scruton's article 'Who are the Real Racists?' is published in the Times, *and Knight writes a reply a fortnight later (*Times, *15 October 1984). In December, Scruton's article 'Punish the Real School Bullies' is published (*Times, *4 December 1984). It is believed that Mrs Thatcher attends a weekend seminar with Scruton early in 1985, and around this time, the Tory line on Honeyford begins to change locally. In May 1985, Scruton confirms that he has visited Drummond Middle School (*New Statesman, *24 May 1985).*

9 November 1984
*Honeyford turns down a verbal offer of a £100,000 package to quit (*Telegraph and Argus, *9 November 1984, 15 November 1984;* Times Educational Supplement, *16 November 1984).*

15 November 1984
*Jim Greenhalf writes a major review of the Honeyford affair so far — 'The head who spoke his mind and the race row that won't go away' (*Telegraph and Argus, *15 November 1984).*

30 November 1984
Knight meets parents and children in City Hall to hear complaints about Honeyford. He later writes to Honeyford to mention the points raised (Director's report to Schools (Education) Sub-committee).

4 December 1984
Mrs Zerina Nawaz (now Miss Rehman), a UK-educated Muslim, is appointed to Drummond Middle School as a first-year class teacher — the school's second Asian teacher (special report to Schools (Education) Sub-committee, 22 March 1985, p. 14; Headmaster's report to governors). In February 1985, Mr A.

Khan is promoted to Scale 3 liaison teacher at Drummond Middle, and expresses willingness to provide a course in Urdu at the school.

17 December 1984   *A special governors' meeting is held to review the first two of the required reports by Honeyford. Further special meetings are held on 11 February and 4 March 1985 to discuss the rest of Honeyford's reports.*

January 1985   *Honeyford's article 'The Right Education' (1985a) is published in* the Salisbury Review. *The article raises questions about comprehensive schooling and the influence of left-wing ideologies on educational policy. He claims that this article had been submitted to* the Salisbury Review *before the Schools (Education) Subcommittee ruling about submitting his articles to Knight for approval. Lambert calls for his suspension as a result of this article.* (Telegraph and Argus, *12 February 1985;* Yorkshire Post, *14 February 1985;* Guardian, *15 February 1985). Around this time, Councillor Goldberg and the Bradford Trades Council also call for Honeyford's dismissal* (Yorkshire Post, *22 February 1985).*

18 January 1985   Considerable publicity is given to an Asian pupil being beaten up on the way home from Greenhead School, Keighley (*Keighley News*, 18 January 1985; *Telegraph and Argus*, 18 January 1985; *Yorkshire Evening Post*, 18 January 1985). Similar attacks are reported as early as 1981 (*Keighley News*, 24 July 1981; *Telegraph and Argus*, 13 August 1981).

21 January 1985   Pickles talks with pride of educational concessions made to Asians in Bradford, and mentions a proposed exchange of teachers between the Indian sub-continent and the UK. He calls for more Asian teachers; currently there are only twenty-five in Bradford (*Jang*, 21 October 1985).

March 1985   *The DPAC publishes a statement claiming that Honeyford has lost the confidence of the majority of parents at his school; made statements that are divisive, insulting and provocative; and contravened Council policies on race and education. In an article entitled 'The Struggle at Drummond Middle School', Olivia Foster-Carter describes the* Salisbury Review *as a 'contentious and obscene right-wing journal' and says that Honeyford has written 'insults which touch the essence of a community's self-respect'. She* gives several references to Marsha Singh's views on the Honeyford affair (Foster-Carter, 1985).

March 1985   Pat McElroy's article, 'The View from a Multi-cultural Inner City Girls' School', is published in *Education Journal*. It describes Muslim demands and the changing nature of Belle Vue Girls' School, of which she is head. The percentage of Muslims in the 1984 intake to her school shows a dramatic increase (*cf Yorkshire Post*, 13 March 1985).

4 March
1985   *The DPAC sets up an alternative school at the Pakistan Community Centre, White Abbey Road. The alternative school is fully supported by the six Labour members of the Schools (Education) Sub-committee. About 250 children attend, and twenty qualified teachers provide lessons on a voluntary basis. It is designed as an 'anti-racist' school (Foster-Carter, 1987), and the lessons include Arabic, Asian languages and Afro-Caribbean culture, but there is no provision for sport or PE. Free meals are provided by local Pakistani restaurants. Access to the school is refused to the Educational Welfare Officer and the Health and Safety Officer, but the six Labour members are allowed admission (*Telegraph and Argus, 4 March 1985, 6 March 1985; Yorkshire Post, 5–7 March 1985; Jang, 8 March 1985; Guardian, 11 March 1985; Director's report to Schools (Education) Sub-committee). The DPAC alienates the NUT by claiming that children have been threatened by teachers for attending the alternative school. The NUT warns it may take action over these claims (Jang, 7 March 1985; Telegraph and Argus, 29 March 1985). The alternative school closes on 8 March (Jang, 9 March 1985).*

18 March
1985   *Honeyford offers to resign — at a price. Eric Pickles visits Liberal leader Kath Greenwood with Bradford's chief executive Gordon Moore, but fails to persuade her to agree to a cash settlement (a package totalling £90,000) for Honeyford (*Telegraph and Argus, 19 March 1985; Yorkshire Post, 26 March 1985*).*

Mid-March
1985   *The Friends of Drummond Middle School (FDMS) is formed as a pro-Honeyford pressure group. Its founders include Mr S. Silverwood, a school governor, and Mrs M. Iqbal, a member of Bradford's Community Relations Council who has spoken out in support of Honeyford (*Yorkshire Post, 5 March 1985, 21 March*

1985, 28 March 1985; Telegraph and Argus, 24 April 1985).
*The NAHT reiterates its support for Honeyford and criticizes the
Council's handling of the case (*Yorkshire Post, 20 March 1985;
Times Educational Supplement, 22 March 1985).

21 March
1985

*A special meeting of Drummond Middle School governors is held
(till midnight) to consider the report of the governors' working
party. Their support for Honeyford is reaffirmed (*Yorkshire
Post, 21 March 1985; Telegraph and Argus, 21 March 1985).

*22 March
1985*

*A special meeting is held at City Hall to consider the advisers' 50-
page report on Honeyford's response to the sub-committee's request
for six reports from him. Knight also presents a confidential report
on the events from October to March. The advisers are openly
critical of Honeyford's response to council policies. After the six-
hour meeting, the Schools (Education) Sub-committee votes 8–7 for
a Labour-sponsored motion of no-confidence in Honeyford. Greenwood supports the motion, though she is later taken to task by the
Baildon Residents' Association for doing so, and so does the co-
opted SDP member Jeffrey Ryan. A three-part Tory motion
supporting the council's race relations policies is passed unanimously (*Yorkshire Post, 23 March 1985; Telegraph and
Argus, 23 March 1985, 12 April 1985; Yorkshire Evening
Post, 23 March 1985; Times Educational Supplement, 29
March 1985; Guardian, 29 March 1985).

23 March
1985

*The Jimmy Young show on race relations in Bradford, including
the Honeyford affair, is recorded at the Queen's Hotel, Leeds, for
transmission the following day. Professor Honey, Carlton Duncan
and Pat McElroy all take part (*Telegraph and Argus, 22 March
1985, 25 March 1985).

Late March
1985

*Honeyford is off school sick for a week, but meanwhile media
attention to the affair continues unabated. Articles are published in*
New Statesman *(15 March 1985),* Education *(15 March
1985), and* Daily Express *(30 March 1985). The* Telegraph
and Argus *publishes 'Life, Times and Turmoil of Ray
Honeyford' (28 March 1985). A string of editorials expresses
sympathy for Honeyford: 'Hunt the Heresy' (*Times, 26 March
1985); *'A Shameful Victory for the Bigots' (*Daily Express, 30
March 1985); *'The Persecution of a Good Man' (*Daily Mail, 3
April, 1985); *and 'The Man Who Dared to Speak his Mind'*

*(Daily Mirror, 9 April 1985). Woodrow Wyatt produces 'This Decent Chap Needs a Pal' (*News of the World, *31 March 1985).*

27 March 1985 · *Nicholas Winterton and Max Madden argue in Parliament over Honeyford (*Telegraph and Argus, *27 March 1985;* Yorkshire Post, *28 March 1985).*

27 March 1985 · *News is leaked to* Yorkshire Post *of a memorandum sent by seven trainers for the Council's racism awareness training courses to the Council's personnel director, Brian McAndrew, and other LEA officers and councillors, saying that Honeyford should not be allowed to attend one of the compulsory racism awareness courses because they did not wish, since it was unlikely that the course would 'make him anti-racist', to empower ' a known racist' to take part in recruitment. In any case, they claim, the handling of the Honeyford affair has been eroding the confidence of Bradford's black community in the Council's race relations policies (*Yorkshire Post, *27 March 1985;* Telegraph and Argus, *1–4 April 1985). Councillor Wightman, chairman of the Race Relations Advisory Group, criticises the memorandum and instructs McAndrew to carry out an investigation. Ten Asian community groups respond by calling for Wightman's resignation (*Yorkshire Post, *13 April 1985;* Telegraph and Argus, *20 April 1985). Meanwhile, Honeyford complains of 'trial by leak' (*Yorkshire Post, *15 April 1985). A disciplinary enquiry into the incident is announced (*Telegraph and Argus, *26 April 1985).*

30 March 1985 · *Frank Kelly starts his one-man campaign in support of Honeyford. Altogether, he collects nearly 10,000 signatures for his petition (*Yorkshire Post, *29 March 1985;* Telegraph and Argus, *30 March 1985).*

1 April 1985 · *Sir Keith Joseph refuses to get publicly involved in the Honeyford affair (*Telegraph and Argus, *1 April 1985), though Granada's TV Eye film about the affair on 2 May reveals that he has called for a full report (*Telegraph and Argus, *3 May 1985;* Times Educational Supplement, *10 May 1985). Sir Keith is said to have made it clear in a private meeting with Eric Pickles around this time that the DES does not want to see Honeyford dismissed.*

3 April 1985 · *Bradford Council invokes its disciplinary procedures and Honeyford is suspended on full pay pending a report to the governing body*

*(*Telegraph and Argus, *3 April 1985;* Yorkshire Post, *4 April 1985). Drummond Middle School reopens after the Easter break with the deputy head, Fred Edmondson, in charge (*Telegraph and Argus, *16 April 1985).*

4 April 1985   *Honeyford supporters hand in two petitions (one organized by Frank Kelly, the other by FDMS) to Bradford Council and demand an enquiry into his suspension (*Yorkshire Post, *2 April 1985, 11 April 1985;* Telegraph and Argus, *4 April 1985, 10 April 1985;* Bradford Star, *5 April 1985).*

9 April 1985   *Jenny Woodward speaks to the press about the DPAC's objections to Honeyford (*Telegraph and Argus, *9 April 1985;* Yorkshire Post, *9 April 1985). She is also due to address a meeting of Rank and File about the activities of the DPAC, but cancels for health reasons and is replaced by Bradford teacher Geoff Robinson (*Yorkshire Post, *10 April 1985, 15 April 1985). She later addresses a fringe meeting at the Liberation Festival at Bradford University (*Telegraph and Argus, *1 May 1985, 13 May 1985).*

10 April 1985   *In a letter to the local press, a Honeyford supporter, Mrs Smith, compares him to Christ; he too is being crucified for speaking the truth (*Telegraph and Argus, *10 April 1985). In another letter, Mrs Wilford implies a similar comparison (*Telegraph and Argus, *27 December 1985).*

12 April 1985   *Jim Greenhalf writes a major review of the Honeyford affair so far — 'Anatomy of a Row that has Split our City' (*Telegraph and Argus, *12 April 1985).*

16 April 1985   *Shipley's Tory MP, Marcus Fox, who has already made various public statements in support of Honeyford, starts an adjournment debate on the Honeyford affair in the House of Commons. The debate breaks up in a bitter row with Bradford West Labour MP Max Madden. Education Minister Dunn has virtually no time to reply (*Yorkshire Post, *3 April 1985, 17–18 April 1985, 22 April 1985;* Telegraph and Argus, *4 April 1985, 17 April 1985;* Times Educational Supplement, *19 April 1985;* Hansard, *16 April 1985, pp. 233–42). On 18 April, Madden's 'The Speech I Never Made' is published in* Telegraph and Argus.

21 April 1985   *The Bradford branch of the NAHT votes almost unanimously (157 members are present) to call for Honeyford's reinstatement,*

and to express concern at the implications of the case for the free speech of all heads *(Yorkshire Evening Post, 24 April 1985; Telegraph and Argus, 24 April 1985; Yorkshire Post, 22 April 1985; Times Educational Supplement, 12 April 1985, 26 April 1985).*

25 April 1985   *Drummond Middle School governors (named in* Telegraph and Argus, *25 April 1985) meet and set a date for hearing evidence regarding Honeyford's suspension (*Telegraph and Argus, *26 April 1985).*

Early May 1985   *Geoff Lawler, Tory MP for Bradford North, attacks the intolerance of both Honeyford and his Labour left-wing opponents (*Telegraph and Argus, *2 May 1985;* Yorkshire Post, *2 May 1985). Bradford Council again attempts to buy Honeyford off. The offer includes boosting his pension to £8,000 a year, plus a lump sum of £27,000. Honeyford turns it down (*Telegraph and Argus, *3 May 1985, 4 May 1985).*

14 May 1985   Simon Pearce criticizes Bradford Conservatives for their multi-cultural policies in his 'Education and the Multi-Racial Society', a policy paper published by the Monday Club. He dismisses multi-culturalism as 'social engineering on a grand scale' (*Yorkshire Post,* 15 May 1985; *Times Educational Supplement,* 17 May 1985).

17 May 1985   *A letter of self-defence by Honeyford (1985c) is published by* Times Educational Supplement *in reply to a letter by C. Billingham (*Times Educational Supplement, *3 May 1985). Councillor Lambert complains of the letter to Richard Knight (*Yorkshire Post, *20 May 1985;* Times Educational Supplement, *24 May 1985).*

22 May 1985   Labour Councillor Muhammad Ajeeb is installed as Lord Mayor (*Telegraph and Argus,* 13 June 1985). His year in office attracts much media attention (*Telegraph and Argus,* 19 May 1986); a BBC2 documentary film is made showing his return to his home village in the Mirpur district of Azad Kashmir (*Bradford Star,* 24 April 1986).

22 May 1985   Liberals on Bradford Council are furious after the Tory and Labour groups vote to exclude them from all sub-

committees and select committees (*Telegraph and Argus*, 26 November 1985).

Late May 1985   *Various articles on the situation in Bradford and the Honeyford affair are published: 'The Melting Pot that Won't Melt'* (Guardian, *23 May 1985); 'Bradford's Test Case', by Helen Jacobus (*New Statesman, *24 May 1985); 'Power Plus Prejudice', by Andrew Brown (*Spectator, *22 June 1985); 'Multi-Cultural Consequences', by Ronald Butt, who argues that radical policies can drive a wedge between the races rather than bring them together (*Times Educational Supplement, *24 May 1985); an article on police and race problems in Bradford (*Race Today, *May–June 1985); and an article by C.L. Husband and others supporting multi-culturalism and opposing Honeyford (*Telegraph and Argus, *28 May 1985). Later, an article appears in* The Economist *on Bradford schools and the Honeyford affair (19 October 1985).*

24 May 1985   *Yorkshire Post publishes a story about the head of Bradford Grammar School being asked by Tory Central Office, and refusing, to speak up for Honeyford.*

Early June 1985   *Councillor Lambert proposes a pay-off deal for Honeyford (£31,000 lump sum, plus £5,200 pension), but the Labour group will not agree; they want to see Honeyford sacked.*

Early June 1985   *Leaflets are distributed in Urdu from five Asian community centres, claiming to be a paraphrase of Honeyford's views, but in fact, according to Mrs Mubarik Iqbal, a total distortion of them. Her re-translation reads, 'Honeyford means we are illegitimate, we are criminals, we are illiterate...volatile...rascals...useless ...scroungers' (*Times Educational Supplement, *13 September 1985;* Times, *3 September 1985).*

6 June 1985   *Liberal education spokesman, John Wells, has a secret meeting with Honeyford at County Hall, Wakefield, about a settlement package. Four days later, they meet again, this time at Bradford's Novotel. He proposes a lump sum of £42,000, plus an enhanced pension of £6,200, with the Council holding the copyright of future articles by Honeyford (*Telegraph and Argus, *8 June 1985, 11 June 1985;* Yorkshire Post, *10 June 1985, 11 June 1985). Labour and Tory leaders sink the Wells initiative on 11 June by ordering the Council*

representative not to attend any more meetings. Instead, Pickles orders chief executive Gordon Moore to open formal talks with Honeyford. The NAHT on Honeyford's behalf suggests an investment by the Council to produce £15,000 per annum for Honeyford. No settlement is agreed (Telegraph and Argus, 12–13 June 1985, 17 June 1985, 24 June 1985; Yorkshire Post, 13 June 1985; Times Educational Supplement, 14 June 1985).

18 June 1985   The NAHT threatens Bradford Council with a libel action over the memorandum produced by the racism awareness trainers unless it pays a substantial sum in damages to Honeyford. Hart (for the NAHT) calls for a full retraction of the document and an undertaking that Council employees will not repeat the offence (Times Educational Supplement, 21 June 1985). The final retirement package agreed with Honeyford in December includes £5,000 paid in connection with this alleged libel (Telegraph and Argus, 14 December 1985).

22 June 1985   Chaired by Councillor Ernest Kinder, the governors' enquiry into Honeyford's suspension begins. It is held at Ilkley College. Police are called to the enquiry after Councillor Goldberg, who has been a governor for only one week, walks out with a confidential file, which he later returns. Three other governors also boycott the meeting (Woodward and two Asians); two others are absent, and one is abroad in Pakistan. The meeting continues with eleven of the eighteen governors present. Goldberg later tries to return as an observer, but the remaining governors have already voted to exclude him. On 25 June, the governors pass a resolution by 7 votes to 4 calling for Honeyford's reinstatement. Councillor Lambert comments, 'To demand his reinstatement is asking for enormous trouble. It is going to divide this city and leave the way open for the new Right Wing to take over education policy' (Telegraph and Argus, 21–26 June 1985; Yorkshire Post, 22–27 June 1985; Sunday Telegraph, 23 June 1985; Times, 24–27 June 1985; Guardian, 25–26 June 1985; Yorkshire Evening Post, 26 June 1985; Times Educational Supplement, 28 June 1985; Daily Mail, 24 June 1985).

1 July 1985   A third petition supporting Honeyford (organized by FDMS, with a further 10,000 signatures) is handed in to City Hall. The first petition (organized by FDMS) had about 3000 signatures, and

*Frank Kelly's had 8–10,000 signatures (*Telegraph and Argus, 2 July 1985; Yorkshire Evening Post, 2 July 1985).

9 July 1985   *The Council agrees to drop further disciplinary action against Honeyford after the threat of an injunction by the NAHT (*Telegraph and Argus, 10 July 1985; Yorkshire Post, 28 June 1985). Pickles says he wants to see Honeyford back at Drummond Middle School (*Telegraph and Argus, 11 July 1985). Norman Roper now has the task of deciding whether or not to accept the governors' recommendation (*Telegraph and Argus, 1 July 1985; Yorkshire Post, 2 July 1985). The NAHT wants the decision about Honeyford taken out of Roper's hands as they consider him biased; he has already presented the case against the head to the governors (*Times Educational Supplement, 12 July 1985). After secret talks on 10 and 13 July between Honeyford, the NAHT and the Council, no agreement is reached on Honeyford's reinstatement. The Council insists that it should be conditional on a 'final warning' disciplinary measure, which could result in his sacking if he transgressed within eighteen months. Honeyford's future is now to be determined in the High Court, and on 16 July, the NAHT serves a writ on Bradford Council (*Yorkshire Post, 11 July 1985, 15 July 1985, 17 July 1985; Yorkshire Evening Post, 10 July 1985; Sunday Times, 14 July 1985; Telegraph and Argus, 16 July 1985; Daily Telegraph, 19 July 1985; Education, 19 July 1985; Times Educational Supplement, 19 July 1985).*

17 July 1985   *The DPAC calls for a ballot of parents to see if they want Honeyford reinstated (*Telegraph and Argus, 18–19 July 1985; Yorkshire Post, 19 July 1985). Meanwhile, Lord Swann calls for an independent enquiry into the Honeyford affair (*Yorkshire Post, 19 July 1985; Telegraph and Argus, 19 July 1985). David Oldman attacks Honeyford's ideas at the Conference for the British Association for the Advancement of Science at Strathclyde University (*Times Educational Supplement, 30 August 1985; cf Oldman, 1987).*

September 1985   *New regulations about school governors are introduced in Bradford. Each school is to have its own governors, instead of one board covering five schools as heretofore. Among Drummond Middle School's fourteen governors will be three parents' representatives* and three community representatives, compared to one from each category previously.

3 September 1985	*Andrew Brown's article on Honeyford is published in the* Times. *It forms the basis of his book* Trials of Honeyford, *which is published on 2 December.*

4 September
1985

*The High Court hearing starts. The following day, the judge, Simon Brown, rules that the Council could not take further legal action and that following the governors' vote of confidence, Honeyford should be reinstated (*Telegraph and Argus, *5–6 September 1985;* Jang, *5–9 September 1985;* Yorkshire Post, *6 September 1985;* Guardian, *6 September 1985;* Times, *6 September 1985;* Daily Telegraph, *6 September 1985;* Bradford Star, *12 September 1985;* Education, *13 September 1985). On 11 September, Bradford Council announces that Honeyford is to return to Drummond Middle School. The acting head, Fred Edmondson, expresses delight. The Council announces that it will appeal against the High Court ruling (*Yorkshire Evening Post, *12 September 1985;* Telegraph and Argus, *12 September 1985;* Times, *12 September 1985;* Times Educational Supplement, *13 September 1985). D. Thompson, the Middle Schools officer, meets the staff at Drummond Middle School on 13 September to discuss the situation (Director's report to governors, November 1985).*

6 September
1985

*The President of Bradford's Council for Mosques, C. Khan, threatens to withdraw all Muslim children from Drummond Middle School (*Telegraph and Argus, *6 September 1985;* Jang, *7 September 1985). The DPAC meets at the Pakistan Community Centre on 13 September to launch a new anti-Honeyford campaign. It discusses the possibility of transferring children to other schools, and plans a boycott of the school from Honeyford's return (*Yorkshire Post, *13 September 1985;* Watan, *local Asian newspaper, 14 September 1985).*

16 September
1985

*Honeyford returns to Drummond Middle School after an absence of five-and-a-half months. There is a noisy reception from demonstrators as the boycott of the school by parents and children begins. Children on the picket line wear anti-Honeyford badges with slogans such as 'Ray-cist' and 'I Hate Honeyford' (*Yorkshire Evening Post, *16 September 1985;* Yorkshire Post, *17*

September 1985; Times, *17 September 1985;* Jang, *18 September 1985;* New Life, *27 September 1985;* Times Educational Supplement, *6 December 1985). On 18 September, fighting breaks out on the picket line outside the school, and Muhammad Ansari is beaten by protestors for taking his children to school (*Telegraph and Argus, *18 September 1985;* Yorkshire Evening Post, *18 September 1985;* Jang, *19 September 1985). On 19 September, demonstrations continue with about 200 on the picket line, many having no connection with the school (*Yorkshire Post, *20 September 1985). On 20 September, the Director of Education issues a press release calling on all parents to return their children to school (*Telegraph and Argus, *20 September 1985). The morning attendance figures for the week are:*

Monday	*– 205 children*
Tuesday	*– 171 children*
Wednesday	*– 181 children*
Thursday	*– 157 children*
Friday	*– 148 children (Director's report to governors, November, 1985;* Jang, *21 September 1985).*

*The Lord Mayor, Councillor Ajeeb, tells a public meeting called by the Community Relations Council that Honeyford should be suspended until the appeal case is over (*Telegraph and Argus, *20 September 1985, 26 September 1985;* Yorkshire Post, *20 September 1985). Later, he gets racist hate mail relating to this and other issues (*Telegraph and Argus, *3 October 1985,* Yorkshire Post, *4 October 1985). On 28 September, he is heckled by football fans shouting 'Honeyford' at Grimsby while receiving a cheque for the disaster fund set up after the Bradford City Football Club fire disaster on 11 May 1985 (*Yorkshire Post, *30 September 1985;* Sunday Times, *15 December 1985).*

22 September 1985   *Honeyford's 'liberalism' is discussed in* Sunday Telegraph.

23 September 1985   *Protesting parents end their boycott to give the Council a fortnight to remove Honeyford (*Yorkshire Evening Post, *23 September 1985;* Telegraph and Argus, *23 September 1985;* Yorkshire Post, *24 September 1985). Children are given a leaflet by the DPAC on their return to school urging them to ignore Honeyford*

or to make up jokes about him. Knight and Pickles both criticize the leaflet (Telegraph and Argus, *24 September 1985).*

24 September 1985

DPAC representatives meet teachers at Drummond Middle School to reassure them of their confidence in the staff. It is reported that the teachers refuse to have anything to do with the anti-Honeyford campaign, though Goldberg says that this is a misinterpretation of what happened at the meeting. Meanwhile, the local branch of the NUT votes to su port Honeyford's dismissal (Telegraph and Argus, *25–6 September 1985).*

28 September 1985

It is announced that Honeyford is to attend an educational seminar at 10 Downing Street on 2 October with the Prime Minister, cabinet ministers and right wing educationalists such as Dr John Marks and Baroness Cox. On the day of the seminar, a group of London teachers and Asians protest outside no. 10 (Telegraph and Argus, *28 September 1985, 3 October 1985;* Yorkshire Evening Post, *30 September 1985;* Yorkshire Post, *3 October 1985).*

30 September 1985

A half-day boycott of Drummond Middle School is held, and about fifty protestors picket the school. Two Asian children display a banner portraying Honeyford as a devil, with the inscription, 'Honeyford writes in the blood of the blacks'. 183 pupils attend the morning session and 350 the afternoon. Goldberg comments that the boycott was held 'just to remind people we can mount a boycott' (Telegraph and Argus, *30 September 1985, 1 October 1985; Director's report to governors.).*

2 October 1985

Three anti-Honeyford parent-governors (N. Naqui, F. Rahman and M. Farooq) are elected to serve on the new governing body (Telegraph and Argus, *3 October 1985;* Times Educational Supplement, *4 October 1985).*

5 October 1985

The Council for Mosques in a letter to Bradford's chief executive, Gordon Moore, withdraws from various Bradford groups, including the Race Relations Advisory Group and the Multicultural Education Support Group, in protest at the Council's handling of the Honeyford affair (Telegraph and Argus, *8 October 1985). On 13 October, the Council for Mosques meets to discuss further action* (Council for Mosques Press Release, *8 October 1985).*

7 October 1985   *An article by members of the Bradford branch of NAME (National Anti-Racist Movement in Education) is published in* Telegraph and Argus, *setting out its objections to Honeyford. Another* Telegraph and Argus *article the same day offers evidence that white children do not suffer when they are a minority in schools. The theme recurs intermittently in other articles (for example,* Guardian, *11 February 1986).*

10 October 1985   *The boycott of the school is reimposed indefinitely. Attendance figures for the next seven days (from a school role of 505) are:*

10 Oct	am	226	pm	212
11 Oct	am	212	pm	212
14 Oct	am	188	pm	193
15 Oct	am	105	pm	109
16 Oct	am	180	pm	193
17 Oct	am	243	pm	246
18 Oct	am	241	pm	211

*(*Telegraph and Argus, *10 October 1985;* Yorkshire Post, *11 October 1985; Director's report to governors.).*

14 October 1985   *Against the recommendation of the local branch of the NUT, an NUT group at Grange School, Bradford, strikes for one day in protest at Honeyford's return to Drummond Middle School (*Yorkshire Post, *12 October 1985;* Telegraph and Argus, *14 October 1985;* Times Educational Supplement, *18 October 1985). Though the members concerned are temporarily suspended for this action (*Yorkshire Evening Post, *18 December 1985;* Yorkshire Post, *19 December 1985;* Guardian, *19 December 1985), a disciplinary hearing in January decides against permanently excluding them (*Telegraph and Argus, *25 January 1986;* Bradford Star, *30 January 1986;* Times Educational Supplement, *31 January 1986). Fights are later reported between Asian pupils at Grange School and White pupils from Thornton School (*Guardian, *23 January 1986).*

15 October 1985   *The DPAC holds a Day of Action to protest against Honeyford. The usual fifty or so demonstrators at Drummond Middle School increase to 250, and a protest march from the school to City Hall attracts nearly twice that number (*Yorkshire Evening Post, *15 October 1985;* Telegraph and Argus, *15 October 1985). Bradford's Council for Mosques calls on all Muslim children in*

Bradford (over 16,000) to boycott school for the day (Council for
Mosques Press Release, 13 October 1985; Yorkshire Post, 10
October 1985, 14 October 1985; Yorkshire Evening Post, 14
October 1985), but only about one in four responds (Telegraph
and Argus, 15 October 1985; Times, 16 October 1985). A call
for a one-day strike by council workers fails to materialize;
NALGO refuses to give official backing (Telegraph and Argus,
11 October 1985, 18 October 1985; Times, 16 October 1985).
The picket reassembles for the inaugural meeting of the new
governing body of Drummond Middle School in the evening; it is
attended by the eleven existing governors together with Richard
Knight and other LEA officials. The main business of the meeting
is to elect three community representatives to the governing body.
The three pro-Honeyford candidates (Tom Brown, a former labour
councillor; Mrs Mubarik Iqbal, a member of the Community
Relations Council; and Azhar Hayat, a lecturer whose two sons
attend the school) are elected by six votes to five. The five votes for
the broadly anti-Honeyford candidates were those of the Labour
party nominees and the parent governors; the six votes for the
elected candidates came from the Tory nominees, the two teacher
governors, the ancillary staff governor and Honeyford himself, who
exercised his right to be on the governing body. When the result
was announced, there were violent scenes both in the school hall
and in the playground, and it was claimed that the election was
rigged. After an adjournment in which Muslim community leaders
helped to restore order, Councillor Eric Sunderland was elected
Chairman of governors, and Tom Brown deputy chairman. In a
brief report, Honeyford discussed the possibility of setting up a
guide and brownie pack in the school (Yorkshire Post, 16 October
1985; Yorkshire Evening Post, 16 October 1985; Telegraph
and Argus, 16 October 1985; Minutes of the governors' meeting
16 October 1985).

Meanwhile, at a meeting of South Glamorgan Council for Racial
Equality, Bradford's Lord Mayor, Councillor Ajeeb, makes a major
speech attacking race relations in Britain and calling for the scrapping
of the Race Relations Act and the Commission for Racial Equality.
Local politicians are offended by his remarks, but C.M Khan, the
president of the Council for Mosques and Tim Whitfield, the
secretary of Bradford's Community Relations Council, both support
him (Telegraph and Argus, 16 October 1985).

16 October   Widespread reaction to the governors' meeting is reported. In a
1985   letter to Gordon Moore, C.M. Khan questions whether the voting
               pattern of the teacher-governors implies that the whole staff at

*Drummond Middle School supports Honeyford. Councillor Lambert raises allegations of corruption and vote-rigging with Councillor Pickles, and an exchange of letters follows (*Telegraph and Argus, *18 October 1985). Tom Brown is threatened with expulsion by the University Ward Labour Party (he has been a member for over forty years) for backing Honeyford (*Yorkshire Post, *18 October 1985;* Telegraph and Argus, *18 October 1985, 1 November 1985).*

16 October 1985

*After reporting threats to his personal safety to the police, Honeyford has an alarm system fitted in his house and in Drummond Middle School, and police keep a watch on his house. Goldberg and Woodward also report that they have received death threats (*Telegraph and Argus, *20 December 1985).*

18 October 1985

*A planned speech on the Honeyford affair by Tory MP Harvey Proctor at Bradford University is called off on the advice of Gordon Moore, who is worried about serious disruption (*Yorkshire Post, *19 October 1985;* Times, *19 October 1985). In the next few months, several other right-wing figures, including John Carlisle (*Telegraph and Argus, *14–18 February 1986) and Roger Scruton (*Telegraph and Argus, *4 March 1986), are unable to address local meetings to which they have been invited, though the media points out that similar restrictions are not placed on speakers from Sinn Fein (*Telegraph and Argus, *28–29 January 1986). Honeyford later writes in defence of John Carlisle's right to free speech (*Telegraph and Argus, *21 February 1986, 14 March 1986), and his own invitation to speak to Conservative students at Bristol Polytechnic is withdrawn (*Telegraph and Argus, *18 February 1986;* Yorkshire Post, *19 February 1986).*

20 October 1985

*The Council for Mosques calls for an end to picketing at the school, for the sake of the children's education (*Council Press Release, *20 October 1985). The Asian Youth Movement issues a statement condemning Honeyford but dissociating itself from the Council for Mosques (*21 October 1985). Bradford Drummond Parents' Support Group (BDPSG) is set up to provide a broader base of opposition to Honeyford. Initially, it calls for demonstrations at the school on 25 October and 7 November (*BDPSG press release). *Meanwhile, about seventy white youths attack people and property in Keighley's Asian district. The police are called after racial incidents outside Greenhead Grammar School in Keighley (*Yorkshire Post, *6 November 1985), and fourteen arrests are made. Gordon Moore commissions the Bradford Campaign against Racist*

> *Attacks (CARA) to write a report on the incident (*Asian Times, *11 April 1986). Later, gang fights between Asian and white pupils at Greenhead Grammar School are linked to the Honeyford affair (*Telegraph and Argus, *11 February 1986).*

23 October
1985

> *News is leaked that Honeyford is ready to leave Drummond Middle School if a suitable cash offer is made (*Telegraph and Argus, *23 October 1985;* Yorkshire Post, *17 October 1985). Soon afterwards, the Labour and Liberal groups on Bradford Council agree that Honeyford should be paid off, but the Tories block the move, saying that he should not go unless he chooses to (*Yorkshire Post, *29 October 1985;* Telegraph and Argus, *29 October 1985;* Bradford Star, *31 October 1985). At a Council meeting on 29 October, Councillor John Wells accuses the Tories of cynically using the Honeyford affair for election purposes, aiming for a 'nasty, right-wing, backlash vote'. 'I urge you to change your position,' he says, 'or you will be accused of fiddling while Bradford burns' (*Yorkshire Post, *30 October 1985).*

25 October
1985

> *Secret talks are held at City Hall between politicians, Chief Constable Colin Sampson and the Bishop of Bradford. Fears are expressed about growing street violence if the Honeyford affair is not resolved (*Telegraph and Argus, *26 November 1985). Eight local clergymen issue a statement expressing anxiety about the damage to the community being caused by the Honeyford affair (*Telegraph and Argus, *25 October 1985).*

1 November
1985

In an article which is strongly anti-Honeyford in tone, Labour Councillor Mohammad Riaz discusses the problems of inner-city children in Bradford (*Telegraph and Argus*, 1 November 1985). In an article entitled 'Lessons in Village Politics for Bradford's Schools', David Selbourne talks of an 'unholy alliance' between Bradford's white left and mosque-led obscurantism (*Guardian*, 21 October 1985). In 'As Others See Us', Mary Stopes-Roe and Raymond Cochrane report on their study of how young Asians see the English (*New Society*, 1 November 1985; *Telegraph and Argus*, 31 October 1985).

4 November
1985

> *The Appeal Court hears the Council's case against the High Court judgment of 5 September (*Times Educational Supplement, *1 November 1985, 8 November 1985). On 13 November, Lord Justice Lawton, Lord Justice Dillon and Lord Justice Mustill rule*

that Bradford Council is entitled to continue Honeyford's suspension, overturning the High Court ruling. After the verdict, demands are renewed for Honeyford's sacking by the BDPSG and the Council for Mosques. The NAHT says it will petition the House of Lords for leave to appeal against the court ruling. Leave to appeal is granted on 28 November (Telegraph and Argus, 13 November; Daily Telegraph, 14 November 1985; Times, 14 November 1985; Guardian, 14 November 1985; Times Educational Supplement, 15 November 1985; Knight's local government reports).

7 November 1985

Bradford and Ilkley College students hold a one-day strike to add weight to calls for Honeyford's dismissal (Telegraph and Argus, 1 November 1985; Yorkshire Post, 1 November 1985). The school is again picketed; children using loud-hailers lead the protest chants against Honeyford (Telegraph and Argus, 7 November 1985). The governors' meeting at the school hears reports from Council officers and from Honeyford on the state of affairs at the school (Telegraph and Argus, 8 November 1985; Yorkshire Post, 8 November 1985). Honeyford appeals to the action groups to direct their campaign away from the staff and the children. In a press statement, Labour's race relations spokesman, Councillor Flanagan says that race relations in the city are on the verge of collapse. He calls for an all-party vote of no-confidence in Honeyford and argues that the financial option agreed by Labour and the Liberal Alliance, but opposed by the Tories, should be dropped (Telegraph and Argus, 26 November 1985). A few days later, Flanagan is sacked as Labour's race relations spokesman (Telegraph and Argus, 19 November 1985).

9 November 1985

Professor Bikhu Parekh, the deputy chairman of the CRE, speaks to the annual meeting of local education authorities in Leeds on the Honeyford affair. Knight and Pickles are among the delegates (Telegraph and Argus, 9 November 1985). Three days later, an article by Michael Meadowcroft, Liberal MP for Leeds West, discusses the dangers to democracy which emerge in the Honeyford affair (Yorkshire Post, 12 November 1985).

17 November 1985

The BDPSG holds a public meeting at Queen's Hall, Bradford, to launch a wider campaign for Honeyford's dismissal (Telegraph and Argus, 26 November 1985). Five days later, it calls another boycott of the school.

18 November 1985   *The Tories deny the rumour that they are about to agree to negotiations for a pay-off deal for Honeyford (*Telegraph and Argus, *26 November 1985). Eight days later, however, Honeyford writes to Pickles expressing willingness to take early retirement if an appropriate package can be worked out. He indicates that he is himself happy to continue, but his wife has been under stress during the last twenty months, and he is also worried about the effects of continued disruption on the children and staff at his school (*Yorkshire Post, *29 November 1985;* Yorkshire Evening Post, *29 November 1985;* Telegraph and Argus, *29 November 1985).*

19 November 1985   *200 members of the Bradford branch of the NUT call on the leaders of the NUT to condemn Honeyford, but vote against asking the national executive to call for his dismissal (*Telegraph and Argus, *20 November 1985;* Times Educational Supplement, *22 November 1985).*

22 November 1985   *Honeyford presents his first report to the new governing body. He calls for more Asian teachers at his school; currently, there are only two out of twenty-seven. His opponents say that his report suggests that Asian children do not naturally belong to Bradford and that the tone is 'deliberately divisive and inflammatory'. There is uproar on the public benches as Honeyford refuses to answer five provocative questions put to him by parent governor Nazim Naqui, such as 'Why haven't you left yet?' (*Yorkshire Post, *23 November 1985;* Telegraph and Argus, *23 November 1985;* Times Educational Supplement, *29 November 1985).*

26 November 1985   *A three-page supplement on the Honeyford debate, prepared by Jim Greenhalf, is published in* Telegraph and Argus. *It includes arguments in support of and against Honeyford, a diary of events, profiles of the main personalities in the affair, a reprint of the crucial* Salisbury Review *article and Honeyford's second* Times Educational Supplement *article, an appraisal of the political implications of the affair, an article about Gill Seidel's work on 'cultural racism' and a statement of the Council's race relations policy. A week later, an article about racism in Bradford, 'Who Wins in the Honeyford Saga?', is published in* New Scientist, *and the first book on the affair, Andrew Brown's* Trials of Honeyford: Problems of Multi-Cultural Education *is published by the Centre for Policy Studies (Brown, 1985;* Telegraph and Argus, *3 December 1985). Its approach is broadly sympathetic to Honeyford. Baroness Cox regrets that*

*Brown does not include either an account of the educationally damaging aspects or an analysis of the political implications of the affair (*Daily Telegraph, *7 December 1985;* Times Educational Supplement, *6 December 1985).*

Late
November
1985

Jonathan Savery, a teacher at a Bristol multi-cultural education centre who wrote an article entitled 'Anti-racism as Witchcraft' which was published in the *Salisbury Review* in the summer, supporting Honeyford and attacking extreme forms of anti-racist education, is investigated by the head of the centre following complaints by other members of staff (*Guardian*, 26 November 1985). In January 1986, he is cleared of making racist remarks to colleagues (*Telegraph and Argus*, 4 January 1986; *Daily Telegraph*, 6 January 1986; *Daily Mail*, 10 January 1986; *Guardian*, 11 February 1986) and in May he is cleared at a disciplinary hearing of Avon Education Committee of allegations of racism arising from the *Salisbury Review* article (*Times Educational Supplement*, 30 May 1986; *Race and Immigration*, July 86). Although he is moved from the multi-cultural education centre to Merry-wood Boys' School, the local branch of the NUT urges its members not to work with him, and Avon County Council plans to move him on again (*Race and Immigration*, December 1986).

4 December
1985

*Honeyford is on sick leave to the end of term with a torn arm ligament sustained in a fall (*Telegraph and Argus, *9 December 1985).*

11 December
1985

Bradford announces a new inner-city school building prog-ramme, forecast as necessary after the phasing out of 'bussing' five years earlier, including a new middle school half a mile away from Drummond (*Telegraph and Argus*, 12 December 1985). A week later, it is announced that three language centres in Bradford are to be closed from Septem-ber 1986. Their pupils will be catered for within existing schools instead. Their premises will be used for the expansion of First School provision in the inner city, along with the new building programme (*Telegraph and Argus*, 18 December 1985).

12 December
1985

Bradford Council takes Jamiyat Tabligh ul-Islam to court to force the closure of three supplementary schools which have been running for five years in terrace houses without planning permission. Four LEA schools have been offered free from 4pm to 6pm until a permanent solution is found, but Councillor Hameed still says that the decision could damage race relations in the district (*Telegraph and Argus*, 12 December 1985).

14 December 1985

*It is announced that Honeyford has accepted a lump sum of £70,900, plus a pension of £6,500 (index-linked from the age of 55) to take early retirement. The official date of retirement is 31 December 1985. The deal is negotiated between David Hart, general secretary of the NAHT, and Bradford's chief executive, Gordon Moore. Agreement is reached on 11 December and ratified in private by the Council on 13 December (*Yorkshire Post, 14 December 1985; Yorkshire Evening Post, 14 December 1985; Telegraph and Argus, 14 December 1985; Sunday Times, 15 December 1985).*

*The two deputy heads are to run the school until the end of term (*Times, 16 December 1985). An acting head, William Haykin, currently head of Calversyke Middle School, Keighley, is appointed, so that a permanent appointment need not be made for a few months (*Telegraph and Argus, 19 December 1985; Yorkshire Post, 20 December 1985; Guardian, 20 December 1985; Times Educational Supplement, 27 December 1985). Haykin avoids contact with the media (*Telegraph and Argus, 6 January 1986). As part of the package, Honeyford agrees not to continue with his appeal to the House of Lords against the Council's original disciplinary action. However, the agreement allows him to carry on writing (*Telegraph and Argus, 16 December 1985). He is said to be writing a book on the affair, and there is speculation that he may join the Centre for Policy Studies or go into full-time politics (*Searchlight, 16 December 1985; Daily Express, 16 December 1985). Ian Murch, secretary of the Bradford branch of the NUT, asks if Honeyford's settlement will be taken from the education budget, and if cuts will be needed to finance it (*Telegraph and Argus, 16 December 1985). Shipley MP Marcus Fox writes to Brian McAndrew, Bradford's Director of Personnel, to ask what action is to be taken against the seven racism awareness training officers who called Honeyford a racist (*Telegraph and Argus, 20 December 1985).*

15 December 1985

The Lord Mayor, Councillor Ajeeb, says, 'I am deeply relieved at his imminent departure'. Ajeeb's house is stoned several times

*(*Telegraph and Argus, *16 December 1985), and later children spit at his mayoral car (*Telegraph and Argus, *11 March 1986).*

19 December   *Two sixteen-year-olds are fined £30 each for daubing anti-*
1985   *Honeyford slogans on the walls of Drummond Middle School in September (*Telegraph and Argus, *20 December 1985).*

Late December   *Ian Jack's article, 'A Severed Head', is published in the* Sunday
1985   Times *magazine (15 December 1985; letter to* Sunday Times *in reply, 22 December). 'The Hounding of Honeyford', a three-part 'exclusive' told by Honeyford himself, is published in* Daily Mail *(16–19 December 1985). Pro-Honeyford letters continue to arrive at the* Telegraph and Argus *and* Yorkshire Post. *Commentary on the Honeyford affair appears in* New Society *(20–27 December 1985).*

20 December   *Two local newspaper reports on school activities symbolize the*
1985   *difference between Honeyford's educational philosophy and that of some of Bradford's more committed multi-culturalists (*Telegraph and Argus, *20 December 1985). One report describes the senior Integrated Studies project at Drummond Middle School entitled 'Where We Live', exploring housing, industry, shops, community care and the emergency services — all in all, little different from a project carried out in 1974 entitled 'Exploring Bradford' (*Telegraph and Argus, *29 March 1974). Meanwhile, the juniors at Drummond Middle School are producing the pantomime 'Jack and the Beanstalk'. The second report is about the nearby Drummond Language Centre, where the end of term play is 'Rama and Sita' (*Telegraph and Argus, *20 December 1985).*

1986   *Honeyford's articles and the protest against him are discussed in numerous articles throughout the year. A satirical article, 'A Bradford Nickleby' is published in* Daily Telegraph *(6 January 1986). Bob Matthews (*Times Educational Supplement, *24 January 1986) claims that news coverage has misrepresented and distorted the real issues in the Honeyford affair, especially the reasons for his suspension; he argues that Honeyford was not suspended because he criticized Bradford's multi-cultural policies, but because of his offensive comments about Asians and West Indians. Frank Pedley (*Times Educational Supplement, *24 January 1986) claims that Bradford's multi-cultural policies had moved too quickly and had lost touch with the electorate; he argues that the LEA was primarily responsible for the inept handling of* the Honeyford affair and for denying heads their traditional right to speak their minds. He mentions that Honeyford was voted the fourth most popular man in Britain in 1985 in a poll by BBC Radio Four's 'Today' programme. S. Collins (Times Educational Supplement, *28 February 1986) discusses how the new Education Bill might affect a Honeyford-type situation. F.H. Mikdadi in a letter to the* Times Educational Supplement *(28 February 1986) interprets the Honeyford affair in terms of freedom to speak one's mind, though at a Community Relations Council meeting, Rev Peter Hawkins condemns this view of the affair* (Telegraph and Argus, *11 February 1986). Michael Meadow-croft (*Times, *10 November 1986) examines the suppression of free speech in connection with Honeyford and Selbourne. An article in the* Telegraph and Argus *(16 December 1986) considers the Honeyford affair a year after. Honeyford's views are also discussed in several books published in 1986, including Gordon and Klug's* New Right, New Racism, *Seidel in Levitas's* The ideology of the New Right, *and Troyna and Williams'* Racism, Education and the State. *The latter also has a significant discussion of Bradford's multi-cultural policies, as does Lynch's* Multi-Cultural Education: Principles and Practice.

January 1986   David Rose (*Guardian*, 23 January 1986) reviews racial tensions in Bradford in the aftermath of the Honeyford affair. Aggression against the Asian community appears to be on the increase. A standing conference on racial harassment is resumed now that the Community Relations Council has withdrawn its ban on co-operation with Bradford Council, which it imposed in protest at the Council's handling of the Honeyford affair (*Bradford Star*, 30 January 1986). The Community Relations Council calls for more initiatives to fight prejudice in Bradford (*Telegraph and Argus*, 11 February 1986). Opening the conference of the Union of Muslim Organizations of UK and Eire in Bradford, the city's Chief Executive Gordon Moore calls race relations the biggest issue facing Bradford (*Bradford Star*, 6 February 1986; *Telegraph and Argus*, 10 February 1986, 14 February 1986, 18 February 1986). Asians express their fear of increased racial attacks when Bradford City return to their football ground (located in a predominantly Asian area) after the rebuilding following the Bradford City Fire Disaster (*Telegraph and Argus*, 12 February 1986). There is argument over whether an attack on an Asian-run amusement hall in Bradford is racist, or simply gang warfare (*Bradford Star*, 20 March 1986, 27 March 1986, 17 April 1986; *Guardian*, 24 March 1986). Racial conflict continues in Heaton, Bradford. Black and white pupils fight outside Belle Vue Boys' School (*Yorkshire Post*, 27 March 1986, 4 April 1986; *Yorkshire Evening Post*, 21 March 1986; *The Next Step*, 4 April 1986; *Telegraph and Argus*, 16 April 1986). The cars and homes of Asian residents are attacked, and an increase in racist attacks on taxi drivers is reported (*Telegraph and Argus*, 20 March 1986, 5 April 1986, 10 April 1986; *Yorkshire Post*, 11 April 1986, 26 April 1986; *New Life*, 4 April 1986, 18 April 1986, 25 April 1986; *Race and Immigration*, June 1986). A gang of Asians attacks three white St Bede's schoolboys (*Telegraph and Argus*, 13 March 1986). Workers Against Racism (WAR), an offshoot of the Revolutionary Communist Party, sets up vigilante patrols to protect blacks from racist attacks (*Telegraph and Argus*, 13 March 1986, 20 March 1986; *The Next Step*, 4 April 1986), though a local communist party member sees this as a 'red rag to racist bulls' (*Bradford Star*, 20 March 1986). Anti-racists claim that there is a conspiracy of silence between press, police and Council to conceal the extent of racist attacks in Bradford (*The Next Step*, 4 April 1986; *Searchlight*, 4 May 1986; cf *Bradford Star*, 17 April 1986). The Chief Constable of West Yorkshire blames a 'hooligan element' for the attacks and says the term 'racial attack' should be avoided (*Guardian*, 5 May 1986). Anti-fascists, with the support of fifteen Labour councillors and Max Madden, MP, are set to disrupt the election campaigns of the two BNP candidates in the May elections (*Bradford Star*, 10 April 1986). A BNP organiser is charged with distributing literature (the leaflet 'If Only We Were Black') likely to stir up racial hatred (*Telegraph and Argus*, 13 May 1986). Meanwhile, it is claimed by a careers adviser that sixth-formers are staying away from Bradford University because the city has a bad name for race relations (*Telegraph and Argus*, 23 April 1986). A major march through Bradford organized by WAR is joined by between 300 and 1,000 people, including Councillor Ajeeb (*Yorkshire Post*, 16 June 1986; *Asian Times*, 27 June 1986, 3 July 1986). In September, Bradford libraries have an anti-racist drive, 'combing children's books for offensive terms and attitudes' (*Bradford Star*, 11 September 1986).

February
1986

Bradford publishes new draft guidelines for worship in schools. Worship is to be removed from whole-school assemblies, and parents are free to opt for their children to attend non-compulsory Christian, Muslim, Hindu or Sikh worship elsewhere on the school timetable. A pilot scheme is initiated with several local schools participating (City of Bradford Metropolitan Council, 1986a; 1986b; *Telegraph and Argus*, 30 January 1986, 7 February 1986). An Interfaith Education Centre for RE teachers and others is opened in Bradford by the Lord Mayor. Headed by David Jackson, it caters for the five main faiths in the city (*Telegraph and Argus*, 27 February 1986, 12 March 1986, 29 March 1986).

February
1986

The number of mosques in Bradford has now reached thirty. Work starts on the first phase of an £8,500,000 mosque complex in the centre of Bradford, planned by the Jamiyat Tabligh ul-Islam group. It will have a prayer hall for 3,000 people, a minaret, a mortuary, and meeting rooms, and when finished will be the largest mosque in Europe (*Telegraph and Argus*, 20 February 1986, 3 March 1986, 8 January 1987; *Times*, 18 August 1987). On a Pennine Radio programme, however, young Asians criticize the plans for expensive mosques in the city (*Telegraph and Argus*, 26 September 1987). Meanwhile, a Muslim businessman in Bradford is reported to be sending his children back to Pakistan for a more religious and disciplined education (*Telegraph and Argus*, 3 February 1986). The story of an indigenous Muslim convert in Bradford receives local press coverage (*Telegraph and Argus*, 7 February 1986). A probe into the financial affairs of the Council for Mosques, which is funded by the MSC, is ordered by Bradford Council (*Telegraph and Argus*, 23 April 1986). The Ahmadiyya sect holds seminars on 'the Muslim Religion' for Bradford sixth-formers, and orthodox Muslims demonstrate angrily against their activities (*Bradford Star*, 1 May 1986; *Telegraph and Argus*, 18 August 1987). The local press reports the disappearance of 16-year-old Yasmin Bibi from home; she returns after a month (*Bradford Star*, 10 July 1986, 31 July 1986). Lucky Ali, aged 15, also goes missing; in a note, she writes, 'Looking at white people outside, they have got freedom, and all I want is a little bit of freedom' (*Telegraph and Argus*, 2 August 1986). A report draws attention to beatings of pupils by imams in Bradford and elsewhere (*Sunday Times*, 10 August 1986). Bradford's Council for Mosques say that traditional forms of discipline will continue to be used in Muslim supplementary schools, whatever the law (*Bradford Star*, 4 September 1986). Single-sex schools remain a top priority for many of Bradford's Muslims (*Telegraph and Argus*, 28 January 1987, 20 July 1987).

12 February 1986

*Tom Brown proposes that Drummond Middle School governors send a vote of thanks to Honeyford for his years of service, but the chairman, Eric Sunderland, wishes to avoid the conflict such an action might produce. Fourteen applications are reported for the post of headteacher, and in April, Leslie Hall, currently head of Wyke Middle School, is appointed for September (*Telegraph and Argus, 12 February 1986, 6 March 1986; Guardian, 17 April 1986).*

24 February 1986

*Jenny Woodward is fined for producing a cannabis plant. She complains that police are trying to discredit her, and mentions hate-mail she has received which includes references to her unborn child (*Telegraph and Argus, 24 February 1986). In March, she refuses to give her talk on 'The Education of Black Children: Honeyford and After' at the Fifth International Book Fair in the presence of two journalists. They leave under protest (*Bradford Star, 13 March 1986; Yorkshire Post, 17 March 1986; Yorkshire Evening Post, 17 March 1986; Telegraph and Argus, 20 March 1986).*

March 1986

Abdul Rehman of Bradford is sentenced for importing heroin from Pakistan (*Telegraph and Argus*, 11 March 1986). Earlier, Pakistani leaders in Bradford echoed General Zia's condemnation of the drug trade (*Telegraph and Argus*, 4 February 1986).

March 1986

A survey of fifth-formers who left school last year shows that one in ten black children got a job, compared to one in three white children (*Telegraph and Argus*, 5 March 1986). 18.2 per cent (1356) of fifth-formers were from ethnic minorities, and 48 per cent of these stayed on at school, compared to 27.7 per cent of whites (*Bradford Star*, 1 May 1986). Only eight-six teachers in the district's 300 schools are from ethnic minorities, and only one in ten governors

are Asian (*Telegraph and Argus*, 29 March 1986). An NAS/
UWT spokesman in Bradford commends the city for
disbanding its language centres and integrating their work
into schools (*Telegraph and Argus*, 17 March 1986). Meanwhile, Bradford University is considering setting up the first
degree course in Asian Studies in the country (*Bradford Star*,
17 April 1986). In an important research paper on Indians in
Bradford, Singh and Ram conclude that the vast majority
have no wish to return to their country of origin (Singh with
Ram, 1986; *Telegraph and Argus*, 12 May 1986; *Bradford Star*,
26 June 1986).

March–
December
1986

Honeyford continues to write articles for Salisbury Review,
Yorkshire Post, Daily Mail, Spectator *and elsewhere (see
Bibliography). In March, he speaks at the annual conference of
Yorkshire Conservative Trades Unionists in Leeds on political
interference in education (*Yorkshire Post, 10 March 1986*). He is
reported to be writing a book on 'Education for All' (the Swann
Report) (*Telegraph and Argus, 14 March 1986;* Yorkshire
Post, 17 March 1986*). In April, he addresses a Rotary Club
lunch at Victoria Hotel, Bradford, and calls for more integration
and an end to multi-cultural education. He is met by WAR
demonstrators (*Telegraph and Argus, 14 March 1986, 5 April
1986;* Yorkshire Evening Post, 5 April 1986;* Yorkshire Post,
5 April 1986, 14 April 1986;* Bradford Star, 10 April 1986*).
He writes a short statement in support of the Conservatives for
their local election newsletter, though Councillor Lambert in
response criticizes the Tories for putting race on the election agenda
(*Telegraph and Argus, 18 March 1986, 25 March 1986, 19
April 1986, 26 April 1986*). In August, Anthony Clare
interviews Honeyford on Radio Four for his series 'In the
Psychiatrist's Chair' (*Listener, 28 August 1986*). In September,
Honeyford is met by 150 protestors when he attends a meeting in
Sheffield to speak on 'The Myths of Anti-Racism' (*Solidarity
Against Racism, journal of the Sheffield Campaign against
Racism, issue 21;* Telegraph and Argus, 26 September 1986;*
Yorkshire Post, 27 September 1986*). In October, Honeyford and
Savery address a lunchtime meeting of Conservative students at
Bristol University. Afterwards, paint is thrown at Honeyford's car
(*Telegraph and Argus, 23–24 October 1986*). In November,
Honeyford speaks for the motion, 'That the aims of the anti-racist
lobby are frustrated by their means', at the Oxford Union. The*

motion is upheld. In December, his chapter entitled 'Anti-Racist Rhetoric' is published in Frank Falmer's Anti-racism – an Assault on Education and Value.

May 1986   *After several years with a hung Council, Labour comes to power in the local elections in Bradford, and Councillor Lambert becomes chairman of the Educational Services Committee. The Liberal leader, Kathleen Greenwood, who is mayor-elect, is heavily defeated by the Conservative candidate in her ward. She claims that the Honeyford affair has been a factor in her defeat, as she had been taken to task locally for voting against Honeyford at a crucial vote of censure in 1985 (Education, 16 May 1986).*

22 May 1986   In a speech to mark his retirement as Secretary of State for Education, Sir Keith Joseph calls for schools to 'transmit British culture', criticizes multi-cultural education and discusses the concept of prejudice. Echoing Honeyford, he argues that the main responsibility for transmitting minority cultures lies in the home and in the minority communities (*Telegraph and Argus*, 22 May 1986; *Race and Immigration*, July 1986).

23 June 1986   Plans are put forward by Councillor Ajeeb, the new chairman of the Race Relations Committee, to disband the Race Training Unit in Bradford and amalgamate its work in the overall training policy of the Council.

15 August 1986   Peter Thorpe, a Keighley teacher, writes an article entitled 'Feminist line baffles me', in which he criticizes Bradford's decision to appoint a Schools' Sex Equality Adviser (*Telegraph and Argus*, 15 August 1986, *cf* 23 July 1986). He is investigated by the directorate of education, but no action is taken (*Yorkshire Post*, 18 August 1986; *Guardian*, 20 August 1986, 23 August 1986; *Daily Mail*, 21 August 1986).

Late 1986   Maureen McGoldrick, the head of Sudbury Infants School in Brent, is suspended in July after allegedly stating that she did not want any more black teachers at her school. In August, the school governors find the allegations unsubstantiated and call for her reinstatement, and in September, NUT members at the school vote to strike in support of her reinstatement.

At a High Court hearing in October, the judge rules that the governors' decision is binding on the Council, and Kenneth Baker then urges the Council to reinstate McGoldrick. She is eventually reinstated in November, and welcomed back to the school by a large crowd of supporters. The affair receives very extensive media coverage, and adds fuel to the growing criticisms of Brent's anti-racist policies. An article by Honeyford in *Daily Mail* (20 October 1986) is strongly critical of Brent's policies (*Guardian*, 6 September 1986, 11 September 1986, 23–5 October 1986, 3 November 1986; *Times Educational Supplement*, 21 November 1986; *Race and Immigration*, November 1986, December 1986; etc.).

December 1986   The all-party consensus on race relations on Bradford Council comes to an end with the publication of a report prepared by a think-tank commissioned by the Race Relations Advisory Group, under its new chairman, Councillor Ajeeb (*Telegraph and Argus*, 27 June 1987).

1987   *Honeyford continues to write articles in the* Salisbury Review, Yorkshire Post *and* Spectator, *and has letters published in the* Times *and* Radio Times *(see Bibliography). Extended accounts of the Honeyford affair are given by Selbourne, Murphy and Foster-Carter. In a book by Gilroy, Honeyford is accused of 'cultural racism'. Further information about immigration to Bradford is given in articles by Dawe and Anwar and in a book by the Bradford Heritage Recording Unit, and an unflattering picture of life in Bradford is provided in West's article, 'Inner City of Dreadful Night'* (Spectator, *27 June 1987), which caused much local resentment.*

May 1987   Two of Bradford's former racism awareness training officers, Ishtiaq Ahmed and Mohammed Salam, who helped to draw up the controversial memorandum which branded Honeyford a racist, are elected chairman and vice-chairman of the city's Community Relations Council. Fears are expressed that the CRC is being taken over by extremists, and Councillor Ajeeb suggests that the CRC may be coming to the end of its useful life (*Telegraph and Argus*, 15 June 1987, 23 June 1987, 27 June 1987, 9 July 1987, 13 July 1987).

June 1987   Controversy develops over the activities of the Black Workers' Collective, a radical pressure group set up in 1986 to organize black workers in the Bradford district and to defend their interests and democratic rights. Its critics say that it is attempting to undermine the Council's efforts to stamp out racism (*Yorkshire Post*, 13 June 1987; *Telegraph and Argus*, 15 June 1987, 27 June 1987).

September
1987

Twenty-six parents in Dewsbury refuse to send their children to Headfield Middle School where about 85 per cent of the pupils are Asian. They claim that their protest is cultural, not racial, and they object to some of the multi-cultural concessions that Headfield has adopted. They wish their children to attend a nearby predominantly white school, Overthorpe Junior, which has spare places, but Kirklees Education Authority refuses. Their daily protests outside Overthorpe receive widespread media coverage. Both Honeyford and Bradford's Muslim Parents' Association express support for the protesting parents, and far-right groups also try to make use of the affair. Kenneth Baker refuses to intervene. Eventually, the children are taught by volunteer teachers in a public house owned by one of the parents. Three months later, the situation is still unresolved (*Guardian*, 21 August 1987, 9 September 1987; *Telegraph and Argus*, 27 August 1987, 2 September 1987, 9 September 1987; *Daily Telegraph*, 8–12 September 1987, 22 September 1987; *Observer*, 13 September 1987; *Independent*, 12 September 1987, 14 September 1987; *Sunday Times*, 6 September 1987, 13 September 1987; *Race and Immigration*, October 1987, December 1987; *New Society*, 27 November 1987; etc.).

October
1987

Bradford Council issues new guidelines for its employees, designed to avoid any further embarrassment from public statements such as Honeyford's and Thorpe's criticisms of Council policies. Any employee criticizing local politicians, Council policy, other employees or the Council's perform-ance may now face disciplinary action (*Telegraph and Argus*, 2 October 1987). At first, it is thought that an article in the *British Journal of Sociology of Education* by David Shepherd, a teacher at Manningham Middle School, is in breach of the guidelines, but it emerges that academic research is not bound by the rules (*Telegraph and Argus*, 9 October 1987).

Late 1987

There is much discussion of the effects of the new Education Bill on minorities in Bradford. NUT members and others point out that one way or another segregated education may result: either white parents may opt not to send their children to schools with a large percentage of Asians, or Muslims and other groups may try to use the opting-out proposals in order to establish distinctively religious schools (*Telegraph and Argus*, 9 June 1987; *Times Educational Supplement*, 20 November 1987). Local Muslims have also expressed concern about the inclusion of drama and music in, and the exclusion of religious instruction from, the planned national curriculum for schools (*Telegraph and Argus*, 1 October 1987).

1988   Honeyford continues to challenge the erosion of free speech and to express his deep suspicions of anti-racism, in both lectures and articles (*Times Educational Supplement*, 26 February 1988, 18 March 1988; *Daily Mail*, 30 March 1988). His name is among the founders of Majority Rights, a pressure group set up in March 1988 to campaign for the protection of the British national identity and the eradication of multi-cultural education (*Guardian*, 18 March 1988). He is reported to be standing as a Conservative counsillor in the forthcoming local elections (*Times Educational Supplement*, 26 February 1988).

Bibliography

ACKERMAN, B.A. (1980) *Social Justice in the Liberal State* New Haven, Yale University Press.

ALLEN, S. (1970) 'Immigrants or workers', in ZUBAIDA, S. (Ed) *Race and Racialism* London, Tavistock.

ALLEN, S., BENTLEY, S. and BORNAT, J. (1981) 'Business activity and the self-employed', in BRAHAM, P., RHODES, F. and PEARN, M. (Eds) *Discrimination and Disadvantage in Employment: the Experience of Black Workers* London, Harper and Row.

ALLPORT, G.W. (1958) *The Nature of Prejudice* New York, Doubleday Anchor.

ALMOND, B. (1987) *Moral Concerns* New Jersey, Humanities Press International.

ANWAR, M. (1979) *The Myth of Return: Pakistanis in Britain* London, Heinemann International.

ANWAR, M. (1987) 'Social picture changes greatly in last decade' *Telegraph and Argus Pakistan Anniversary Supplement*, 14 August.

ARBLASTER, A. (1974) *Academic Freedom* Harmondsworth, Penguin.

ARONSFELD, C.C. (1981) 'German Jews in nineteenth-century Bradford', *Yorkshire Archaeological Journal*, 53, pp. 111–7.

ASHRAF, S.A. (1985) *New Horizons in Muslim Education* London, Hodder and Stoughton.

ASHRAF, S.A. (1986) 'Foreword' to: HALSTEAD, J.M. *The Case for Muslim Voluntary-aided Schools: Some Philosophical Reflections* Cambridge, Islamic Academy.

ASHRAF, S.A. (1988a) 'Editorial: The Islamic approach to education and the national curriculum' *Muslim Education Quarterly*, 5, 2, pp. 1–7.

ASHRAF, S.A. (1988b) 'The conceptual framework of education: The Islamic perspective' *Muslim Education Quarterly*, 5, 2, pp. 8–18.

ASHRIF, S. and YASEEN, M. (1987) 'The case for Islamic Studies' *Muslim Education Quarterly*, 4, 2, pp. 23–27.

ASIAN YOUTH MOVEMENT (1983) *Policy Statement on Religious/Separate Schools* Bradford, Asian Youth Movement.

ASIAN YOUTH MOVEMENT (1984) *Reading, Riting, Rithmetic, Race: Racism and Schools* Bradford, Asian Youth Movement.

BAILEY, C. (1980) 'The autonomous teacher', in SOCKETT, H. (Ed) *Accountability in the English Educational System* London, Hodder and Stoughton.

BAILEY, C. (1983) 'Education, accountability and the preparation of teachers' *Cambridge Journal of Education*, 13, 2, pp. 10–19.

BAILEY, C. (1984) *Beyond the Present and the Particular* London, Routledge and Kegan Paul.

BANDURA, A., ROSS, D. and ROSS, S.A. (1961) 'Transmission of aggression through aggressive models' *Journal of Abnormal Social Psychology*, 63, 3, pp. 575–82.

BANTON, M. (1985) *Promoting Racial Harmony*. Cambridge, Cambridge University Press.

BARKER, M. (1981) *The New Racism* London, Junction Books.

BEAUMONT, G. (1976) 'Bilingualism in Bradford', in *Bilingualism and British Education: the Dimensions of Diversity*, Report No. 14, CILT London, Centre for Information on Language Teaching and Research.

BECHER, A. *et al.* (1979) *Accountability in the Middle Years of Schooling* Working Papers, Final Report to the SSRC, University of Sussex.

BECHER, A., ERAUT, M. and KNIGHT, J. (1981) *Policies for Educational Accountability* London, Heinemann.

BELL, D. (1987) 'Acts of union: Youth sub-culture and ethnic identity amongst protestants in Northern Ireland' *British Journal of Sociology*, 38, 2, pp. 158–183.

BENTLEY, A.F. (1908) *The Process of Government* Chicago, University of Chicago Press.

BENTLEY, S. (1981) 'Industrial conflict, strikes and black workers: Problems of research methodology', in BRAHAM, P., RHODES, E. and PEARN, M. (Eds) *Discrimination and Disadvantage in Employment: the Experience of Black Workers* London, Harper and Row.

BEN-TOVIM, G. (1978) 'The struggle against racism: Theoretical and strategic perspectives' *Marxism Today*, July, pp. 203–213.

BERGER, P.L. and LUCKMANN, T. (1967) *The Social Construction of Reality* Harmondsworth, Penguin.

BERLIN, I. (1969) *Four Essays on Liberty* London, Oxford University Press.

BILLINGHAM, C. (1985) 'Honeyford's views' Letter to *The Times Educational Supplement*, 3 May.

BOEKE, J.H. (1953) *Economics and Economic Policy of Dual Societies* New York, Institute of Pacific Relations.

BONNETT, M. (1979) 'Reply to David Bridges' *Journal of Philosophy of Education*, 13, 2, pp. 165–168.

BOWEN, D.G. (1981) The Hindu community in Bradford. In BOWEN, D.G. (Ed) *Hinduism in England* Bradford College.

BRADFORD HERITAGE RECORDING UNIT (1987) *Destination Bradford: a Century of Immigration* Bradford, Libraries and Information Service.

BRIDGES, D. (1978) 'Participation and political education' *Cambridge Journal of Education*, 8, 2–3, pp. 117–130.

BRIDGES, D. (1979) 'Some reasons why curriculum planning should not be "left to the experts"'. *Journal of Philosophy of Education*, 13, 2, pp. 159–164.

BRIDGES, D. (1980) 'Accountability and the politics of the staffroom', in SOCKETT, H. (Ed) *Accountability in the English Educational System* London, Hodder and Stoughton.

BRIDGES, D. (1981) 'Accountability, communication and control', in ELLIOTT, J. *et al.* (Eds) *School Accountability: the SSRC Accountability Project* London, Grant McIntyre.

BRIDGES, D. (1982a) 'So truth be in the field...?' Approaches to controversy in world studies teaching', in HICKS, D. and TOWNLEY, C. (Eds) *Teaching World Studies* London, Longman.

BRIDGES, D. (1982b) 'Accountability and schools', *Where*, July/August, pp. 12–14.

BRIDGES, D. (1984) 'Non-paternalistic arguments in support of parents' rights', *Journal of Philosophy of Education*, 18, 1, pp. 55–61.

BROWN, A. (1985) *Trials of Honeyford: Problems in Multi-cultural Education* London, Centre for Policy Studies.

BULLIVANT, B.M. (1984) *Pluralism: Cultural Maintenance and Evolution* Clevedon, Multilingual Matters.

BULLOCK, D. (1985) 'Still muddling on', *The Times Educational Supplement*, 13 December, p. 19.

BURGESS, C. (1986) 'Tackling racism and sexism in the primary classroom', in GUNDARA, J., JONES, C. and KIMBERLEY, K. (Eds) *Racism, Diversity and Education* London, Hodder and Stoughton.

BUTT, R. (1985) Multi-cultural consequences *The Times Educational Supplement*, 24 May.

CAMPBELL, M. and JONES, D. (1983) *Asian Youths in the Labour Market: a Study in Bradford* Bradford College.

CARMICHAEL, S. and HAMILTON, C. (1967) *Black Power* New York, Vintage.

CARROLL, P. (1986) 'The scramble from the ghetto' *Telegraph and Argus*, 4 February.

CARTER, A. (1973) *Direct Action and Liberal Democracy* London, Routledge and Kegan Paul.

CASEY, J. (1982) 'One nation: The politics of race', *The Salisbury Review*, 1, pp. 23–28.

CASHMORE, E.E. and TROYNA, B. (1983) *Introduction to Race Relations* London, Routledge and Kegan Paul.

CAUDREY, A. (1987) 'Dewsbury Drama' *New Society*, 27 November.

CENTRE FOR CONTEMPORARY CULTURAL STUDIES (1982) *The Empire Strikes Back: Race and Racism in 70s Britain* London, Hutchinson.

CITY OF BRADFORD METROPOLITAN COUNCIL (1983) *Ethnic Minorities in the District's Schools* Bradford, CBMC Educational Research Information Unit.

CITY OF BRADFORD METROPOLITAN COUNCIL (1984a) *District Trends 1984: the Changing Face of Bradford* Bradford, CBMC.

CITY OF BRADFORD METROPOLITAN COUNCIL (1984b) *Bradford in Figures* Bradford, CBMC.

CITY OF BRADFORD METROPOLITAN COUNCIL (1984c) *Race Relations in Bradford: the Council's Approach* Bradford, CBMC Policy Unit.

CITY OF BRADFORD METROPOLITAN COUNCIL (1984d) *Community Languages in Bradford*, Bradford, CBMC.

CITY OF BRADFORD METROPOLITAN COUNCIL (1984e) 'Report of Advisers' inspection of Drummond Middle School', Bradford, CBMC Directorate of Education.

CITY OF BRADFORD METROPOLITAN COUNCIL (1985) *A Chance to Speak: A Report to the Race Relations Advisory Group and Sex Equality Advisory Group* Bradford, CBMC.

CITY OF BRADFORD METROPOLITAN COUNCIL (1986a) *Assembling the School in a Multi-Faith District.* Bradford, CBMC Directorate of Education.

CITY OF BRADFORD METROPOLITAN COUNCIL (1986b) *School Assembly: Guidelines (Draft)* Bradford, CBMC Directorate of Education.

CITY OF BRADFORD METROPOLITAN COUNCIL DIGEST (1981) *Turning Point: A Review of Race Relations in Bradford* Bradford, CBMC.

CITY OF BRADFORD METROPOLITAN COUNCIL SOCIAL SERVICES DIRECTORATE (1983) *European Immigrants in Bradford* Bradford, CBMC.

CLARE, A. (1986) 'In the psychiatrist's chair', *The Listener*, 28 August.

COARD, B. (1971) *How the West Indian Child is Made Educationally Subnormal in the British School System* London, New Beacon Books.

COHEN, B.G. and JENNER, P.J. (1981) 'The employment of immigrants: A case study within the wool industry', in BRAHAM, P., RHODES, E. and PEARN, M. (Eds) *Discrimination and Disadvantage in Employment: the Experience of Black Workers* London, Harper and Row.

COLE, G.D.H. (1917) *Self-Government in Industry* London, Bell.

COMMISSION FOR RACIAL EQUALITY (1980) *Mother Tongue Teaching Conference Report*, Bradford College, 9–11 September, 1980, London, CRE.

COONS, J.E. and SUGARMAN, S.D. (1978) *Education by Choice: the Case for Family Control* Berkeley, University of California Press.

COOPER, D.E. (1980) *Illusions of Equality* London, Routledge and Kegan Paul.

COUNTER INFORMATION SERVICES (1976) 'Leeds and Bradford: The darker sky', in *Racism: Who Profits?* (Anti-Report No. 16). London, CIS.

CRITTENDEN, B. (1978) 'Autonomy as an aim in education', in STRIKE, K.A. and EGAN, K. (Eds) *Ethics and Educational Policy* London, Routledge and Kegan Paul.

CRITTENDEN, B. (1982) *Cultural Pluralism and Common Curriculum* Carlton, Melbourne University Press.

CROSS, J. (1984) 'When in Bradford...' *The Times Educational Supplement*, 25 May, p. 19.

DAHL, R.A. (1956) *A Preface to Democratic Theory* Chicago, Chicago University Press.

DAWE, A. (1987) 'Faith, hope and poverty: Islam in Britain', *The Times*, 18 August, p. 8.

DEARDEN, R.F. (1966) ' "Needs" in education' *British Journal of Educational Studies*, 14, 3, pp. 5–17.

DEARDEN, R.F. (1968) *The Philosophy of Primary Education: an Introduction* London, Routledge and Kegan Paul.

DEEM, R. (1984) *Coeducation Reconsidered* Milton Keynes, Open University Press.

DEPARTMENT OF EDUCATION AND SCIENCE (1975) *A Language for Life* (The Bullock Report) London, HMSO.

DEPARTMENT OF EDUCATION AND SCIENCE (1977) *A New Partnership for our Schools* (The Taylor Report) London, HMSO.

DEPARTMENT OF EDUCATION AND SCIENCE (1985) *Education for All* (The Swann Report) Cmnd 9453, London, HMSO.

DEPARTMENT OF EDUCATION AND SCIENCE (1987) *The National Curriculum 5–16: a Consultation Document* London, DES.

DESPRES, L. (1967) *Cultural Pluralism and Nationalist Politics in British Guiana* Chicago, Rand McNally.

DEWEY, J. *(1920) Reconstruction in Philosophy* New York, Henry Holt.

DHONDY, F. (1978) 'The black explosion in schools', *Race Today*, May.

DOBZHANSKY, T. (1973) 'Differences are not deficits', *Psychology Today*, December.

DREW, D. (1986) 'Storm erupts as "Star" flies flag of racism' *Solidarity Against Racism*, 21, pp. 6–7.

DUNCAN, C. (1985a) 'Portrait of a multi-cultural school: Some implications for practice' in CORNER, T. (Ed) *Race and the Curriculum* Glasgow, University Department of Education.

DUNCAN, C. (1985b) 'One school's response to the needs of Muslim children' *Multicultural Teaching*, 3, 3, pp. 20–22.

DUNLOP, F. (1979) 'On the democratic organization of schools'. *Cambridge Journal of Education*, 9, 1, pp. 43–54.

DWORKIN, R. (1977) *Taking Rights Seriously* London, Duckworth.

EGGLESTON, J., DUNN, D. and ANJALI, M. (1986) *Education for Some: the Educational and Vocational Experiences of 15–18 year-old Members of Minority Ethnic Groups* Stoke-on-Trent, Trentham Books.

ELLIOTT, J. (1980) 'Who should monitor performance in schools?' in SOCKETT, H. (Ed) *Accountability in the English Educational System* London, Hodder and Stoughton.

ELLIOTT, J. *et al.* (1981a) *School Accountability: the SSRC Accountability Project* London, Grant McIntyre.

ELLIOTT, J. *et al.* (1981b) *Case Studies in School Accountability* Vols I, II and III, Cambridge, Institute of Education.

ELLIS, T. *et al.* (1976) *William Tyndale: the Teachers' Story* London, Writers and Readers Publishing Cooperative.

ESSIEN-UDOM, E.U. (1966) *Black Nationalism: the Rise of the Black Muslims in the USA* Harmondsworth, Penguin.

EVANS, P. (1971) *Attitudes of Young Immigrants* London, Runnymede Trust.

FAIRHALL, J. (1986) 'It would not resolve a Poundswick, but it could prevent a Tyndale', *The Guardian*, 25 February.

FEINBERG, J. (1980) *Rights, Justice and the Bounds of Liberty* Princeton, Princeton University Press.

FIGGIS, J.N. (1905) 'The church and the secular theory of the state,' *Church Congress Report*, pp. 189ff. Reprinted as Appendix One in NICHOLLS, D. (1975) *The Pluralist State* London, Macmillan.

FIGGIS, J.N. (1913) *Churches in the Modern State* London, Longmans.

FISHKIN, J.S. (1983) *Justice, Equal Opportunity and the Family* New Haven, Yale University Press.

FITZPATRICK, B. and REES, O.A. (1980) 'Mother tongue and English teaching project' *Disadvantage in Education*, 3, 1, pp. 7–8.

FLEW, A. (1986) 'Clarifying the concepts', in PALMER, F. (Ed) *Anti-Racism — an Assault on Education and Value* London, Sherwood Press.

FLEW, A. (1987) ' "Education against racism": Three comments', *Journal of Philosophy of Education*, 21, 1, pp. 131–7.

FOSTER-CARTER, O. (1985) 'The struggle at Drummond Middle School', *Critical Social Policy*, 12, pp. 74–78.

FOSTER-CARTER, O. (1987) 'The Honeyford affair: Political and policy implications', in TROYNA, B. (Ed) *Racial Inequality in Education* London, Tavistock.

FRASER, P. (1986) 'Black perspectives on British education', in GUNDARA, J., JONES, C. and KIMBERLEY, K. (Eds) *Racism, Diversity and Education* London, Hodder and Stoughton.

FREEMAN, M. (1983) 'The concept of children's rights', in GEACH, H. and SZWED, E. (Eds) *Providing Civil Justice for Children* London, Arnold.

FURNIVALL, J.S. (1948) *Colonial Policy and Practice* Cambridge, Cambridge University Press.

GAINE, C. (1987) *No Problem Here: a Practical Approach to Education and 'Race' in White Schools* London, Hutchinson.

GARNETT, C.W. (1983) *Irish Immigration and the Roman Catholic Church in Bradford. 1835–1870* Sheffield Polytechnic MA thesis (unpublished).

GAUS, G. (1983) *The Modern Liberal Theory of Man* London, Croom Helm.

GEACH, H. and SZWED, E. (eds) (1983) *Providing Civil Justice for Children* London, Arnold.

GIBSON, R. (1980) 'Teachers as employees' in SOCKETT, H. (Ed) *Accountability in the English Educational System* London, Hodder and Stoughton.

GILROY, P. (1987) *There Ain't No Black in the Union Jack: the Cultural Politics of Race and Nation* London, Hutchinson.

GLAZER, N. (1983) *Ethnic Dilemmas, 1964–1982.* Cambridge, Massachusetts, Howard University Press.

GOLDSTEIN, J., FREUD, A. and SOLNIT, A.J. (1973) *Beyond the Best Interests of the Child* New York, Free Press.

GOLDSTEIN, J., FREUD, A. and SOLNIT, A.J. (1979) *Before the Best Interests of the Child* New York, Free Press.

GOLDSTEIN, J., FREUD, A., SOLNIT, A.J. and GOLDSTEIN, S. (1986) *In the Best Interests of the Child: Professional Boundaries* New York, Free Press.

GOODALL, J. (1968) 'The Pakistani background', in OAKLEY, R. (Ed) *New Backgrounds* London, Oxford University Press.

GOODMAN, P. (1971) 'What rights should children have?' *New York Review*, 23 September.

GORDON, P. and KLUG, F. (1986) *New Right, New Racism* London, Searchlight Publications.

GREENHALF, J. (1985a) 'Anatomy of a row that has split our city', *Telegraph and Argus*, 12 April.

GREENHALF, J. (1985b) 'The Honeyford debate', Supplement to *Telegraph and Argus*, 26 November.

GRETTON, J. and JACKSON, M. (1976) *William Tyndale: Collapse of a School or a System?* London, Allen and Unwin.

GRIBBLE, J. (1969) *Introduction to Philosophy of Education* Boston, Allyn and Bacon.

GRIGG, M. (1967) *The White Question* London, Secker and Warburg.

GRIZZARD, N. (1983) *Follow Bradford's Jewish Heritage Trail* Available in Bradford Central Library.

GUTMANN, A. (1980) *Liberal Equality* Cambridge, Cambridge University Press.

HALDANE, J. (1986) 'Religious education in a pluralist society: A philosophical examination', *British Journal of Educational Studies*, 34, 2, pp. 161–181.

HALSTEAD, J.M. (1986) *The Case for Muslim Voluntary-aided Schools: Some Philosophical Reflections* Cambridge, Islamic Academy.

HALSTEAD, J.M. (1987) *Radical Feminism, Islam and the Single-sex School Debate* Unpublished paper presented to graduate seminar at the University of Cambridge Department of Education.

HALSTEAD, J.M. and KHAN-CHEEMA, M.A. (1987) 'Muslims and worship in the maintained school' *Westminster Studies in Education*, 10, pp. 25–40.

HARE, R.M. (1963) *Freedom and Reason* Oxford, Clarendon.

HARRIS, J. (1982a) 'A paradox of multi-cultural societies' *Journal of Philosophy of Education*, 16, 2, pp. 223–233.

HARRIS, J. (1982b) 'The political status of children' in GRAHAM, K. (Ed) *Contemporary Political Philosophy: Radical Studies* Cambridge, Cambridge University Press.

HATCHER, R. (1985) 'On "Education for Racial Equality" ' *Multiracial Education*, 13, 1, pp. 30–46.

HAYDON, G. (1987) 'Towards a Framework of Commonly Accepted Values' in HAYDON, G. (Ed) *Education for a Pluralist Society: Philosophical Perspectives on the Swann Report* Bedford Way Paper 30, London, University of London Institute of Education.

HEILBRON, M.R. (1975) *Jews and Judaism in Bradford* Bradford Metropolitan District Community Relations Council.

HMI (1987) *Report on Muslim Girls' High School, Bradford* (inspected 29 September – 1 October 1986), Stanmore, DES.

HEY, C. (1987) 'A history of the West Indian community in Bradford', in *Moving Stories: Towards a History of the Many Peoples of the English Cities.* Leeds, City Council (Continuing Education Section) Multi-cultural Education Centre.

HILL, M. and ISSACHAROFF, R. (1971) *Community Action and Race Relations.* London: Oxford University Press.

HIRST, P.H. and PETERS, R.S. (1970) *The Logic of Education* London, Routledge and Kegan Paul.

HOBSON, P. (1984) 'Some reflections on parents' rights in the upbringing of their children', *Journal of Philosophy of Education*, 18, 1, pp. 63–73.

HOLT, J. (1975) *Escape from Childhood* Harmondsworth, Penquin.

HONDERICH, E. (Ed) (1976) *Social Ends and Political Means* London, Routledge and Kegan Paul.

HONEYFORD, R. (1972) 'Class talk', *British Journal of Disorders of Communication*, 7, pp. 206–12.

HONEYFORD, R. (1973a) 'Graffiti in the classroom', *Use of English Quarterly*, 24, pp. 240–3.

HONEYFORD, R. (1973b) 'Against objective teaching', *Use of English Quarterly*, 25, pp. 17–20, 26.

HONEYFORD, R. (1974) 'Progress reports in English teaching', *Use of English Quarterly*, 25, pp. 295–300.

HONEYFORD, R. (1980) 'Listening in the classroom', *British Journal of Disorders of Communication*, 15, pp. 45–50.

HONEYFORD, R. (1982a) *Starting Teaching* London, Croom Helm.

HONEYFORD, R. (1982b) 'Suppression of research', Letter to *The Times Educational Supplement*, 23 July, p. 13.

HONEYFORD, R. (1982c) 'Explanations needed', letter to *Telegraph and Argus*, 30 July.

HONEYFORD, R. (1982d) 'Multiracial myths?' *The Times Educational Supplement*, 19 November, pp. 20–1.

HONEYFORD, R. (1983a) 'Multi-ethnic intolerance', *The Salisbury Review*, 4, Summer, pp. 12–13.

HONEYFORD, R. (1983b) 'When east is west', *The Times Educational Supplement*, 2 September, p. 19.

HONEYFORD, R. (1983c) 'The school attendance of British/Asian schoolchildren', *The Head Teachers' Review*, Winter, pp. 16–19.

HONEYFORD, R. (1984a) 'Education and race – an alternative view,' *The Salisbury Review*, 6, Winter, pp. 30–32.

HONEYFORD, R. (1984b) 'Teacher and social worker – an inevitable conflict', *The Salisbury Review*, 7, Spring, pp. 20–1.

HONEYFORD, R. (1984c) 'Irrational outcry', letter to *Telegraph and Argus*, 10 April.

HONEYFORD, R. (1984d) 'Taking the risk of telling the truth', *Yorkshire Post*, 7 June.

HONEYFORD, R. (1985a) 'The right education?' *The Salisbury Review*, 3, 2, pp. 28–30.

HONEYFORD, R. (1985b) letter to *Telegraph and Argus*, 11 April.

HONEYFORD, R. (1985c) 'None immune from criticism in a free society', letter to *The Times Educational Supplement*, 17 May, p. 17.

HONEYFORD, R. (1985d) 'The hounding of Honeyford — the head's own story', *Daily Mail*, 17–19 December.

HONEYFORD, R. (1986a) letter to *Telegraph and Argus*, 21 February.

HONEYFORD, R. (1986b) 'The anti-racist myth', *Yorkshire Post*, 21 April.

HONEYFORD, R. (1986c) 'The Gilmour syndrome', *The Salisbury Review*, 4, 3, pp. 11–14.

HONEYFORD, R. (1986d) 'Ray Honeyford speaks out', statement in *Election in Touch*, April.

HONEYFORD, R. (1986e) 'Classroom crisis', *Yorkshire Post*, 26 May.

HONEYFORD, R. (1986f) 'Voucher bonus', *Yorkshire Post* 16 June.

HONEYFORD, R. (1986g) 'The facts of life', *Yorkshire Post*, 13 August.

HONEYFORD, R. (1986h) 'Watch your language', *The Spectator*, 13 September. Adapted as: 'Children who put the race lobby to shame', *Daily Mail*, 12 September.

HONEYFORD, R. (1986i) 'This most evil force in Britain', *Daily Mail*, 20 October.

HONEYFORD, R. (1986j) 'Anti-racist rhetoric', in PALMER, F. (Ed) *Anti-Racism: an Assault on Education and Value* London, Sherwood Press.

HONEYFORD, R. (1986k) 'Culture and Religion in a Multicultural Society: a Dilemma for Pupils' *Education Today*, 36, 3, pp.31–36.

HONEYFORD, R. (1987a) 'Muslims in the swim', *The Spectator*, 3 January.

HONEYFORD, R. (1987b) 'In black and white' (review of SARUP, M. (1986) 'The Politics of Multi-Racial Education', Routledge and Kegan Paul) *The Salisbury Review*, 5, 2, pp. 64–6.

HONEYFORD, R. (1987c) Oxford Union Debate, letter to *The Times*, 28 February, p. 9.

HONEYFORD, R. (1987d) 'FAILED: the proof that comprehensives damage more than just education', *Daily Mail*, 1 May.

HONEYFORD, R. (1987e) 'The Swann fiasco', *The Salisbury Review*, 5, 3, pp. 54–6.

HONEYFORD, R. (1987f) Race to the top (review of DENCH, G. (1986) 'Minorities in the Open Society', Routledge and Kegan Paul) *The Salisbury Review*, 5, 4, pp. 66–7.

HONEYFORD, R. (1987g) 'Lessons of a mother tongue', *Yorkshire Post*, 29 July.

HONEYFORD, R. (1987h) 'Balance needed in the debate on racism', letter to *Radio Times*, 8–14 August.

HONEYFORD, R. (1987i) 'Contrary notions on British racism', *Yorkshire Post*, 8 September.

HONEYFORD, R. (1988) 'Has anti-racism become a travesty of itself?', letter to *The Times Educational Supplement*, 18 March.

HOULGATE, L.D. (1980) *The Child and the State: a Normative Theory of Juvenile Rights* Baltimore, John Hopkins University Press.

HOURANI, G.F. (1985) *Reason and Tradition in Islamic Ethics* Cambridge, Cambridge University Press.

HUBBUCK, J. and CARTER, S. (1980) *Half a Chance: A Report on Job Discrimination against Young Blacks in Nottingham* Nottingham, CRC and London, CRE.

HUMPHREY, D. and JOHN, G. (1971) *Because They're Black* Harmondsworth, Penguin.

HUSAIN, S.S. and ASHRAF, S.A. (1979) *Crisis in Muslim Education* London, Hodder and Stoughton.

HUSBAND, C. (Ed) (1982) *'Race' in Britain: Continuity and Change* London, Hutchinson.

HUSBAND, E. (1985) 'Doing her job', letter to *Telegraph and Argus*, 3 October.

IQBAL, M. (1975) *Islamic Education and Single Sex Schools* London, Union of Muslim Organizations of UK and Eire.

JACK, I. (1985) 'A severed head?' *Sunday Times Magazine*, 15 December, pp. 28–35.

JACOBS, B.D. (1986) *Black Politics and Urban Crisis in Britain* Cambridge, Cambridge University Press.

JENSEN, A.R. (1969) 'How much can we boost IQ and scholastic achievement?' *Harvard Educational Review*, 39, 1, pp. 1–123.

JENSEN, A.R. (1973) 'The differences are real' *Psychology Today*, 7, 7.

JONES, M. (1985) 'Education and racism', *Journal of Philosophy of Education*, 19, 2, pp. 223–234.

JOSEPH, SIR K. (1984) *Educating People for Peace* press notice 32/84. Reprinted in NCWGB (ed) *A Report of a One-Day Conference on Peace Education in Schools* London, National Council of Women of Great Britain.

KENT, E. (1976) 'Respect for persons and social protest,' in HONDERICH, E. (Ed) *Social Ends and Political Means* London, Routledge and Kegan Paul.

KERR, C. (1955) *Industrial Relations and the Liberal Pluralist* Berkeley, Institute of Industrial Relations.

KHAN-CHEEMA, M.A. *et al.* (1986) *The Muslims and 'Swann'* London, the Council of Mosques, UK and Eire.

KIRP, D.L. (1979) *Doing Good by Doing Little : Race and Schooling in Britain* Berkley, University of California Press.

KITWOOD, T. and BORRILL, C. (1980) 'The significance of schooling for an ethnic minority', *Oxford Review of Education*, 6, 3, pp. 241–53.

KNOWLES, L.L. and PREWITT, K. (Eds) (1969) *Institutional Racism in America* Englewood Cliffs, Prentice-Hall.

KOGAN, M. (1986) *Educational Accountability: an Analytic Overview* London, Hutchinson.

LASKI, H.J. (1917) *Studies in the Problem of Sovereignty* New Haven, Yale University Press.

LASKI, H.J. (1919a) *Authority in the Modern State* New Haven, Yale University Press.

LASKI, H.J. (1919b) 'The pluralistic state', *Philosophical Review*, 28, pp. 562*ff.* Reprinted as Appendix Two in NICHOLLS, D. (1975) *The Pluralist State* London, Macmillan.

LE BON, G. (1960) *The Crowd* (1st edition 1895), New York, Viking.

LE LOHÉ, M. (1979) 'The effects of the presence of immigrants upon the local political system in Bradford 1945–77', in MILES, R. and PHIZACKLEA, A. (Eds) *Racism and Political Action in Britain* London, Routledge and Kegan Paul.

LEVITAS, R. (1986) *The Ideology of the New Right* Cambridge, Polity Press.

LINGUISTIC MINORITIES PROJECT (1983) *Linguistic Minorities in England: A Report* London, ULIE and Heinemann Educational Books.

LITTLE, A. and WILLEY, R. (1983) *Studies in the Multi-Ethnic Curriculum* London, Schools Council.

LOP (Leeds Other Paper) (1982) *The Campaign to Free the Bradford 12* Leeds Alternative Publications Ltd.

LUSTGARTEN, L.S. (1983) 'Liberty in a culturally plural society', in PHILLIPS GRIFFITHS, A. (Ed.) *Of Liberty* Cambridge, Cambridge University Press.

LYNCH, J. (1986) *Multicultural Education: Principles and Practice* London, Routledge and Kegan Paul.

McELROY, P.M. (1985) 'The view from a multi-cultural inner city girls school', *Education Journal*, 6, 3, pp. 6–9.

McLAUGHLIN, T.H. (1984) 'Parental rights and the religious upbringing of children', *Journal of Philosophy of Education*, 18, 1, pp. 75–83.

McLAUGHLIN, T.H. (1985) 'Religion, upbringing and liberal values: A rejoinder to Eamonn Callan' *Journal of Philosophy of Education*, 19, 1, pp. 119–128.

MAHONEY, P. (1985) *Schools for the Boys? Co-education Reassessed* London, Hutchinson.

MAITLAND, F.W. (1911) *The Collected Papers* Cambridge, Cambridge University Press.

MARCUSE, H. (1968) *One Dimensional Man* London, Sphere.

MARCUSE, H. (1969) 'Repressive tolerance', in WOLFF, R. *et al.* (Ed) *A Critique of Pure Tolerance* London, Cape.

MATTHEWS, R. (1986) 'Bad news for race relations', *The Times Educational Supplement*, 24 January, p. 28.

MEADOWCROFT, M. (1985) 'The other debate at Drummond', *Yorkshire Post*, 12 November.

MEADOWCROFT, M. (1986) 'Keeping it in the family', *The Times*, 10 November.

MILES, R. and PHIZACKLEA, A. (1984) *White Man's Country: Racism in British politics* London, Pluto.

MILL, J.S. (1972a) *Considerations on Representative Government.* (first published 1861), London, Dent.

MILL, J.S. (1972b) *On Liberty* (first published 1859), London, Dent.

MORRELL, F. (1984) 'Policy for schools in Inner London', in GRACE, G. (Ed) *Education and the City* London, Routledge and Kegan Paul.

MORRIS, G., HUSSAIN, A. and AURA, T.G. (1984) 'Schooling crisis in Bradford' *Race Today*, July/August, pp. 8–11.

MULLARD, C. (1980) *Racism in society and schools: History, policy and practice*, Occasional Paper No. 1, London, Centre for Multicultural Education, University of London Institute of Education.

MULLARD, C. (1984) *Anti-Racist Education: The Three O's* Cardiff, National Association for Multiracial Education.

MURPHY, D. (1987) *Tales from Two Cities* London, John Murray.

MURRAY, H.A. *et al.* (1938) *Explorations in Personality* New York, Oxford University Press.

NATIONAL ANTI-RACIST MOVEMENT IN EDUCATION (NAME) (Bradford branch) (1985) 'Freedom of speech is not the issue', *Telegraph and Argus*, 7 October.

NATIONAL UNION OF TEACHERS (1978) *Race, Intelligence and Education: A Teacher's Guide to Facts and the issues* London, NUT.

NAYLOR, D. (1968) 'The other immigrants', *Yorkshire Post*, 4–5 June.

NIAS, J. (1981) 'The nature of trust', in ELLIOTT, J. *et al.* (Eds) *School Accountability: The SSRC Accountability Project* London, Grant McIntyre.

NICHOLLS, D. (1974) *Three Varieties of Pluralism* London, Macmillan.

NICHOLLS, D. (1975) *The Pluralist State* London, Macmillan.

NIXON, J. (1985) 'Education for a multicultural society: Reviews and reconstructions', *Curriculum*, 6, 2, pp. 29–36.

NORRIS, S.E. (1976) 'Being free to speak and speaking freely', in HONDERICH, E. (Ed) *Social and Political Means* London, Routledge and Kegan Paul.

NOZICK, R. (1974) *Anarchy, State and Utopia* Oxford, Oxford University Press.

O'NEILL, O. and RUDDICK, W. (eds) (1979) *Having Children: Philosophical and Legal Reflections on Parenthood* New York, University Press.

OLDMAN, D. (1987) 'Plain speaking and pseudo science: The 'New Right' attack on anti-racism', in TROYNA, B. (Ed) *Racial Inequality in Education* London, Tavistock.

PALMER, F. (Ed) (1986) *Anti-Racism — An Assault on Education and Value* London, Sherwood Press.

PAREKH, B. (1985) 'The gifts of diversity', *The Times Educational Supplement*, 29 March, pp. 22–3.

PARSONS, T. (1951) *The Social System* London, Routledge and Kegan Paul.

PATEL, A. and SHAHID, R. (eds) (1982) *Transformation of Muslim Children* Bradford, Muslim Parents Association.

PATEMAN, C. (1970) *Participation and Democratic Theory* Cambridge, Cambridge University Press.

PEDLEY, F. (1986) 'Bad news for race relations', *The Times Educational Supplement*, 24 January, pp. 28–9.

PERKS, R. (1984) 'A feeling of not belonging': Interviewing European Immigrants in Bradford, *Oral History*, 12, 2.

PERKS, R. (1987) 'You're different, you're one of us: The making of a British Asian', *Oral History*, 15, 2.

PIERCE, G. (1982) 'Out of Court' *The Guardian*, 21 June.

PLASCOW, M. (1985) *Life and Death of the Schools Council* Lewes, Falmer Press.

POSTMAN, N. (1983) *The Disappearance of Childhood* London, W.H. Allen.

PRATT, M. (1971) *The Influence of the Germans on Bradford* Bradford College.

PRIESTLEY, J.B. (1977) *English Journey* Harmondsworth, Penguin (first published by Heinemann, 1934).

RAM, S. (1983) *A Geographical Analysis of Indians in Bradford* Working Paper No. 373, Leeds, University School of Geography.

RAM, S. (1984) *A Geographical Analysis of Indians in Bradford: Spacial Distribution and Temporal Trends (1971–81)* Working Paper No. 384, Leeds, University School of Geography.

RAM, S. (1985) *The Geography of the Indian Community in Britain with Special Reference to Bradford* PhD Thesis, University of Leeds.

RAWLS, J. (1972) *A Theory of Justice* Oxford, Oxford University Press.

RAZ, J. (1986) *The Morality of Freedom* Oxford, Clarendon.

REES, O.A. and FITZPATRICK, F. (1981) *Mother Tongue and Teaching Project Summary of the Report. Vols. I and II* Bradford, Bradford College.

RICHARDS, J.R. (1980) *The Sceptical Feminist: a Philosophical Enquiry* London, Routledge and Kegan Paul.

RICHARDSON, C. (1968) 'Irish settlement in mid-nineteenth century Bradford', *Yorkshire Bulletin of Economic and Social Research*, 20, 1, pp. 40–57.

RICHARDSON, C. (1971) 'The Irish in Victorian Bradford', *Bradford Antiquary*, 11, pp. 294–316.

ROSE, S., LEWONTIN, R.C. and KAMIN, L.J. (1984) *Not in Our Genes* Harmondsworth, Penguin.

SAIFULLAH KHAN, V. (1975) *Pakistani Villagers in a British City: the World of the Mirpuri Villager in Bradford and in his Village of Origin* Unpublished PhD Thesis, University of Bradford.

SAUNDERS, M. (1982) 'Education for a new community', *New Community*, 10, 1, pp. 64–71.

SAVERY, J. (1985) 'Anti-racism as witchcraft', *Salisbury Review*, July, pp. 41–2.

SCANLON, T. (1972) 'A theory of freedom and expression', *Philosophy and Public Affairs*, 1, pp. 204ff.

SCHAUER, F. (1982) *Free Speech: a Philosophical Enquiry* Cambridge, Cambridge University Press.

SCHUMAN, H. and HARDING, J. (1964) 'Prejudice and the norm of rationality' *Sociometry*, 27, pp. 353–71.

SCRIMSHAW, P. (1980) Making schools responsible', in SOCKETT, H. (Ed) *Accountability in the English Educational System* London, Hodder and Stoughton.

SCRIMSHAW, P. and HORTON, T. (1981) *William Tyndale: the System Under Stress* E200, 14, Milton Keynes, Open University Press.

SCRUTON, R. (1984) *The Meaning of Conservatism* (2nd edition), London, Macmillan.

SCRUTON, R. (1986) 'The myth of cultural relativism', in PALMER, F. (Ed) *Anti-Racism — an Assault on Education and Value.* London, Sherwood Press.

SEIDEL, G. (1986) 'Culture, nation and 'race' in the British and French new right', in LEVITAS, R. (Ed) *The Ideology of the New Right* Cambridge, Polity Press.

SELBOURNE, D. (1984a) 'The culture clash in Bradford', *New Society*, 26 April, pp. 135–139.

SELBOURNE, D. (1984b) 'Misplaced intent', letter to *Yorkshire Post*, 22 August.

SELBOURNE, D. (1985) 'Lesson in village politics for Bradford's schools', *The Guardian*, 21 October.

SELBOURNE, D. (1987) *Left Behind: Journeys into British Politics* London, Cape.

SELDON, A. (1986) *The Riddle of the Voucher* London, Institute of Economic Affairs.

SELZNICK, P. (1969) *Law, Society and Industrial Justice* New York, Russell Sage.

SHALLICE, J. (1984) 'Racism and education, in ALTARF (Ed) *Challenging Racism* London, All London Teachers against Racism and Fascism.

SHEPHERD, D. (1987) 'The accomplishment of divergence', *British Journal of Sociology of Education*, 8, 3, pp. 263–276.

SIEGHART, P. (1985) *The Lawful Rights of Mankind* Oxford, Oxford University Press.

SINGH, R. (1978) *The Sikh Community in Bradford* Bradford College.

SINGH, R. with RAM, S. (1986) *Indians in Bradford: the development of a community* Bradford and Ilkley Community College.

SKILLEN, A. (1982) 'Freedom of speech', in GRAHAM, K. (Ed) *Contemporary Political Philosophy*, Cambridge, Cambridge University Press.

SMITH, M.G. (1960) 'Social and cultural pluralism', in RUBIN, V. (Ed) *Social and Cultural Pluralism in the Caribbean* New York, Annals of the New York Academy of Sciences.

SMITH, M.G. (1965) *The Plural Society in the British West Indies* Berkeley, University of California Press.

SOCKETT, H. (1980) 'Accountability: The contempory issues', in SOCKETT, H. (Ed) *Accountability in the English Educational System* London, Hodder and Stoughton.

SOCKETT, H. (1982) 'Accountability', in COHEN, L., THOMAS, J. and MARIAN, L. (Eds) *Educational Research and Development in Britain 1970–1980* Windsor, NFER.

SOWELL, T. (1977) *Race and Economics* New York, Longman.

SPEARS, A.K. (1978) 'Institutional racism and the education of blacks', *Anthropology and Education Quarterly*, 9, 2, pp. 127–136.

SPENCER, D. (1983) 'How Bradford held on to its lead in race', *The Times Educational Supplement*, 7 October, p. 10.

SPENCER, D. (1984) 'The man who went too far, too fast', *The Times Educational Supplement*, 16 November, p. 9.

SPENDER, D. and SARAH, E. (1980) (Eds) *Learning to Lose: Sexism and Education* London, The Women's Press.

ST. JOHN-BROOKS, C. (1987) 'The standard bearers', *New Society*, 15 May, pp. 20–1.

STONE, M. (1981) *The Education of the Black Child in Britain: the Myth of Multicultural Education* London, Fontana.

STRIKE, K.A. (1982a) *Liberty and Learning* Oxford, Martin Robertson.

STRIKE, K.A. (1982b) *Educational Policy and the Just Society* Urbana, University of Illinois Press.

SUTHERLAND, C. (1986) 'Protest against racism in education', *Solidarity Against Racism*, 21, p. 5.

SWANN REPORT See DEPARTMENT OF EDUCATION AND SCIENCE (1985)

TAYLOR, J.H. (1976) *The Half-Way Generation: A study of Asian Youth in Newcastle upon Tyne* Slough, NFER.

TAYLOR, L. and NELSON, S. (1978) *Young People and Civil Conflict in Northern Ireland* Belfast, DHSS.

TAYLOR, M.J. with HEGARTY, S. (1985) *The Best of Both Worlds: a Review of Research into the Education of Pupils of South Asian Origin* Windsor, NFER/Nelson.

TELEGRAPH AND ARGUS (1986) 'Bradford and District Citizen's Guide', Bradford, Telegraph and Argus.

TROYNA, B. and WILLIAMS, J. (1986) *Racism, Education and the State* London, Croom Helm.

TRUMAN, D. (1951) *The Governmental Process* New York, Knopf.
TWITCHIN, J. and DEMUTH, C. (1981) *Multi-cultural Education*, London, BBC.

VAN DEN BERGHE, P. (1967) *Race and Racism*. New York, John Wiley.
VAN DEN BERGHE, P. (1969) 'Pluralism and the polity', in KUPER, L. and SMITH, M.G. (Eds) *Pluralism in Africa* Berkeley, University of California Press.
VERMA, G.K. and BAGLEY, C. (Eds) (1984) *Race Relations and Cultural Differences*, London, Croom Helm.
VERMA, G.K. *et al.* (1986) *Ethnicity and Educational Achievement in British Schools*. London, Macmillan.

WALD, M. (1979) 'Children's rights — a framework for analysis', *University of California Davis Law Review*, 255.
WALKER, M. (1977) *The National Front* London, Fontana.
WALKLING, P.H. (1980) 'The idea of a multicultural curriculum', *Journal of Philosophy of Education*, 14, 1, pp. 87–95.
WARNOCK, M. (1979) 'Cultural relativism and education', *Westminster Studies in Education*, 2, pp. 35–44.
WEDGE, P. and PROSSER, H. (1973) *Born to Fail?* London, Arrow Books.
WELLMAN, D.T. (1977) *Portraits of White Racism* Cambridge, Cambridge University Press.
WEST, R. (1987) 'Inner city of dreadful night', *The Spectator*, 27 June.
WHITE, J. (1973) *Towards a Compulsory Curriculum* London, Routledge and Kegan Paul.
WHITE, J. (1980) 'Should schools determine their own curricula?' in SOCKETT, H. (Ed) *Accountability in the English Educational System* London, Hodder and Stoughton.
WHITE, J. (1987) 'The quest for common values', in HAYDON, G. (Ed) *Education for a Pluralist Society: Philosophical perspectives on the Swann Report* Bedford Way Paper 30, London, University of London Institute of Education.
WHITE, P. (1983) *Beyond Domination: an Essay in the Political Philosophy of Education* London, Routledge and Kegan Paul.
WILLEY, R. (1984) *Race, Equality and Schools* London, Methuen.
WILLIAMS, J. and CARTER, R. (1985) ' "Institutional racism": New orthodoxy, old ideas', *Multiracial Education*, 13, 1, pp. 3–8.
WILSON, A. (1981) 'Bradford black youth "on trial for beliefs" '. *New Statesman*, 4 September.
WILSON, A. (1982) 'Evidence of racialism examined', *New Statesman*, 11 June.
WILSON, J. (1986) 'Race, culture and education: Some conceptual problems', *Oxford Review of Education*, 12, 1, pp. 3–15.
WOLFF, R.P. (1968) *The Poverty of Liberalism* Boston, Beacon Press.
WOODWARD, J. *et al.* (1984) 'Racism in Bradford', *The Times Educational Supplement*, 4 May, p. 20.
WOODWARD, J. (1985) 'Diary of a race storm', *Yorkshire Post*, 9 April.
WRINGE, C. (1981) *Children's Rights* London, Routledge and Kegan Paul.

ZEC, P. (1980) 'Multicultural education: What kind of relativism is possible?' *Journal of Philosophy of Education*, 14, 1, pp. 77–85.
ZELLICK, G. (1987) 'Free speech that may go too far', letter to *The Times*, 23 February.

Index

NOTE. Drummond Middle School is abbreviated to DMS, Ray Honeyford to RH.

absenteeism, Asian schoolgirls' 29, 34, 35, 48, 233, 246, 249
accommodationism 49–50, 53–54, 63, 193
'accomplice in racism' 149, 156
accountability 106, 167–8, 182–202
  autonomy and 185, 189, 195–9
  Central Control model 188, 194
  Chain of Responsibility Model 189–90, 191, 193, 194, 198, 199
  concept of 184–8
  Consumerist Model 189, 194
  contractual 183, 187, 189, 194
  moral and legal 183
  Partnership Model 192–3, 199–200
  professional 185, 189, 195–9
  Professional Model 190–2, 193, 195, 198
  responsive 183–4, 187, 194; *see also* Chain of Responsibility Model
  Self Accounting Model 189, 194
Adams, F.J. 33
advisers, LEA 55, 188, 194, 245
  see also Drummond Middle School
Africa, Asians from 11, 14
aftermath of RH affair 111–16, 125, 160
age of immigrant population 14
aggression 111, 119, 120, 139
Ahmadiyya movement 13, 278

Ahmed, Ishtiaq 113–14, 282
aims of education 23, 162, 197–8
Ajeeb, Councillor Muhammad
  and bussing 39, 234
  and Community Relations Council 114, 282
  Lord Mayor 12, 260
  race relations initiative, 1986 113
  race relations speech, Oct 1985 268
  and Race Training Unit 281
  and RH affair 91, 106, 114–15, 127–8, 247, 274–5
  threats, abuse and attacks on house 106, 108, 111, 119, 265, 274–5
  on voluntary-aided schools 52
  joins WAR protest march 125, 277
AKMAB *see* Azad Kashmir Muslim Association of Bradford
Al Falah (Islamic Youth Movementt) 250
Ali, Lucky 278
alienation, social 158–9
Almond, B. 180
animal rights 31, 46, 242, 247
Ansari, Muhammad 105, 118, 265
answerability 185, 186, 187
anti-racism 41–4, 52, 62
  RH's attack on 62, 65, 176–8
  politicized 125
  teaching 204, 243

anti-sexist teaching 56
anxiety; cause of racism 120–1, 139
'Any Questions' radio programme 239
Appeal Court 108–9, 129, 270–1
Arabic teaching 32, 39
art teaching 36
Arthur, Councillor 234
articles of government 103, 106, 109,
129, 130, 263
Ashraf, S.A. 27, 201, 209, 229, 230
Asian Workers' Support Group 68, 74,
93, 252
Asian Youth Movement
campaign against RH 74, 76, 86, 91,
107, 133, 249, 250, 269
foundation 11, 235–6
pamphlet on education 246–7
politicization 125
on racism 17, 42
and voluntary-aided schools 30, 44,
241
Asians
cultural identity 9, 10, 25–6, 26–7, 64
population statistics 10, 15, 16,
231–2, 242
RH's descriptions 58, 60, 61, 67, 68,
69–70, 84, 179
see also under individual aspects
assemblies, school
Bradford draft guidelines 28–9, 278
excusing from 36, 151, 206, 238, 239
worship moved from 112–13
assimilation 47–9, 146, 208, 212, 214
see also integrationism
Austrian immigrants 6, 7
autonomy
of academic discipline 229
and accountability 185, 189, 195–9
child's 209, 215, 220, 221–2, 223–4
personal and moral; Muslims and
229
professional 55, 84, 96–7: erosion 65,
67, 77, 96, 165, 183; pluralism
and 184, 195–202; RH on 65, 67,
96, 193, 195, 249
AYM *see* Asian Youth Movement
Azad Kashmir Muslim Association of
Bradford 17, 41–2, 74, 76, 125, 239
Azam, Sher 242

Bailey, C. 185, 195–9, 201
Baker, Kenneth, MP, 112, 190, 282,
283
Bangladeshis 12–13, 14
Bangladeshi People's Association 12,
250
Baptist church 8
Bashir, Abu 68, 93, 252
Batley 241
BDPSG *see* Bradford Drummond
Parents' Support Group
Behrens, Jacob 5
Belle Vue Boys' Upper School 42, 111,
243–4, 277
Belle Vue Girls' School 34–5, 233, 238,
246, 256
proposed merger with boys 242,
243–4
voluntary-aided proposal 44, 240–1
Beloff, Michael, QC 104
Bendall, P. 37
Bengalis 15
Bharatiya Mandal 11
Bibi, Yasmin 278
bilingual education 40, 51
see also mother-tongue
biological determinism 140, 143, 144–
5, 157
Birdsall, Councillor Doris 238, 239
birth rate 13, 16
Bishop of Bradford 108, 270
'black'; use of term 7–8
Black Heritage 8
black immigrants in Bradford 7–16, 26
current statistics 14–16
see also: Asians; West Indians
Black Muslims 145
Black Workers Collective 113–14,
282–3
books, school and library 42–3, 163
colour-blind racism and 153
at DMS 246
institutional racism and 149
library 43, 277
RH on 58, 59, 96
working group on 244
boycotts
of meetings 101–2, 262
see also Drummond Middle School

Bradford *see under individual topics*
Bradford Chamber of Commerce 5
Bradford City AFC 106, 276
Bradford College 40, 236
Bradford Drummond Parents' Support
　Group 74, 107, 109, 269, 271
Bradford Girls' Grammar School 34
Bradford Grammar School 5, 101, 261
Bradford Heritage Recording Unit 7,
　114, 282
Bradford and Ilkley Community
　College 109, 271
Bradford Metropolitan District Council
　accountability models 194
　and Asian community groups 30,
　　126–7, 251, 266, 273–4, 276, 278
　Asian councillors 12, 125
　charged with discrimination 8, 12
　consultation and lack of 18, 30,
　　132–3, 134, 193; RH on
　　'diktats' 22, 67, 77
　'District Trends' 236, 253
　education policies 23–32, 275–6, 281;
　　changes 31, 132
　employees' responsibility 182, 193
　hung 122-3
　pragmatism 121, 126–7
　press guidelines 112, 283
　race relations policies 16–20, 21–54,
　　83–4, 113, 121, 134, 275–6;
　　accommodationism 49–50, 53–4,
　　63, 193; failure? 76, 79, 100; integ-
　　rationism 26, 33, 47–9, 232; pace-
　　setter (1970s) 21–2, 243;
　　separatism 51–4, 63
　recruitment 18, 113, 237, 245–6
　and RH affair 67–8, 76, 84, 86,
　　126–7; and DPAC 74, 76, 86–7,
　　133, 194; mishandling 95, 132–4,
　　266; and NAHT 77, 88, 99; res-
　　tricts publication by RH 62, 89,
　　92, 93, 169, 239, 251, 253–4, 274
　right to dismiss head 108–9
　see also under individual committees,
　　councillors, departments, officers and
　　policies
Bradford North Ward 16
Bradford Observer 4

Bradford Trades Council 255
Bradford Twelve 17–18, 24, 238
Bradford University
　Asian Studies course proposed 280
　bad name for race problems 111, 277
　Mirpuri research project 13, 235
　MOTET project 40, 236
　H. Proctor speech cancelled 111, 269
　Woodward addresses 100, 259
Brent 53, 62
　McGoldrick affair 112, 190, 281–2
　voluntary-aided schools 229, 241
Bridges, D. 184–5, 199–200, 224, 228
Bristol; 1981 riots 23
　RH to speak in 111, 112, 169, 269
British Association for the
　Advancement of Science 263
British Broadcasting Corporation
　'Any Questions' 239
　documentary on Ajeeb 260
　'The Heart of the Matter' 45
　'In the Psychiatrist's Chair' 63, 118,
　　139, 207, 280
　'Jimmy Young Show' 257
　Panorama 87, 176, 251
　'Poles Apart' 252
　'Today' 276
British Journal of Disorders of
Communication 55
British National Party 17, 42, 124, 246,
　277
British Nationalist 244
British traditional values
　and cultural racism 146
　free speech as 167
　RH on 69–70, 119, 124, 167, 207,
　　208, 215, 284
　Swann Report on 215–16
Brixton 18, 23
Brown, Andrew 80, 264, 272
Brown, Mr Justice Simon 104, 264
Brown, Tom 107, 268, 269, 279
Bullock Report 27
Burke, Edmund 175
businesses, Asian 9
bussing 27, 37–9, 48–9, 152, 155, 231
　abandonment 11, 28, 37–9, 51,
　　234–5, 273; DMS after 64, 237
　RH on 58, 64, 67

Cambridge Accountability Project 189
Campaign Against Racist Attacks 86,
    133, 269–70
Campbell, Bernard 248
Cardiff; Ajeeb speaks in 106, 268
Carlisle, John 269
Channel Four TV 52
Checkpoint (West Indian community
    centre) 8, 56–7, 239
Chief Constable of Bradford 108, 270
Chief Constable of West Yorkshire 277
child; autonomy of 209, 215, 220,
    221–2, 223–4
    see also needs
Chinese immigrants 14
Christ; RH compared to 128, 259
Church of God of Prophecy 8
churches *see individual denominations and
    sects, and* clergymen
circumstances, RH as victim of 77
citizenship, RH on 65, 180–1
City Hall, Bradford 86, 101, 249
Clare, Anthony 63, 118, 139, 207, 280
Clarke, Michael 75, 84–5, 247
class; affair in terms of 127–8
clergymen, Bradford 74, 108, 270
clothing *see* Physical Education
co-education
    Abdullah Patel's protest 47–8
    concessions over 27, 49, 206
    Muslim objections 13, 24, 34–5,
        233–44, 242, 249, 279
    Sikhs and 11
    see also voluntary-aided
cognitive dissonance 141
colonialism, British 57, 59, 138, 152
colour, skin 10, 16, 26
colour-blind racism 42, 43, 153–5, 157
Commission for Racial Equality
    Ajeeb calls for scrapping 268
    and bussing 39, 234
    and mother-tongue teaching 236
    praises Bradford's policies 21, 237
    RH on 60, 207
common education 50, 199–201, 208
    Muslims and 126, 229–30
Communist Party 125
community groups, immigrant 6–7, 12
    Asian 13, 30, 85, 126–7, 231
    see also under names of groups

Community Relations Council 10,
    42
    and bussing 234
    and Council 87, 113, 251, 276
    and extended visits question 238
    new political slant 113–14, 282
    and RH affair 85, 87, 90, 113, 247,
        251
    and voluntary-aided schools 44, 241
comprehensive schools 56, 255
concessions, cultural 205–6, 225–6
    RH's 59, 63, 89, 205–6
    see also: assemblies; Physical
        Education; Religious Education;
        worship
conflict
    avoiding home/school 25, 35, 222
    see also culture; racist behaviour;
        violence
Conservative party
    court black vote? 24
    and freedom of speech 174
    in local elections 123, 280
    and parental choice 198
    racial attitudes 121
    and RH's retirement 110, 270, 272
    RH supports 55–6, 113, 123, 125,
        215, 280, 284
    on Schools Education Subcommittee
        91, 92
    support for RH 121–2
consultation, Council 18, 30, 132–3,
    134, 193
contact, inter-racial 51
    see also: bussing; friendships
control of education 130, 131–2
    and accountability 184–5, 185–6, 187
controls, immigration 11
Coons, J.E. and Sugarman, S.D. 189,
    194, 200, 222, 224
Council for Mosques 12
    and Bradford Council 113, 266, 278
    calls to end DMS picketing 107, 269
    campaign against RH 59, 74, 76,
        102–3, 104–5, 106, 109, 247, 250,
        267–8, 271
    and Community Relations Council
        114
    and girls' education 34, 249
    meetings on education 242, 249
    politicization 125

Council for Mosques (continued)
on supplementary schools 279
and voluntary-aided schools 30, 44, 241
see *also* Khan, Choudhury M.
courts *see*: Appeal; High; Parliament
Cox, Baroness 124, 266, 272–3
critical awareness 164
criticism of ethnic groups 178–81, 206
Crittenden, B. 217–18, 224, 228
crowd mentality 119
culturalism 146
culture
  Asian distinctiveness 9, 10
  clash 19, 25–6, 31, 65, 209, 236–7
  freeing child from restricting 25–6,
    31, 196, 205, 209, 215, 220, 221–2,
    226
  German Jews and Bradford's 5
  preserving distinct 9, 25–6, 26–7, 64
  race differentiated from 204, 205
  transmission of minority 57–8, 59,
    60, 64, 206, 281
  undervaluing of minority 146, 162
  see *also* racism (cultural)
curriculum
  accommodationism 50
  democracy in determining 199–201
  national 188, 284

Daily Mail 56, 62, 275
debate on multi-cultural education,
  need for 73–83, 108, 115
decision-making, educational 198–201
Delius, Frederick 5
democracy
  and decision-making 199–201
  diversity essence of 210
  RH as going against 86, 177, 181
Department of Education and Science
  and bussing 27, 37
  and definition of 'needs' 27
  funds MOTET project 40
  and professional autonomy 96–7
  and single-sex schools 47, 233
  statistics on ethnic origins 153
Dewsbury affair 52, 63, 112, 190, 198,
  283
'diktats', Council 22, 67, 77
Dillon, Lord Justice 108–9, 270–1

Director of Educational Services *see*:
  Adams; Knight; Parker
  Assistant *see*: Bendall; Roper
disadvantage, white
  children in racial minority at school
    52, 61, 65, 70, 89, 267
  lower working class 150–1
disciplinary procedures 88, 103, 129,
  130, 131, 251, 263
discrimination
  Council accused of 8, 12, 41
  C19th against Irish in Bradford 4
  in employment 9–10, 16, 19, 140
  housing 140
  positive 53, 134, 152; RH on 57, 59,
    64, 65
  and prejudice 141, 144
  racism and 140, 157
dismissal procedures 129–31
dispersal *see* bussing
distortion in written sources 78–83
  essence of democracy 210
  in liberal pluralism 219
  Swann report and 214, 215–16
  in multi-cultural education 49–50, 60
    203
diversity, genetic 143
dominance
  cultural 28, 37, 49
  in pre-reflective gut racism 139–40
drama teaching 36, 284
dress, Asian 10, 11, 29, 36, 239
  see *also under* Physical Education
drugs 70, 279
Drummond Language Centre 111, 248,
  250, 275
Drummond Middle School
  activities 111, 246, 275
  advisers' inspection 51, 87–8, 250,
    251; report 76–7, 88–90, 128, 209,
    251–2; implementation 91–3, 96–7
  after RH affair 110–11, 114, 279
  aims, educational 162
  alternative school, DPAC 94–5, 120,
    129, 254, 256
  assemblies 206
  boycott 105, 106, 109–10, 177, 264–8
    passim
  concessions, RH's cultural 206

Drummond Middle School (continued)
Educational Welfare Officer 58, 93–4
ethnic composition 51, 53, 64, 94, 100, 237, 252
governors *see separate entry*
liaison teacher 91, 94, 254–5
meetings; on extended visits (1981) 41, 60, 118, 237–8; Knight's with parents (1984) 93
parents: communication with 59, 91, 94, 96; support for DPAC 73
picketing and protests 73, 74, 107, 119–20, 125, 269, 271, 275; pupils affected 109, 119–20, 195, 271; violence 105, 118, 177, 264–5
Religious Education 59, 63, 89, 206
RH appointed head 84, 237
Scruton visits 254
staff 74, 97, 105, 107, 195, 266, 268–9; picketing and 109, 195, 271
voluntary-aided proposal 44, 240
West Indian Saturday classes 8
see also: Bradford Drummond; Drummond Parents'; Friends; governors, DMS
Drummond Parents' Action Committee
and accountability models 194
and advisers inspection 90, 93, 251
alternative school 94–5, 120, 129, 254, 256
and class aspects of affair 127
and Council 74, 76, 86–7, 133, 194
and freedom of speech 177–8
and governors' meetings 91, 106–7, 109–10
mass request for pupil transfers 129–34, 176–7, 252
1984 campaign 85–6, 91, 249, 250, 252
1985 campaign 94, 100
and press 77, 86, 101, 250, 255, 259, 279
protest action 74, 87–8, 106–7, 176, 251; marches 87–8, 250, 267; picketing *see under* Drummond Middle School
and RH's reinstatement 102–3, 105, 263, 264

support of parents for 73–4
see also Woodward
Duncan, Carlton 52, 101, 244–5, 257
Dworkin, R. 172–3

Eccleshill Upper School 42, 84, 244
Edmondson, Fred (acting head) 104, 259, 264
education *see under individual aspects, and* multi-cultural
Education Acts
(1944) 44, 51, 232
(1959) 41
(1980) 28, 188
(1986) 131–2, 175, 192
Education Bill (1987) 53
and accountability 188, 189
opting-out 112, 189, 198, 229–30, 283–4
Education Today 62
Educational Services Committee *see*; Bradford MDC; Gilmour; Pickles; Lambert
Educational Welfare Officer, DMS Asian 58, 93–4
EEC bi-lingual teaching project 40
Eid ul-Fitr 36, 37, 151
elections, local
(1986) 86, 113, 122, 123, 277, 280, 281
(1988); RH may stand in 56, 284
voting power of blacks 24, 121
emotion
pre-reflective gut racism 139, 140, 141
response to RH's articles 66, 118
RH's language 84, 108, 170, 178, 179
employment
Asians 9–10, 11
Bradford Council 18–19, 113, 237, 245–6
discrimination in 9–10, 16, 19, 140
female 8, 11
RH on equipping immigrant pupils for 57, 59–60, 63, 64, 206, 220
Sikhs 11
textile industry 8, 11
West Indians 8
engineering industry 8, 11

engineering industry 8, 11
English language in schools
  advisers on DMS 89
  cross-cultural friendships and 64
  parents' priority 39
  as prime medium for teaching 235
  see also Language Centres
equality
  colour-blind racism and 153
  RH's belief 65, 96, 128, 205
  of concern and respect 172–3
  see also: injustice; justice
ESN schools, black children in 151
Estonian immigrants 6,7
ethnic minorities in Bradford 3–19
  demands 32–46
  fears 24
  needs 23, 25–31
  see also: Asians; Europeans; *and under
    individual aspects and nationalities*
ethnicity 204
Eurich, Professor Frederick 5
Eurich, Richard 5
European Convention on Human Rights
  and Fundamental Freedoms 170–1
European immigrants to Bradford 3–7,
10, 15, 26, 57
examination results and
accountability 188
expectations, educational
  Asians 42, 162
  West Indians 70, 140, 145, 175, 179
experiences, use of pupils' in school 90,
91,   153, 163, 203, 209
expertise, professional 196–7, 198–9
extended trips to subcontinent *see* visits

Farley, Councillor Ronnie 245
Farooq, M. 106, 266
fear
  cause of racism 120–1, 139, 140
  ethnic minorities' 17–18, 24, 238
  see also vigilante patrols
Federation of Bangladeshi Youth
  Organizations 247
Federation of Sikh Organizations 114
Fellowes, Alex 83, 248
feminism 128–9, 153
festivals, religious 151
  absence for 29, 36–7, 51, 239

Flanagan, Councillor Tommy 110, 271
Foster-Carter, O. 82–3, 246, 255, 282
Fox, Sir Marcus, MP
  and campaign for RH 75, 99, 259,
    274
  on LAM 6/83 29–30, 245
Free, Councillor Norman 46, 75, 86,
  91, 121, 247
freedom
  group 210
  individual 53, 179
  negative and positive 213
  of opinion 75, 77, 96, 97, 98, 169–70
  and pluralism 210
  and respect of persons 53
  see also: autonomy; speech
Friends of Drummond Middle School
  74, 95, 99, 256, 259, 262–3
friendships, cross-cultural 37–8, 48, 64,
  89, 164

Gadaffi, Colonel 114
gambling 29, 36
Garnett, Stanley 17, 42, 124, 246
genetic superiority 140, 143, 144–5,
  157
German Evangelical Church 5, 6
German Jews in Bradford 4–6
ghetto schools 35, 38, 39, 48, 67
Gilmour, Peter
  on heads' diminished autonomy 183
  loses seat 87, 250
  meets Muslim parents (1983) 242
  and Perry case 245
  on pragmaticism of racial policies 24,
    193
  and RH 75, 85, 86, 121, 247; fails to
    act in time 84, 132; interviews
    with 58, 240
  RH's book on 68
  support for single-sex schools 249
  and Whittaker 87, 240
girls
  equal opportunities 96, 128, 205
  separate schools for Muslim 13, 24,
    34–5, 233–4, 242, 249, 279
Goldberg, Councillor Reuben 81, 97,
  113, 125, 255
  and boycotts 101–2, 105, 262, 266

Goldberg, Councillor Reuben (continued)
  comments 105, 109, 110, 114
  threats made to 108, 269
goods
  common 219
  principal 224–5
governing bodies, school
  and control of education 108–9, 130
  Education (No. 2) Act (1986) 131,
    192
  ethnic mix 43, 52–3, 100, 243,
    279–80
  RH on head's relationship with 55
  see also: articles; governors, DMS
government; role in affair 122
  see also state
governors, DMS 86, 129–31
  articles of government, new (1985)
    263–4; elections under 106–7,
    118–19, 193, 266, 268
  ethnic composition 53, 100
  meetings: *1984* (6 Apr) 249; (16 Oct)
    91, 253; (Dec 1984 – Mar 1985)
    96, 255, 257; *1985* (25 Apr) 260;
    (22–5 June) 101–2, 262; (15 Oct)
    106–7, 118–19, 268, 269; (7 Nov)
    109, 271; (22 Nov) 109–10, 272
  parent 193, 266; J. Woodward 86,
    251
  press and public at meetings 129
  reinstate RH 101–2, 262
  support for RH 74, 249
  and vote of thanks to RH 279
Grange School 106–7, 267
Greenhalf, Jim 75, 80–1, 254, 259, 272
Greenhead Grammar School, Keighley
  111, 225, 269–70
Greenwood, Councillor Kathleen
  loss of seat 98, 113, 257, 281
  and RH's retirement 96, 122–3, 256
groups
  Muslim view 229
  in pluralist society 210–14
Guardian, The 45
guilt, racial 60, 138, 149, 156–7, 168
Gujeratis 11–12, 15
Gurdwaras (Sikh temples) 11
Gurmukhi, Punjabi (language) 15
halal meat 13

animal rights and 31, 46, 242, 247
campaign for 30, 36, 84, 242
Council policy 24, 29, 45–6, 49–50,
  126, 247; RH criticizes 58, 67
introduction 163, 239, 243
Hall, Leslie 114, 279
Halstead, Mark 27, 45, 129, 216, 228,
  229, 230
Hameed, Councillor 39, 41, 234, 274
Hanson Upper School 233–4
Haringay Black Pressure Group on
  Education 60, 240
Harrington, Patrick 179
Hart, David 99, 251, 274
Hawkins, Professor 38, 234
Hay, Courtney 152
Hayat, Azhar 107
Haykin, William 110–11, 114, 274
head teachers, Bradford 127
  autonomy 96–7, 183, 184, 195
  and freedom of speech 100, 260
  and LAM 6/83 29–30, 43, 84, 165,
    245
  Racism Awareness training 43, 44,
    245–6
Head Teachers' Review 41, 59, 238, 244
Headfield Middle School *see* Dewsbury
Heart of the Matter, The 45
High Court 103–4, 129, 263, 264, 282
Hindu Cultural Society 11
Hindu Society 39
Hundus in Bradford 11–12, 15
HMI *see* Inspectors
holidays, religious *see* festivals
Honey, Professor 257
Honeyford, Ray
  articles 55–83, 193, 275, 280–1, 282,
    284; interpretations 73–83;
    misrepresented by critics 68–9; on
    race and education 56–63; under-
    lying assumptions 64–6; what
    found offensive 66–71; *see also*
    *under names of journals, and list in
    Bibliography*
  appointed head of DMS 84, 237
  Asians offended by 58, 60, 61, 67,
    68, 69–70, 84
  background and education 55–6,
    127–8

Honeyford, Ray (continued)
  and Bradford Council 67–8, 76, 79,
    84, 86, 126–7, 177, 193, 249; claims
    right to criticize 181–2; mishand-
    led by 95, 132–4, 266
  competence questioned 76–7, 88,
    102, 169
  Conservatism 55–6, 113, 123, 125,
    215, 280, 284
  and Director of Educational Services
    84, 177, 193, 195, 249; publication
    restricted by 62, 88, 92, 93, 169,
    239, 251, 253–4, (end of
    restriction) 62, 110, 274;
    reprimanded by 57, 58, 59, 240
  early retirement 62, 119, 195;
    negotiations 91, 96, 100, 110,
    129–30, 253, 254, 256, 260, 261–2,
    270, 271, 272, 274
  insensitive 102, 115, 118, 121, 181
  language 84, 108, 170, 178, 179
  later career 114
  lectures 63, 111–12, 169, 269
  letters to press *see under names of
    journals*
  over-simplistic thought 64–5
  racism, accused of 76, 99, 137, 169,
    258, 262, 274
  radio and TV interviews *see under*
    BBC; Channel Four; Yorkshire
    TV
  reports called for by advisers 78, 80,
    91–2, 94, 96, 97, 253, 255, 257
  suspension 93–8, 258–9;
    re-instatement after 98–104, 264
  views *see under individual topics*
Honeyford affair, perspectives on
  legal and administrative 129–34
  political 121–5
  psychological 118–21; effect on
    pupils 109, 119–20, 195, 271
  sociological 126–9
Hooper, Baroness 53
House of Lords *see under* Parliament
housing 9, 10, 13, 16, 19, 140
Hungarian immigrants 6,7
Hussain, Councillor Manawar 12, 38,
  234

identity, distinct cultural 9, 25–7, 64
ignorance and racism 140
imams 80, 128
  and integration 13, 153, 235
  lead prayers in school 29, 33
  punishment, corporal 279
  Selbourne on 108
Immigrant Language Centres *see*
  Language Centres
immigration to Bradford
  statistics 10, 13, 15, 16, 231–2, 242
  *see also under individual nationalities,
    and*: Asians; European
Immigration Acts 9
Indian immigrants 11, 14, 233, 280
Indian Workers' Association 11, 125
indoctrination 163, 239
industry; education accountable to 187
  see also: engineering; textile
inequality and racism 157
injustice
  of inappropriate equal treatment 65
  racism as 65, 153, 155–60
Inner London Education Authority
  131, 189
Inspectors, Her Majesty's 34, 188, 243
instinct, tribal 144
*Instrument of Government of Various
  County Middle Schools, 1985* 103, 106,
  109, 129, 130, 263–4
integration
  bussing and 37
  community leaders prevent 13, 235
  Indian attitudes to 11, 12, 233
  multi-cultural education and 204
  Muslim attitudes 12, 13, 233, 235
  RH on 208, 280
  West Indians' attitude 8
integrationism 47–9
  and analysts' view of 'needs' 26
  and RE policy 33, 232
  RH and 54, 63, 64
intent and racism 148, 149–50, 156, 157
Inter-faith Education Centre 36, 113,
  278
intermarriage 7, 10
IQ, racial differences in 144–5

Iqbal, Mrs Mubarik 95, 100, 107, 125, 128, 256, 261
Iqbal, Muhammad 235
Irish immigrants 4, 7, 34
Islam 10
    centrality 12–13, 218–19, 228, 229
    and 'foreignness' of blacks 26
    in curriculum 32–3, 47, 50, 232
    see also Muslims
Islam, Yusuf (Cat Stevens) 44
Israelitism, British 142
Italians in Bradford 7, 34

Jack, Ian 81, 275
Jackson, David 278
Jamiyat Tabligh ul-Islam 34, 273–4, 278
Jensen, Professor Arthur 144–5
Jews in Bradford 4–6, 57
Jimmy Young Show 257
John, Gus 158–9
Joseph, Sir Keith
    limits of intervention 190
    on multi-cultural education 208–9, 281
    role in RH affair 75, 99, 129, 190, 249, 258
    and voluntary-aided schools 241
Judaism 5
justice 108, 157–60
    and positive discrimination 53
    racial 162–5, 204
Justices of the Peace, Asian 11

Keighley
    black population 12, 16
    Gilmour loses Council seat 87, 250
    racist attacks 111, 255, 269–70
Kelly, Frank 98, 258, 259
Kenyan Asian immigrants 11, 14
Khan, A. (DMS teacher) 91, 94, 254–5
Khan, Azia 240
Khan, Choudhury M. 12, 68, 109
    and RH's reinstatement 104–5, 264
    on support of DMS staff for RH 107 268–9
    supports speech by Ajeeb 106, 268
Khan-Cheema, Akram 52, 201, 228
Kinder, Councillor Ernest 94, 101, 262
King, Martin Luther 159

Kinnock, Neil, MP 249
Kirklees Council 229, 241, 283
Kirp, D.L. 38, 151, 155
Knight, Richard 78, 93, 97, 98, 104, 243, 254, 268
    and DMS advisers 87–8, 97, 250
    and DPAC 95, 105, 265, 266
    and Perry case 245
    and Peter Thorpe 112
    and RH's publications 62, 92, 169, 239, 251, 253–4
    RH warned by 57, 58, 59, 240

Labour group, Bradford Council
    court black vote 24
    control Council (1986) 123, 281
    and girls' education 35
    on *halal* meat 46, 247
    and picketing 125
    Press guidelines 174–5
    racial attitudes 121, 141
    and RH 88, 100, 110, 121–2, 261, 270
    and Schools (Education) Sub-committee 91, 92, 95, 256
Labour Party
    Bradford 102–3, 234
    Bradford West 85, 247
    national 45, 241, 249
    University Ward 107, 269
Labour Party Young Socialists' Asian Youth Conference 250
LAM No. 2/82 28, 33, 36, 89, 239–40
LAM No. 6/83 43, 131–2, 244
    and heads' autonomy 29–30, 67, 84, 165
    RH and 67, 89, 249
Lambert, Councillor John 87, 103, 107 262, 269
    Education Services chairman 113, 281
    and local elections 113, 280, 281
    on RH's publications 93, 255, 260
    and RH's retirement 100, 253, 261
language
    Council documents in minority 18
    development, and bussing 64
    emotive 77–8, 82; RH's 84, 108, 170, 178, 179
    information for parents in own 28

language (continued)
  options in school 50
  'racism'; definition problems 138–9
  RH on opponents' 60, 62, 207,
    281
  statistics 4, 12, 13, 15, 242
  see also: English; mother-tongue
Language Centres 27, 33, 40, 47, 152,
    231–2
  closing of 43, 52, 273, 280
Latvian immigrants 6,7
Lawler, Geoff, MP 101, 260
Lawton, Lord Justice 109, 270–1
Le Bon, Gustave 119
lectures
  freedom of speech 175
  RH gives 63, 111–12, 169, 269
Lee, Professor Terence 28
left-wing groups, extreme 74, 125
  see also under individual names
Lewis, Linda Lee 88, 252
Liberal group, Bradford Council
    122–3, 260–1
  and early retirement settlement 110,
    261–2, 270
  see also: Greenwood; Wells
liberalism
  and freedom of speech 178, 181
  on groups 210
  and multi-cultural education 209,
    225–7
  Muslim challenge to 227–30
  and pluralism 212–15, 219
  on professional autonomy 195
  and rationality 218
  and rights of child 223–5
  and shared values 216–17
libraries, Bradford City 43, 277
Lickley, Kenneth 244
Linguistic Minorities Project 15, 40,
    242
Lithuanian immigrants 6, 7
Little Horton Ward 16
Liverpool 18, 23
Local Administrative Memoranda *see*
  LAM
Local Education Authorities
  advisers; RH on 55
  annual meeting 1985 108
  and control of education 108–9, 130

  and professional autonomy 96–7
  see also Bradford MDC
London; radical policies 150–1, 173
  see also Brent
Lord Mayor *see*: Ajeeb; Free
loyalty
  clash of, for young blacks 19, 25–6,
    31, 65, 209, 236–7
  RH's lack of, to Council 102

McAndrew, Brian 99, 258, 274
McElroy, Pat 256, 257
McGoldrick, Maureen 112, 190, 281–2
Madden, Max, MP 75, 99, 247, 253,
    277
  speeches 87, 250, 258, 259
Mahoney, Graham 244
majoritarianism 199, 210, 219, 227
Majority Rights group 284
Manningham Middle School 112, 237,
    283
marches *see under* protest
Marcuse, H. 173–4, 177, 210, 211
marriages, arranged 10
Matthews, Robert 68–9, 275
Meadowcroft, Michael, MP 271, 276
media 75, 77
  Council on RH's use of 67, 86
  see also under individual media
Melville-Williams, John, QC 104
Merrick, J. 17
Mekdadi, F.H. 276
Mill, John Stuart 179, 199, 223
Mirpuris 8–9, 12, 13, 235, 260
mixed-ability teaching 56
Monday Club 124, 260
Moore, Gordon 21
  cancels H. Proctor speech 111, 269
  and Greenhead School violence
    269–70
  inquiry into handling of affair 251
  and RH's retirement 91, 100, 110,
    123, 256, 262, 274
  and RH's reinstatement 103, 104
  on RH's stubbornness 119
  speech on race relations Feb 86 276
moral commitment to racial justice 164
moral responsibility in racism 156–7
moral training 160, 164
Mortimer, Dr 56, 145, 175, 239

mosques 12–13, 278
schools 32, 33, 35, 39, 51, 232
Mother Tongue and English Teaching
for Young Asian Children Project
(MOTET) 40, 236
mother-tongue teaching
Council policy 39–40, 51, 126, 241
experimental introduction 28, 163
in mosque schools 32
in multi-cultural education 203
RH and 59, 60, 62–3, 64, 67, 206
Mothers against Racism 250
motivational dispositions 139–40
Multi-Cultural Affairs Officer 236
multi-cultural education 36–7, 203–30
anti-racist compared 204
Bradford's motivation to 121
criticism of: Sir K. Joseph 281;
Majority Rights 284; Muslims
227–30; RH 96, 205–9, 227
justifiability 225–7
LAM 2/82 on 239–40
liberalism 225–7
Muslim challenge 227–30
and paternalistic racism 152
RH on 22, 57–8, 60, 62, 204, 205–9,
215, 227
two types: for ethnic minority
children 23, 36–7, 203–4, 225–6;
for all children 23, 203–4, 206–8
Multi-Cultural Education Support
Group 113, 127, 266
multi-culturalism 21–54, 76, 83–4, 260
Council actions 32–46
underlying trends 46–54
multi-racialism
Bradford's policies 21–2, 76
RH on 'multi-racial lobby' 62,
175–6, 207, 208, 215, 227
Murch, Ian 274
Murphy, Dervla 81–2, 282
music 5, 10, 36, 284
Muslim Association of Bradford 13,
33, 34, 232, 242
Muslim Education Trust 33, 232
Muslim girls' school 13, 34, 233–4, 242
Muslim Parents' Association 36, 74
and Dewsbury affair 112, 283
and girls' education 34, 233, 235

'The Transformation of Muslim
Children' 238
and voluntary-aided schools 13, 30,
44, 84, 240
Muslims 12–13
and feminists 128–9
'foreignness' 26
and integration 13
and liberalism 227–30
in pluralism 212
politicization 125
and shared values 217, 229
Socialists' alliance with 127
see also: co-education; Islam
Mustill, Lord Justice 270–1
myths, racial 140, 141

Naqui, Nazim 59, 106, 107, 110, 243,
266, 272
National Anti-Racist Movement in
Education 106, 267
National Association of Head Teachers
on disciplinary letter 88, 251, 263
and House of Lords appeal 109, 271
libel writ against Council 77, 99,
129, 262
local branch 90–1, 246, 252, 259–60
and RH's reinstatement 100,
103–4, 259–60
and RH's retirement 100, 110, 262,
274
on Roper's over-involvement 87,
263
supports RH 74, 90–1, 95, 101, 252,
257
National Association of Local Government Officers 106, 268
National Association of Schoolmasters/
Union of Women Teachers 280
National Front 17, 42, 143, 160, 179
and bussing 38, 234
decline in support 124, 125
National Union of Teachers
and DPAC 74, 95, 106, 129, 256
Grange School strike 106–7, 267
local branch on RH 85, 247, 266,
272, 274
and McGoldrick affair 281
and Savery 273

National Union of Teachers (continued)
and voluntary-aided schools 241
Nawaz, Mrs Zerina 94, 254
needs 26–7
 Bradford's view of immigrant 23,
  25–31, 49
 child/parent discrepancy 25–6, 31,
  196, 205, 209, 215, 220, 221–2, 226
 common, of all children; RH on 58,
  64, 206; *Swann Report* 214, 215
 RH on need of immigrant child to
 compete 57, 59–60, 63, 64, 206, 220
New Right 22, 55–6, 75, 111, 124–5,
 146
New Testament Church of God 8
North London Polytecynic 179
Northern Ireland 120
Nozick, R. 172

objectivity, need for 73–83, 108, 115
Ockenden Venture 14
offence given by RH 66–71, 84, 179
opinion, freedom of 96, 97, 169–70
opportunism, political 24, 121, 126,
 133, 251
opting out *see* Education Bill
outcome; in racism 148, 150–1, 157
Overthorpe Junior School 283
Oxford Union 63, 280–1

Pakistan Community Centre 12, 105,
 256
Pakistanis
 immigration 8–9, 12–13, 14
 and integration 233
 number intending to return home
  232–3
 political divisions 12, 30
 RH's offensive remarks 61, 68, 70–1
Palmer, Frank 62, 138, 281
'Panorama' TV programme 87, 176,
 251
Parekh, Professor Bhikhu 108, 115,
 152–3, 160–1, 209, 226–7, 271
parents *see under*: Drummond Middle
 School; needs; rights
Parker, B.J.R. 34–5
Parliament 75, 79, 258, 259
 House of Lords; leave to appeal

81–2, 109, 271; RH forgoes
 110, 129–30, 274
 see also under names of members, and:
  Education Acts; Education Bill;
  Immigration Acts; Race Relations
  Act
Patel, Abdullah 47–8, 233–4
paternalism 221, 223, 224
Pathans 12
Peace Studies 56, 190
Pedley, Frank 53, 275–6
Pentecostal church 8
permissiveness 35, 127
Perry, Christopher 244–5
petitions 74, 98–9, 126, 262–3, 258, 259
philosophy, value of 160, 163
physical differences and racism 140
 see also colour
Physical Education
 DMS; advisers report 89
 covering body for 29, 36, 58, 63, 89
 separate for girls 24, 239–40
picketing
 of Bradford Conservative offices 125
 of governors' meetings 109–10, 253
 see also Drummond Middle School
Pickles, Councillor Eric 95–6, 87, 107,
 250, 255, 269
 meets Sir K. Joseph 99, 249, 258
 political dexterity 98, 123
 on 'Pupils' Charter' 105, 266
 and RH's retirement 100, 122–3,
  256, 262
 and RH's suspension 103, 263
pluralism 210–15
 American Model 210
 Colonial Model 211
 and educational decisions 198–201
 English Model 211–12
 liberalism and 178, 219
 multi-cultural education and 203,
  206–8, 226
 and professional autonomy 184, 195–
  202
 RH on 206–9
 voluntary-aided schools and 228
polarization of views
 on Council race policies 21–2
 on RH 121–2

polarization of views (continued)
  view of racism as injustice prevents
    159
'Poles Apart' (radio programme) 252
police 107, 108, 269, 270, 277
  'Thought' 75, 77, 98, 169–70
Policies Development Officer *see*
  Whittaker
Policy Statement on Race Relations
  18–19, 42, 49, 94, 237
Policy Unit, Bradford Council 237,
  244
Polish immigrants 6, 7, 34
political understanding, child's 164
politicization
  of Asians 125
  of education, RH on 62, 175–6, 207,
    208, 215, 227
politics, local
  Asian 11, 12, 125, 126
  impact of affair 113, 121–2, 160
  opportunism 24, 121, 126, 133, 251
  Pickles' dexterity 95–6, 98
  and retirement settlement 100, 270
politics, national; RH affair and 126
population statistics 10, 13, 15, 16
  schoolchildren 231–2, 242
Poundswick affair 132
Powell, Enoch, MP 144, 239
power in racism 146, 157
prejudice
  identifying criterion in racism 157
  C19th Irish in Bradford 4
  and discrimination 141, 144
  in employment 9–10
  Joseph on 281
  morally reprehensible per se? 141
  multi-cultural education and 204
  RH on 121, 144
  vetting school books for 42–3
press 63, 75, 98, 167, 248, 279
  guidelines: Council 112, 283; Labour
    group 174–5
  see also under names of journals
pressure groups
  Asian 125
  effect on Council policies 30–1
  school 126
  see also under names of groups

Priestley, J.B. 5–6
Proctor, Harvey, MP 111, 269
propaganda, political 163
protest, techniques of 176–8
  against RH 106–7, 126
  direct action/petitions 126
  effect on participants 120
  marches 42, 87–8, 101, 111, 125,
    250, 267, 277
  petitions 86–7, 126
  publicity 176
  see also picketing
psychological approach 118–21
public meetings disrupted 111, 269
publication; Council guidelines 112,
  283
  see also under Honeyford
publicity
  for Bradford's race policies 134
  technique of protest 176
punishment, corporal 35, 279
Punjabi immigrants 10–11
'Pupils' Charter' 105, 265–6
'purdah mentality' 60, 69, 205, 208
Pushtu population; statistics 15

Qureshi, Amin 86, 101, 114

race/culture distinction 204, 205
race relations
  all-party consensus ended 113, 282
  budget 246
  education on 121, 163
  'industry' 98, 147
  lobby; RH on 62, 124, 168, 175–6,
    207, 208, 215, 227
  see also under Bradford MDC
Race Relations Act 268
Race Relations Advisory Group 18–19,
  42, 86, 238, 244, 258
  Asians withdraw from 127, 266
  on LAM 6/83 84, 245
  race relations initiative, 1986 113
Race Relations Board 38, 234
Race Relations Committee 281
Race Relations Policy Statement (1981)
  18–19, 42, 49, 51, 94, 237
Race Today 21
Race Training Unit 281

racialism *see* racism, pre-reflective gut
racism 137–65
    Asian fear of 17–18
    colour-blind 42, 43, 153–5, 157
    concept of 138–60
    cultural 41, 42, 124, 145–7, 204, 220
    distinguishing criteria 155–6, 157
    in education; dealing with 84, 89,
      160–5
    extent in Bradford 17, 43, 239
    factors fostering 16–17
    as injustice 155–60
    institutional 17, 41, 42–4, 66, 139,
      147–51, 156–7
    intent 148, 149–50
    in minority ethnic groups 138
    moral judgment 155, 156–7
    multi-cultural education and 204
    outcome 148, 150–1
    paternalistic 151–3
    post-reflective gut 142–5
    pre-reflective gut 139–42
    RH on 62, 63, 65–6, 67, 125, 137,
      144, 230; accused of 76, 99, 137,
      169, 258, 262, 274
    Sikhs and protests against 11
    unintentional 41, 42–4, 153–5, 157
    Wyke Manor School 42, 84, 244–5,
      248
    see also: discrimination; prejudice;
      stereotyping
Racism Awareness Training Courses
    43, 44, 82, 237
    abolished 113
    headteachers and 30, 169, 245–6
    for recruitment staff 19, 245–6
    training officers 113–14, 282:
      memorandum on RH 76, 77, 99,
      137, 169, 258, 262, 274
racist behaviour 140, 142, 164–5
    conspiracy of silence on? 42, 111
    Council policy 29–30, 41–3, 244
    violence 84, 111, 244, 267, 276–7
    Wyke Manor School 42, 84, 244–5,
      248
racist myths 236
radicalism in multi-racial education; RH
    on 62, 175–6, 207, 208, 215, 227
radio *see* British Broadcasting

Rahman, F. 106, 266
Rank and File 91, 100, 259
Rashid, Johnny 235
Rastafarianism 8
rationality 140, 218
Rawls, J. 158, 159, 160, 224
razzismo 157
records, ethnic 153, 155
    see also population
Religious Education
    dilution 37, 50
    excusing from 28, 238, 239
    in Islam 29, 32–3, 47, 50
    Muslim misgivings 36, 284
    national curriculum excludes 284
    new agreed syllabus 33, 36, 50, 63,
      232, 240
    Race Relations Policy Statement 51
    RH's, at DMS 59, 63, 89, 206
referendum, RH proposes 62, 207, 208
Rehman, Abdul 279
Rehman, Miss Zerina 94, 254
relativism, cultural 207, 208, 226–7
religion
    European immigrants 4, 5, 7
    Hindus 10, 11
    right to bring up child in own 220,
      222
    Sikhs 10, 11
    West Indian immigrants 8
    see also individual denominations and
      sects
repatriation 4, 146, 232–3
representation 131
research, suppressed 56, 145, 175, 239
resistance 176–7
respect of persons 53
responsibility 180–1, 186–7
    and accountability 184–5
Revolutionary Communist Party 30,
    42, 125
    see also Workers Against Racism
Rhodes, Councillor 38, 234
Riaz, Councillor Mohammad 82–3,
    270
rights 129
    child's 209, 215, 220, 221–2, 223–4
    of criticism; RH on 65, 176, 178–81,
      181–2, 206

rights (continued)
  governors' 108–9
  in multi-cultural education 209
  in pluralism 220–4
  individual, and state 172
  LEA 108–9
  parents' 28, 30–1, 35, 112, 194, 198;
    on liberal view 215, 20, 221–2,
    225; on religion 32–3, 220; RH
    on 56, 65, 207, 220
  religious 44, 220, 222
riots, race 21, 23, 78
Robinson, Geoff 259
Roman Catholics 4, 7, 8
Roper, Norman
  and extended visits 238
  NAHT objections to 87, 263
  and RH 86–7, 98, 102, 103, 243,
    249
  statutory role in dismissal 130, 131
Rothenstein, Sir William 5
Rumanian immigrants 6
Russian immigrants 6
Russian Orthodox church 7
Ryan, Jeffrey 257
Ryan Street Muslim girls' school 13,
  34, 233–4, 242

St Joseph's College, Bradford 34
Salam, Mohammed 113–14, 282
Salisbury Review, The 124
  RH's articles 56; (1983) 59–61, 242;
    (1984 Winter) 41, 59–61, 69, 168,
    246, (Urdu paraphrase) 69, 100;
    (1984 Spring) 250; (1985) 93, 255;
    (1986) 62; (1987) 62
  Savery's article 112, 273
Salmon, John 240, 243
Sampson, Colin 108, 270
Save the Children Fund 14
Savery, Jonathan 111–12, 273, 280
Sawyer, Pauline 88, 240, 251
scapegoating 140–1, 142
Schauer, F. 171, 172, 173, 179, 181
schools
  building programme 38, 39, 273
  role in tackling racism 160–5
  see also under names of schools, and:
    Muslim girls'; supplementary;

voluntary-aided
Schools Council 192
Schools Education Subcommittee 77,
  78
  and alternative school 95, 256
  and implementation of advisers'
    report 91–2, 122–3, 253, 257
  vote of no confidence in RH 97–8,
    257
Schools' Sex Equality Adviser 112, 281
Scruton, Roger 93, 111, 124, 171–2,
  254, 269
SDP; role in hung council 122–3
segmentation 211, 212, 214
segregation in schools
  de facto 52
  end of bussing promotes 38, 39
  through opting-out 229–30
  see also separatism
Selbourne, David 77–8, 91, 108, 252
  on Asian/Socialist alliance 127
  on Labour racist opinions 121, 141
  Left Behind 79–80, 282
  New Society article, Apr 84 248
  on politics of anti-racial lobby 270
self-concept, immigrants' 59–60, 120
Semon, Charles 5
separatism 8, 51–4, 63
sex education 29, 35, 124, 238, 242
sexual codes 35, 127
Shahid, Riaz 48, 233, 238
Sheffield; RH speaks in 111, 280
Shepherd, David 9, 42, 112, 283
Shree Prajapati Samaj 11
Sichel, Ernest Leopold 5
Sikh Parents' Association 11
Sikhs in Bradford 10–11, 15, 235
Silverwood, Stephen 95, 256
Singh, Marsha 11, 235–6, 248, 256
Singh, Ramindar 42, 235, 244
single-sex education *see* co-education
Smith, David 101, 261
social avoidance in racism 140, 142
social control 37–8, 152–3, 260
social services 18, 19
Socialist Education Association 241
Socialist Federation 86
Southall riots 18, 23
Spectator, The 62

speech, freedom of 167–82
  accepted by RH's opponents 177–8
  constraints of public office 67, 170
  headteachers' concern over 100, 260
  issue in RH affair 76, 95, 102, 276
  legal perspective 170–1
  liberal principles and 181
  political perspective 171–5
  public speeches cancelled 111, 269
  RH on 60–1, 62, 167, 168–70, 175,
    181
Sri Sathya Sai Baba Mandir 11
standard of living, immigrants' 5,
  10–11, 11–12, 13, 19
standards, declining educational 124
state
  authority of, and free speech 171–2
  and control of education 221–2
  paternalism 223
statistics
  collection of ethnic 153, 155
  see also population
stereotyping 42
  in cultural racism 145
  and educational expectations 162
  knowledge to replace 164
  in pre-reflective gut racism 140
  by RH 69–70, 178, 179
  vetting school books for 42–3
Stevens, Cat (Yusuf Islam) 44
Strauss, Rev Dr Joseph 5
Strike, K. 221, 222, 224–5, 229
strikes
  Bradford and Ilkley College 109, 271
  DPAC 251
  Grange School 106–7, 267
  October 1985 106–7, 268
  Wyke Manor Upper School 42
stubbornness, RH's 119, 133
Sudbury Infants School *see* McGoldrick
Sunderland, Councillor Eric 77, 107,
  268, 279
supplementary schools, Muslim 39
  Council finances 33, 241–2
  discipline 279
  planning regulations 29, 273–4
  Swann, Lord; and RH affair 101, 263
  Swann Committee and Report 28
  accommodationism 53

Bradford represented on 28
on Britishness 215–16
on bussing 38
Carlton Duncan on 245
on colour-blind racism 153
on democratic decision-making 201
dissenting statement 52
drops research into West Indian
  achievement 56, 145, 175, 239
on institutional racism 148, 151
on pluralism 213–14
on racism amongst minorities 141
RH criticizes 62
on shared values 209
on transmission of culture 206
on voluntary-aided schools 228
on worship in schools 229
swimming 30, 36, 62, 238, 239–40
Swindlehurst, Councillor Albert 33
Sylhets 14
synagogue, Bradford 5

tact, need for teachers' 29, 43–4
Taylor Report 192–3
teachers
  allegations of racism 42, 244–5
  beliefs, Council control of 92
  black 52–3, 151, 255, 272, 279
  colour-blind racism 43, 153
  expertise 196–7, 198–9
  in-service training on racism 43
  oppose Council policy changes 31
  see also: autonomy, professional;
    Drummond Middle School;
    headteachers
Telegraph & Argus 75, 78, 101
  Greenhalf's reviews: (12 Apr 1985)
    259; (26 Nov 1985) 78, 80–1, 272
  RH's letters and interviews 56, 85,
    61, 78, 239, 248, 249
television *see* British Broadcasting;
  Channel Four; Yorkshire TV
temples, Indian 11
T.F. Davies Teachers' Centre 37
textile industry 3–4, 4–5, 7, 8, 9, 11
Thatcher, Margaret 47, 75, 105–6, 124,
  125, 233, 254
Thompson, Donald 92, 101, 102, 104,
  107, 264

Thorne, Councillor Barry 84, 92, 238, 241, 245
Thornton School 267
Thorpe, Peter 112, 281
thought, Council on RH's 96, 97
'Thought Police' 75, 77, 98, 169–70
threats 77, 107–8, 265, 269, 279
Times Educational Supplement; articles and correspondence
    on Bradford's race policies 21
    by Gilmour 86
    by Pickles 95
    by RH: (1982) 56, 57–8, 239, 240; (1983) 58–9, 243; (1984) 62; (1985) 65, 100, 260
    on voluntary-aided schools 45
    by Woodward 86, 250
tokenism and paternalistic racism 152
tolerance
    limits of reasonable 179–80
    RH on 64, 168
Toller Ward 16
totalitarianism; RH on anti-racist 65
trade unions, Asians in 9
Trades Council 234
transfers, requests for school
    DMS 129–34, 176–7, 252
    William Tyndale case 131, 189
trust in teacher 197
Turkish immigrants 6
TV Calendar programme 244
TV EYE programme 99, 258
Tyndale affair 131, 189
Tyndall, John 143, 146

Uganda, Hindu immigrants from 11
Ukrainian immigrants 6–7, 34
Ukrainian Video Archives Society 7
unemployment 9, 13, 16, 236, 279
uniform, school 10, 11, 29, 36, 206, 239
Union of Muslim Organizations of UK and Eire 235, 276
United Black Youth League 17
United States of America 188
University Ward 16, 107, 269
Urdu language
    RH's article paraphrased 69, 100, 133–4
    speaker statistics 15, 242
    taught at DMS 206
    Use of English Quarterly 55

values, shared 197–8, 208–9, 214, 215–19, 229
Vietnamese immigrants 14
vigilante patrols 30, 111, 125, 277
violence 118–19, 177
    inter-racial 17, 84, 111, 244, 276–7
    on picket-line 105, 118, 177, 264–5
    RH affair and 111, 269, 276–7
visits to sub-continent, extended
    advisers on effect of 89–90
    Council policy 29, 118, 132, 237–8
    DMS meeting 41, 60, 118, 237–8
    institutional racism and 151
    RH on 59, 60, 64, 65, 67, 206
voluntary-aided schools 52–3
    Ajeeb on 52
    campaign for 13, 52–3, 84, 127, 229, 240
    Council policy 44–5, 240–1
    Dewsbury affair renews calls for 112
    Education Bill (1987) and 52–3, 284
    Swann Committee on 228
vote, immigrant 24, 121
voucher system 56, 124, 189

wages, Asian 9
Wall, Pat 250
Walthamstow 18
War, First World 5–6
War, Franco–Prussian 5
War, Second World 6
Wells, Councillor John 100, 110, 123, 261–2, 270
West Indian immigrants 8, 34
    and Asians 41
    discrimination against 10, 41, 239
    population statistics 14
    research dropped 56, 145, 175, 239
    RH's comments on 56, 57, 60, 61, 68, 69–70, 145, 179, 239
    school population; statistics 15
    stereotypes 69–70, 140, 179
    and white working class 41
West Indian Parents' Association 8, 250
West Yorkshire County Council 12

White, J. 199, 217–18, 219, 225
White, P. 220–1, 223
white activists 31
white children in minority in school 52, 61, 65, 70, 89, 267
white working class 41, 127–8, 150–1
Whitfield, Tim 85, 88, 100, 106, 250, 268
Whittaker, Michael 22, 84–5, 183, 240, 247, 248
  Gilmour's partnership with 87, 132
  seconded to Home Office 87, 250
  tells press about RH's article 84–5, 247
Wightman, Councillor 99, 258
William Tyndale school 131, 189
Winterton, Nicholas, MP 75, 99, 258
Wolfe, Humbert 5
women, Muslim 13, 32
Woodman, Shirley 246
Woodward, Jenny 94, 97, 100, 101, 177, 259, 262
  chairperson of DPAC 85–6, 249
  feminism 128–9
  later career 114, 279
  parent governor, DMS 86, 251
  and press 77, 86, 101, 250, 259, 279
  threats to 108, 269, 279
wool trade 3–4, 4–5, 7, 8, 9
Workers Against Racism 125
  Asian membership 125

demonstrations 111, 277, 280
vigilante patrols 30, 111, 277
working class, white lower 41, 127–8, 150–1
World Islamic Mission 34, 235
worship in schools 36
  draft guidelines 112–13, 278
  experimental proposals 28, 37
  Muslim, led by imams 29, 51, 239
  RH on 64
  Swann Report suggests optional 229
  right to withdraw child 28
written sources; distortion 78–9, 83
Wyke Manor Upper School 37, 42, 84, 244–5, 248
  see also Duncan, Carlton

Yorkshire Campaign to Stop Immigration 17, 124–5
Yorkshire Conservative Trades Unionists 280
Yorkshire Post 75, 84–5, 101
  Knight in 67
  Racism Awareness training officers' memo 99, 258
  RH in 56; (1984) 61, 88, 251; (1986) 62; (1987) 62–3
  on RH's *Salisbury Review* article 84–5, 247
Yorkshire Television 99, 258
Yugoslav immigration to Bradford 6, 7